THE MIND OF DAVID HUME

THE MIND
of
DAVID HUME

A Companion to Book I

of

A TREATISE OF HUMAN NATURE

Oliver A. Johnson

UNIVERSITY OF ILLINOIS PRESS   URBANA AND CHICAGO

© 1995 by the Board of Trustees of the University of Illinois
Manufactured in the United States of America
1 2 3 4 5 C P 5 4 3 2 1

This book is printed on acid-free paper.

Excerpts from David Hume, *A Treatise of Human Nature,* 2d ed.,
ed. L. A. Selby-Bigge and P. H. Nidditch (Oxford: Oxford University Press, 1978) are included by permission of Oxford University Press.

Library of Congress Cataloging-in-Publication Data

Johnson, Oliver A.
    The mind of David Hume : a companion to book I of A treatise
of human nature / Oliver A. Johnson.
        p.   cm.
    Includes bibliographical references and index.
    ISBN 0-252-02156-8 (alk. paper). — ISBN 0-252-06456-9 (pbk.
: alk. paper)
    1. Hume, David, 1711-1776. Treatise of human nature. Book 1.
2. Knowledge, Theory of. 3. Philosophy of mind. I. Title.
B1489.J64   1995
128—dc20   94-24329
                                                                    CIP

In Memoriam Mentis Magnae

Contents

PREFACE

My interest in the philosophy of David Hume is almost as old as my interest in philosophy. In 1946, just after my return from the war in the Pacific, I enrolled in a seminar at the University of Oregon in which we read Descartes and Hume. I had little trouble understanding the Frenchman but the Scot baffled me. Innocent as I was then of the issues of epistemology and metaphysics, I could not understand what had led Hume to come to conclusions that seemed to me quite outrageous. I realize now, nearly a half-century later, that my consternation was mainly a result of my own ignorance. Probably I should have waited until I was better versed in philosophy before I attempted to unravel the *Treatise*.

For a number of years after my unfortunate introduction to Hume, my main philosophical concentration took me away from epistemology and metaphysics into ethics. Since I found that Hume's writings on this subject held little of interest to me, I turned my attention to other philosophers. First attracted to intuitionism, I gradually came to the conclusion that the appeal to "moral insight" was not a viable basis for ethical theory. But, then, what was? This question led me to concentrate on the question of moral knowledge, which in turn led me to the broader question of knowledge in general. I became an avid reader of the writings of the sceptics, trying to devise some way in which a cognitivist could respond to their denial of the possibility of knowledge. Since the literature on scepticism was full of references to Hume, and particularly to Book I of the *Treatise*, I finally decided to return to this work that had proved so puzzling to me early in my studies. For the last ten years I have tried to analyze and understand Book I. The result of my labors is *The Mind of David Hume*.

I think that this book fills an important gap in the literature on Hume. Although there are countless commentaries on his philosophy, nothing has been published comparable, say, to Paton's book on Kant's *Critique of Pure Reason*. Rather, most commentators either concentrate on a particular aspect of Hume's metaphysics and epistemology or approach his philosophy from a special point of view. No one has undertaken the task of going through Book I fully, systematically, and in detail, following directly in the footsteps of Hume. This I have tried to do; or, to shift the metaphor, I have tried to get inside the mind of Hume as he wrote Book I. Through doing this I think I have shown Book I to be a highly complex but sustained argument devoted to the attempt to answer most of the fundamental questions of philosophy. I have also, I believe, uncovered many important facets of Hume's thought that have received little attention in the critical literature. To mention just a few of these, I have distinguished between two meanings of "the determination of the mind"; I have pursued the extraordinary consequences of Hume's conception of belief; I have emphasized the ontological significance of Section IV of Part IV; I have separated Hume's two metaphors of the mind; and I have established the essential connection between his total scepticism and his "true" scepticism.

Although this book is devoted mainly to an exposition and analysis of Hume's argument in Book I, it would not be complete, as a philosophical work, if it did not include some evaluation of that argument and of Hume's epistemology and metaphysics. So I have examined some of his central theories and arguments critically, in order to provide an assessment of his philosophy. But limitations, not only of space but also of my own analytical ability, have, I realize, brought many of my criticisms to a premature end. Perhaps other Hume scholars, better equipped than I, will find in these critical comments hints they can pursue further, to draw out the implications of Hume's philosophy to their final end.

Needless to say, Book I is very difficult to understand, for many reasons, not least of which is Hume's penchant for irony, of which he was an acknowledged master. At times, particularly when he is talking about religion, his irony becomes almost embarrassingly heavy but at other times it rivals that of Socrates in subtlety. But irony seems to have the peculiar quality of being infectious, especially when an ironist himself invites irony. I fear that I may have on occasion succumbed to the infection in the pages that follow; if so, I beg the indulgence of my readers.

Many people have contributed, in many ways, to this book. Most important is my wife, Carol, without whose encouragement and active support over the years (including the many hours she spent in mastering the complexities of a personal computer) I doubt that the book would ever have been finished. I also appreciate the help I received from a large number of members of the Hume Society; I learned a great deal about both Hume and contemporary Hume scholarship from their questions and comments during meetings of the society, as well as in personal conversations with individuals. I should like to express my special appreciation to the following Hume scholars who have been particularly helpful to me in this project: To my colleagues at the University of California, Alexander Rosenberg and Barry Stroud, with whom I have discussed many aspects of Hume's philosophy; to Robert Anderson, with whom I have had long talks about Hume over forty years; to Daniel Flage, for his views on the central notion of memory in the *Treatise;* to Robert Hurlbutt, for his insights into the nuances of Hume's thought; to Manfred Kuehn, for his knowledge of the history of empiricism; to David Norton, for the wealth of his bibliographical information; and to Richard Popkin, for his encyclopedic memory of the history of scepticism. All of these have helped me immeasurably. Finally, I owe a special debt of gratitude to Sandra Borders, whose bibliographical knowledge and experience saved me many hours of library research.

I dedicate this book, with love, to my grandchildren. May they always be philosophical, even if never philosophers.

The Mind of David Hume

INTRODUCTION:
ON THE INTERPRETATION
OF THE *TREATISE*

1. THE DIFFICULTY OF BOOK I OF THE *TREATISE*

David Hume published Books I and II of *A Treatise of Human Nature* anonymously, in 1739, when he was twenty-eight years old.[1] The first substantive English review of the work appeared later the same year, in a publication called *History of the Works of the Learned.* In his long, unsigned commentary, which dealt only with Book I of the *Treatise,* the reviewer, who combined a supercilious attitude toward Hume with an abject failure to understand him, did succeed in making one perceptive remark. He complained about Hume's "inscrutability."[2]

Similar remarks about the difficulty of the *Treatise* can be found in the works of many subsequent Hume commentators. For example, the scholar John Passmore, writing over two hundred years after the publication of the *Treatise,* begins his book *Hume's Intentions* with the following statement: "Hume is one of the most exasperating of philosophers. Each separate sentence in his writings—with very few exceptions—is admirable in its lucidity: the tangled syntax and barbarous locutions which bedevil the reader of Kant and Hegel are completely absent. And yet, although in a different way, Hume is at least as difficult as Hegel."[3] I leave it to those who understand Hegel to judge whether Passmore is correct in claiming that Hume may be even more difficult than he is; what can safely be said is that Passmore finds Hume hard to comprehend.[4]

Although these assessments of Hume's difficulty are justified, they do not apply to all of his writings. Quite the contrary. His *Enquiry Concerning the Principles of Morals* and his *Dialogues Concerning Natural Religion,* for example, are models of clarity. As for the *Treatise* itself, Books II and III are readily understandable. When commentators deplore Hume's difficulty, they invariably have one piece of his writing in mind—Book I of the *Treatise.* I agree. That it is by far the most difficult of his works is the conclusion I have come to after many years of study; it is one of my main reasons for writing this book. In it I will endeavor to accomplish two aims: (1) To clarify Hume's philosophy in Book I by following the progress of his thought closely from the beginning to the end, attempting to elucidate his meaning and the logic of his argument, as I understand these, appealing throughout directly to the text itself, and (2) to examine his arguments in order to provide an evaluation of his epistemology and metaphysics as he develops them in Book I. Most of the book will be devoted to the first task; however, I will include sufficient critical commentary to justify some judgments concerning the success of Hume's philosophy.

2. Reasons for the Difficulty of Book I of the *Treatise*

There are several reasons for the difficulty of Book I. Obviously, the problems with which it is concerned are inherently difficult, so no attempt to deal with them adequately can be easy. Witness to this fact can be found in the philosophical writings of Hegel or, for that matter, of Aristotle or Spinoza or Kant. Yet such an answer does not explain the special difficulty of Hume, for other philosophers, including both Locke and Berkeley, managed to write about these subjects in a relatively understandable way. Why, then, is the Hume of Book I so hard to comprehend?

One source of difficulty lies in Hume's frequent use of two literary devices—metaphor and irony. Book I is liberally sprinkled with picturesque metaphors, for example, that of the self as a group of actors strutting on a nonexistent stage, that of reason as a monarch sitting on a shaky throne, or that of the philosopher as a sailor about to put to sea in a leaky boat. Although such metaphors brighten the text, they can mislead readers into thinking they have understood an argument more clearly than they have. Hume's irony poses a more serious problem.[5] That he is being ironical in certain passages, particularly in his discussions of religion, is apparent but in other passages, although one may suspect irony, it is often hard to be sure. For readers this uncertainty poses a dilemma: If they interpret a passage as irony, they may miss an important point Hume is trying to make; if, on the other hand, they take it seriously, they may expose themselves to ridicule for being obtuse. In this book I lean toward reading Hume conservatively; that is, I assume he means just what he says, unless his irony is *patent*. This procedure may take some of the adventure out of reading the text but it lessens the danger of falling into egregious errors of interpretation.

Other problems arise from Hume's terminology. For instance, he sometimes uses terms that are central to his argument loosely and ambiguously, with the result that a reader is left unsure as to what he means. One of the most perplexing of these ambiguities concerns the word "object"; sometimes

Hume uses it as the equivalent of "perception" and at other times of "physical object." Often the sense in which he is using it in a given passage is far from clear.[6] Other important terms Hume uses ambiguously include "cause," "memory," "imagination," "probability," "reason," "inference," "mind," in fact most of the central concepts of Book I.

A closely related difficulty arises because Hume often develops his meaning of central terms only late in Book I. Unaware that Hume will give a special meaning to a certain concept, readers understandably interpret it according to its ordinary meaning, only later to find that Hume gives the concept a meaning quite different from what they had assumed. As a result readers belatedly realize that they may have misunderstood much of what they have read and that, if they are to comprehend Hume, they must not only alter the meanings they normally give to commonly used words but must also go back and reread the text with these new meanings in mind. Although Hume continues, on some occasions, to use such words with their ordinary meanings, even after he has redefined them, they now have meanings for his philosophy different from those of normal usage. Obviously such changes in meaning can result in confusion, for readers are faced with such questions as these: Is Hume, on a given occasion, using a term in its ordinary or its special sense? If the latter, has he always been doing so? If he has, how do we reinterpret our original understanding of the text? And can we assume that he will continue to use the term in its special sense? Book I gives rise to such questions about several of its central terms. To alert readers to the fact that Hume has changed the meaning of a commonly used word, giving it a new and special meaning, I will label such words *technical* terms of his philosophy.

Another kind of problem with Book I results from its organization. Although the argument follows a line of progression that must have seemed logical to Hume, that logic may well escape readers. Several impediments stand in the way of their following Hume's line of thought. Perhaps most apparent are the digressions, of which there are several. Some of these are relatively minor, for example, Hume's occasional discussions of religion and theology, as well as some of his brief excursions into history and literature. Others, however, are substantial. Most notably, Hume's long arguments regarding the infinite divisibility of space and time and the idea of a vacuum that occupy most of Part II do not add greatly to the positive philosophy he develops in Book I. Sometimes, however, appearances are deceiving. The apparent "digression" entitled "Of the reason of animals" (Part III, Section XVI), which seems to have little connection with his main argument, in fact makes an important point about Hume's view of human nature.

The general organization of Book I, also, is disconcerting. After laying down, in the first five sections of Part I, the epistemological principles that will guide his inquiry in the remainder of the book, Hume changes the subject in Sections VI and VII to add a brief discussion of the notions of substance and abstract ideas. He then turns, in Part II, to a lengthy account of the nature of space, time, and mathematics, which interrupts the development of his general argument. One of the most important topics of this general argument—our knowledge of and belief in an external world—is treated in two widely separated parts of the book—Section VI of Part II and Sections II–IV of Part IV. He also gives two different accounts of the nature of memory and its difference from imagination, separated from each other by about seventy-five pages of text. Another example of the peculiarities of organization appears in Part IV, with Hume's general form of scepticism. Although Sections I and VII of that part clearly form a connected argument, the conclusions of the former leading directly to Hume's final position in the latter, the two sections are separated from each other by several sections devoted to a variety of different topics.

Another source of difficulty, and one that poses particularly delicate problems of judgment for the interpreter, is Hume's frequent apparent inconsistencies. Some of these can be dealt with quite easily by showing that the inconsistency is only verbal, resulting from Hume's loose use of language, and that his thought can be reformulated in a consistent way. Others, however, are harder to resolve. Even though one reads Hume sympathetically, making every effort to interpret him in a way that supports the consistency of his argument, the conclusion that he is contradicting himself seems difficult to avoid. Sometimes these contradictions are relatively minor so that, although they mar the argument, they do not detract seriously from Hume's central views. Others, however, seem to be fundamental. These leave the interpreter, despite efforts to the contrary, forced to recognize that there may be deep and apparently intractable flaws in Hume's philosophy. Passmore puts the point bluntly: "Hume . . . had a quite extraordinary insensitivity to consistency; few men are so ready to announce a general principle and admit exceptions to it, all in a single breath, or, having admitted exceptions, still to proceed as if they did not exist."[7] Interpretation that has to contend with the possibility of inconsistencies on a large scale, particularly if these involve crucial points in the author's theory, poses vexing and difficult problems for commentators. It is hard for them to avoid the thought that, if they had *really* understood the writer, they would have realized that the problems they believe they have found have been resolved. The best they can do, and what I will do in this book, is to face any inconsistencies that may appear as they arise, dealing with each in a way that seems both appropriate and fair.[8]

Before concluding this section I should like to make some remarks about the attitude I believe a commentator who is trying to interpret a writer as difficult as Hume should take toward his or her subject. As I have indicated, one should read Hume sympathetically, and I will try to do so to the extent that I can, consistent with maintaining my philosophical integrity. In practice, however, "sympathetic reading" is not a simple matter. Obviously, it involves the attempt to interpret Hume, as often as possible, in a way that will make him consistent and to avoid emphasizing inconsistencies that are either just verbal or of minor theoretical importance. But I think it means more than this; in particular, it requires that the interpreter understand Hume in his own context and terms—those of an eighteenth-century writer. One must avoid the temptation, to which some commentators have succumbed, of reading concepts and theories back into Hume that did not appear in the literature until centuries later. Although Hume may have been the precursor of later ideas, these are not—indeed, could not be—a part of his own thought and therefore should not be represented to be.

3. The Problems of Interpretation

Faced with the task of interpreting Hume, commentators on the *Treatise* have understandably sought ways of approaching the text that can resolve some of the difficulties it presents. Often this effort has led them to seek a single point of view or thesis in terms of which they can interpret the *Treatise*—a kind of master key with which to unlock the labyrinth of Hume's thought. The secondary literature on Hume's epistemology and metaphysics, beginning with the anonymous critique in the *History of the Works of the Learned*, growing relatively slowly in the eighteenth and nineteenth centuries, but increasing to a veritable flood in the twentieth, has resulted in a plethora of interpretations of his philosophy. Almost everyone seems to have a different picture of the essential Hume. He has been called an empiricist, a phenomenalist, a subjectivist, an idealist, a realist, a nominalist, a dualist, a naturalist, an associationist, a materialist, a neutral monist, an atomist, a rationalist, an irrationalist, a positivist, a Newtonian, a solipsist, a sceptic, a representationalist, a common-sense philosopher, and more.[9] Although these labels encompass most of the main positions in epistemology and metaphysics, the remarkable fact is that each commentator who has applied one of them to Hume can offer strong textual evidence from the *Treatise* to support his or her interpretation. The explanation of this bewildering array of interpretations can, I think, be found in the fact that Hume was a multifaceted genius.

Although these different interpretations have given insights into his thought and have aided our understanding of Hume, this understanding has been bought with a price. To the extent that a commentator approaches the study of Hume's philosophy as a whole from the perspective of any one of its multiple facets, he or she runs the risk of emphasizing passages and arguments that fit in with a particular interpretation and giving insufficient attention to those that do not. The result can be a distortion of Hume's philosophy. Although the distortion is not intended, it can easily give the reader an oversimplified view of Hume that fails to do justice to the diversity and richness of his mind.

I will call the kind of perspectival approach to Hume I have just described *pre-textual interpretation*. By this term I mean a commentary that adopts a *general* point of view or perspective *at the outset* that molds and guides the commentator's interpretation throughout his or her study. Such an approach can be contrasted with *post-textual interpretation*, which starts without any preconceived general view but, if it does arrive at interpretative generalizations, does so only *after* completing its study, deriving these from the text itself. Although I recognize the value of pre-textual interpretations of Hume, I have reservations about them. Yet, numerous Hume commentators, going all the way back to Thomas Reid in the eighteenth century, have employed them. At the beginning of his book *Hume's Philosophy of Common Life* Donald Livingston puts the point I am making very nicely: "More than any other modern philosopher, Hume has appeared as the construct of the conceptual frameworks that interpreters have imposed upon him."[10]

Pre-textual interpretations are, of course, not limited to Hume but can be found in the critical literature on all the major philosophers. However, the *Treatise*, because of the ambiguities, complexities, and variety of views it contains, has been an unusually fertile ground for their nourishment. In addition there is another, completely different and quite remarkable reason why many commentators have concluded that a master key with which the *Treatise* can be unlocked must exist. This special reason is provided by Hume himself but almost surely unwittingly. I will discuss it in the next section.

4. Hume's "New Scene of Thought"

In 1729, when he was eighteen years old, Hume suffered a neurophysical breakdown, which continued for a period of about five years, with a variety of symptoms, some of which caused him considerable pain and all of them anguish. His biographer, Ernest Mossner, describes his affliction as a "deep-set emotional and physical disorder."[11] However Hume's youthful illness may be diagnosed, it affected him seriously, interfering with the studies in which he was engaged prior to embarking on the *Treatise*. So unnerved had he become that in 1734 (just before his departure for France to write the *Treatise*) he composed a letter to a physician in London in which he described his recurrent illness. The letter is long and somewhat rambling. In addition to descriptions of his physical ailments, it includes a brief account of his intellectual pursuits during the same years.[12] This account contains a passage that has captured the imagination of a number of Hume scholars. They believe it provides the vital clue to the correct understanding of the *Treatise*. Specifically, they have concluded that Hume, at the age of eighteen, made a remarkable discovery that was to become the foundation for the new philosophical system he would present in his book. All that is needed is a proper interpretation of the passage; once this has been provided, commentators will have in their hands the master key with which they can unlock the *Treatise*. Naturally, this is an exciting prospect for any scholar. But a problem remains: How should the passage be interpreted? Before we can address that question, we need to see just what Hume writes. The crucial sentences read as follows:

> From my earliest Infancy, I found alwise a strong Inclination to Books & Letters. As our College Education in Scotland, extending little further than the Languages, ends commonly when we are about 14 or 15 Years of Age, I was after that left to my own Choice in my Reading, & found it encline me almost equally to Books of Reasoning & Philosophy, & to Poetry & the polite Authors. Every one, who is acquainted either with the Philosophers or Critics, knows that there is nothing yet establisht in either of these two Sciences, & that they contain little more than endless Disputes, even in the most fundamental Articles. Upon Examination of these, I found a certain Boldness of Temper, growing in me, which was not enclin'd to submit to any Authority in these Subjects, but led me to seek out some new Medium, by which Truth might be establisht. After much Study, & Reflection on this, at last, when I was about 18 Years of Age, *there seem'd to be open'd up to me a new Scene of Thought, which transported me beyond Measure*, & made me, with an Ardor natural to young men, throw up every other Pleasure or Business to apply entirely to it.[13]

The sentence in this passage that has excited scholars is, of course, the last, in which Hume refers to a "new scene of thought" that transported him "beyond measure." Here is the key; properly interpreted, the sentence can unlock the *Treatise*. However, the key is well hidden, because the sentence is quite vague, containing no hint as to the nature of the new scene of thought that had opened before Hume. The commentators who have seized on this passage, believing it contains the vital clue to Hume's philosophy, have taken the responsibility of drawing conclusions from it, first, by assuming that the phrase "new scene of thought" refers to a revolutionary philosophical discovery Hume had made and, second, by concluding what that discovery was. Having reached their conclusions they can then apply them to interpret the *Treatise*. Thus Hume has contributed, by his youthful "Letter to a Physician," to what I have called the pre-textual interpretation of the *Treatise*.

The "new scene of thought" passage has beguiled several commentators, including eminent Hume scholars. In my reading through the secondary literature I have found no fewer than six different interpretations of it.

> The initial discovery, too, that filled Hume with such transports of joy and opened a whole new prospect to him, we can readily identify. It was surely the fact . . . that man is vastly presuming whenever he uses the maxim of cause and effect. (C. W. Hendel)[14]

> The "Letter to a physician" clearly shows that the "new scene of thought" which so "transported" Hume was his discovery of the resources of the inductive, experimental or Newtonian method in the entire domain of human nature. (J. Laird)[15]

> The thesis for which I shall argue is . . . that [Hume] was led to recognise that judgments of moral approval and disapproval, and indeed judgments of *value* of whatever type, are based not on rational insight or on evidence, but solely on feeling; and that what then "open'd up to [him] a new Scene of Thought, which transported [him] beyond Measure" (giving birth in due course to the *Treatise*), was the discovery that this point of view could be carried over into the theoretical domain. (N. K. Smith)[16]

> What was "the new Scene of Thought" that seemed to be opened up to Hume at eighteen? . . . It is I think fairly safe to assume that some notion of how the study of Human Nature could be used to settle the age-long disputes of philosophy formed at least the setting of Hume's new scene of thought. (D. G. C. Macnabb)[17]

> Perhaps one can make one more contribution to the problem of "Hume's intentions" by suggesting that the two main currents of advanced speculation in Scotland at that time: natural law teaching and Newtonian or Baconian experimental science came together, and allied to Hume's religious scepticism, produced his famous "new scene of thought." (D. Forbes)[18]

> [Hume] tells us that "about the age of 18 years of age" there seemed to be opened up to him "a new scene of Thought." It is not possible quite definitely to determine in what this "new scene of thought" consisted. . . . But . . . we may more than suspect that associationism was the "new scene of thought." (J. Passmore)[19]

My purpose in reproducing these interpretations of what Hume "must have meant" by his "new scene of thought" statement is not to impugn the scholarship of their authors. All are eminent Hume commentators and all offer arguments in support of the interpretations they give. Yet two facts remain. First, nothing Hume says in the statement or elsewhere regarding it offers any evidence confirming any one of the interpretations, so we must conclude them to be the creative work of the commentators themselves. Second, since each of the six interpretations is different from the other five, we must—unless we assume that Hume had unfolded before him six new scenes of thought—conclude that at least five, and quite possibly all six, of these interpretations are inaccurate. Hume scholars notwithstanding, the fact remains that nothing Hume says in the passage in question supports any view about what, if anything, he may at that time have been planning to write in his *Treatise*.

These diverse efforts to read a special meaning into Hume's statement, although they are of considerable interest, are not themselves of crucial importance in the interpretation of the *Treatise*. Rather, their significance lies in the consequences their authors draw from them when they put them to work as master keys to unlock Hume's thought. I will not pursue the implications each of these different commentators may have drawn from the statement but will limit myself to a brief account of one—that of Norman Kemp Smith. In the same introductory chapter of his book in which he offers his interpretation of the "new scene of thought" passage, Smith writes: "What is central in [Hume's] teaching is not Locke's or Berkeley's 'ideal' theory . . . but the doctrine that the determining influence in human, as in other forms of animal life, is feeling, not reason or understanding."[20] A little later, after having quoted extensively from Hume's "Letter to a Physician" and given his interpretation of the "new scene of thought" passage, Smith concludes: "The evidence in support of this reading of the *Treatise* [the one I have just reproduced] is partly internal and partly external. As *external evidence* we have the draft letter [to a physician] which Hume composed while in London in March or April 1734."[21]

Accepting the "external evidence" (or rather his own interpretation of it), Smith devotes most of his book, first, to offering internal evidence to justify his thesis that he has found the clue to an understanding of the *Treatise* in the interpretation he gives and, second, to explicating the text from the perspective of that interpretation. His argument is novel and impressive and has exercised a powerful influence on Hume scholarship in the twentieth century. Nevertheless, it is clearly a pre-textual interpretation of the *Treatise*. Rather than developing out of the text itself, it is applied to the text from the outset, forming a perspective from which Smith views its arguments and theories and into whose contours he then shapes them. Objective though the commentator may try to be, the very fact that he believes himself to have a master key to the *Treatise* in his hand from the start cannot help but exert pressures leading him to an interpretation of the text that supports his hypothesis. That these pressures have actually had such a result can be verified by examining the commentaries of writers, like Smith, who have leaned heavily in the direction of pre-textual interpretation.

Before leaving Hume's "new scene of thought" statement and its various interpretations I must add one further comment. All six interpreters, although they differ in their explanations of the passage, assume that it refers to a philosophical discovery made by the youth. But, ironically, this shared assumption itself could be mistaken. This is the opinion of Reinhard Brandt. In a paper entitled "The Beginnings of Hume's Philosophy"[22] Brandt carefully analyzes the language Hume uses in the passage, other remarks he makes in the letter, and details of his intellectual activities during the year about which he was writing (1729). Brandt reaches two conclusions: (1) That the "new scene of thought" Hume describes was literary criticism rather than philosophy and (2) that Hume did not turn to philosophy and begin the studies that led to the *Treatise* until 1731, or two years later. As Brandt sums up his conclusions: "Hume himself places the beginnings of his philosophy in 1731. . . . It seems probable that in 1729 Hume let himself get involved in the adventure of trying his hand at literary criticism, writing in the exalted and enthusiastic style of a young genius who was trying to express his experience of the Great and Sublime. . . . I think this is the only explanation of the content of the 'new scene of thought' that is based on the texts of Hume and not in the imagination and thoughts of the interpreter."[23]

My point in introducing Brandt's critical thesis is not simply to agree with him. Although he presents a strong case for his view—stronger, I believe, than any of the pre-textual interpreters he is criticizing—questions can also be raised about his reading of the passage. My concern here is not with details but with the larger issue of whether the "new scene of thought" passage can provide a firm basis for *any* conjectures (whatever they may be) about Hume's intentions in writing the *Treatise*. My conclusion is that it cannot, because there is nothing in it that gives us any information at all on this matter.

5. Post-textual Interpretation

I have dwelt on Hume's "new scene of thought" statement not for its own sake but rather to emphasize the problems involved in pre-textual interpretations of his philosophy. Although these can yield illuminating insights into the *Treatise*, they can also impede a full and balanced understanding of it. Nevertheless, Book I of the *Treatise* calls for interpretation. The obvious alternative is post-textual interpretation, the method I will employ in this book. Instead of beginning with a general explanatory formula, into which Hume's views are to be fit, I will make no prejudgments about what Hume "must" have meant but rather I will read and then try to understand what he actually said. From this study certain broad generalizations will emerge. Indeed, it may turn out that one of the interpretations I reproduced in section 4 does succeed in capturing his thought. But that is for the text itself to show. So I will make it my aim as an interpreter of Hume to allow him to speak for himself, keeping any assumptions I might have about his philosophy in abeyance and using my commentary mainly as an aid to the reader in overcoming the difficulties of the text in the hope that the author's thought will lose at least a part of its "inscrutability."

It would be naive, however, to think I wrote this book without having some initial ideas about what is of most importance in the *Treatise*. If I were to attempt a full commentary, including everything Hume wrote in Book I, it would occupy several volumes. Since I cannot do that, I must forgo complete coverage of the text, devoting considerably less attention to certain parts than to others. So I must make some judgments at the outset regarding the relative importance of various parts of Book I. Without going into details here, I think there would be general agreement among Hume scholars that *at least* the following ten topics merit the commentator's closest attention (I list them roughly in the order in which Hume introduces them in Book I): (1) The empiricist theory of ideas; (2) the functions of imagination; (3) the doctrine of association of ideas; (4) space, time, and mathematics; (5) the external world; (6) knowledge and probability or opinion; (7) causation; (8) belief and, especially, natural belief; (9) scepticism; (10) the mind or self. In this book I will devote a substantial part of my discussions to these topics. However, I will not assume that they exhaust the important philosophical issues of Book I. If, in the course of my reading, I discover other topics of importance, I will devote comparable attention to them. On the other hand, I will pay relatively little attention to Hume's digressions, particularly into history, literature, religion, anthropology, and so on, which he uses to illustrate and embellish his central philosophical arguments. These discussions are often highly perceptive and of considerable interest in themselves but, with some exceptions, do not add substantively to an understanding of Hume's philosophy. They can, in any case, usually be grasped by an attentive reader without the need of commentary.

6. Plan of the Book

Given the number of secondary works written about Hume's philosophy, particularly during the twentieth century, one might well ask: Why another book on Hume? I have already answered this question in part, with my critique of pre-textual interpretations of the *Treatise*. But that, in itself, is not a sufficient justification for this book, if for no other reason than that many Hume commentators do not adopt such a procedure.

I had quite another reason for writing the book; namely, that it will fill a significant gap in the literature on Hume. Book I of the *Treatise*, because of its philosophical importance as well as its difficulty, justifies the kind of treatment I give it in this book. Although it has been discussed repeatedly by commentators, to the best of my knowledge no one has yet undertaken the task of following Hume's argument in Book I systematically and in detail, beginning with Section I of Part I and continuing directly in Hume's footsteps all the way through to Section VII of Part IV. That is what I propose to do in this book.[24] After I have presented some introductory material, here and in chapter 1, I will divide the main body of my commentary into four parts, coinciding with the four parts of Book I (but giving them my own titles). Although my commentary will follow Hume's argument step-by-step, I will depart from his organization in one, relatively minor way. I will separate my book into chapters and sections that often do not coincide with his section divisions (giving these my own titles also). My reason for doing so is that Hume's own organization is often perplexing and hard to follow. Throughout this book I attempt to divide the material into chapters and sections in such a way that each division and subdivision has reasonably homogeneous subject matter, but at the same time following the course of Hume's argument. Since, finally, I will be directly concerned only with Book I, I will limit my comments on other parts of the *Treatise* and on Hume's other writings to occasional comparisons between views he expresses elsewhere and those that appear in it.[25]

A question might be raised about the feasibility of limiting a critical commentary to Book I of the *Treatise*, without including the other two books as well. It is true that Book I is part of a larger work, just as, for example, the Transcendental Analytic is part of the *Critique of Pure Reason*. Nevertheless, I believe it contains a complete and comprehensive argument devoted to the central questions of epistemology and metaphysics, which can profitably be examined and evaluated on its own. Although I limit my commentary to Book I, I fully recognize that there is much more to Hume's thought than it contains, not only in Books II and III of the *Treatise* but in his later writings as well. Nor does it represent his most mature thought on all of the issues with which it is concerned; he later changed his mind on at least some points. Yet it is in its own right a classic in fundamental philosophy, and worthy of the attention that generations of scholars have given to it.

In my book I will only occasionally address some of the many complex and controversial issues that have been raised by scholars in their attempts to explicate Hume's philosophy. Instead I will concentrate my attention almost wholly on the text of the *Treatise* itself. Nevertheless, despite my relatively few explicit references to the secondary literature, I have gained immeasurably in my understanding of the *Treatise* from my reading of that literature. I trust that this book will reveal my indebtedness to many Hume scholars, both past and present.

Although my book is meant to serve as an aid to the understanding of Hume, it is not intended to be an introductory textbook, in the ordinary sense of that word. To read it profitably, one needs to have solid grounding in the central problems of epistemology and metaphysics, as well as a background in the history of philosophy in the early modern period, and considerable acquaintance with the thought of Hume himself. My commentary, if it is to succeed in penetrating the complexities of Hume's arguments, will itself often have to become quite complex, hence will not be easy reading. I trust that the comprehension of Hume it will yield for readers will compensate for the difficulties they may encounter in working their way through it. I would even hope that Hume scholars may on occasion find things I say in it worthy of their consideration.

To a certain extent, then, this book may be viewed as an *explication de texte*, in the classical sense of the phrase. But it is more than that. Since Hume was a philosopher, any adequate commentary on his work must be philosophical as well. As a commentator, I will not limit myself to an elucidation of the text but will criticize and evaluate it as well. Such critical evaluation will form an integral part of the body of this book; I will engage in it concurrently with my explication of the text. The passages devoted to critical evaluation will take two forms. I will examine specific arguments Hume offers on various major issues in the course of his exposition. I will also attempt a general assessment of the central philosophical conclusions he reaches in Book I, considered as a whole. Hume himself was convinced, and rightly, that he was presenting a revolutionary philosophical system to the world. Although he does not make many references in the text of the *Treatise* itself to the fact that he is offering a new philosophical theory, it is obvious that he saw himself as doing that. Two statements he makes bear on this point. The first appears in the Introduction, where he writes: "In pretending . . . to explain the principles of human nature, *we in effect propose a compleat system of the sciences, built on a foundation almost entirely new,* and the only one upon which they can stand with any security" (xvi—italics added). And, at the end of the last section of Book I, he writes, with modesty: "We might hope to establish *a system or set of opinions,* which if not true (for that, perhaps, is too much to be hop'd for) might at least be satisfactory to the human mind, and might stand the test of the most critical examination."²⁶ Hume clearly believed himself not only to have originated a new philosophical system, which departed radically from earlier philosophies, but hoped that, unlike these, it could stand "the most critical examination." In my critical examination, I will raise a central question: Does Book I contain a philosophy that is self-consistent or does it break down into irreconcilable contradictions?

Earlier in this Introduction I emphasized that a commentator should read Hume sympathetically. I wish to reiterate that point here but add that such a requirement is consistent with critical evaluation. If Book I is important enough to merit the detailed exposition I will give it, as I am convinced it is, it is also important enough to be subjected to philosophical examination. Hume, I am confident, would agree with this.

7. THE MIND OF DAVID HUME

I will conclude this introductory chapter with a few remarks about the title I have given to my book. My use of the word "mind" in it serves a dual purpose. First, Hume entitles Book I of the *Treatise* "Of the Understanding." Although he does not define the term "understanding," it is clear from the contents of the book that he is writing about that part of human nature concerned with thinking, in contrast to the emotional side of our nature, his concern in Book II, which bears the title "Of the Passions." Furthermore, in his inquiry into the understanding in Book I Hume bases many of his arguments and conclusions on the discoveries he makes through probing into his own mind. By acts of introspection, he repeatedly makes the mind of David Hume the object of his scrutiny. Mind in general and Hume's mind in particular thus form the central focus of Book I.

But I will be interested in Hume's mind in another, quite different way. I hope to "get inside" of that mind in this book, in order to illuminate the manner in which it works, as it does philosophy, by following its path, section by section, through the intricate ways and byways that make up Book I of the *Treatise*.

1

INFLUENCES
AND INTENTIONS

Hume wrote the *Treatise* during a three-year sojourn in France (1734–37), first at the cathedral city of Reims in Champagne and later, for most of his stay, at the town of La Flèche in the Loire Valley. René Descartes had been a student at La Flèche somewhat over a hundred years before but there is no evidence that Hume chose it because of its connection with the great French philosopher. Rather his reasons for settling there seem to have been that it offered him a place to work in a country retreat in which his expenses would be modest; he had to live on a very small income from an inheritance. As he describes his travels in the brief autobiography he wrote a few months before his death:

> I went over to France [in 1734], with a View of prosecuting my Studies in a Country Retreat; and I there laid that Plan of Life, which I have steddily and successfully pursued: I resolved to make a very rigid Frugality supply my Deficiency of Fortune, to maintain unimpaired my Independency, and to regard every object as contemptible, except the Improvement of my Talents in Literature.
>
> During my Retreat in France, first at Reims, but chiefly at La Fleche in Anjou, I composed my *Treatise of Human Nature*. After passing three Years very agreeably in that Countrey, I came over to London in 1737.[1]

So much, briefly, for the physical setting in which the *Treatise* was written. Much more important is the intellectual setting from which it sprang. Before beginning my commentary on Book I, I will describe this setting in some detail, concentrating on two features of the intellectual background of the *Treatise* that can help to explain why Hume wrote as he did: (1) The general intellectual climate of the early eighteenth century and in particular the writers who most deeply influenced Hume's thought and (2) Hume's own goals as he set about composing the *Treatise*. Chapter 1 will be devoted to these topics, under the headings "Influences" and "Intentions."

Influences

1. SOURCES FOR DETERMINING THE INFLUENCES ON HUME'S THOUGHT

Anyone attempting to trace the influences that helped to shape Hume's thought in the *Treatise* is faced with two major obstacles. First, Hume, following general eighteenth-century custom, is very lax in citing references. Book I contains only about a dozen footnotes in which earlier writers are mentioned by name, and several of these are references to the same individual. Also, although it is obvious in many instances that Hume is referring to the views of other writers in the text itself, on occasion even paraphrasing their language, he rarely acknowledges his indebtedness to them—an omission in the *Treatise*, incidentally, for which Hume compensates in later works. So the commentator trying to trace the influences of others on Hume must often rely on inference or circumstantial evidence.

The second obstacle is even more formidable. We know, mainly from his "Letter to a Physician,"[2] that Hume, for several years immediately before his retreat to France to write the *Treatise*, spent most of his time reading literature and philosophy, jotting down his thoughts in copious notes. As he describes his labors and accomplishments during this period in the letter:

> Within these three Years [1731–34], I find I have scribled many a Quire of Paper, in which there is nothing contain'd but my own Inventions. This with the Reading most of the celebrated Books in Latin, French & English, & acquiring the Italian, you may think a sufficient Business for one in perfect Health; & so it wou'd, had it been done to any Purpose: But my Disease was a cruel Incumbrance on me. I found that I was not able to follow out any Train of Thought, by one continued Stretch of View, but by repeated Interruptions, & by refreshing my Eye from Time to Time upon other Objects. Yet with this Inconvenience I have collected the rude Materials for many Volumes.[3]

It is reasonable to conclude that during this period Hume generated at least some of the ideas he later incorporated into his book. Many of these ideas were his own and novel; others were drawn from the thought of earlier writers. Assuming, on the basis of his remarks in the "Letter," that his voracious reading of "the celebrated books" during these crucial years helped to mold his thinking, it would be of inestimable value to know just what books he read and what his reactions to them were. Unfortunately, we have very little information on the subject. One clue Hume gives us about his reading during this period appears in a cryptic remark in his autobiography, written over forty years later. "My studious Disposition, my Sobriety, and my Industry gave my Family a Notion that the Law was a proper Profession for me: But I found an unsurmountable Aversion to every thing but the pursuits of Philosophy and general Learning; and while they fancyed I was poring over Voet and Vinnius, Cicero and Virgil were the Authors which I was secretly devouring."[4]

Among other sources of information about Hume's reading during these years, one deserves mention even though it tells little about the influences on his thought. As he mentions in his "Letter," he wrote a large number of memoranda or notes as he was reading. Unfortunately, he destroyed most of them several years later. A few, however, have survived. E. C. Mossner, Hume's biographer, has published these with a commentary, devoted mainly to dating the time of their composition.[5] According to Mossner, forty-nine were written before Hume left for France to compose the *Treatise*. They consist of short statements (two or three lines) on a variety of subjects, mostly concerned with religion, but referring occasionally to philosophical and scientific questions. In addition to a number of ancients, whom he discusses briefly, Hume directly cites five writers of his own time on issues of possible philosophical interest—Pierre Bayle, Ralph Cudworth, Jean-Baptiste Dubos, François Fénelon, and William King. However, most of these citations have very little connection with the views he developed in the *Treatise* and, with the exception of Bayle (whom I will discuss later in this chapter), none of the writers seems to have influenced the argument of Book I to any noticeable extent. As Mossner sums up their contributions in his biography of Hume: "Among the moderns, five names from the 'Philosophy' section [of the memoranda] will be commented on briefly, not because I wish to make claims for any of them as 'sources' for Hume, rather, on the contrary, because I wish to stress the danger of looking for the unique source by indicating the wide range of influences to which he was deliberately subjecting himself."[6]

To supplement these meager bits of information about the influences on Hume's thought, the commentator can turn to several other sources for further evidence. One such source can be found in a letter Hume wrote anonymously defending the views he had expressed in the *Treatise*, when he was an unsuccessful candidate for a professorship at the University of Edinburgh in 1745. In this letter he cites the names of a number of thinkers, both ancient and modern. Among the latter he includes Hobbes, Clarke, Descartes, Malebranche, Locke, Berkeley, Newton, Cudworth, Wollaston, and Hutcheson.[7] Another letter, this one to Michael Ramsay, written in 1737, is of importance. In it Hume tells his friend: "I desire of you, if you have Leizure, to read once over le Recherche de la Verité of Pere Malebranche, the Principles of Human Knowledge by Dr Berkeley, some of the more metaphysical Articles of Bailes Dictionary; such as those . . .

[of] Zeno, & Spinoza. Des-Cartes Meditations woud also be useful but don't know if you will find it easily among your Acquaintainces. These Books will make you easily comprehend the metaphysical Parts of my Reasoning."[8]

We can glean information about Hume's academic background from the curriculum of the University of Edinburgh in the early eighteenth century, where he was a student from 1723 to 1725 or 1726.[9] From extant records we can determine fairly accurately the subjects he studied at the university as well as the professors who taught them. It is a reasonable inference that these studies and teachers had some influence on the development of his young mind.

In addition we have information from which we can draw inferences about Hume's intellectual interests and activities during the time between his leaving the university and writing the *Treatise*. Although he found the study of law distasteful, he ostensibly devoted the years from 1726 to 1729 to this subject; from his later writings it is apparent that his study was by no means barren. But we know that at the same time he had other, quite different interests. He belonged to at least one literary club in Edinburgh and numbered among his circle of friends many of the young intellectuals who were later to become influential in the Scottish enlightenment. Finally, he had access to the books in several libraries, including the Physiological Library at the University of Edinburgh; the Advocates' Library, also at Edinburgh; and a substantial collection of books in his own library.

From all these sources scholars have drawn some fairly well warranted conclusions regarding the main influences that helped to shape Hume's thinking as he set about to write the *Treatise*. I will not pursue these possibilities further here. Partly because of space limitations but mainly because I am concerned in this book with philosophy rather than with the history of ideas, I will limit myself in the sections that follow to a discussion of a small number of writers who seem to be of major importance to an understanding of Hume's thought, omitting others whom he *may* have read and profited from but whose influence was either relatively minor or cannot be substantiated. While recognizing that Hume was undoubtedly influenced by many earlier writers going back to classical times, it must never be forgotten that the *Treatise* is *Hume's* book, a work not only of genius but also of originality.[10]

2. THE BRITISH EMPIRICISTS

To talk of the "influence" of the British empiricists on Hume may seem odd; after all he was one of them. Indeed, the notion of an empiricist triumvirate—Locke, Berkeley, and Hume—has become so embedded in the history of philosophy that the three are often depicted as though they form a logical sequence, each succeeding thinker carrying the implications of the empiricist position a step beyond those of his predecessor. This logically neat interpretation of the relationships among the three, although it may be a pedagogically convenient device (providing teachers with a foil to cross with that of the triumvirate of continental rationalists), is nevertheless an oversimplification of a complex historical development. Careful scholarship, particularly by writers in the twentieth century, has made it abundantly clear that the simple notion of an empiricist assumption working itself out historically through three minds not only overlooks the many other, quite diverse influences that affected the thought of each but also fails to do justice to the originality of those minds, especially that of Hume. Nevertheless, although the philosophies of Locke, Berkeley, and Hume diverge from each other in a number of ways, it is still fair to describe each (with appropriate qualifications) as an empiricist and to recognize the substantial influence the earlier two had on Hume, particularly in Book I of the *Treatise*.

Turning to Book I (including the introduction) we find that, in the few footnote references it contains, twelve persons are named. Of these Locke is referred to five times, far more than anyone else. Berkeley is named only once, but in the passage in the text to which the footnote is appended Hume calls him "a great philosopher" who is responsible for "one of the greatest and most valuable discoveries that has been made of late years in the republic of letters."[11]

Hume's references to earlier writers do not in themselves imply that he was influenced by the person cited in the narrow sense of agreeing with him; indeed, several citations are appended to passages in which Hume rejects the views of the individual he is citing. Nevertheless, these references are evidence that he was aware of the writer's opinions, had thought seriously about them, and had something of his own to add, whether in agreement or disagreement, to them. In the case of his British predecessors, in particular, an additional point needs to be recognized. Often when Hume disagrees with one of them (which he does on several occasions), his disagreement occurs within the context of a broader agreement. To cite one example: At the beginning of the *Treatise*, Hume points out that Locke has "perverted" the meaning of the term "idea" and that he will restore it to its original sense.[12] This disagreement does not mean that Hume is rejecting Locke's epistemology; rather it is a terminological change that clarifies the theory of knowledge they both accept.

Although both Locke and Berkeley influenced Hume's arguments in various ways throughout Book I, by far their greatest single influence lies in their empiricism, or their view regarding human knowledge or understanding—its origin, nature, and, by implication, its scope and limits. This shared position is often referred to as the "empiricist theory of ideas" or the "empiricist theory of knowledge." Each of these philosophers formulates its basic postulate in a (relatively) succinct statement. Because we will find this postulate to be fundamental to Hume's argument—reiterated at crucial points throughout Book I—I will refer to it frequently in this book. For simplicity's sake I will give it a name, calling it the Empiricist Principle. Locke states the Principle in the following colorful language: "Let us then suppose the mind to be, as we say, white paper, void of all characters, without any ideas:—How comes it to be furnished? Whence comes it by that vast store which the busy and boundless fancy of man has painted on it with an almost endless variety? Whence has it all the *materials* of reason and knowledge? To this I answer, in one word, from EXPERIENCE. . . . [External observation and the internal operations of our minds] are the fountains of knowledge, from whence all the ideas we have, or can naturally have, do spring."[13] Berkeley's statement of the Empiricist Principle, although more prosaic, is almost identical in content with that of Locke: "It is evident to any one who takes a survey of the objects of human knowledge, that they are either ideas actually imprinted on the senses, or else such as are perceived by attending to the passions and operations of the mind, or lastly ideas formed by help of memory and imagination, either compounding, dividing, or barely representing those originally perceived in the aforesaid ways."[14] Finally, we find Hume offering a statement of the Empiricist Principle that, although formulated more tersely and in slightly different terms, captures the essential point he shares with his predecessors: "*All our simple ideas in their first appearance are deriv'd from simple impressions, which are correspondent to them, and which they exactly represent.*"[15] The extent to which Hume was influenced by Locke and Berkeley depends on two related points: The first is the way he interprets the Empiricist Principle and the role he gives it in his theory of knowledge. These topics occupy him primarily in Sections I to V of Part I; I consider them in the next chapter. The second point pertains to the conclusions he derives from the empiricist theory of ideas in the remainder of Book I, particularly regarding the scope and limits of knowledge but also about what exists. Awaiting our detailed discussion of these topics we can say in a preliminary way that this influence is profound—directly as it relates to his theory of knowledge and indirectly as it contributes, through Hume's pursuit of the implications of the Principle, to conclusions that his predecessors had not drawn (or probably even contemplated). One of my main objectives as I go about tracing Hume's argument will be to understand the nature of his empiricism and to see how and why his acceptance of the

Empiricist Principle led him to the conclusions it did, in both epistemology and metaphysics.[16]

3. ISAAC NEWTON

The "scientific revolution," which had begun during the Renaissance, reached its climax with the publication of Isaac Newton's *Philosophiae Naturalis Principia Mathematica* in 1687. This epochal work made Newton's name a household word; during the century that followed, every educated European was at least acquainted with his theories about the universe and the ranks of his followers grew with the passing years.

Certainly Hume was exposed to Newtonianism and was probably conversant with the main views of the new science. But we have little *direct* evidence that he had studied Newton in any depth or was influenced by his thought to any appreciable degree in the *Treatise*. Hume nowhere mentions Newton's name in the book, although he refers briefly to "*the Newtonian* philosophy" in the appendix, in connection with a point about the nature of a vacuum.[17] However, *indirect* evidence can be amassed that supports the view that Hume was not only well acquainted with Newtonian thought but was substantively influenced by it. Newton's new science spread quickly from Cambridge after the *Principia* was published, particularly to other universities, including Edinburgh. During his student days there Hume undertook a course of study that included, in its final year, a concentration on natural philosophy, or science. The instructor was Professor Robert Stewart, who, when Hume was a student, was an adherent of Cartesian science but who later shifted over to Newtonianism. During Hume's time Stewart was undoubtedly conversant with Newton's theories and probably referred to them in his lectures. Also, Hume may well have taken a course in mathematics, which was offered as an elective. The instructor in that course in all probability was Colin Maclaurin, an enthusiastic follower of the Newtonian science who was nominated for his teaching position at Edinburgh by Newton himself. Although we know, from Hume's own description, that his education at Edinburgh did not advance far beyond an elementary level, we can still reasonably infer that during his three years there he was introduced to the new science of Newton.[18]

We have little information about Hume's studies after he left the university—except that he read voraciously. Yet it is not unreasonable to assume that works about the new science were included on his reading lists. Certainly many books were available. A second, revised edition of the *Principia*, edited by Robert Cotes, was published in 1713. This edition contained a preface by Cotes, introducing its readers to the Newtonian system. Henry

Pemberton edited a third edition in 1728 and, in 1729, Andrew Motte published the work in an English translation.[19] In addition, a number of commentaries on Newton's scientific work appeared during these years.

It seems clear that Hume had ample opportunity to study Newton and almost surely did. But was he influenced by Newtonianism? Again, we can appeal to indirect but persuasive evidence that Newton influenced Hume in two quite different ways—methodologically and substantively. The main evidence for this conclusion can be found in the *Treatise* itself.

On the question of methodology one has no further to look than the title page to discover Hume's debt to Newton. The full title of the work is *A Treatise of Human Nature: Being an Attempt to introduce the experimental Method of Reasoning into Moral Subjects*. In the introduction, elaborating his reason for giving the *Treatise* the subtitle he does, Hume refers to Francis Bacon as the individual who first applied the experimental method to scientific subjects in modern times, thus acknowledging his indebtedness to him;[20] but it was Newton who both employed this method rigorously and laid it down as a canon of scientific procedure, one that was to have profound effects on all subsequent scientific thought.

Newton's famous dictum *"Hypotheses non fingo"* (I fashion no hypotheses) is a succinct expression of the new scientific methodology.[21] It does not, of course, mean that Newton was averse to *scientific* hypotheses; quite the contrary, he fashioned some of the most original and important hypotheses in the history of science. Instead he was rejecting *speculative* hypotheses, or alleged explanations of physical phenomena that cannot be confirmed by empirical observation.[22] When we turn to Hume we find him attempting to apply this methodological principle of the new science to the study of human nature. In a repeated injunction, first stated in the introduction to the *Treatise,* he emphasizes that "the only solid foundation we can give to [the science of human nature] must be laid on experience and observation" (xvi). I will elaborate this point later in the chapter (under Hume's "Intentions").

Turning to Newton's influence on Hume in substantive matters, Hume's theory of association of ideas, which forms a central feature of his analysis of human nature, is an apparent adaptation of a basic principle of Newtonian physics—the theory of gravitation. At the very beginning of the *Treatise* (Section IV of Part I) Hume introduces the concept of association, to explain how certain simple ideas join together to form complex ones. At the end of the discussion he comments: "Here [in the association of ideas] is a kind of ATTRACTION, which in the mental world will be found to have as extraordinary effects as in the natural, and to shew itself in as many and as various forms" (12–13). Although Hume mentions neither Newton nor gravitation in this passage, it requires only the slightest inference to make the connection, especially when one remembers that Newton described his gravitational theory in terms of the mutual *attraction* among physical bodies. The analogy between the two concepts is, however, not exact. Gravitation is an attraction that holds between all bodies; association does not hold between all ideas, at least not in the same sense in which gravitation does in the physical world. Also, the force of gravitation can be formulated in precise mathematical terms, but no such precision is possible in the case of association. This weakness of the analogy points up a general problem with Hume's attempt to introduce the experimental method of reasoning into moral subjects; namely, that the differences between the worlds of physical nature and human nature may prove so great that a method capable of providing a satisfactory explanation of the first may not be an adequate instrument to explain the second. Nevertheless, Hume clearly thought he could make the transfer.

Hume's attempt to apply Newton's theory of gravitation to moral philosophy suggests an additional point on which we can postulate a Newtonian influence on him. Although this influence cannot be documented textually, because of its close connection to the one just described it seems reasonable to add it. According to Newton, the basic components of the universe are physical atoms, or particles. As he puts it: "It seems probable to me, that God in the Beginning form'd Matter in solid, massy, hard, impenetrable, moveable Particles."[23] Gravitation affects atoms, causing them to coalesce, thus forming complex bodies. Once again, appealing to analogy one could argue that Hume, in his analysis of human nature, conceived of our simple ideas as the counterpart, in the mental realm, of Newton's atoms in the physical realm. Just as gravitation brings the physical atoms together to form larger bodies, according to Newton, so association brings the mental atoms, or simple ideas, together to form complex ideas, according to Hume.

4. FRANCIS HUTCHESON

In his influential book *The Philosophy of David Hume,* Norman Kemp Smith writes: "The thesis which I propose to maintain is that it was [Hutcheson's view that all moral and aesthetic judgments rest not on reason but solely on feeling] which opened out to Hume the 'new Scene of Thought' of which he speaks in his letter of 1734. For there is a path that leads directly from them *to all that is most fundamental in his philosophy.*"[24] Smith is unquestionably right in his claim that Hutcheson exerted an influence on Hume; that the influence was most fundamental to Hume's entire philosophy is, however, a different—and more arguable—matter.

As with Newton, we have almost no direct but substantial indirect evidence of Hutcheson's influence on Hume. The lack of direct evidence is apparent; Hume mentions Hutcheson only once in the *Treatise*, in a footnote in the introduction, where he is listed along with four other writers as having "begun to put the science of man on a new footing."[25] This reference, although it establishes that Hume was acquainted with Hutcheson's writings and recognized his importance, does not acknowledge a major Hutchesonian influence on his own thought.

Before turning to the indirect evidence of Hutcheson's influence on Hume, a few remarks should be inserted about the personal relationship between the two men. Francis Hutcheson was appointed Professor of Moral Philosophy at the University of Glasgow in 1729, where he gained fame as a teacher and as a leading moral philosopher of his time, developing the "moral sense" theory of ethics, on the foundations laid by Shaftesbury at the beginning of the eighteenth century.[26] Hume, seventeen years his junior, did not know Hutcheson personally at the time he was composing the *Treatise* but after publishing the first two volumes sought his acquaintance in 1739 to get his advice about Book III ("Of Morals"), which he was then preparing for publication. Hutcheson made a number of critical comments about Hume's manuscript and helped him find a London publisher, who brought the volume out in 1740.[27] Correspondence between Hume and Hutcheson, who had met and become friends, continued until 1744 when Hume applied for the Chair of Ethics and Pneumatic Philosophy at the University of Edinburgh, a position he failed to obtain. He became convinced that a part of the reason for his failure was Hutcheson's opposition to his appointment. In a letter he wrote at the time, he complained: "For as to Mr Hutcheson, all my Friends think, that he has been rendering me bad Offices to the utmost of his Power. . . . What can be the Meaning of this Conduct in that celebrated & benevolent Moralist, I cannot imagine."[28] After rejecting Hume's candidacy the university offered the professorship to Hutcheson himself but he declined it. Understandably, the unpleasantness arising from this incident apparently ended the friendship between the two.

The evidence we have of the personal relationship between the men, particularly in Hume's letters, gives us strong grounds for inferring that Hume was well acquainted with Hutcheson's work in ethics and found his views congenial. To support the conclusion that Hutcheson's moral philosophy influenced Hume's thought in Book I of the *Treatise* (which was published before the two became personally acquainted), however, we have to make two inferences: (1) That Hutcheson influenced Hume's *moral* philosophy and (2) that this influence extended to his epistemology. For our purposes, since we are concerned with Book I, the second inference is the more important.

It is generally agreed that the moral theories of Hutcheson and Hume are quite similar. Hutcheson held that our beliefs about what is good and evil spring from a moral sense. He describes this as an inner sense, analogous to such outer senses as sight and hearing in that it is an original feature of human experience. As an inner sense it differs from our other five senses in being a feeling or emotion rather than a sensation. Finally, and of great importance, our moral sense does not rest on reason. We do not come to the conclusion that something is good or evil through any process of thought; rather we immediately *feel* approval or disapproval of it when we confront it. Hutcheson's view, thus, is a form of ethical nonrationalism. In his own summary of it he writes: "We are not to imagine, that this *moral Sense,* more than the other Senses, supposes any *innate Ideas, Knowledge,* or *practical Proposition:* We mean by it only *a Determination of our Minds to receive amiable or disagreeable Ideas of Actions, when they occur to our Observation.*"[29]

Turning to Hume's ethics we find a clear parallel with Hutcheson. In Book III of the *Treatise*, Hume adopts a moral-sense theory, explicitly based on feeling or passion. He entitles Section II of Part I "Moral distinctions deriv'd from a moral sense" (470). Describing his moral-sense view he writes: "Morality, therefore, is more properly felt than judg'd of. . . . To have the sense of virtue, is nothing but to *feel* a satisfaction of a particular kind from the contemplation of a character. The very *feeling* constitutes our praise or admiration" (470–71). On the question of the relationship of our moral sense to reason, Hume is equally explicit. The title of Section I of Part I is "Moral Distinctions not deriv'd from Reason" (455).

The similarities in their views makes it reasonable to conclude that Hutcheson did influence Hume in his moral philosophy. But, given the paucity of direct information on the subject, we cannot be sure how strong this influence was. Hume read widely prior to composing the *Treatise* and he may have been inspired by some other predecessors, particularly the classical writers whose views on morality he generally held in high esteem.[30] On the positive side, we have the evidence that, before its publication, he submitted Book III of the *Treatise* to Hutcheson for his comments and, after receiving them, wrote to him: "I am much oblig'd to you for your Reflections on my Papers. I have perus'd them with Care, & find they will be of use to me."[31]

To establish Hutcheson's influence on Book I of the *Treatise*, however, we must make a further inference; namely, that Hume expanded his moral-sense theory beyond the realm of ethics, applying it to his epistemology as well. Evidence can be found in Book I that lends credence to this inference, even though it rests on the assumption that Hume's ethics, despite the organization of the *Treatise*, is the heart of the book and his epis-

temology and metaphysics derivative from it. The argument for the
Hutchesonian interpretation of Book I rests mainly on Hume's theory of
natural belief, which he holds to be a product not of a rational process but
rather of feeling. Thus, if one assumes that this theory is the core of Hume's epistemology, one might well conclude that the argument of Book I
is founded on Hume's interpretation of our moral judgments in Book III.
Since I will be discussing the theory of natural belief at length later in my
book, I will not devote further space to it here.

To sum up this section, we can conclude that Hutcheson did exercise a
fundamental influence on Hume in Book I of the *Treatise*—*if* Hume derived his moral-sense theory of ethics, with its nonrationalism, from him,
if his conclusions regarding epistemology and metaphysics rest on his theory of natural belief, and *if* this theory in turn is derived from his nonrational ethics. A case can be made for all of these hypotheses but, on the
evidence we have, the second and the third, in particular, seem open to
question.

5. THE CLASSICAL SCEPTICS

Scepticism makes its appearance in a number of places throughout Book
I, as Hume examines and finds wanting the reasons we give for various
beliefs we hold. The sceptical conclusions he reaches are usually based on
the epistemological foundation of his theory of ideas in Part I, in particular the Empiricist Principle. To the degree, therefore, that he was influenced by other thinkers in drawing these conclusions, the influence came
primarily from the earlier British empiricists. In each of these cases his
scepticism is directed toward a specific item of belief, so constitutes only a
partial rather than a total scepticism.

Besides these partial scepticisms, however, a quite different kind of scepticism, not based on his empiricism, appears in Section I of Part IV. Hume
labels it "total" scepticism, and in Section VII of that part (the last section
of Book I) makes an addition to this total scepticism that he calls "true"
scepticism. Unlike his other sceptical views in Book I, these two are not
limited to any specific objects of belief but are completely general in their
scope. In Section I it is apparent that the setting for Hume's total scepticism is the scepticism of the ancients, in particular the Pyrrhonists.[32] That
Hume was acquainted with classical Pyrrhonism is evidenced, first, in his
direct reference to it in the section. Although he does not mention them
by name, it is obvious that he is referring to the Pyrrhonists when he writes:

> My intention then in displaying so carefully the arguments of that fantastic
> sect, is only to make the reader sensible of the truth of my hypothesis . . . *that*

belief is more properly an act of the sensitive, than of the cogitative part of our
natures. I have here prov'd, that the very same principles, which make us form
a decision upon any subject . . . when carry'd farther, and apply'd to every
new reflex judgment, must . . . at last reduce it to nothing, and utterly subvert all belief and opinion. If belief, therefore, were a simple act of the
thought . . . it must infallibly destroy itself, and in every case terminate in *a*
total suspense of judgment. (183–84—second italics added)

That Hume had Pyrrhonism in mind when he wrote these words is clear
from the phrase with which he concludes the passage—"a total suspense
of judgment." This is a close paraphrase of a thesis appearing in the *Out-*
lines of Pyrrhonism by Sextus Empiricus, the chronicler of classical Pyrrhon-
istic scepticism. Sextus writes: "Scepticism is an ability, or mental attitude,
which opposes appearances to judgements in any way whatsoever, with the
result that, owing to the equipollence of the objects and reasons thus opposed, we are brought firstly to a state of mental suspense and next to a
state of 'unperturbedness' or quietude. . . . 'Suspense' is a state of mental
rest owing to which we neither deny nor affirm anything."[33]

Fuller, but somewhat less direct evidence of Hume's acquaintance with
Pyrrhonist thought is provided by the form taken by his "true" scepticism
of Part IV, Section VII. Without describing this scepticism in detail here
(something I will do in chapter 18), it is enough to note that the intermittent suspension of judgment involved in that "true" scepticism, relieved by
an equally intermittent pursuit of philosophy, is a variant form of the suspension of judgment advocated by the Pyrrhonists.

Although the influence of the Pyrrhonists on Hume is evident, it must
be qualified; he did not consider himself to be a Pyrrhonist. That he dis-
associated himself from Pyrrhonism is strongly suggested by his reference
to it, in the passage I reproduced above from Section I, as "that fantastic
sect." Furthermore, he writes, in that same section: "Shou'd it here be ask'd
me . . . whether I be really one of those sceptics, who hold that all is uncertain, and that our judgment is not in *any* thing possest of *any* measures
of truth and falshood; I shou'd reply, that this question is entirely superfluous, and that neither I, nor any other person was ever sincerely and constantly of that opinion" (183). But it has to be added that this disavowal
comes immediately after Hume has reached a conclusion that echoes a
central thesis found repeatedly in the writings of Sextus: "All the rules of
logic require a continual diminution, and at last a total extinction of belief
and evidence."[34]

Perhaps more important to the thesis that Hume was substantially influenced by the Pyrrhonists is the context and form in which he develops
his "true" scepticism in Section VII. Convinced, on the one side, that none
of our beliefs can be rationally justified, he was impelled in the direction

of a Pyrrhonic suspension of judgment. But equally convinced, on the other side, that we must believe and hence judge, he drew back from the Pyrrhonic extreme. His compromise was to find a position in which both belief and its suspension play their successive roles. It is in this middle way between Pyrrhonic suspension and belief, which he calls "true" scepticism, that Hume comes to rest.

6. Pierre Bayle

Evidence of the influence on Hume of the French philosopher and man of letters, Pierre Bayle (1647–1706), can be found in several places in the *Treatise*. Bayle exerted his main influence on three quite different topics discussed in Book I: (1) The analyses of space and time and of a vacuum, which appear in Part II; (2) the critique of the notion of simple substances, especially in Section V of Part IV; and (3) the defense of scepticism, particularly that stemming originally from ancient Pyrrhonism (which I have just discussed). We have direct (or almost direct) evidence of all of these influences. To begin, we know from Hume's own testimony that he was acquainted with Bayle's thought before he wrote the *Treatise*, because he cites him by name on no less than sixteen of the numbered memoranda that have survived from his period of independent study just prior to his departure for France in 1734.[35] We also have the evidence from Hume's letter of 1737 to Michael Ramsay, which lists a number of writers, including Bayle, to whom he was indebted.[36]

Turning to the *Treatise* itself, and concentrating on the three topics I have listed, the evidence for Bayle's influence on Hume regarding the first rests on similarities in their discussions of space and a vacuum. These are so marked that they make the conclusion that Hume was acutely aware of the arguments found in Bayle's article "Zenon d'Elée" in his *Dictionaire Historique et Critique* virtually certain.[37] To mention some specific examples, Bayle claims that there are three possible theories regarding the nature of space and that all of them can be shown to lead to contradictions. Hume accepts the same three possibilities and, following Bayle, rejects two as being untenable but argues, against him, that the third can be made viable.[38] On the question of the possibility of a vacuum, both offer similar arguments designed to show inconsistencies in the concept itself but, even more specifically, Hume employs the same example Bayle had used—that of a room surrounded by walls from which all the air has been evacuated.[39]

Bayle's second influence on Hume is quite specific. In Section V of Part IV, entitled "Of the immateriality of the soul" (232), Hume questions whether the notion of substance, either material or immaterial, is intelligible. His argument leads him into a discussion of the Spinozistic theory of substance, which he criticizes at length. In the course of this criticism, he inserts one of his few footnotes in Book I, writing "See *Bayle's* dictionary, article of *Spinoza*."[40] Many of the points Hume makes in the section can be found in Bayle's article; for example, that Spinoza was an atheist, that he attempted to locate what is made up of parts in a simple substance, that modes cannot be distinguished from the substances in which they inhere, and others. On one occasion Bayle and Hume use the same illustration, both denying that the substance of a round table can be identical with that of a square table.[41] On another, they use almost identical language in castigating Spinoza, Bayle describing his metaphysics as "la plus monstrueuse Hypothese"[42] and Hume calling it a "hideous hypothesis" (241). Although Hume goes beyond Bayle in Section V, applying the same kinds of arguments Bayle had used against Spinoza's view of material substance to the theologians' doctrine of an immaterial soul-substance, the important point is that the evidence, even without Hume's own footnote reference, clearly supports the conclusion that his arguments in that section are often patterned after those of Bayle's article "Spinoza."[43]

The third main influence Bayle exerted on Hume concerns his relationship to scepticism, in particular that of the classical Pyrrhonists. On this issue the primary reference is Bayle's *Dictionaire* article "Pyrrhon."[44] This influence is particularly important, not simply because it may well have been through Bayle that Hume became interested in the classical sceptics, but also because of the close relationships between Hume's scepticism and that of the ancients. I have already discussed this connection in section 5; here I will simply add a brief comment about the role played by Bayle in a central sceptical argument Hume used in Section I of Part IV—his attempt to employ reason to destroy reason.

In Note (B) of his article "Pyrrhon," particularly in a long discussion purportedly between two abbés, Bayle shows how a Pyrrhonist can undermine both logic and mathematics, thus destroying reason. In a summary of the results of the discussion he writes: "A learned theologian who was there . . . concluded that it was a waste of time to dispute with the Pyrrhonists and that their sophisms could not easily be eluded by the mere force of reason; that before everything else it was necessary to be made sensible of the weakness of reason in order to have recourse to a better guide; namely, faith."[45] In Section I, Hume, like Bayle, offers a series of arguments designed to show that reason can be turned against reason, leading to its ultimate self-destruction. He concludes: "'Tis happy, therefore, that nature breaks the force of all sceptical arguments in time, and keeps them from having any considerable influence on the understanding. Were we to trust entirely to their self-destruction, that can never take place, 'till they have first subverted all conviction, and have totally destroy'd human reason" (187). It should be noted that neither Bayle nor Hume rests content with the total scepticism to which their arguments have led them. The former seeks refuge in faith; the latter in nature.

7. THE CARTESIANS

Given Hume's antipathy to classical rationalism, it might seem reasonable to conclude that he was not markedly influenced by Cartesianism. This, at least, is the view of some Hume scholars. Others recognize a strong influence, and at least one—Antony Flew—believes that influence to be a dominating force in Hume's thought. In his book *David Hume*, Flew writes: "Almost all [Hume's] conclusions are, for better or for worse, conditioned and sometimes determined by an interlocking set of Cartesian assumptions."[46] Some confirmation of Flew's opinion can be found in Hume's writings, particularly in the passage from his letter to Michael Ramsay, which I have reproduced in section 1, in which he cites "le Recherche de la Verité of Pere Malebranche" and "Des-Cartes Meditations" (as well as works of Berkeley and Bayle) and concludes: "These Books will make you easily comprehend the metaphysical Parts of my Reasoning."

Turning to the *Treatise* we find that, although Descartes is never mentioned in Book I, the name of Nicholas Malebranche (1638–1715) appears twice. The first citation occurs in Section XIV of Part III, "Of the idea of necessary connexion," and the second in Section V of Part IV, "Of the immateriality of the soul." In both of these sections Hume is discussing metaphysical problems.

In the first passage in which he cites Malebranche[47] Hume is examining the standard view that, in every cause-effect relation, the cause possesses some force or energy that produces the effect. After pointing out that, because we have no impression of any such causal efficacy in bodies, we can have no idea of it, he proceeds to attack a variety of explanations of this force given by earlier philosophers, writing: "There are some, who maintain, that bodies operate by their substantial form; others, by their accidents or qualities; several, by their matter and form; some by their form and accidents; others, by certain virtues and faculties distinct from all this. . . . the supposition of an efficacy in any of the known qualities of matter is entirely without foundation" (158). Turning with Hume in his footnote to Book VI, Part 2, Chapter 3, of Malebranche's *Recherche de la Vérité*, we find the author criticizing the view that material bodies can have any causal efficacy. Like Hume he cites a variety of theories that attempt to explain this causal power, such as "substantial forms," "real qualities," "faculties," "virtues," and so on.[48] He concludes: "There are then no forces, powers, or true causes in the material, sensible world; and there is no need to admit the existence of forms, faculties, and real qualities in order to produce effects that bodies do not produce."[49] In this instance Hume acknowledges his debt but, even without his citation, it is clear that Hume's argument borrows heavily from that of Malebranche.[50]

Hume's second citation of Malebranche, in Section V of Part IV, concerns a point on which the two disagree; namely, the causal efficacy of God, which Malebranche affirms and Hume denies.[51] Hume's main argument against Malebranche and other Cartesians rests on an appeal to the Empiricist Principle; to have an idea of God's causal power we must have an impression from which it is derived, but there is no such impression. His most forceful statement of this objection actually appears earlier in Book I, where he writes: "The supposition of a deity can serve us in no stead, in accounting for that idea of agency. . . . For if every idea be deriv'd from an impression, the idea of a deity proceeds from the same origin; and if no impression, either of sensation or reflection, implies any force or efficacy, 'tis equally impossible to discover or even imagine any such active principle in the deity."[52]

Despite this disagreement, both writers share a related view about the nature of causality. In the same chapter of his *Recherche* in which he raises objections to the causal powers of bodies, Malebranche rejects the view that finite minds can be causes. He writes: "Now to me it appears very certain that the will of minds is incapable of moving the smallest body in the world; for it is evident that there is no necessary connection between our will to move our arm, for example, and the movement of our arm."[53] Hume uses the same kind of illustration to reach the same conclusion. In his words: "Some have asserted, that we feel an energy, or power, in our own mind. . . . The motions of our body, and the thoughts and sentiments of our mind, (say they) obey the will. . . . But to convince us how fallacious this reasoning is, we need only consider, that the will being here consider'd as a cause, has no more a discoverable connexion with its effects, than any material cause has with its proper effect."[54]

In summary, Malebranche was a major source for Hume's arguments dealing with two of the most important critical conclusions of Book I—the denial that we can have any knowledge that either bodies or minds exert causal power—conclusions at radical variance with most of the philosophical wisdom of the age. Having agreed on these conclusions, however, the two parted company. Malebranche (as well as other Cartesians), apparently convinced that the universe must contain a real causal power, located it in the will of God. But Hume was unwilling to accept such an answer, finding the causality of God's will as inexplicable as that of bodies or of finite wills. So he devised an entirely novel explanation of the causal relationship.

Before leaving the Cartesians I should add a note of a different kind.

Although, particularly through Malebranche, they influenced Hume in positive ways, they also exerted a strong negative influence on his thought. Throughout Book I we find him repeatedly voicing his rejection of the rationalistic approach to philosophy embodied in the Cartesian tradition.

Intentions

To preface my study of the *Treatise* with a statement of Hume's intentions might well seem inconsistent with the post-textual character of the interpretation I said I would undertake in this book. Indeed it would be, if I were to base my statement of his intentions on my own preconceived notion of his philosophy. Fortunately I do not have to do that because Hume states his intentions himself, although only in very general terms, at the outset of his book. He offers the first clue to these intentions in its title. The subject with which he will be concerned is *human nature*. The subtitle, *An Attempt to introduce the experimental Method of Reasoning into Moral Subjects*, is more revealing of his intentions.[55] I have mentioned this subtitle already, in connection with my review of Newton's influence on Hume. Here I will expand on those earlier remarks, basing my discussion on Hume's own statements regarding his intentions in writing the *Treatise*, which he develops (all too briefly) in his introduction to the book.[56]

These intentions can be divided into three main parts: First, as the book employs the experimental method of reasoning; second, as it applies this method to the subject matter of human nature; and, third, as this application affects our study of other realms of intellectual inquiry. I will take these topics up in order, noting, however, that the issues they raise are closely interrelated.

As far as the experimental method is concerned, Hume accepts the basic position of Newton and the new science. As he puts it, "The only solid foundation we can give to this science itself [the science of man] must be laid on experience and observation" (xvi). But he recognizes a complication resulting from the attempt to apply the experimental method to a study of human nature, making that application much more difficult than it is in the study of physical nature. Whereas the physical scientist can use the method of controlled experiment, the moral scientist cannot. The reason for this difference is obvious; the physicist, say, can manipulate his materials in his laboratory but the social scientist, whose materials are human beings, can rarely even put them in a laboratory, let alone manipulate them to suit his purposes. If he tries to avoid this difficulty by making himself the subject of his experimentation, he finds that the attempt to be both observer and observed distorts his data. So the only version of the experimental method of the natural sciences available to the social scientist is the careful observation of human behavior as people go about living their daily lives. In Hume's words: "Moral philosophy has, indeed, this peculiar disadvantage, which is not found in natural, that in collecting its experiments, it cannot make them purposely, with premeditation. . . . We must therefore glean up our experiments in this science from a cautious observation of human life, and take them as they appear in the common course of the world, by men's behaviour in company, in affairs, and in their pleasures."[57]

In spite of these methodological limitations, Hume is sanguine about the possibilities of a science of human nature. He concludes his introduction on an optimistic note: "Where experiments of this kind [cautious observation of human life] are judiciously collected and compared, we may hope to establish on them a science, which will not be inferior in certainty, and will be much superior in utility to any other of human comprehension" (xix). Behind this apparent optimism, however, lies a deeper pessimism. Although students both of human nature and of physical nature should probe their respective subject matters as far as their experimental methods will permit, they must realize that they can never penetrate beyond the range of experience, hence can never comprehend the ultimate principles either of human beings or of the natural world: "We cannot go beyond experience; and any hypothesis, that pretends to discover the ultimate original qualities of human nature, ought at first to be rejected as presumptuous and chimerical. . . . But if this impossibility of explaining ultimate principles should be esteemed a defect in the science of man, I will venture to affirm, that 'tis a defect common to it with all the sciences" (xvii–xviii).

Nevertheless, Hume does not feel that these limitations on our ability to understand either the human or the natural world fully should seriously concern us. Once we recognize that we cannot probe either to its utmost depths, we lose the desire to do so, remaining contented with a level of understanding that can be gained by any ordinary person without special study at all. As Hume concludes: "When we see, that we have arrived at the utmost extent of human reason, we sit down contented; tho' we be perfectly satisfied in the main of our ignorance, and perceive that we can give no reason for our most general and most refined principles, beside our experience of their reality; which is the reason of the mere vulgar, and what it required no study at first to have discovered" (xviii).

So much, then, for what Hume means by the experimental method, the way in which it can be applied to a study of human nature, and the limitations of any such study. The final question about Hume's intentions in the *Treatise*, as he describes them in the introduction, concerns the conclusions he hopes to establish about the relationship between our understanding of human nature, limited though it may be, and the progress we can make in the other sciences. This relationship establishes, for Hume, the importance of the undertaking on which he is about to embark. Put briefly, Hume's thesis is that the science of human nature is fundamental to all the other sciences for the simple reason that these sciences are enterprises carried on by human beings. Therefore, unless we first understand human nature, we can never succeed in reaching an understanding of the nonhuman world. Hume presents his case in the following forceful terms: "There is no question of importance, whose decision is not compriz'd in the science of man; and there is none, which can be decided with any certainty, before we become acquainted with that science. In pretending therefore to explain the principles of human nature, we in effect propose a compleat system of the sciences, built on a foundation almost entirely new, and the only one upon which they can stand with any security" (xvi).

This is indeed a bold thesis. Certainly a case can be made that, in some areas of study Hume mentions, such as natural religion, morals, criticism, and politics, progress is dependent on a clear conception of humanity and the human condition. But the foundational nature of human studies for other areas of the sciences is considerably less apparent. To what extent would Newton have been aided in his astronomical investigations by a prior understanding of human nature? A similar question can be raised about logic and mathematics, whose comprehension, Hume contends, must also rest on the same foundation. Yet, although we may express reservations about the claim Hume makes for the fundamental importance of a study of human nature, we should recognize the novelty of his thesis. When he writes that, by making this study the basis of all others, he is proposing a foundation for them "almost entirely new," he is surely not overstating his case. Hume is indeed embarking on a new, important, and, needless to say, extraordinarily difficult intellectual enterprise in the *Treatise*. Even though he warns us not to expect it to result in an understanding of the "ultimate principles of the soul" (xvii), he still wants us to know that his intent in the book will be to provide, through the deepest study of human nature of which the human mind is capable, a foundation for "a compleat system of the sciences."

One qualification must, however, be made. Although Hume believed that our understanding of human nature would provide the foundation for a complete system of the sciences, he did not propose to develop such a system in the *Treatise*. Rather, he limited his enterprise to the realm of the moral sciences. In the "Advertisement" he inserted into the beginning of the *Treatise* he described his project in the following terms:

My design in the present work is sufficiently explain'd in the introduction. *The reader must only observe, that all the subjects I have there plann'd out to my self, are not treated of in these two volumes. The subjects of the* understanding *and* passions *make a compleat chain of reasoning by themselves; and I was willing to take advantage of this natural division, in order to try the taste of the public. If I have the good fortune to meet with success, I shall proceed to the examination of* morals, politics, *and* criticism; *which will compleat this* Treatise of human nature. (xii)

Hume, in fact, completed only three of the five volumes projected for the *Treatise*, adding the third, "Of Morals," to the first two in 1740. However, in later years he wrote extensively in the fields of politics and criticism, including two volumes of *Essays, Moral and Political* (1741, 1742), a volume of *Political Discourses* (1752), *Four Dissertations*, one dealing with tragedy and another with the standard of taste (1757), plus other related works.

If one is to have any prospect of completing the kind of project Hume outlines in his "Advertisement" and then continuing to develop a system of the sciences based on a foundation of human nature, one must have a clear conception of the instrument one is to employ in this task, including a just appreciation of its powers and a realization of its limitations. One must start with an examination of the human mind as an instrument of reasoning. Hume is fully aware of this need. So he writes in the introduction: "'Tis evident, that all the sciences have a relation, greater or less, to human nature. . . . 'Tis impossible to tell what changes and improvements we might make in these sciences were we thoroughly acquainted with the extent and force of human understanding, and cou'd explain the nature of the ideas we employ, and of the operations we perform in our reasonings" (xv). Thus, to carry out the project he set for himself in the *Treatise*, it is perfectly appropriate for Hume to begin as he does, with an examination of human understanding and reasoning. This is the subject matter of Book I, which he entitles "Of the Understanding."

Part 1

HUME'S EMPIRICIST EPISTEMOLOGY

Book I of *A Treatise of Human Nature* examines the cognitive side of our nature, in contrast to the emotional side, to which Book II is devoted. Hume entitles Book I "Of the Understanding," dividing it into four parts: "Of ideas; their origin, composition, abstraction, connexion, &c."; "Of the ideas of space and time"; "Of knowledge and probability"; and "Of the sceptical and other systems of philosophy." These titles, as we will discover as we progress through Book I, are not fully representative of the parts themselves, whose contents are considerably richer and more diverse than they suggest, including discussions of most of the central problems of epistemology and metaphysics. Although this is least true of Part I, the part itself falls naturally into two subdivisions, which I have recognized by dividing my commentary on it into separate chapters (2 and 3). Of the two subdivisions, the first (which consists of Sections I through V) is the more important because in it Hume sets forth the epistemological foundations of his philosophy in Book I, including the main conclusions he will reach about the extent and limits of our knowledge and about the nature of reality. In the second subdivision of the part (which consists of Sections VI and VII) he begins to put his theory of ideas to work, applying it to some classic issues in epistemology and metaphysics.

Part I is the shortest of the four parts of Book I, occupying only twenty-five pages of text. This causes serious difficulties for an adequate understanding of Hume's philosophy. The material contained in the part is not only of fundamental importance but is quite complex as well. But Hume treats it in a cursory way. Central concepts are often not adequately explained and relationships between these concepts left obscure. As a result the commentator has the burden of filling the gaps in a way that seems most consonant with Hume's thought. One is tempted to ask: Why did Hume devote so little space to his explanation of the epistemological foundations of his system? I cannot, of course, answer that question but will venture the following hypothesis: In the early eighteenth century, when Hume wrote the *Treatise*, the dominant philosophical book in the English-speaking world was Locke's *Essay Concerning Human Understanding*. Everyone with philosophical pretensions had either read it or was acquainted with its contents. In this monumental work Locke had devoted over four hundred pages to the exposition and defense of an epistemological theory much like the one Hume offers in Part I of the *Treatise*. Under these circumstances it is understandable that Hume should assume he was writing for a knowledgeable audience, so should conclude that it was not necessary to elaborate his epistemological position in lengthy detail.

I have entitled part 1 of this book "Hume's Empiricist Epistemology." A few remarks should be made about the word "empiricist." Although Hume is called an "empiricist" by almost all commentators, he does not use that term to describe himself. Neither it, nor the word "empiricism," appears in Book I or (as far as I have found) anywhere else in Hume's philosophical writings. This raises an interesting question: When and where did the term originate as a label for Hume's philosophy, as well as those of Locke and Berkeley? The term itself is old, its etymology going back to classical times, the Greek word from which it is derived meaning "observational experience." It is enshrined in the history of philosophy in the name Sextus Empiricus, the second-century Pyrrhonist. But who first applied it in modern philosophy to Locke, Berkeley, and Hume—the so-called "British empiricists"? This is an intriguing question for those interested in the history of ideas but one that falls outside the scope of my present study, and so I will not pursue it here.[1]

2

THE ELEMENTS OF
HUME'S PHILOSOPHY

(Part I, Sections I–V)

Introduction

In a summary statement Hume describes the contents of Part I as "the elements of [his] philosophy" (13). If we understand by the term "elements" the basic conceptions that form the foundations on which a philosopher will construct his or her system, it is clear that these may be of several different kinds. With some philosophers they are metaphysical, with others theological; some have turned to science and yet others to logic or mathematics to lay the foundations of their systems. The elements of Hume's philosophy are epistemological. That this should be so is understandable. In Book I Hume is concerned with the understanding, or that faculty in human nature with which we think or reason. He is also concerned with knowledge—its scope and limits. To lay the groundwork for the theories he will develop later in the book, he begins with an analysis of the understanding and of the materials with which it works in its attempts to gain knowledge of the world.

The main subject of this analysis is what Hume calls "perceptions." This is a general term he uses to identify the contents of human consciousness. He divides perceptions into "impressions" and "ideas." The most important epistemological theory he states concerns the relationship between these two types of perception. I have labeled it the Empiricist Principle.[1] Hume employs the Principle throughout the remainder of Book I as a pivotal argument in his critique of traditional philosophers and in drawing many of his own philosophical conclusions. Although perceptions and the Empiricist Principle are the main theoretical elements in Hume's epistemology, the first five sections of Part I include several other basic concepts that are critical to an understanding of his philosophy in Book I. I will discuss these generally in the order in which he introduces them, but arrange my exposition in some instances somewhat differently from his.[2]

Text

1. PERCEPTIONS: IMPRESSIONS AND IDEAS (SECTION I)

Hume begins Book I of the *Treatise* with an explanation of three central concepts of his epistemology. The first four sentences read as follows:

> All the perceptions of the human mind resolve themselves into two distinct kinds, which I shall call IMPRESSIONS and IDEAS. The difference betwixt these consists in the degrees of force and liveliness, with which they strike upon the mind, and make their way into our thought or consciousness. Those perceptions, which enter with most force and violence, we may name *impressions;* and under this name I comprehend all our sensations, passions and emotions, as they make their first appearance in the soul. By *ideas* I mean the faint images of these in thinking and reasoning. (1)

Each of the terms Hume introduces in this passage needs comment. "Perception" is a general term; it means whatever we are aware of, whatever "appears before the mind" or is the content or object of consciousness.[3] Thus we can say that, for Hume, a person's experience is made up of all the perceptions he has. Perceptions are divided into two subclasses—impressions and ideas. Every perception one has is either an impression or an idea, so one's life experience is the total of one's impressions and ideas. Because they are more specific in their meanings, these two concepts give us more detailed information than does the broader term "perception." As a result they become the primary working concepts of Hume's epistemology. So I will concentrate my attention on them, first explicating each individually, then turning to a discussion of their differences, their relationships, and their ontological status.

Impressions as they first appear in consciousness are of two kinds, either sensations or passions and emotions. Because Book I is devoted to the understanding, Hume is concerned almost exclusively with the first kind, deferring his discussion of the second to Book II. I will follow him in this, equating the term "impression," as it refers to an original content of consciousness, with the term "sensation." Sensations are primarily the impressions we experience through our five senses—sight, hearing, touch, taste, and smell—but they also include such feelings as heat or cold, thirst or hunger, and pleasure or pain (8). The special feature of impressions, distinguishing them from ideas, is their force or liveliness or, to add a term Hume himself uses frequently throughout Book I, their vivacity. Hume does not attempt to define these terms, descriptive of our sensations, but assumes that we understand what they mean. Our visual experience of a bright light shining in our eyes is certainly lively, as is our auditory experience of a clap of thunder or our olfactory experience of an agitated skunk. These impressions enter our minds, as Hume says, "with most force and violence."

Equally as important as our impressions are our ideas. That Hume wishes to emphasize the central role they will play in his philosophy is clear from the fact not only that he entitles Section I "Of the Origin of our Ideas" but also that he gives all of Part I the title "Of Ideas. . . ." In what, then, does the importance of ideas lie? The answer is to be found in the title of Book I: "Of the Understanding." The understanding is the thinking part of human nature, and ideas are the tools we use in thinking. As he writes in the passage with which I began, "By *ideas* I mean the faint images of [impressions] in thinking and reasoning." Later in Book I he equates our forming an idea of something with our conceiving it.[4] Thus, for Hume the term "idea" can be considered equivalent to the term "concept." This identity has an important consequence for his view concerning the scope of human knowledge. Since to know anything we must be able to conceive it, and since to conceive it we must form an idea of it, the range of what we can know is limited by the range of our possible ideas. Whatever lies beyond that range is unknowable because it is inconceivable. As he elaborates the point later in the *Treatise* (in the passage I referred to above): "Now since nothing is ever present to the mind but perceptions, and since all ideas are deriv'd from something antecedently present to the mind; it follows, that 'tis impossible for us so much as to conceive or form an idea of any thing specifically different from ideas and impressions" (67). It is vital to our understanding of Hume that we grasp what he means here. When he claims that it is impossible to conceive of anything specifically different from the impressions or ideas we have, he means something quite definite. Although he uses somewhat vague terms, like "inconceivable" and "unintelligible" throughout Book I to convey this view, the epistemological point is clear. Since the only things that are "present to the mind" are perceptions, any word that does not refer to an impression or an idea is simply a noise to us, conveying nothing, because, where a perception would normally be, corresponding to it, nothing exists in our mind but a blank void. This is a point of fundamental importance, which shapes Hume's views about the range of our possible knowledge throughout Book I.[5]

The distinguishing difference, then, between impressions and ideas is that the former are forceful and lively and the latter are faint. But this mark of distinction, Hume adds, is not a rigid one. Rather, one might more accurately consider the situation as being a spectrum, both impressions and ideas having different degrees of force among themselves but with the place occupied by the different degrees of force falling within the range of impressions being higher on the spectrum than that of ideas. Because the force of perceptions within the total spectrum is a gradually descending scale from very high to very low rather than a sharp demarcation between two types of perceptions, it can sometimes become difficult in particular instances to decide whether a perception should be labeled an impression or an idea. Hume mentions two instances of this difficulty. Sometimes in sleep or in fever or in madness our ideas become very forceful; one can picture here the images of a nightmare. On the other hand, our impressions are sometimes quite faint; one can think of the visual impressions we have in a dense fog. Nevertheless, this ambiguity does leave a problem. If relative force is the only mark distinguishing impressions from ideas, we might, on occasion, take one to be the other.

This problem can, however, be mitigated because we have other ways to help us in distinguishing the two. Most impressions enter our consciousness through our five senses, hence any perception that we see, hear, touch, taste, or smell must be an impression. Hume takes note of this difference between impressions and ideas by the remark, "I believe it will not be very necessary to employ many words in explaining this distinction [between impressions and ideas]. Every one of himself will readily perceive the difference betwixt feeling [sensing] and thinking."[6]

A second difference between impressions and ideas is a temporal one. In Hume's words, "simple impressions always take the precedence of their correspondent ideas, but never appear in the contrary order" (5) and, again, "our simple impressions" are prior to their correspondent ideas" (7). To illustrate this relationship he describes the way in which we introduce new ideas to children. Suppose the idea is the color "orange." We hold an orange in front of a very young boy (i.e., present him with the impression "orange") so that he can see it. A few repetitions, perhaps including other examples of the color "orange," will implant the idea of this color in his mind. What we do not do is to attempt to arouse the idea "orange" in his mind first in order to make it possible for him to generate the visual impression of that color.

The temporal priority of impressions to ideas introduces the first of two other important relationships between them. Ideas, for Hume, are copies or images of the impressions from which they are derived. As he writes, in the passage I reproduced at the beginning of the section, "By *ideas* I mean the faint images of [impressions]" (1). In Hume's view the resemblance between an impression and its corresponding idea is total. Ideas are not just vaguely like the impressions they copy but exactly duplicate them. Hume makes this point very definite: "The first circumstance, that strikes my eye, is the great resemblance betwixt our impressions and ideas in every other particular, except their degree of force and vivacity. The one seem to be in a manner the reflexion of the other; so that all the perceptions of the mind are double, and appear both as impressions and ideas" (2–3). Generalizing, he writes, "these two species of perception [impressions and ideas] are exactly correspondent."[7]

Hume's copy theory of ideas yields important evidence about his conception of the nature of human thought. Our thoughts, being our ideas, are just like our impressions. So, to understand the nature of these thoughts we must focus our attention on that of our impressions. What is an impression like? The sense of sight gives us both the clearest and most important example, and it is the one Hume employs as his primary exemplar of our impressions. Sight yields "pictures." I look out my study window and see a panorama of shapes and colors, some stationary and others moving, which I variously label sky, houses, trees, people, and so on. These are mental presentations, or pictures within my consciousness. When I close my eyes I can reproduce these pictures within my thought. They then become ideas. As Hume says, "When I shut my eyes and think of my chamber, the ideas I form are exact representations of the impressions I felt" (3). The important point is that our ideas, because they exactly replicate our impressions, are, like them, pictures. And, since our ideas are the objects that constitute the content of our thought, we can conclude that, for Hume, most of the time we think in pictures.

The second relationship between impressions and ideas is their causal connection. It is not fortuitous that an idea always follows and never precedes its correspondent impression. The reason it does so is that "our impressions are the causes of our ideas, not our ideas of our impressions" (5). Since Hume elaborates the notion of the causal connection from impressions to ideas in detail in his defense of the Empiricist Principle, I will postpone any further discussion of this relationship until section 3, where my topic will be that Principle.

So much for now about the distinguishing features of impressions and ideas, and the relationships between the two. I turn next to a quite different point that applies to both, as perceptions. What, in technical terminology, is their ontological status? Or, put more simply, what kind of existence or reality do they have? Although Hume does not answer this question explicitly in Part I, he gives some clues to its answer. Unfortunately, these clues are ambivalent. Returning to the passage I reproduced at the beginning, we find Hume writing (and I excerpt to capture his point): "All the perceptions of the human mind . . . strike upon the mind, and make their way into our thought or consciousness. Those perceptions, which enter with most force and violence, we may name *impressions;* and under this name I comprehend all our sensations, passions and emotions, as they make their first appearance in the soul." The proper interpretation of this passage may seem reasonably clear, particularly if we concentrate on what

Hume says in the final clause of the second sentence. Impressions "make their appearance" in the soul. Thus they—and the ideas that follow them— are mental phenomena, or contents of consciousness. In his footnote on the following page Hume adds the even more straightforward statement that "perceptions are produced in the soul" (2 n. 1). That is, they originate there. Later in Section I he adds another element to this description, writing: "where-ever by any accident the faculties, which *give rise to* any impressions, are obstructed in their operations, as when one is born blind or deaf; not only the impressions are lost, but also their correspondent ideas; so that there never appear in the mind the least traces of either of them" (5—italics added). The operative expression here is "give rise to"; a natural interpretation of it would be that Hume means that impressions do not have any existence before they are brought into being by the faculties of the perceiver. When these faculties are absent so too are the impressions. Even, however, if we interpret Hume to mean simply that the faculties are necessary conditions for the existence of the impressions, we can still infer from this passage that the impressions themselves must be simply mental in nature.

What, then, is the problem? There seems no doubt that Hume thinks of our perceptions as mental entities. The question that remains is this: Are they mental entities *only* or do they also have another, nonmental form of existence? Two considerations make the second interpretation a possibility we cannot eliminate at this time. The first is implied in the opening sentences of Part I, which we have just been examining. Perceptions, Hume writes, "strike upon the mind," they "make their way into our thought," and so on. This language suggests the picture of some external entity forcing its way into our consciousness, to be labeled there a perception. If this is correct, then these entities would seem to have an independent reality, existing either as perceptions or in some other unspecified form, *before* they enter our consciousness.

Such an interpretation of Hume's account of what perceptions are seems, however, to be at variance with the general tenor of his thought in Part I. Perhaps it can be understood simply as a dramatic and picturesque way in which Hume begins his book and not to be taken literally. That such a reading cannot be accepted as definitive at this point, nevertheless, results from a second consideration. Later in Book I Hume has more to say about the ontological status of perceptions—some of it raising the possibility of their having an extramental existence. Since I will discuss these views in detail later in the book, I will not pursue the topic further here.[8] For the present it seems reasonable to conclude that his view in Part I is that perceptions are strictly mental entities. It is regrettable, however, that he left some doubts on this important metaphysical question.

Before ending this section I must raise the specter of another problem, one that will haunt us throughout our study of Book I. In the third paragraph of Section I Hume introduces a central term of his philosophy—"object." The problem is: Just what is an object? Ordinarily, when we use the term "object" we are referring to a physical object—a book, a chair, a mountain. But there are, of course, other kinds of objects, including mental objects. Hume's "perceptions" are cases in point. In the passage in which he first introduces the term "object" Hume is referring to them. The sentence in question reads: "Having by these divisions [of perceptions] given an order and arrangement to our objects, we may now apply ourselves to consider with the more accuracy their qualities and relations" (2). A few pages later he writes: "To give a child an idea of scarlet or orange, of sweet or bitter, I present the objects, or in other words, convey to him these impressions" (5). It is apparent from these passages that Hume is identifying the objects to which he is referring with perceptions. This is particularly true in the second passage, in which he makes it clear that when he presents a child with an orange what he is in fact placing before him is the impression "orange."[9]

But now we come to the problem. As we delve further into Book I, it will become increasingly apparent that Hume is using the same term to refer to physical objects. This second usage, while it is obviously congenial to our ordinary way of thinking and talking, raises three issues, which are not only difficult in themselves but are crucial to our understanding of Hume. First, Hume repeatedly uses the term "object" loosely and ambiguously so that it is often almost impossible to determine whether he is referring to a mental or a physical object. Second, in interpreting Hume we have to try to understand how he pictures the relationship between mental objects and physical objects. Closely related to the second issue is the third problem: Given the Empiricist Principle, how does Hume explain the way in which we acquire knowledge of physical objects? We will have to wrestle with all of these problems in due course.

2. SIMPLE AND COMPLEX PERCEPTIONS (SECTION I)

It is obvious that Hume's account of our perceptions, as I have just described it, is an oversimplification. It simply does not explain the nature of our experience as we actually find it to be. Hume was, of course, well aware of this fact; in the second paragraph of Section I he supplements his original account by adding to the notion of *simple* perceptions that of *complex* perceptions.

Two main reasons can be given why such a complication is necessary. First, simple impressions and ideas do not constitute more than a small fraction of our conscious experience. How often is our consciousness, even for a moment, occupied solely by one simple impression, say, the visual sensation of a certain shade of red or the auditory impression of B-flat? Or, how often do we have such simple impressions as the sole ideas in our minds? Such occurrences are not the normal situations of consciousness but rather are quite rare. For most of our lives our conscious states are quite—indeed, extraordinarily—complex, consisting of myriads of sensations arising out of several of our senses simultaneously accompanying equally complex and changing ideas. Although Hume does not make this point in Section I, he would undoubtedly agree with it. He would probably also acknowledge that simple impressions and ideas are abstractions from a much richer context of consciousness, but then add that they were necessary starting points from which to launch his project of developing his philosophy from its basic elements.

The second point concerns Hume's thesis that our impressions and ideas replicate each other. Although this generalization is true of our simple impressions and ideas, it does not extend to those that are complex. As he puts it, "Upon a more accurate survey I find I have been carried away too far by the first appearance, and that I must make use of the distinction of perceptions into *simple and complex,* to limit this general decision, *that all our ideas and impressions are resembling*" (3). Many of our impressions are not followed by ideas exactly like them; many of our ideas have no impressions of which they are exact copies. Hume illustrates both kinds of exception to his original thesis. He has an idea of Paris, which is a copy of his impression of Paris. But it is an imperfect copy, missing many of the details of his original impression. In the reverse way, he has an idea of the New Jerusalem, but he has never had any impression of such a city. Hume explains these facts by introducing complex impressions and ideas into his theory. Whereas simple perceptions contain no internal distinctions but are completely single and pure so that they cannot be divided into parts, complex perceptions do have parts, thus can be subdivided into constituents and ultimately into their basic elements, the simple perceptions of which they are composed.

The introduction of complex perceptions easily handles both issues I have just raised. We can simply note, in response to the first, that almost all of the perceptions human beings actually experience, whether they be impressions or ideas, are complex. We can, furthermore, usually break these down into their simple constituent parts and experience these parts in isolation if we are willing to make the effort and find it worth our while to do so. The problems raised by our ideas of Paris and the New Jerusalem require a bit more extensive explanation. The reason why the ideas Hume has of Paris after he has gone on to La Flèche do not replicate the impressions he had when he was in the fair city is that many of the details or parts of those complex impressions have faded from his memory. The reason why he can have an idea of the New Jerusalem even though he has had no impression of any such city is that, by the use of his imagination, he can join together separate impressions he has had—of pavements and walls, of gold and rubies—to form one composite, complex idea of that imaginary metropolis.

A final point needs to be noted regarding the formation of complex perceptions out of simple ones. It is illustrated best by the New Jerusalem example in which several simple ideas, which are replicas of simple impressions, come together to form the complex idea of the city. The question is: How is the verb "come together" to be understood? Do these ideas just happen to fall into a pattern or is some agency at work putting them together? If the latter, what is the agency? I will return to these questions in section 7, where the discussion will center on Hume's theories of memory and imagination.

3. The Empiricist Principle (Section I)

This section will be devoted to the central component of Hume's empiricist epistemology—the Empiricist Principle.[10] His discussion of the Principle in Section I can be divided into four parts: (1) His preamble to the Principle; (2) the Principle itself; (3) his defense of it; and (4) an exception to it. All of these are brief, taking up altogether about two pages of text. In this section I will concentrate on the first three parts, turning to the fourth in the next section. I will begin with parts (2) and (3), leaving (1) until the end of the section. The Empiricist Principle (with its preamble) reads as follows:

> Let us consider how [simple impressions and ideas] stand with regard to their existence, and which of the impressions and ideas are causes and which effects.
>
> The *full* examination of this question is the subject of the present treatise; and therefore we shall here content ourselves with establishing one general proposition, *That all our simple ideas in their first appearance are deriv'd from simple impressions, which are correspondent to them, and which they exactly represent.* (4)

In spite of his emphasis on its importance, Hume states the Empiricist Principle quite briefly. It constitutes the italicized proposition that concludes the passage I have reproduced. The Principle states the relationship between simple ideas and simple impressions, drawing two connections between them and making one qualification about these connections. The qualification, to begin with it, is that the connections between these types of perception apply only to simple ideas in their *first* appearance. This is not an important point. Hume probably inserted it to emphasize that the Principle is concerned with the basic elements of human consciousness as these originally appear to us. This leaves open the possibility, which he elaborates a bit later in the section, that other ideas may be derived from ideas, rather than directly from impressions.

Concerning the two connections between simple impressions and ideas, Hume affirms a point I have already discussed—the copy theory of ideas. Simple ideas "exactly represent" their "correspondent" impressions; i.e., those of which they are the images. The second connection affirms another feature of great importance; namely, that simple ideas *are derived from* simple impressions. The significance of this connection becomes quickly apparent; in his defense of the Principle, which follows immediately afterward, Hume devotes his arguments wholly to its establishment. Before we turn to them, however, we need to understand what Hume means by "derived from," as he uses the term in the Principle. There can be little doubt that he is talking about a causal connection between impressions and their correspondent ideas. This is clear from what he says in the preamble, as well as from his arguments that follow.

Turning next to part (3), Hume's defense of the Principle, we find it to proceed in two stages. In the first stage his object is to establish a causal connection between correspondent impressions and ideas. This he does by pointing to the evidence of the constant conjunction of the two, which he claims would not occur if the conjunction were due simply to chance. "Such a constant conjunction, in such an infinite number of instances, can never arise from chance; but clearly proves a dependence of the impressions on the ideas, or of the ideas on the impressions" (4–5). In the second stage he raises the question of the direction in which the influence runs and concludes that the causal dependence is one of ideas on impressions rather than of impressions on ideas. He offers two arguments in support of this conclusion.

The first argument is based on temporal priority. Impressions always precede their correspondent ideas; ideas never precede their correspondent impressions. Since a cause always precedes its effect, it follows that impressions are always the causes of their correspondent ideas, which are their effects. "The constant conjunction of our resembling perceptions, is a convincing proof, that the one are the causes of the other; and this priority of the impressions is an equal proof, that our impressions are the causes of our ideas, not our ideas of our impressions" (5).

The second argument turns on the fact that when persons do not or cannot employ certain faculties—they are, for example, born blind or deaf—

they not only do not have any visual or auditory impressions but are lacking as well in visual or auditory ideas. This argument is particularly important to the case Hume builds on the Principle throughout the remainder of Book I. It does not turn, as does its predecessor, on a direct appeal to the causal relationship between an impression and its correspondent idea. Instead, Hume shifts the point to another relationship between the two, which stresses the logical connection between impressions and ideas. What he is concerned to establish is that impressions are necessary conditions for the existence of their correspondent ideas. As he puts it in a remark with which he concludes the argument: "We cannot form to ourselves a just idea of the taste of a pine-apple, without having actually tasted it" (5). This "necessary condition" feature of the Principle is, as we will see, particularly important because Hume constantly appeals to it in Book I, rather than to the cause-effect connection between impressions and ideas, to support his conclusions regarding the nature and scope of human knowledge.

We can now return to part (1) of Hume's account of the Empiricist Principle—the preamble to it. To have it before us for examination I repeat it.

> Let us consider how [simple impressions and ideas] stand with regard to their existence, and which of the impressions and ideas are causes and which effects.
>
> The *full* examination of this question is the subject of the present treatise.[11]

Unfortunately, these statements are not free from ambiguity. Hume begins the preamble by noting that two points about impressions and ideas are to be considered: (a) How they stand with regard to their existence and (b) which of the impressions and ideas are causes and which effects. We have already learned that his answer to (b) is that all simple impressions are causes and simple ideas in their first appearance their effects. But it is not clear how the Principle relates to (a), mainly because the point itself is obscure. One can only speculate about what Hume means by the phrase "stand with regard to their existence"—unless, of course, he is referring to the causal relationship between impressions and ideas. If so, (a) and (b) are not really different but collapse into (b). Or, perhaps he is referring to the temporal priority of impressions.

Fortunately, the problem posed by Hume's lack of clarity does not affect his argument, for the central features of the Principle are its statement of the causal connection between impressions and ideas and the copy theory of ideas. Therefore we can pass on to the second sentence of the preamble, which is obviously of the very greatest importance to our understanding of the *Treatise*. In it Hume states what the subject of the *Treatise* is; namely, the *full* examination of the question he has just raised. Even acknowledging some ambiguity in this question, we can conclude that Hume is informing his readers in his preamble to the Principle that the *Treatise* will have for its subject the full examination of his thesis that all of our simple ideas are exact copies of simple impressions, which are their causes. With this statement of his purpose in the preamble, the central role of the Empiricist Principle in our study of Book I becomes abundantly evident. To summarize, we can say that Hume regards the Principle as setting a standard or constituting a criterion of intelligibility and, hence, of possible knowledge. Any word we use, if it is to have a meaning that is conceivable, must stand for some idea that is derived from simple ideas that are in turn derived from simple impressions, which are their causes and of which they are exact copies.

4. An Exception to the Empiricist Principle (Section I)

As soon as he has stated and briefly defended the Empiricist Principle, Hume notes an exception to it. This exception consists in the fact that we can have a certain idea in our minds even though we have not previously experienced its correspondent impression. The example he gives is this: Consider an individual who has for years experienced the color "blue" in a variety of different shades but has never seen one particular shade of that color. Next, suppose he is presented with a spectrum of blue color patches, ranging from very light blue at one end to very dark blue at the other. The spectrum is so arranged that each step from one shade of blue to the next is identical to the others—with one exception. Along the spectrum the precise shade of blue the individual has never seen before is omitted. Hume agrees that the person will be able to spot the gap in the spectrum where that particular shade of blue is missing. But will he, Hume then asks, be able to generate a mental picture, or an idea, of the missing shade of blue, even though he has never seen it before? Hume answers: "I believe there are few but will be of opinion that he can" (6). Thus Hume candidly brings to his readers' attention an exception he has discovered to his Empiricist Principle.

We must agree with Hume that the situation he describes in this counterexample is possible. The critical question is: How significant is it as an objection to the Empiricist Principle? Hume does not himself consider it defeating; on the contrary, he dismisses it as of negligible importance: "The instance is so particular and singular, that 'tis scarce worth our observing, and does not merit that for it alone we should alter our general maxim" (6). Before we can accept this conclusion we need to examine the situation further, because the exception to the Principle he has found may not be so negligible as he supposes.

First, it is obvious that the counterexample Hume gives is not limited to a specific shade of blue but can be generalized to cover any other shade. Further, it is not limited to the color blue but can be applied to all colors. Also, a similar if not so sharp counterexample can be offered in connection with shapes as well as colors. For example, suppose we were to construct a spectrum of shapes enclosed by curved lines, ranging from a perfect circle to an extremely elongated ellipse, but with one shape omitted from the spectrum. Could we not find someone who had never seen that particular shape but who would still spot the gap in our spectrum where it should fit and be able to form an idea of it? Or, turning to sound, think of the possibilities of a spectrum of notes ranging from very high to very low on a scale but with one note missing. The sense of taste offers the possibility of still other counterexamples. Although most of us, who are not trained, would probably be unable to fill a gap in a spectrum of relative dryness or sweetness of different wines, would we want to deny that ability to an expert wine-taster? With the sense of smell, too, we have the case of experts in various perfumes, who undoubtedly can make distinctions of similar kinds far beyond the capabilities of the average person. To sum up, the counterexample Hume describes in the color spectrum of blue is not the isolated case he takes it to be.

Nevertheless, it does not follow that we should therefore depart from Hume and abandon the Principle. Granted there are exceptions to it, we have to determine how important these are. Hume does not pursue this question, but it can be answered in a way that will allow us to accept his conclusion that we need not abandon or even alter the Principle because of them. To justify this judgment we must take a brief look ahead, into the argument of Book I. There we would find that Hume uses the Principle repeatedly, at crucial points in his argument, to establish a conclusion or to refute a philosophical theory. But nowhere have I found him using it in such a way that his doing so would force him to deny the existence of the counterexamples I have described. So their existence does not affect the arguments that he will employ the Principle to support in the remainder of Book I.

At the end of Section I, after discussing his color blue counterexample, Hume makes an important statement about the Empiricist Principle, writing: "This then is the *first principle* I establish in the science of human nature; nor ought we to despise it because of the simplicity of its appearance" (7—italics added). In describing it as the *first* principle, Hume is undoubtedly referring to the fact that it is the first general thesis about human nature that he asserts in Book I. But we can also conclude, from the evidence of his preamble to the Principle, that, by calling it "first," he means to imply as well that it is the most basic and important principle of the science of human nature, one to which he will have constant recourse in the development of his philosophy as he considers humans as thinking beings with some potential for knowledge, throughout the remainder of Book I.

5. Impressions of Sensation and Reflection (Section II)

Going on with Hume in Section II to a description of the elements of his philosophy, we find him again adding a complication to his account, this time based on a distinction between impressions of *sensation* and impressions of *reflection*. Impressions of sensation—or, simply, sensations—the type we have been discussing until now, are original; impressions of reflection are derived, their immediate source being ideas. To illustrate what these impressions of reflection are Hume gives an example: Suppose we feel a pain. This is an impression of sensation. The mind takes a copy of this feeling, which is an idea of pain. When we think of this idea of pain later it can cause us to feel aversion or fear. These are impressions of reflection. They, in turn, Hume adds, give rise to ideas, which are their copies, from which further impressions of reflection may be generated. Impressions of reflection, thus, are ultimately derived from impressions of sensation, but through the medium of ideas.

One might ask why Hume introduced impressions of reflection into the elements of his philosophy. The answer lies in their nature; they are, as he says, "passions, desires, and emotions" (8). What Hume is doing through his theory of impressions of reflection is to explain the emotional side of human nature and, specifically, to give an account of how our emotions are aroused. Our emotions are original, in the sense that they are feelings that occupy our consciousness; we directly experience fear or anger or pity and so on. That is why it is appropriate to call them impressions. But they are derived, in the sense that they are the consequences of other experiences we have already had, being aroused when we think about those experiences. Since the passions form the subject of Book II of the *Treatise* and, with one notable exception (which I will discuss in chapter 12), do not enter directly into Hume's argument in Book I, I will have little further to say about them in this study.

Before leaving Section II, I should make a brief comment on a remark Hume inserts into his discussion of impressions of sensation and reflection, because it is perhaps subject to misinterpretation. He writes: "The examination of our sensations belongs more to anatomists and natural philosophers [scientists] than to moral; and therefore shall not at present be enter'd upon" (8). His reference, particularly to anatomists, might seem to suggest that Hume means here that the examination of sensations involves a study of the human body. But, from what he has said about perceptions in the preceding section, this may seem odd because he holds sensations to be mental phenomena. Why, then, should they be the province of anatomists? Answered in Hume's terms (as far as his argument so far has taken us), the explanation would run along the following lines: When we think, whether we are doing moral or natural philosophy, the entities we employ in our thinking are ideas. These ideas are derived from impressions or sensations. The special province of anatomists is to study the sensations themselves, which are the original sources of our thought. When they do this they are employing one mental phenomenon (ideas) to understand another mental phenomenon (sensations).

6. The Causes of Our Sensations (Section II)

Although Section II is relatively unimportant to the argument of Book I, it contains one sentence of potentially great significance for an understanding of Hume's philosophy. This section will be devoted to a commentary on that sentence, which reads as follows: "The first kind [i.e., impressions of sensation] arises in the soul originally, from unknown causes" (7). Its philosophical significance should be obvious.[12]

Hume's statement raises a question: Why does he maintain that the causes of our impressions are unknown? Is this a contingent truth or a necessary truth? If it were the former, it would remain possible that, although we do not know the causes of our impressions, we *might* come to know them. That Hume would reject such a view, however, is apparent from the logic of his argument up to this point. We have seen that to know something requires that we have an idea of it and that a necessary condition of our having an idea of anything is to have a previous impression of it, of which our idea is a copy. But the causes of our impressions cannot themselves be impressions for that would generate a vicious infinite regress. Hence we can have no ideas of these causes. They are unknown to us because they are, according to Hume's theory of ideas, intrinsically unknowable. This conclusion, of course, diverges dramatically from our ordinary, commonsense beliefs, but that is hardly a criticism of it. More important for our understanding of Hume is the way in which he develops the position later in Book I.

Nevertheless, in saying that the causes of our impressions are unknown, Hume is not saying we cannot know entities—for example, physical objects—that are different from our impressions, but which those impressions resemble. Although the statement at least suggests the contrary, it still leaves open the possibility of such knowledge.

7. The Ideas of Memory and Imagination (Section III)

Hume devotes the first two sections of Part I to explaining the elements that constitute the basic building blocks of his epistemology. But that is only half of his task in the opening sections of Part I. In the next three sections he describes how these elements come together to form human experience and thought. That Hume needs to take a second step in the development of his epistemology is apparent. He has identified two basic elements in his theory—impressions and ideas—differentiating them from each other on the grounds that the latter are less lively than the former and follow them in time, and relating them together by the tie of causation and the copy theory of ideas. His concern in the following sections is to develop in further detail his account of the relationships between impressions and ideas. The questions he sets forth to answer are two: (1) What are the "mechanisms" by which ideas are related to impressions, and (2) What kinds of relations result? He devotes Sections III and IV to the first question and Section V to the second.

Ideas follow their correspondent impressions in time. First we have the impression, say, of a red barn, and later its copy in the idea of a red barn. "We find by experience, that when any impression has been present with the mind, it again makes its appearance there as an idea" (8). How is this possible? What are the agencies that reproduce our impressions as ideas? Hume gives two answers: The memory and the imagination. He refers to both of these as "faculties." One might take issue with this term, because it connotes what has come since Hume's time to be considered an outmoded psychology. We should not allow changing fashions in terminology or even improvements in psychological theory to be stumbling blocks to us here because the point Hume is trying to convey can be expressed equally well by saying that we have the capacity or the ability to reproduce our impressions as ideas and we can exercise this capacity in two different ways, either through memory or imagination. That he is attributing such a capability to us is evident from the sentence in which he introduces the concepts of memory and imagination into his theory. "The faculty, by which we repeat our impressions in the first manner, is called the MEMORY, and the other the IMAGINATION" (8–9).

Two points should be noted about this passage. First, by saying that we repeat our impressions as ideas, Hume seems to be giving an active role to the mind in experience, which it exercises through the faculties of memory and imagination. Second, since thoughts are the same as ideas, Hume is telling us that we think either through the exercise of memory or through the use of imagination. Two questions occur on this point: (a) How much of our thought is memory and how much is imagination?

(b) Is there no other faculty besides these two that we can use when we think?

Memory and imagination, Hume continues, differ from each other in two ways: First, memory ideas are more "lively and strong" than imagination ideas; the former are "forcible," the latter "faint and languid" (9). Hume even goes so far as to suggest that memory ideas are so strong that they are not really ideas at all. "[A memory idea] retains a considerable degree of its first vivacity, and is somewhat intermediate betwixt an impression and an idea" (8). I do not think we should take Hume literally here, since that would require the introduction of another mental entity into his theory, occupying a position midway between impressions and ideas, a possibility he never pursues further. Rather, we should interpret the passage as Hume's way of emphasizing that memory ideas are *much* more forceful and vivacious than imagination ideas.

The second difference between the two kinds of ideas involves a constraint on memory ideas not shared by imagination ideas. As Hume describes the difference: "There is another difference betwixt these two kinds of ideas . . . namely that tho' neither the ideas of the memory nor imagination . . . can make their appearance in the mind, unless their correspondent impressions have gone before to prepare the way for them, yet the imagination is not restrain'd to the same order and form with the original impressions; while the memory is in a manner ty'd down in that respect, without any power of variation" (9). This distinction between memory and imagination is easily understandable. If we claim to remember some past experience, the idea we have—if we are legitimately to call it a memory idea—must replicate the experience. I cannot, for example, correctly say "I remember climbing the pyramid of Cheops" if I have never visited Egypt. If my idea does not reproduce any impression I have had, or reproduces it in a distorted way, I am *mis*-remembering. Imagination, on the other hand, although it may reproduce impressions as they originally were experienced, is not bound to do so. As long as its ideas are derived from previous impressions, it is free to put them together as it pleases, to create such images as "winged horses, fiery dragons, and monstrous giants" (10).

This account of the second difference between memory and imagination presents two problems, one minor and the other major. The minor problem (which is perhaps better described as a puzzle about Hume's meaning) arises from his terminology when he makes his distinction between the two. He says that the imagination, unlike the memory, need not reproduce its ideas in the same *order* and *form* as that of the impressions from which they are derived. Later in the section he speaks of the liberty of the imagination "*to transpose and change its ideas*" (10). The power of the imagination to transpose its ideas raises no problems. Suppose I have an idea of a horse derived from an impression of a horse and an idea of a bird derived from an impression of a bird. Both of these are complex ideas, having parts, so they can be separated into their parts. I can imaginatively take that part of my idea of a bird which consists of its wings and attach it to my idea of a horse to create a new imagination idea—that of a winged horse. As Hume explains: "Nor will this liberty of the fancy [imagination] appear strange, when we consider, that all our ideas are copy'd from our impressions, and that there are not any two impressions which are perfectly inseparable. Not to mention, that this is an evident consequence of the division of ideas into simple and complex. Where-ever the imagination perceives a difference among ideas, it can easily produce a separation [and a recombination]" (10).

But what would it mean for the imagination to give an idea a different *form* from its impression? It is difficult to understand just what Hume intended by his use of this word because it seems to imply that the imagination has the power to alter the nature or character of an impression (in contrast to rearranging its parts). If that is Hume's meaning, we face the problem of how this possibility can be made consistent with his view that all of our ideas are exact copies of their correspondent impressions. It might be said that the copy theory applies only to simple impressions and ideas and that the imagination operates only on complex ones. But this distinction seems incapable of solving the problem because the imagination in its activity of changing complex ideas through transpositions of their parts is not changing the nature or form of the ideas so transposed. These either are themselves simple ideas or are reducible by further analysis to simple ideas and such simple ideas are, according to the copy theory, beyond the power of the imagination to alter. The only interpretation that can resolve the difficulty caused by Hume's terminology about the power of the imagination is to assume that he does not mean by the "form" of an idea what I have here taken him to mean. Instead, when he talks about the imagination's ability to change the "form" of an impression, he should be understood to mean nothing essentially different from its power to transpose its parts. The problem then is simply one of his failure to communicate clearly.[13]

The second problem arising from Hume's distinction between memory and imagination is more serious. Before I can address it, however, I must clarify a preliminary point. Hume has stipulated two different marks distinguishing the memory from the imagination. Does an idea have to satisfy both of these marks to be labeled a memory idea or will one suffice? From what he says in Section III there seems no problem *in principle* about the first mark. Although we may not always be able in practice to draw a line that will permit us to decide whether a certain idea is a memory idea or should instead be classified as an imagination idea, we know the basis on which we should draw the line. A memory idea is forcible and vivacious, an imagination idea faint and languid. The second distinction is another matter, chiefly because Hume's account of it is ambiguous. We can confidently say of any idea that, if it is to qualify as a memory idea, it must exactly replicate its correspondent impression. If it does not it must be an imagination idea. But what of imagination ideas? Must they (because of their transpositions of our simple ideas) always *fail* to replicate the impressions from which they are derived? If that is correct we have in principle a clear criterion to distinguish between the two kinds of ideas. But Hume does not state the distinction in this way. Rather, he writes (in the passage already reproduced): "The imagination is not restrain'd to the same order and form with the original impressions." Although he says that the imagination can transpose ideas derived from impressions, he seems to imply in the passage that it need not do so. If this reading is correct, we cannot use the criterion that an idea has the same order and form as its correspondent impression as an infallible basis for concluding that it is a memory idea because it could meet this condition and still be an imagination idea. In that case we are left with only one mark distinguishing the two—that of their relative force and vivacity. I do not know just how to interpret Hume on this point; an illustration in the text would have been helpful.[14] Nevertheless, I think it reasonable to infer that Hume believes that the imagination usually does transpose and recombine its impressions to form complex ideas. So to answer the question with which we began this discussion, we can conclude that an idea, to be a memory idea, must (1) be forceful and (2) replicate its impression. An imagination idea, on the other hand, (1) must be faint and (2) may or may not replicate its impressions, but ordinarily does not.

We can turn now to our main problem, which is simply that Hume's distinction between memory and imagination differs in an important way from the distinction people commonly draw between the two. The issue does not turn on his requirement that memory ideas replicate the impressions from which they are derived. That view, however formulated, is consonant with the accepted meaning of memory. No one can *remember* a past event that did not take place, or did not have the characteristics one's "memory" attributes to it. The problem arises rather from a person's distinction between memory ideas and imagination ideas based on their relative force and vivacity. It can be put in terms of the following question: May we ever legitimately label a *faint* idea a memory idea and a *vivacious* idea an imagination idea? If we mean by the terms, memory and imagination, what people ordinarily mean by them, the answer to both questions is affirmative. Turning to examples, we do call many ideas we have memory ideas even though they are quite faint. For instance, I am convinced that I remember the first view I had of Edinburgh Castle, even though my memory of this long-past experience is dim. Conversely, people often have very forceful ideas that we believe to arise from their imaginations. Several nights ago I had a nightmare, in which I dreamed I was falling from a high cliff. My idea, which was all too vivid, involved a subconscious combination of previous impressions I had had—of falling and of cliffs. There is no question that we all use these terms in ways like those I have just described and that our usage runs directly contrary to Hume's distinction between memory and imagination.

If we agree that Hume's relative vivacity criterion, as a device to distinguish memory from imagination, marks a departure from ordinary usage, what conclusions should we draw from this fact? The first point to be noted is that Hume has made "memory" and "imagination" *technical* terms of his philosophy. By this I mean that he has taken two ordinary words, which have accepted meanings in our normal vocabulary, and given them meanings different from those normal meanings, doing so in order to use the terms in question in the development of his philosophy. Such a procedure is perfectly acceptable as long as one is aware that it is taking place. Problems can arise, however, when a reader, seeing the familiar words in the text, understands them in their ordinary sense, hence fails to appreciate that Hume is giving them new, nonordinary meanings.

But there is another, more serious problem involved here. Consider the first of my two examples. If Hume is right, I do not now remember my first sight of Edinburgh Castle. Since the only other way in which one can repeat a previous impression is through imagination, I must be imagining it. But at one time—before my memory idea faded—he would say that I did remember it. Now it seems odd to say that I once remembered an event but now only imagine it. One is inclined to ask: Just when did my memory of the event turn into my imagination of it? The nightmare example raises a similar but slightly different question. I could not have been remembering my falling off a cliff because this had never happened to me. No more could I be imagining such an experience because my idea was too vivacious to have been an imagination idea. But, since the only means we have for repeating our impressions as ideas are memory and imagination, it would seem to follow, on Hume's view, that I could not have had my nightmare at all.

Since his account of memory and imagination not only runs counter to our ordinary way of thinking and talking but also raises serious problems of its own, Hume must have had good reasons for putting it forward. Unfortunately, he does not directly say what those reasons are so we must look to his general theory for an explanation. When we do this we can recognize that he must have concluded that his account of them was required by his theory of ideas. A fundamental thesis of his epistemology, on which he insists from the beginning of the *Treatise,* is that all perceptions are, in themselves, alike, the only difference between them (other than their specific content) being their relative force and vivacity. This difference distinguishes impressions from ideas and also distinguishes ideas from each other. Therefore, if Hume wishes to establish a criterion to distinguish between memory ideas and imagination ideas capable of allowing us to separate one kind from the other, it is almost inevitable that he should find it in the one difference to which he can appeal—the relative amount of force or vivacity the ideas have.

We must conclude that there are problems in Hume's theory of memory and imagination. The points I have raised are fairly specific but they suggest a more general issue. Hume is attempting in the *Treatise* to develop a theory of human nature, including an explanation of human experience. It is questionable whether his account of memory and imagination in Section III succeeds in making a positive contribution to his goal.[15]

8. The Association of Ideas (Section IV)

In Section III Hume has distinguished the imagination from the memory in part by its ability to join various simple ideas together in many kinds of combinations, to create innumerable complex ideas, some of a fantastic nature like "winged horses, fiery dragons, and monstrous giants." Since the simple ideas of which these complex ideas are composed are different from each other, they can be separated by the imagination and then put together again in whatever way the imagination pleases. But experience has shown us that we do not normally combine our ideas in a haphazard way; we rarely, for example, imagine winged horses. Rather, our imagination usually puts simple ideas together to form complex ideas according to regular patterns. In Section IV Hume is concerned with the reason why we do this and the principles according to which we do it.

Turning to the first point, Hume finds that our ideas themselves, although distinct and separable, contain an associating quality that leads the imagination to join certain ones naturally together. "Were ideas entirely loose and unconnected, chance alone wou'd join them; and 'tis impossible the same simple ideas should fall regularly into complex ones (as they commonly do) without some bond of union among them, some associating quality, by which one idea naturally introduces another" (10).

Hume seems to be appealing here to two quite different characteristics of ideas, which together can explain why the imagination regularly, but not always, combines certain simple ideas to form complex ones. First is a "bond of union" among ideas; some ideas naturally join together. For example, the idea of fire brings up in the imagination those of light and heat. Later in the section Hume draws a famous analogy between the association of ideas and the Newtonian concept of gravitation. "[In association] is a kind of ATTRACTION, which in the mental world will be found to have as extraordinary effects as in the natural, and to shew itself in as many and as various forms" (12–13). But there is a significant difference between gravitation in the physical world and association in the mental. In the former the causal connection is universal and exceptionless; all bodies in the universe attract each other in accordance with a precise mathematical formula. This kind of rigid cause-and-effect relation cannot be found in the realm of ideas. Ideas are intrinsically independent of each other. As a result they are separable by the imagination, so, although it ordinarily does combine them in certain patterns, it need not always do so. The causal connection uniting ideas is much looser than gravitation; Hume describes it in the following way: "This uniting principle among ideas is not to be consider'd as an inseparable connexion; for that has been already excluded from the imagination: nor yet are we to conclude, that without it the mind cannot join two ideas; for nothing is more free than that faculty: but we are only to regard it as a gentle force, which commonly prevails" (10).

In the *Abstract* this point is put in a way that reveals the enigmatic nature of Hume's epistemology on this important issue. The passage reads, "There is a *secret tie* or union among particular ideas, which causes the mind to conjoin them more frequently together" (662—italics added). Putting aside any distinction between a secret tie and a gentle force, the question naturally arises: What is this secret tie? Although Hume in the text attempts to explain the connection among ideas (a point I will consider in the next paragraph), the fact that it can be described as being "secret" should serve as a warning that he may be taking a step in his epistemology that, on his account of the nature of perceptions, he will not be able to explain satisfactorily.

To continue with the text, since the imagination regularly forms its complex ideas from simple ones because of a kind of connection between those ideas, the next step is to discover what special features of the ideas themselves lead us to join them together as we do. Hume finds three. "The qualities, from which this association arises, and by which the mind is after this manner convey'd from one idea to another, are three, *viz.* RESEMBLANCE, CONTIGUITY in time or place, and CAUSE and EFFECT" (11). He then proceeds to explain the first two. However, he does not elaborate on the relation of cause and effect in Section IV, because he will discuss it at great length later in Book I, but contents himself with one observation: "There is no relation, which produces a stronger connexion in the fancy [imagination], and makes one idea more readily recall another, than the relation of cause and effect betwixt their objects" (11).

Although Hume writes as if these three relations are "qualities" of ideas, he does not mean that they are qualities that directly attach to our ideas, in the sense that the quality "red" characterizes our idea of an apple. Rather than being descriptive of ideas themselves, they stand between ideas, linking them together and thus facilitating the work of our imagination in moving from one to another.

To sum up Hume's theory of the association of ideas, he sees this association to be accomplished through the joint contributions of two different agencies: (1) The activity of our imagination, which has the ability to take different simple ideas and put them together to form complex ideas. This is what we do, Hume points out, when we think (11). (2) The ideas themselves, which, although they are distinct and separable, are linked together by a "bond of union," resulting from certain of their "qualities," leading the imagination to associate them. As a result of this cooperation, our simple ideas regularly (but not always) become joined together to form the same complex ideas.

This analysis seems to be incomplete. Why, from the mere fact, say, that two ideas resemble each other, should the imagination join them together? The problem can be illustrated in this way: On a clear night with a full moon both I and my cat can observe shadows on the moon's surface. However, only I see the "man in the moon"; my cat presumably does not. Why the difference—when we are both looking at the same object? The answer is that I recognize that the shadows resemble a man's face and my cat is unable to do so. In other words, there is a gap in Hume's argument. It is not enough that two ideas resemble each other for us to associate them together; it is essential as well that we recognize the resemblance between them. Thus the weight of Hume's theory of association falls on the activity of the imagination; the "uniting principles" among ideas do no more than make it possible for it to exercise its ability.

With one exception the remainder of Section IV adds little to the elements of Hume's philosophy. He points out that the three relations among ideas can be extended beyond ideas directly related to each other to those that are linked together through intermediary ideas but adds that, as the links in the chain of intermediaries multiply, the strength of the relation diminishes. He then extends the causal relationship by noting that it includes not only the action of one thing on another but its power of so acting. This leads him into a short digression into human relationships and the power structures of a society.

Near the end of the section Hume emphasizes one important methodological point, concerning our ability to probe into the causes of our association of ideas. He writes: "[The] effects [of association] are every where conspicious; but as to its causes, they are mostly unknown, and must be resolv'd into *original* qualities of human nature, which I pretend not to explain" (13). He then issues a general warning against the attempt to probe too deeply into causes, arguing that such an attempt will lead to "obscure and uncertain speculations" (13). Hume is emphasizing to his readers that, although his aim in the *Treatise* is to explain human nature, there are limits beyond which neither he, nor anyone else, can safely go in giving such an explanation.

9. PHILOSOPHICAL RELATIONS (SECTION V)

As we have just seen, Hume finds three "qualities" of ideas that lead the imagination naturally from one to another, enabling it to form complex ideas. These can be called *natural relations*. At the beginning of Section V he adds another dimension to his theory of relations by introducing what he calls *philosophical relations*, describing them in the following somewhat obscure way: "That particular circumstance, in which, even upon the arbitrary union of two ideas in the fancy, we may think proper to compare them" (13). Fortunately, he clarifies what he means by such philosophical relations in the sentences that follow. Simply put, his point is that, because the imagination is not restricted in its power of combining ideas but can join together any that it pleases, it may associate ideas that lack a "connecting principle" (14). To contrast these relations, which are arbitrary rather than natural, with natural relations, he labels them philosophical relations.

Given the liberty of the imagination to unite ideas as it pleases, it would seem that there would be an endless number of possible philosophical relations. Hume's main aim in Section V is to bring some order into the scene, by reducing these relations to a few types. He distinguishes seven: (1) Resemblance, (2) Identity, (3) Space and Time, (4) Quantity or Number, (5) Degrees of Quality, (6) Contrariety, and (7) Cause and Effect.

Hume's list of philosophical relations merits a few comments. First, not all of these relations are arbitrary, two—resemblance and cause and effect—are natural relations as well. Space and time is ambiguous in this regard. Contiguity, which is subsumed under it, is a natural relation but distance, which is also subsumed, is not. Resemblance has a special status among the philosophical relations, being a necessary condition of the others. "[Resemblance] is a relation, without which no philosophical relation can exist; since no objects will admit of comparison, but what have some degree of resemblance" (14). Hume notes a minor problem about the relation of resemblance. Because it underlies all the other relations, even including contrariety, resemblance must be a very broad relation, applying to almost any thing about which we can think. Because of its very breadth resemblance sometimes fails to lead the imagination into associating ideas. Since so many ideas resemble each other, the imagination occasionally has trouble in putting any two together as being *particularly* resembling of each other.

Since Hume will be discussing all of the philosophical relations (particularly cause and effect) later in Book I, I will not comment here on each one individually. However, we cannot leave the subject without considering a problem raised by his theory of relations. According to Hume, relations, both natural and philosophical, perform a central role in our thought. Complex ideas combined together by the imagination in the patterns formed by the seven relations constitute the primary objects of our thought, or the contents of our consciousness when we are thinking. Because of the indispensable role that they play, relations must themselves be thinkable entities. Put in the reverse direction, we cannot employ relations as the linkages among our simple ideas allowing us to join these together to form complex ideas unless we can bring these relations themselves into our thought. Were we unable to do this, they would be inconceivable. Although we could, for example, hear the word "resemblance," it would be simply an unintelligible sound in our ears. If relations are to be conceivable, they must exist as ideas in our minds. Since all of our ideas, according to the Empiricist Principle, are derived from our impressions, to have an idea of a relation we must, therefore, first have an impression of it.

We now come to our problem. Do we have impressions of relations? In examining this difficult question I will limit myself to the basic relation of resemblance. There seems to be no question about the fact that we can discern resemblances between different things. Suppose that I were confronted with a set of twins. I would quickly notice a remarkable physical resemblance between them. The question that has to be answered is, How do I recognize this resemblance and, more to the point, how could Hume recognize it? I could say things like: They both are of a certain height and weight; both have dark brown eyes and wavy black hair; both have deep voices. Hume, presumably, would say approximately the same things. After having seen them and heard them talk he could later describe these physical characteristics. He would have ideas of the two individuals derived from his impressions of them. So far there is no problem; he has seen each of the twin's eyes and heard their voices and so on. But what about the resemblance each bears to the other? If Hume is to have an idea of this, he must derive it from some impression. If it is a visual impression, like the color of eyes, he must be able to see it; if it is an auditory impression, like the sound of a voice, he must be able to hear it. But although the twins' resemblance of each other is associated in some way with these—for how else could I recognize that they resemble each other?—it just does not seem to be either identical with or reducible to any or all of them. The resemblance between the two appears not to be anything we see, hear, touch, taste, or smell. But if we have no impression of it, we cannot, according to the Empiricist Principle, have any idea of it either.

A serious consequence seems to follow from this conclusion. Since our ideas are the objects with which we think, if we cannot have any idea of resemblance, we cannot use this relation in our thinking processes. Furthermore, since resemblance is a necessary condition for the existence of all the other relations, we seem forced to the conclusion that they too are unthinkable. Finally, since these relations provide the links that lead the imagination to combine simple ideas into patterns in its formation of complex ideas, their elimination from the thought process would leave us with nothing but arbitrary combinations as our complex ideas. Under such circumstances, what would we mean by "thought"?

I do not know just how to evaluate the problem that seems to beset Hume's theory of relations. Obviously the difficulty is serious. I doubt that Hume would accept the conclusion I have just reached. Rather, we must assume that, when he introduces relations in Section V, he believes that the Empiricist Principle is not inconsistent with their appearance as ideas in our mind. If we accept this, we must also assume that he does actually perceive the relation of resemblance through his senses. If so, he is different from me because I am sure that I do not. Although I certainly recognize that twins resemble each other, my recognition is not accomplished through my senses in the way in which Hume's epistemology requires. The process is much more complex than this and involves the active participation of my mind. If I am right, Hume's epistemology fails to give a satisfactory account of our recognition of relations.

Summary

In the first five sections of Part I Hume lays the foundations on which he will erect his philosophy. These foundations, the empiricist theory of ideas, are epistemological. He begins by listing the basic building blocks—*perceptions*—divided into two kinds—*impressions* and *ideas*—which are distinguished from each other in the first instance by their relative force and vivacity. He then introduces two complications into this initial picture of the contents of our consciousness, distinguishing, first, between *simple* and *complex* perceptions, and, second, between *impressions of sensation* and *impressions of reflection*.

Having listed the parts that make up the contents of our consciousness, Hume then turns to a description of the relationships among them. The central thesis he sets forth is the *Empiricist Principle:* That our simple ideas in their first appearance are all exact copies of their correspondent impressions, which are their causes. Turning to the mechanisms by which ideas copy impressions, he explains the different roles played by *memory* and *imagination.* The ability of the imagination to associate simple ideas in various ways to form complex ideas is of particular importance because imagination is the faculty with which we normally think or reason. The *association* of ideas by the imagination is not haphazard but guided by principles, or the *relations* of ideas. Hume concludes his account by listing seven types of relation in terms of which the imagination associates ideas.

Several problems have arisen from Hume's statement of the elements of his philosophy. Six of these may be mentioned. (1) Hume's account of the ontological status of perceptions is to some degree ambiguous, although it seems that he considers them to be mental phenomena. (2) The Empiricist Principle is not exceptionless, as Hume makes clear in his "shade of blue" counterexample. Although this particular exception does not raise problems for him later in Book I, it raises the possibility that there may be others that do. (3) Consistently with his theory of ideas, in the early portion of Part I Hume uses the term "objects" to mean mental objects or perceptions. But toward the end of his presentation he appears to use it to designate physical objects. This ambivalence, which barely shows itself in Part I, later becomes more pronounced, causing serious difficulties for the understanding of his philosophy. (4) The marks by which Hume distinguishes memory from imagination do not clearly separate the two and seem to lead to the awkward consequence that some of our ideas are products of neither our memory nor our imagination. (5) Hume's theory of the association of ideas seems incomplete, because it does not emphasize that, if a relation is to lead us to associate two ideas, it must first be recognized as a relation by us. (6) Although relations perform a central function in Hume's account of human understanding, a serious question can be raised whether, on his theory of ideas, they can ever enter the mind as impressions and, hence, function there as ideas.

The six items I have listed should not be taken to be criticisms of Hume but rather problems raised by his statement of the elements of his philosophy in Part I. Some are the result, I believe, of his failure to communicate his thought clearly and others of the sheer brevity of his exposition. Fortunately, Hume will address almost all of the issues I have raised later in Book I. Thus as we progress, we will be able to discover how he resolves them.

3

First Fruits
of the Empiricist
Principle

(Part I, Se&ions VI–VII)

Introduction

When we move from Section V of Part I to Section VI we can sense a break in Hume's argument. Instead of continuing to describe the elements of his philosophy, he begins the section with a criticism of the views of others. The break, nevertheless, is only temporary. After his sharp critical comments at the beginning of the section, he returns to his constructive task. He does not add any new elements to his philosophy but instead draws out some important implications of the Empiricist Principle about the nature of three concepts—substance, modes, and abstract ideas. He deals with the first two quite briefly but engages in a lengthy, quite complex discussion of the third.

The reason why I have given this chapter the title I have should be apparent from the first paragraph of Section VI. In it Hume puts the Empiricist Principle to work, using it in a detailed way to reach a conclusion about one of the central concepts in the history of metaphysics, reaching back to the pre-Socratic philosophers. Continuing to use the Principle in Section VII, he develops an account, which he acknowledges to be derived from Berkeley, of a basic epistemological concept of equal philosophical importance and almost equally ancient origin.

Text

1. The Idea of Substance (Section VI)

Hume's first and main concern in Section VI is with the idea of substance. His question is: Do we have any such idea and, if so, what is its nature? His immediate answer, which is directed against the traditional view of substance, is negative. He writes: "We have . . . no idea of substance, distinct from that of a collection of particular qualities, nor have we any other meaning when we either talk or reason concerning it" (16). Hume's conclusion is based on a direct appeal to the Empiricist Principle. If we are to have an idea of substance as it has traditionally been conceived, we must have some prior impression of which that idea is a copy. As Hume ironically asks believers in the traditional notion of substance: "I wou'd fain ask those philosophers . . . whether the idea of *substance* be deriv'd from the impressions of sensation or reflexion?" (15–16). Since we obviously have no impression of substance, we can have no idea of it. It is inconceivable.[1]

In order to appreciate Hume's critique of the traditional notion of substance we need to have a fuller understanding of that concept. Although the classical account is found in Aristotle, the dominant view in the British philosophical world of the early eighteenth century was that of Locke. It can be found in Book II of his *Essay Concerning Human Understanding*.

> The mind being . . . furnished with a great number of the simple ideas . . . takes notice also that a certain number of these simple ideas go constantly together; which being presumed to belong to one thing, . . . are called, so united in one subject, by one name; which, by inadvertancy, we are apt afterward to talk of and consider as one simple idea, which indeed is a complication of many ideas together: because, . . . not imagining how these simple ideas *can* subsist by themselves, we accustom ourselves to suppose some *substratum* wherein they do subsist, and from which they do result, which therefore we call *substance*.[2]

This account, whatever its inadequacies, is close to the commonsense view. To take an example used by both Locke and Hume, we ordinarily think of something like a piece of gold as a material object that has certain qualities, such as its color, weight, hardness, and so on. The gold, we believe, is not reducible to its qualities; rather it is something distinct from them that possesses these qualities. It is the substance "gold."

To this Lockean, commonsense view of substance, Berkeley had raised serious objections. Attacking the possibility of our having any knowledge of material substances (things like gold), Berkeley, in his *Three Dialogues between Hylas and Philonous*, asks two (rhetorical) questions: "Either you perceive the being of matter [material substance] immediately, or mediately. If immediately, pray inform me by which of the senses you perceive it. If mediately, let me know by what reasoning it is inferred from those things which you perceive immediately."[3] Hume, in the first paragraph of Section VI, follows in Berkeley's footsteps in his criticism of Locke's theory of substance in general, raising the same objection to it that Berkeley had and using the same reason to support the objection. Having rid his philosophy of the traditional concept of substance, Hume is left with a problem. Even though we might acknowledge that we have no idea of substance, we all persist in using the concept constantly. We talk about such things as houses and people and gold nuggets as though they were real entities distinct from the impressions and ideas we have. How are we to explain this in a way consistent with the Empiricist Principle? Hume's answer is quickly forthcoming.

In the paragraph following his attack on the traditional view, Hume offers his own, alternative account of the idea we have of substance. "The idea of a substance . . . is nothing but a collection of simple ideas, that are united by the imagination, and have a particular name assigned them, by which we are able to recall, either to ourselves or others, that collection" (16). Thus the idea of substance is a complex idea made up of a collection of simple ideas, with a name attached to it. To illustrate, Hume refers to our idea of gold. This is not an idea of a material object, as we in our commonsense view suppose it to be. Rather it is a composite made up of the ideas (derived from our senses) of yellow color, heavy weight, malleability, and fusibility, all joined together by the relations of contiguity and causation. Because of these relations among them, our imagination collects the ideas together and then gives the collection a name by which we identify it later and communicate about it to others. Although he rejects the traditional conception of substance, Hume does not eliminate the word from his philosophical vocabulary. Instead he redefines it, in a way consistent with the requirements of the Empiricist Principle. It becomes, as a result, a technical term of his philosophy.

Hume's accomplishment in Section VI is threefold. First, he rejects the traditional concept of substance—of a gold nugget that exists distinct from its yellow color, heavy weight, and so on. As far as our possible knowledge is concerned, these are not qualities of the nugget; rather they *are* the nugget. Second, he identifies these qualities with mental phenomena; they are impressions and ideas in our minds. Third, he gives an account, based on his theories of imagination and the association of ideas, to explain why we think and talk in substantival terms, referring to gold and houses and people as though they are real things themselves, even though all we can meaningfully think and talk about are collections of perceptions in our minds.

There seems to be a fourth point of importance Hume makes about substance in Section VI. Although his argument is mainly epistemological, he draws a metaphysical conclusion from it. Not only is the traditional concept of substance meaningless to us, but substances—as real, independent entities—apparently do not exist. At least he seems to suggest this in his statement that "the particular qualities, which form a substance, are commonly refer'd to an unknown *something,* in which they are supposed to inhere; or granting this fiction should not take place, are at least supposed to be closely and inseparably connected by the relations of contiguity and causation" (16). The crucial word in this statement is "fiction." By labeling the "unknown *something*" in which we suppose particular qualities to inhere a fiction, he seems to be telling us that such a reference is a mistake because the "something" in question (e.g., the gold nugget) does not exist. Later in Book I Hume will have more to say on the subject of substance; one of our tasks will be to determine whether he continues to adhere to the negative ontological conclusion about the existence of substances he appears to be expressing in Section VI.

2. THE IDEAS OF MODES (SECTION VI)

Hume devotes only a short paragraph to the ideas of modes (17). Since they are not important to an understanding of his philosophy in Book I, I shall simply describe here what he takes them to be. For an explanation of modes we must again begin with Locke. In the *Essay* he defines them as follows: "*Modes* I call such complex ideas which, however compounded, contain not in them the supposition of subsisting by themselves, but are considered as dependences on, or affections of substances;—such as are the ideas signified by the words triangle, gratitude, murder, &c."[4]

Locke's examples help to clarify his somewhat turgid definition of modes. The difference between our ideas of substances and those of modes is that, while we think of the former—such things as houses and people— as being independent existences, we do not so consider the latter; rather we view their existence as being dependent on that of substances. Thus we do not regard murder as a thing but as an event that happens to people. The same is true of gratitude; it is an emotion people feel. "Triangle" is a bit harder to explain. Presumably, what Locke was thinking of, in calling it a mode, was the attribute "triangularity," which we do not view as a thing but as a shape characterizing certain physical objects.

Returning to Hume, he apparently has adopted Locke's conception of modes and so contents himself with explaining one difference between them and substances. When we contemplate an idea of substance, such as our complex idea of gold, and discover a new idea, like dissolubility in *aqua regia* connected with the other ideas that make it up, we add this new idea to our collection with the result that our complex idea of gold becomes even more complex. But we do not do this in the case of our ideas of modes. Rather, if we have an idea of a dance or of beauty (both modes) and discover a new idea connected with them, we give the modes a new name.

3. Abstract or General Ideas: The Problem (Section VII)

In Section VII Hume discusses a second issue that has its roots in classical thought. Ever since Plato developed his theory of Forms, philosophers have disputed about the ontological status of abstract or general concepts and the manner in which the mind can apprehend them. This is the traditional "problem of universals."[5] Hume's objective in Section VII is to provide an explanation of universals that satisfies the epistemological requirements laid down by the Empiricist Principle. As a prelude to his own discussion he acknowledges his debt to Berkeley, beginning the section with the claim that Berkeley's theory of general ideas is "one of the greatest and most valuable discoveries that has been made of late years in the republic of letters" and adding that his intention in the section is "to confirm it by some arguments, which I hope will put it beyond all doubt and controversy."[6]

To understand the problem of abstract or general ideas, as it appeared to Hume, it is best to begin by noting that we use general terms (words that apply to more than one entity) constantly in our ordinary, everyday discourse. To mention some of Hume's examples, we talk about "man," "triangle," "body," "figure," "color," and so on. If these words are to express general concepts, which we must possess in order to think, we must be able, *in some sense,* to form general ideas, because ideas, according to Hume, are the concepts with which we think. Hume's goal in Section VII is to explain how this is possible. The issue is a difficult one for him since he has already established that all of our ideas, because they are copies of impressions, must be particular. So the problem for him becomes this: If all our ideas are particular, *in what sense* can we have the general ideas we need in order to think?

Hume begins his argument by presenting a dilemma. Consider, he suggests, our abstract or general idea "man." This idea represents all individual men, whatever their special attributes (sizes and qualities) may be. Two explanations can be given of how such an idea is possible. Either (1) our general idea represents all possible human sizes and qualities or (2) it represents no particular one at all. The alternative generally accepted, continues Hume, is (2), (1) being rejected because the mind, lacking an infinite capacity, could not contain such an idea. Hume, however, disagrees, rejecting (2) in favor of (1). To justify his stand he recognizes he must do two things: First, show why (2) is unacceptable and, second, develop a viable rendition of (1), which, without assuming an infinite mind, can explain how "we can at once form a notion of all possible degrees of quantity and quality, in such a manner at least, as, however imperfect, may serve all the purposes of reflexion and conversation" (18).

Hume offers three reasons for rejecting (2), all based on the theory of ideas he has developed earlier in Part I. His first argument is somewhat hard to follow but can be understood by considering the illustration he uses. Suppose we wish to form the general idea "line" from our particular ideas of a line. According to (2) our general idea will be of a line of no particular, or precise, length. To form such an idea it is necessary to separate that part of our particular idea of a line that consists in its length from our total idea of the line. We can accomplish this separation only if that part of the idea is distinguishable from the total idea. But it is not; we cannot distinguish the length of a line from the line itself. Therefore we cannot separate it. So any general idea we form of a line must be one of a line of a particular length, which is inconsistent with (2). The same condition applies to all general ideas we form, so all must possess particular, determinate qualities or characteristics. Hume's second argument is quite straightforward. All our ideas are copies of our impressions, differing from them only in relative vivacity. Our impressions are always determinate in their quantity and quality, for example, our impression of a line being always of one having a certain specific length and so on. It follows that all our ideas of a line must be the same. Therefore we can form no general idea of a line that represents no particular quantity or quality, as (2) requires. To think otherwise, Hume notes, is to embrace a contradiction (19). Hume's third argument makes an appeal to the external world. If everything in nature is individual, the notion of general objects (like a triangle lacking precise proportions) is absurd. Since to form an idea of an object and to form an idea is the same thing, the idea we form (when we think about an object) must be individual also. The supposition that the idea could be general, thus, is impossible.

To sum up Hume's case, his objection to (2) is that, by interpreting general ideas as representing no particular quantities and qualities of the ideas they generalize, it requires that we be able to form an indeterminate idea, one that has no precise nature, like the idea of a line without any particular length. But we can form no such idea because, according to the Empiricist Principle, all of our ideas are copies of our impressions and our impressions are always precise and determinate.

4. How Individual Ideas Become General in Their Representation (Section VII)

Led by his epistemology to adopt the theory that general ideas represent all possible quantities and qualities, Hume is left with the problem: How can this interpretation be made consistent with his view that all of our ideas, including general ones, are particular in nature? He states his solution to the problem in the following way: "Abstract ideas are therefore in themselves individual, however they may become general in their representation. The image in the mind is only that of a particular object, tho' the application of it in our reasoning be the same, as if it were universal" (20). To render this theory viable Hume must show how individual or particular ideas can become general or universal "in their representation." He does this mainly through an appeal to the activity of the imagination, aided by custom or habit. To explicate his argument I shall use an example, his case of the general idea "man." After having experienced a number of individuals—Smith, Jones, Brown, and so on—and recognizing that they resemble each other, we generate a name, "man," that applies to them all, whatever individual differences—in size, color, and so on—there may be among them. The use of the general term "man" becomes habitual to us, so whenever we hear it, an image of some particular person, say, Smith, appears in our mind. This image of Smith is a particular determinate idea but it stands for or represents the ideas of Jones, Brown, and so on. Although we are not aware of their images, we can bring them to consciousness just in the way we do that of Smith. Whatever individual we bring to mind when we hear or use the word "man," that individual idea represents all others of a similar kind, so, although we never possess anything but particular, individual ideas, some of these ideas, because they bear a resemblance to other ideas, become general in their representation. They stand for all other ideas of a similar kind that we may have. In our communication we give them general names, like "man," "triangle," "body," "figure," "color." As Hume summarizes his view: "A particular idea becomes general by being annex'd to a general term; that is, to a term, which from a customary conjunction has a relation to many other particular ideas, and readily recalls them in the imagination" (22).

Having stated his theory of general ideas, Hume acknowledges that a problem remains. How can we explain the custom or mental habit that enables us to call to mind such particular ideas as Smith, Jones, or Brown when we hear the word "man"? After noting that we cannot give any explanation of the ultimate causes of our mental acts, Hume adds that we can, however, provide examples of analogous types of mental activity. He mentions four: (1) We have no adequate ideas (images) of very large numbers but we can make use of such numbers in our reasoning. In a similar way we can reason with general ideas even though we do not possess them. (2) Through habit we are able to recite a long poem we have once learned but since forgotten, if we are given the first line. (3) When we use very complex ideas like "government" or "church" we are not consciously aware of all the simple ideas of which these complexes are composed. Nevertheless, we can use them, as we use general ideas, intelligibly. (4) The power of imagination enables us to gather together ideas that resemble each other "from one end of the universe to the other" (24), collecting them and then using them under one general term. Hume considers these kinds of mental activity to be analogous to our generation of general ideas. Although the mind is, in his opinion, capable of accomplishing prodigious feats (as evidenced particularly by geniuses), we cannot in any way explain how it does so. Indeed, this power seems to him magical.

> Nothing is more admirable, than the readiness, with which the imagination suggests its ideas, and presents them at the very instant, in which they become necessary or useful. . . . One would think the whole intellectual world of ideas was at once subjected to our view. . . . There may not, however, be any present, beside those very ideas, that are thus collected by a kind of magical faculty in the soul, which . . . is however inexplicable by the utmost efforts of human understanding. (24)

Hume concludes the statement of his theory of abstract or general ideas with some remarks that indicate that he may feel somewhat hesitant about its adequacy. Instead of emphasizing its strength, he acknowledges possible difficulties in it but argues that it is the only theory we have that can account for such ideas. "But to tell the truth I place my chief confidence in what I have already prov'd concerning the impossibility of general ideas, according to the common method of explaining them. We must certainly seek some new system on this head, and there plainly is none beside what I have propos'd" (24).

Is Hume justified in being hesitant about his theory of general ideas? Critics have raised a variety of objections to it; one seems important enough to be considered here. Hume maintains that all of our ideas, because they are copies of impressions, must be particular and determinate. Thus we have no general ideas. Nevertheless, we have general words, like "man" and "triangle," that we use in our thinking and communication. We generate these words because we recognize resemblances between individual ideas, like those of Smith and Jones, or equilateral and isosceles three-sided figure, which lead us to group these individual ideas together and give them the same general name. Through the operation of custom or habit, whenever we hear a certain general term, like "man" or "triangle," it brings to mind a particular, individual idea (or image), like "Smith" or "equilateral three-sided figure," which stands for or represents all ideas of a resembling kind— "Jones" and "Brown" and so on or "isosceles" and "scalenum" three-sided figures and so on.

The problem with this theory, which is meant to explain how we can think in general terms without possessing general ideas, seems to be that it presupposes what it claims to be impossible; namely, our possession of such ideas. The crucial point turns on the concept of "resemblance." Assuming for purposes of our discussion that we have an idea of resemblance,[7] we can say, of any two entities, that, if they are to resemble each other, they must have something in common, some feature or characteristic they share.[8] Consider Hume's example of a triangle. Triangles share many common features; they are geometric figures, they are composed of three lines, their lines are straight, their lines enclose a space, they have angled corners, the sum of their angles equals 180 degrees, and so on. Suppose we conduct an experiment in which we are presented with a geometrical figure. This figure exhibits a characteristic common to triangles—it has angled corners. So we might label it a triangle. But now suppose we notice that it is made up of four rather than three lines. Immediately we would deny that it should be called a triangle, because it does not exhibit another common feature of triangles. Let us repair this omission by presenting a three-sided geometrical figure (which has angled corners). Now we could claim that we have a triangle before us. But again we notice an omission; our three-sided figure does not enclose a space (there is a gap between its lines). Once more, we would withdraw the label "triangle." And so on.

So we can raise the question: Why do we refuse to call either of these two figures triangles, even though they share common features of triangles? The answer is clear: Geometrical figures that resemble each other, to be called triangles, must resemble each other in certain ways; specifically they must exhibit *all* of the characteristics that *define* triangles. If we have an idea of a geometrical figure before our consciousness and ask ourselves if it is a triangle, to answer our question we check to see whether it satisfies the conditions necessary to qualify it as a triangle. We cannot answer our question by contemplating the particular idea before us alone. It has no label on it marking it "triangle." Rather our ability to reach a decision on the question of whether or not it is a triangle presupposes that we *already* know what a triangle is; i.e., what its defining characteristics are. So Hume's explanation of the generation of general terms and his account of general concepts seems to be backwards. He says that we explain the concept of a triangle from the fact of our being presented with a geometrical figure that represents or stands for all other figures that resemble it. But, unless we already possessed the concept of a triangle, we could not know which of our presented figure's many characteristics that resemble those of other figures was the one that qualified it to be called a triangle, rather than a square or an open-ended figure and so on. Thus Hume's theory seems to presuppose our possession of the general ideas or concepts it is meant to eliminate.

Although he presumably did not recognize the fact, Hume actually offers a criticism of his own account of the generation of general ideas that

closely parallels the one I have just given. The passage, in which he phrases his point in figurative terms, appears just after he has completed the
initial exposition of his theory of general ideas. He writes:

> For this is one of the most extrordinary circumstances in the present affair,
> that after the mind has produc'd an individual idea, upon which we reason,
> the attendent custom, reviv'd by the general or abstract term, readily suggests
> any other individual, if by chance we form any reasoning, that agrees not with
> it. Thus, shou'd we mention the word, triangle, and form the idea of a partic-
> ular equilateral one to correspond to it, and shou'd we afterwards assert, *that
> the three angles of a triangle are equal to each other,* the other individuals of a
> scalenum and isoceles, which we overlook'd at first, immediately crowd in
> upon us, and make us perceive the falshood of this proposition. (21)

Since Hume is surely correct in his conclusion, we are left with the question: *Why* should we be forced to recognize the falsehood of the statement
about the angles of a triangle? Any satisfactory answer must assume that
we already possess the general concept of a triangle, with its defining characteristics—a concept we cannot have derived from particular impressions
of geometrical figures—which requires us to recognize that scalenum and
isoceles figures are equally as authentic triangles as equilateral figures, even
though they are not equiangular.[9] The consequences of this point are serious. If Hume's attempt to account for general concepts is not successful,
we are left with the problem of how thought is possible. Perhaps we could
still think even though we never possessed general ideas, but our thought
would be severely constricted.

5. Distinctions of Reason (Section VII)

Hume concludes Section VII by introducing a somewhat puzzling concept—that of a *distinction of reason*—in order to resolve a problem in his
theory of ideas. This problem can be seen most easily through an examination of the illustration he gives. Consider the following three objects: (1)
a white globe, (2) a black globe, and (3) a white cube. We can recognize
that (1) and (2) resemble each other in that both are globes; we can also
recognize that (1) and (3) resemble each other in that both are white. The
problem is that the particular ideas we have of these three objects are such
that the color and form of each appear in our consciousness together and
cannot be separated from each other. For example, "When a globe of white
marble is presented, we receive only the impression of a white colour
dispos'd in a certain form, nor are we able to separate and distinguish the
colour from the form" (25). Yet, in order to recognize the resemblances just
noted, we must separate the color from the form. How is this possible?

Hume solves his problem through an appeal to a distinction of reason: "we begin to distinguish the figure from the colour by a *distinction of reason;* that is, we consider the figure and colour together, since they are in effect the same and undistinguishable; but still view them in different aspects, according to the resemblances, of which they are susceptible" (25). A bit later in the paragraph he speaks of this distinction of reason as a "kind of reflexion" (25) that accompanies our ideas. One might say that what we do, when we recognize the resemblance between our ideas of a white and black globe, is to concentrate our attention on the form of these ideas rather than their color and when we recognize the resemblance between our ideas of a white globe and a white cube we concentrate our attention on the color of our ideas rather than their form.

No one would disagree with Hume about our ability to do what he describes. Nevertheless, his appeal to distinctions of reason raises some problems. First, he seemingly acknowledges that his introduction of such distinctions is at odds with his view that ideas (like color and form), which are not distinguishable, cannot be separated. He writes: "A person, who desires us to consider the figure of a globe of white marble without thinking on its colour, desires an impossibility" (25). It would have been helpful if he had clarified the matter further. He seems also to be in danger of compromising his original theory of ideas through his introduction of distinctions of reason. As he puts it, "By this means [distinctions of reason] we accompany our ideas with a kind of reflexion, of which custom renders us, in a great measure, insensible."[10] Again, further explanation would have been helpful. If the mind can concentrate its attention on certain perceptions presented to it to the exclusion of others, rather than simply receive them and recombine them through memory and imagination, it has powers that Hume has not fully explained in Part I. Such powers could be important. Not only may they open the door to further activities of the mind but their relationship to Hume's original theory of ideas, particularly the Empiricist Principle, needs to be made clear.

Summary

In Sections VI and VII of Part I Hume turns his attention to two concepts of fundamental importance to philosophy—substance and abstract or general ideas—offering explanations of them based on his theory of ideas, summarized in the Empiricist Principle. (His discussion of modes in Section VI is of minor importance.) After rejecting the Lockean, commonsense view of substance on the grounds that substance, so understood, can never form the content of an idea and hence is inconceivable, he offers his own theory of substance; namely, that it is a complex idea made up of a collection of simple ideas united together by the imagination and given a name. Substance, as a reality independent of the mind, must be accounted a "fiction."

Hume's account of general ideas is an attempt to combine the recognition that we need such ideas to think and communicate with his conclusion that all our ideas, because they are copies of impressions, which are particular, must be particular as well. Again, Hume rejects the commonsense view in favor of the theory that general ideas are only particular ideas that become general in their representation, by standing for similar particular ideas. He explains how this is possible through a psychological analysis based on an appeal to resemblance and custom or habit. The main difficulty with Hume's theory of general ideas is that the whole process he describes to account for their generation seems to presuppose their existence.

Hume concludes Part I with the introduction of what he calls distinctions of reason. He says little about such distinctions but they raise the possibility that he will have further things to say later in Book I about the active powers of the mind.

Part 2

SPACE, TIME, AND EXISTENCE

Part II of the *Treatise* is puzzling, for several reasons. Hume entitles it "Of the Ideas of Space and Time" but devotes much of it to an analysis of space and time themselves, which are not the same as their ideas. Also, he discusses a number of other subjects in it, some related to the topics in his title, others with little connection to them. The part begins in an unexpected way, considering the structure of the preceding part. Assuming that Hume would have continued to develop the implications of his theory of ideas, as he had commenced doing at the end of Part I with his analysis of substance and abstract ideas, one would expect him to have launched immediately into similar analyses of the ideas of space and time, an expectation naturally aroused by the title he gives to Part II. Instead he begins the part by addressing himself to a more particular and seemingly subordinate issue, the question of whether the ideas of space and time are infinitely divisible, to which (with the companion question of whether space and time themselves are infinitely divisible) he devotes much of the part. Finally, in the last section he leaves space and time altogether to consider the ideas of existence and external existence. Because the subject matter of this section is quite different from what has gone before, and, more important, because it concerns matters of great significance to an understanding of Hume's philosophy, I will devote chapter 5 to it.

Part II may appear to the reader (as it has to many Hume commentators) to be an unfortunate element in Book I, which, besides doing little to advance Hume's philosophy, is itself subject to serious criticisms.[1] Why, then, did Hume insert this material, with its special and limited focus, into the book almost immediately after he had begun to develop and apply his empiricist theory of ideas? He may have had two reasons, quite different from each other, for doing so. The first is readily understandable, for the part does mark a legitimate (although somewhat unexpected) progression from Part I. Having at the end of that part begun the task of working out the implications of his theory of ideas, Hume could well have decided that he should continue by turning his attention to three of the most basic ideas that occupy the human mind, those of space, time, and existence. That he was motivated to develop his argument along these lines because he recognized them as a logical continuation of his thought is evidenced not only by the fact that the Empiricist Principle forms the constant background against which his discussion throughout the part is conducted but also by the fact that he appeals to it repeatedly in his arguments there.

The second reason why Part II (with the exception of the final section) has the form and content it has is, I suggest, historical. Hume was concerned about developments in mathematics and science that had occurred in the preceding century. He was convinced that some of these were clearly mistaken—as, indeed, they had to be if Hume's epistemology is sound— and undertook in the part to show why they were wrong and what needed to be done to correct them. Two developments, in particular, agitated Hume—the mathematical theory of infinite divisibility and the physical theory of a vacuum, or empty space. Both were subjects of intense discussion and controversy in the years preceding the publication of the *Treatise*, with natural scientists, mathematicians, philosophers, and theologians contributing to the literature. The seminal figures in these debates were Isaac Newton and two continental thinkers—G. W. Leibniz and René Descartes.

The controversy concerning infinite divisibility had its immediate origins in the infinitesimal calculus—or the theory of fluxions, as it was then called—a major advance in the history of mathematics, which was achieved independently and almost simultaneously in the latter part of the seventeenth century by Newton and Leibniz.[2] The question of a vacuum arose earlier, with the cosmological theories of Descartes in the first half of the century. According to Descartes, the universe is a plenum, or completely filled with matter, hence empty space does not exist. Later in the century Newton championed the opposite view: all the bodies in the universe are in motion in empty space. During the years that followed, disciples of these three great thinkers continued to debate the issues in science and mathematics their work had generated. In Part II Hume joins these debates with characteristic vigor and subtlety of thought. His arguments, which put him at odds with Newton, whom he undoubtedly admired, were derived mainly from two sources, his own empiricist epistemology from Part I and the arguments contained in the *Dictionaire Philosophique et Critique* of Pierre Bayle.[3]

4

Space and Time and Their Ideas

(Part II, Sections I–V)

Introduction

Hume begins Part II with two sections devoted to the twin issues of the infinite divisibility of our ideas of space and time and then of space and time themselves. In Section III he examines the sources, in our impressions, of these two ideas, returning to questions of infinite divisibility in Section IV. His pursuit of problems connected with these concepts at times becomes quite complex and often difficult to follow. It leads him into a long, involved account of the nature of mathematics, in which he presents a novel theory of geometry that is at variance with the views of most geometers, both before and after his time. In Section V he completes his discussion of the idea of space with an analysis of the concept of a vacuum. The main topics that occupy Hume in the first five sections of Part II, although they are of historical interest and give us information about his reactions to intellectual currents prominent in his day, do not contribute significantly to the development of his philosophy in Book I. However, Hume does raise an issue of major importance to his epistemology and metaphysics in these sections. I will discuss it in some detail in this chapter. In my commentary on Sections I to V, I will in general concentrate on points that directly affect Hume's philosophy in Book I.

Text

1. Are the Ideas of Space and Time Infinitely Divisible? (Section I)

Hume entitles the first section of Part II "Of the infinite divisibility of our ideas of space and time" (26). He begins with a sharp criticism of "philosophers," who like to exhibit their superiority to the common herd by propounding *outré* and paradoxical theories, and of their disciples, who greedily embrace these theories. The term "philosophers" Hume uses here should not be understood narrowly; rather, he was undoubtedly referring to intellectuals in general and, given the concluding sentence of his polemic, with its reference to the doctrine of infinite divisibility, to mathematicians in particular.[1]

Hume begins his argument by stating two assumptions, which he takes to be obvious, that will guide his discussion of the infinite divisibility of space and time and of our ideas of both in Part II.[2] The first reads: "The capacity of the mind is limited, and can never attain a full and adequate conception of infinity" (26). This statement may seem so evident that one might question why Hume bothered to insert the qualifying adjectives "full" and "adequate" into it. Further thought, however, might raise doubts about it. If, one might ask, the human mind cannot have a conception of infinity, how do we explain the fact that mathematicians use the concept successfully and fruitfully in their calculations? Although this objection is serious, Hume was prepared to meet it. According to the Empiricist Principle, all of our ideas, or conceptions, are copies of our impressions. Thus, if we are to have a conception of infinity, we must first have an impression of it. But this we cannot have because none of our five senses can grasp such an impression. "Infinity" (or an infinite object) is simply not something we can see, and so on.

Hume's second assumption is more complex and involves him in a longer discussion than the first. He writes:

> Whatever is capable of being divided *in infinitum*, must consist of an infinite number of parts, and . . . 'tis impossible to set any bounds to the number of parts, without setting bounds at the same time to the division. It requires scarce any induction to conclude from hence, that the *idea*, which we form of any finite quality, is not infinitely divisible, but that by proper distinctions and separations we may run up this idea to inferior ones, which will be perfectly simple and indivisible. (26–27)

This second assumption can be shown to follow from the first. Suppose we have an idea of a certain magnitude. This idea, no matter how large it is, must nevertheless (according to the first assumption) be finite. Suppose next that we begin to divide our idea into parts. No matter how far we try to divide it, we can end only with a finite number of smaller parts, because only an infinite magnitude is capable of division into an infinite number of parts. The second assumption is also derivable directly from the Empiricist Principle. Since all our ideas are copies of prior impressions, to divide any idea infinitely we must be able to divide its impression infinitely. But this we cannot do; there is a limit to how far we can go before our senses fail us.

Hume goes on to elaborate his thesis concerning divisibility, using two examples taken from our ideas and one from our impressions. The first involves our idea of a grain of sand, which is later repeated (with a significant difference) with our idea of a mite. His argument is obscure and appears to contain an inconsistency. He begins by saying that, just as we can have an idea of a grain of sand, so we can have the ideas of the numbers we use when we talk about exceedingly small parts of a grain of sand. This point is not helpful, unless we assume he means that we can have ideas of exceedingly small parts of a grain of sand just as we have one of the grain itself—ideas that necessarily would be much smaller than our idea of the grain of sand. But he rejects this explanation, writing: "When you tell me of the thousandth and ten thousandth part of a grain of sand . . . the images [ideas] which I form in my mind to represent the things themselves, are nothing different from each other, nor inferior to that image, by which I represent the grain of sand itself" (27). Hume confuses the situation further by his second example of an idea, that of a mite, which appears on the following page. In his discussion of that example he writes:

Taking the impressions of those minute objects, which appear to the senses, to be equal or nearly equal to the objects, and finding by reason, that there are other objects vastly more minute, we too hastily conclude, that these are inferior to any idea of our imagination or impression of our senses. *This however is certain, that we can form ideas, which shall be no greater than the smallest atom of the animal spirits of an insect a thousand times less than a mite.* (28—italics added)

According to the mite illustration, we can form ideas much smaller than our idea of a mite. Why then can we not form ideas much smaller than our idea of a grain of sand? What has caused Hume to make this shift from one page to the next? He speaks in the mite example of our "finding by reason" that there are objects much smaller than things the size of mites. But this is not helpful unless we understand what he means by "finding by reason." Obviously, on his epistemological theory the only meaning this phrase can have is that we are in possession of some idea of the entity in question through having had a prior impression of it. That this interpretation of the illustration, besides being consonant with his general epistemology and with his line of thought in these passages, succeeds in erasing the apparent inconsistency between his grain of sand and mite examples, is shown by an illustration he gives between the two, in which he defends the ultimate indivisibility of our impressions.

Try the following experiment, suggests Hume. Put a small ink spot on a piece of paper, tack the paper on a wall, and then gradually back away from the wall. Your impression of the ink spot will gradually diminish in

size until you reach a point at which it vanishes. At your last step backward before it vanishes, Hume claims, your impression is "perfectly indivisible" (27). It follows from this that you cannot divide your impression
or, consequently, your idea into smaller parts (parallel to the grain of sand
case) but it nevertheless is possible for you to have an impression and,
hence, an idea of a smaller spot (parallel to the mite case). This possibility
results from the use of aids to vision, such as telescopes and microscopes.
With the proper magnifying device the ink spot that to the naked eye has
become invisible assumes substantial proportions. Under a microscope the
mite likewise becomes a formidable beast. "A microscope or telescope,
which renders [bodies] visible . . . both gives parts to impressions, which
to the naked eye appear simple and uncompounded, and advances to a
minimum, what was formerly inperceptible" (28). So we can conclude that,
although each one of us can say what our smallest impressions and, hence,
ideas are when we appeal to our unaided vision, no one can predict how
far we can carry our sight, when we make use of such magnifying devices
as microscopes and telescopes. Nevertheless, if we could reach an absolutely
minimum perception, this would, Hume maintains, be indivisible.

To sum up Hume's argument in Section I, the alleged notion of infinite divisibility is incomprehensible because, to comprehend it, we should
have to be able to divide our impressions and ideas infinitely. But such a
possibility is precluded by his two assumptions, both of which rest on the
Empiricist Principle. However, Hume's attack on infinite divisibility does
not exhaust the contents of Section I. Toward the end of the section he
raises a quite different issue, of major importance to his epistemology. I
will turn to it in section 2.

2. Error and Truth (Section I and Section II, Paragraph 1)

In the last paragraph of Section I Hume introduces a new and puzzling
element into his philosophy. In a statement that occurs during his discussion of a mite, he raises the problem of error, writing: "The only defect of
our senses is, that they give us disproportion'd images of things, and represent as minute and uncompounded what is really great and compos'd of
a vast number of parts."[3] Hume seems clearly to be saying in this sentence
that our senses (sometimes) give us false perceptions of things, or entities
in the external world. If this is what he means, he has introduced an important new kind of entity into his metaphysics—physical objects, or a
material world—whose reality he had questioned in Part I (16).

That Hume did intend to explain error by reference to the nature of
external reality seems to be confirmed by a statement he makes at the beginning of Section II (in the paragraph immediately following the one in

which his account of error appears). The passage reads: "Wherever ideas are adequate representations of objects, the relations, contradictions and agreements of the ideas are all applicable to the objects; and this we may in general observe to be the foundation of all human knowledge."[4] If, for example, I have the idea that a mite is smaller than an ant, I can legitimately claim to know this only if a mite is in fact smaller than an ant. My idea can be true, hence something I can know, only if it adequately represents a fact about an independently existing world. Thus Hume in this statement seems to be affirming the traditional correspondence theory of truth. If he is doing so he is also affirming both the existence of physical objects and our possible perception of them through our senses.[5]

Obviously, the two statements I have cited raise a problem for our understanding of Hume. To appreciate the problem we must return to Part I and Hume's theory of ideas. We found in chapter 2 that the central concept of Hume's epistemology is "idea." Ideas are things we perceive; they are contents of our consciousness. They are also copies or images of impressions, which are contents of consciousness as well. The causes of these impressions are unknown, indeed unknowable. Finally, nothing that is not a perception (an impression or an idea) is conceivable by the human mind.[6]

With these epistemological assumptions in mind, let us return to Hume's statement about error. In order to explain error—or, equally, to explain truth—we need a standard against which to measure any perception we have, whether it be an impression or an idea. In the sentence in question Hume provides such a standard. Our senses are in error, he says, when they give us incorrect images of things. But to employ this standard we must be able to compare the image with the thing; otherwise we could never recognize our error. To do this we must be able to conceive the thing, in this situation the external physical object. But the only things that are conceivable, on Hume's epistemology, are perceptions and these are mental entities, not external physical objects. Thus, if he employs external objects as standards for the detection of perceptual errors, Hume is appealing to a criterion that is, according to his epistemology, inconceivable. The same judgment must be made about his introduction of the correspondence theory of truth. To be able to say of any idea that it is true, we must be able to compare the idea with its object, to determine that it corresponds to that object, but this we cannot do if the object in question is an external reality and the only things we can conceive of are perceptions.

To sum up these observations, Part II appears to introduce a new dimension into Hume's thought, one inconsistent with the epistemological foundations he laid down in Part I. This apparent inconsistency leaves commentators in a quandary. Should we conclude that Hume has changed his position, abandoning his epistemology of Part I? If we were to do so, however, we would be faced with an insuperable difficulty. Not only in Part II but throughout the remainder of Book I, Hume repeatedly appeals to his original epistemology, and particularly to the Empiricist Principle, at crucial points in his argument. He obviously does *not* repudiate Part I. The best thing we can do at this point is to keep this problem in mind as we proceed, remaining alert to the possibility that later Hume may give some explanation to resolve the issue. The question needing an answer is: Does Hume later in Book I develop a theory that (1) affirms the existence of an external world (2) that is knowable to us and (3) that can be known by means of his theory of ideas? As we continue our study I will keep this issue in mind, addressing it directly wherever the text of the *Treatise* makes doing so appropriate.[7]

Before leaving this question, another point needs to be recognized. In my interpretation of the passage that appears to affirm the correspondence theory, I assumed that Hume means by the word "objects" in it "external physical objects." But perhaps he does not and instead means "impressions," which are the "objects" of our "ideas." Then the problem I have raised would not exist. This alternative interpretation, however, faces at least two objections. First, in the statement Hume implies that the question of whether an idea adequately represents its "object" is an open one but we already know from Part I that all ideas are exactly correspondent to their impressions. Second, in the statement about error in the previous paragraph Hume is talking about a defect not of our ideas but of our impressions; our senses sometimes deceive us about the sizes of things. Unfortunately, Hume did not make himself clear but, as we will see, he has much more to say on this point later in Book I.

3. The Infinite Divisibility of Space and Time (Section II)

The title of Section II supports the suggestion I have just made, of a shift in the focus of Hume's epistemology early in Part II. In Section II he seems clearly to be concerned not with our ideas of space and time but with space and time themselves, as realities independent of our consciousness. He raises the same question about them that he had raised in Section I about our ideas of them: Are they infinitely divisible? Assuming the correspondence theory of truth, which implies that the "relations, contradictions and agreements of the ideas are all applicable to the objects" (29), he sets out to establish that, since the infinite divisibility of our ideas of space and time is impossible, so too must be the infinite divisibility of space and time themselves.

Turning his attention first to "extension"—a term he uses synonymously with "space" throughout Part II—Hume offers two arguments against its infinite divisibility. In the first he contends that it is contradictory to sup-pose that a finite extension is infinitely divisible. If, he says, he starts with the smallest idea of extension he can form, then doubles, triples, and con-tinues to increase the size of the idea, he would, if he could produce such an idea, end with an infinite idea of extension. Anything short of this would be a finite idea of extension containing a finite number of parts. Since ex-tension itself must be in agreement with our adequate ideas of it, it follows that a finite extension must be composed of a finite number of parts and so cannot be infinitely divisible.[8] His second argument, which he describes as "very strong and beautiful" (30), he attributes to a "Mons. *Malezieu*."[9] Ex-tension is a number and has no existence other than that possessed by the units of which it is composed, just as the existence of twenty men is reduc-ible to that of the individual men of which the group of twenty is composed. Hence, if there is to be any extension at all, there must be individual units of extension, therefore extension cannot be infinitely divisible.

Hume notes an objection to this argument, to the effect that any unit of extension can be divided infinitely through the use of fractions, but re-jects it on the grounds that this would permit twenty men, or even the whole universe, to be considered as a unit and such a supposition intro-duces a fictitious notion of a unit, one that cannot exist alone, because it is identical to a number. Hume's argument here does not seem to offer a persuasive objection to the possibilities created by fractions. Could not a mathematician take one of Hume's "indivisible" units and fractionalize it endlessly?

At this point Hume leaves the subject of extension or space, to offer some brief remarks about time. After noting that the same two arguments he had just used to disprove the infinite divisibility of space apply equally to time, he adds a further argument. It is of the essence of time that its parts (the moments that make it up) succeed each other. They cannot be coexistent, as the parts of space are. It follows from this that the parts of time must be indivisible for, if time were conceived to be infinitely divisi-ble, it would consist of an infinite number of coexistent moments, hence there could be no succession and thus no time.[10]

Leaving the subject of time, Hume inserts a short homily on the dif-ference between demonstrations and arguments from probabilities in which he says of the former, "[A demonstration is] either irresistible, or has no manner of force" (31). He then concludes Section II by offering a general argument to demonstrate that space, rather than being infinitely divisible, is composed of ultimate parts that are indivisible. In this argument, after making the point that anything of which we can have an idea can exist (e.g., a golden mountain) but nothing of which we cannot have an idea is pos-sible (e.g., a mountain without a valley), he presents the following argument: (1) We can conceive (have an idea) of extension, (2) our conception of extension is not infinitely divisible, therefore (a) a conception of extension composed of indivisible parts is possible and (b) a real extension so composed is also possible. It follows from these conclusions that "all the arguments employ'd against the possibility of mathematical points are mere scholastick quibbles, and unworthy of our attention."[11]

Two comments about this argument are in order. If sound, it establishes that the attempt to *demonstrate* the infinite divisibility of extension must fail because Hume's opposed view offers an alternative account that is possible. But mathematicians might counter by replying that their arguments are not meant to constitute a demonstration of infinite divisibility but only to provide a better theory of extension than that of Hume. Hume's response to such a counterargument would appear to be that infinite divisibility is inconceivable, for he writes: "'Tis likewise certain, that this idea [of extension], as conceiv'd by the imagination . . . is not infinitely divisible, nor consists of an infinite number of parts: For that exceeds the comprehension of our limited capacities" (32). Because we can have no idea of an infinitely divisible extension, it is inconceivable to us.

4. The Idea of Space or Extension (Section III, Beginning and End)

In Section III Hume returns to the topic of our ideas of space and time, but not to the question of their infinite divisibility, with which he had begun Part II. Instead he concentrates on the nature of these ideas and offers an explanation of their origin, based on his empiricist epistemology. He discusses both in the section, beginning with the idea of space, then moving to that of time, and finally returning to space. To simplify my exposition I will separate my discussion into two parts, devoting this section to the idea of space and section 5 to that of time.

Hume begins Section III with a reaffirmation of the Empiricist Principle, noting that he will base his analysis of the ideas of space and time on it. "No discovery cou'd have been made more happily for deciding all controversies concerning ideas, than . . . that impressions always take the precedency of them, and that every idea, with which the imagination is furnish'd, first makes its appearance in a correspondent impression. . . . Let us apply this principle, in order to discover farther the nature of our ideas of space and time" (33). Applying the Principle, he launches his analysis of the idea of space or extension, writing: "Upon opening my eyes, and turning them to the surrounding objects, I perceive many visible bodies; and upon shutting them again, and considering the distance betwixt these bodies, I acquire the idea of extension."[12] He continues by pointing out that this idea of extension must, like all ideas, be derived from some impression, either of sensation or reflection. Since the latter can be ruled out, to trace the origin of the idea, we must start with our sense impressions. When I look, for example, at a table, what do I see? Hume answers: "My senses convey to me only the impressions of colour'd points, dispos'd in a certain manner."[13] Since this is all I see, he concludes, "we may conclude with certainty, that the idea of extension is nothing but a copy of these colour'd points, and of the manner of their appearance" (34).

Although Hume may appear to be saying here that we have a direct impression of extension, of which our idea is a copy, the explanation he then gives of these passages makes it clear that he is not. Hume's visual impression of a table (or any other material object) is complex, consisting of two components, (1) colored points and (2) the manner of their arrangement, or their "composition" or "disposition" (34). His account of the idea of extension consists in an analysis of both of these components of our sense impressions. He takes them up in reverse order, turning immediately to (2) but leaving (1) until after he has discussed the idea of time. I will also discuss these components in reverse order.

Hume's purpose in his analysis of component (2) is to explain the origin of our general idea of space, an idea that applies to all complex objects of visual sensation. He begins by noting that the colored points, whose composition we see in a table, are of a certain color, say, purple. But then we see other tables whose points have a similar order or disposition but a different color. After such experiences we eliminate the differences in the color of the points and concentrate on the resemblance of their dispositions and thus form the idea of space. This is an *abstract* idea; that is, it is a particular idea, which, being annexed to a general term, can stand for other ideas that share the same feature.

I turn next to Hume's account of the "colour'd points" component (1) of our impressions and, hence, our ideas of space; this occurs near the end of Section III, after his discussion of the idea of time. He writes: "Let us take one of those simple indivisible ideas, of which the compound one of *extension* is form'd, and separating it from all others, and considering it apart, let us form a judgment of its nature and qualities" (38). He makes four points about this idea. (1) It is indivisible. Being an ultimate part of our idea of extension, which is a compound or complex idea, it must, because our idea of space is not infinitely divisible, be a simple, indivisible idea. He describes these simple ideas as ideas of "mathematical points" (38). (2) It is real. As he puts it, "The idea of extension consists of parts; and this idea, according to the supposition, is perfectly simple and indivisible. Is it therefore nothing? That is absolutely impossible. For as the compound idea of extension, which is real, is compos'd of such ideas; were these so

many non-entities, there wou'd be a real existence compos'd of non-entities; which is absurd" (38). (3) It is colored. This quality follows from the
fact that the idea of such a point is a copy of a visual impression and our
eyes can see nothing unless it is colored. (4) It is not the idea of extension.
The idea of extension is a compound idea, made up of indivisible parts,
and this idea is one of those parts. Being indivisible it cannot itself be an
idea of extension. In Hume's summary account of these indivisible points
that are the building blocks of our idea of extension: "If a point be not
consider'd as colour'd or tangible, it can convey to us no idea; and consequently the idea of extension, which is compos'd of the ideas of these points,
can never possibly exist. But if the idea of extension really can exist, as we
are conscious it does, its parts must also exist; and in order to that, must
be consider'd as colour'd or tangible" (39).

Hume's account of the idea of space contains some obscurities, which
cast doubt on his conclusion that he has any such idea. He makes it clear
that he has no ordinary idea of space itself, because he has no impression
from which it can be derived. "The ideas of space and time are . . . no separate or distinct ideas" (39). Therefore it must be an abstract idea, generated from the two components he has described. In fact, Hume argues, it
is derived from component (2). "[We] found an abstract idea [of space]
merely on that disposition of points, or manner of appearance, in which
[various colored objects] agree" (34). The terms Hume uses here are obscure. What does he mean by "the disposition of points" or their "manner
of appearance"? Is he describing their spatial relationships? If so, he has a
direct impression of space but this is something he denies he possesses. If
he is not talking about spatial relationships when he uses the phrases, as
he apparently is not, just what does he mean by them?

Hume's account raises a further problem. He says that "space" is an
abstract idea. But how can it be? If we return to his theory of abstract ideas
in Part I, we find him writing: "Abstract ideas are . . . in themselves individual, however they may become general in their representation. The
image in the mind is only that of a particular object."[14] Explaining further,
he argues that the abstract idea "man" is an idea, derived from an impression, of an individual man, which stands for or represents all other like
individuals. To have an abstract idea "man," therefore, we must have ordinary ideas of individual men. When we try to apply this analysis to the
abstract idea of space, however, we run into difficulties. To have such an
idea, or the idea of space in general, we must have ideas of individual "spac-
es." But these, Hume claims, we do not have. So he has failed to give a
satisfactory explanation of how space can be an abstract idea. Since it is
not an ordinary idea either, we are left to conclude that Hume has no idea
of space at all.

5. The Idea of Time or Duration (Section III, Middle Portion)

Hume's discussion of the idea of time—or "duration," a term he uses as a synonym—occupies the middle portion of Section III. In its main aspects it parallels his analysis of the idea of space; nevertheless, there are differences between the two. I will note these when they appear.

Like the idea of space, that of time is an abstract idea (35). Unlike it, however, it is derived not simply from sense impressions but from perceptions of every kind, ideas as well as sensations. "As 'tis from the disposition of visible and tangible objects we receive the idea of space, so from the succession of ideas and impressions we form the idea of time" (35). The reason for this difference becomes apparent when we consider the two components that give rise to the idea of time. The first is our perceptions themselves (analogous to the "coloured points" in the idea of space); the second is the notion of "succession" (analogous to the "manner" or "disposition" of the colored points in the idea of space). Hume is attempting to explain that our perceptions, of *whatever* kind, appear in our mind successively (one after another) and that from this feature of them we acquire the idea of time. He writes of "the idea of time, being deriv'd from the succession of our perceptions of every kind" (34–35). Because we can have no idea of time without a perception of succession and succession entails change, we can never derive the idea of time from an unchangeable object. Hume devotes a good part of his discussion to establishing this conclusion, emphasizing the indispensable role played by our perception of succession in the generation of our recognition of time. In his words, "We may conclude, that time cannot make its appearance to the mind, either alone, or attended with a steady unchangeable object, but is always discover'd by some *perceivable* succession of changeable objects."[15]

The passage I have just quoted reveals another feature of the idea of time. It is not a separate idea we have. It cannot be because that would require us to have a separate impression of time as its source and this we do not have. Hume offers an illustration to clarify this point, writing:

> The idea of time is not deriv'd from a particular impression mix'd up with others, and plainly distinguishable from them; but arises altogether from the manner, in which impressions appear to the mind, without making one of the number. Five notes play'd on a flute give us the impression and idea of time; tho' time be not a sixth impression, which presents itself to the hearing or any other of the senses. . . . since [the idea of time] appears not as any primary distinct impression, [it] *can plainly be nothing but different ideas, or impressions, or objects dispos'd in a certain manner, that is, succeeding each other.* (36–37—italics added)

A final feature of the idea of time is that the ultimate parts that make it up—the separate, successive "moments" (39) of time—are indivisible. Hume does not expand on this view here, presumably because he had already dealt with it in Section I and will return to it in Section IV. We can also conclude, although Hume does not make the point explicitly, that these indivisible moments are, like the extensionless colored points of our idea of space, themselves durationless. That this must be his view follows from the fact that these moments of time are indivisible, thus contain no parts, and any bit of time that has a duration must be made up of shorter parts.

Hume's account of the idea of time gives rise to a serious problem. Assuming that time is an abstract idea,[16] it still must have its source ultimately in some impressions. We have seen that Hume turns to two components of our original impressions that give rise to this idea, the perceptions themselves and the particular order in which they appear, which is one of succession. That Hume has perceptions is indisputable, but what of the second component—the succession of his perceptions? He must, if he is to conceive of this succession, find an original impression from which its idea is derived. To do so he must perceive *succession* itself through one of his senses. As he has said, "[Time] is always discover'd by some *perceivable* succession of changeable objects" (35). But this succession cannot be perceived, either through sight, hearing, touch, taste, or smell. It follows that Hume can have no idea of succession, hence—since having such an idea is a necessary condition for his acquiring the idea of time—we seem forced to conclude that he can have no such idea.

Since this problem is serious, I will pursue it further, by looking more closely at the illustration Hume gives, of five notes played on a flute. To repeat a sentence from that illustration: "Five notes play'd on a flute give us the impression and idea of time; tho' time be not a sixth impression, which presents itself to the hearing or any other of the senses." What we *actually hear* is not, as Hume claims, *five* flute notes but rather only flute note—flute note—flute note—flute note—flute note. We have no sense impression of anything else. Hume is mistaken in claiming that we *hear five* notes, following *in succession* one after the other. We do not *hear* anything other than the flute notes themselves. Thus he has no grounds for his conclusion that our hearing these five successive sounds gives rise in us to the idea of time. This illustration calls for three further comments: (1) To be able to recognize that the *five* notes are played and played *in succession*, we must be aware that each note *follows after* the one preceding it.[17] But "following after" is a temporal concept, hence our very awareness that one note follows after another, and thus that the notes are *successive*, presupposes our possession of the idea of time. So we cannot derive our idea of time from that of succession; rather we could never be aware of succession unless we already had an idea of time. (2) We do not, in fact, have a Humean idea of succession. As a purported component of the source of our idea of time, it must be an idea copied from an impression. But, as I argued in the previous paragraph, we have no impression of succession, so can have no idea of it. (3) Hume's analysis of the five successive flute notes presents him with a dilemma. If he follows the Empiricist Principle, which he took pains to reaffirm at the beginning of his argument in Section III, he can never account for our recognition that the notes succeed each other or, as a result, for our having any idea of time at all. If, on the other hand, he claims—as he does—that we have such an idea, he is in violation of the foundations of his own epistemology. He cannot have it both ways.

6. Infinite Divisibility versus Mathematical Points (Section IV)

In Section IV Hume returns to the topic of space and time themselves, addressing two different but closely related topics. In the earlier portion of the section he defends his view that space and time are not infinitely divisible but are composed of ultimate, indivisible parts; in the latter portion he develops a theory of the nature of geometry, based partly on his conception of space. However, he does not draw a sharp distinction between these two topics; the shift from the first to the second in the course of the section is primarily one of emphasis. In this section I will discuss his arguments regarding infinite divisibility, turning to his conception of geometry in section 7.

Before launching into the defense of his view, Hume summarizes the main points of his theory of space and time, using these as the bases on which he will mount his argument. They are: (1) (a) It is possible for space and time to be composed of a finite number of indivisible parts because our ideas of both are so composed and whatever is conceivable is possible, and (b) it is certain that they are so composed because their infinite divisibility is "utterly impossible" (39). (2) It follows from (1) that the indivisible parts of our ideas of space and time must be filled with something real and existent because they are "nothing in themselves" (39). In saying that these parts are nothing in themselves Hume is not denying their reality, but only emphasizing that they are not themselves spatial or temporal in nature. As we have already seen, he holds that the indivisible parts of our ideas of space are filled with color and those of our ideas of time with the contents of all of our perceptions. Accepting these conclusions Hume next offers three objections to his theory of space. The first two he answers quite summarily, the third at greater length.

The first objection is not so much an objection as the statement of a problem about the ultimate constitution of space. Hume maintains that his conception of space is the only one that is viable, because it can avoid the absurdities of the two alternative theories. These theories are (1) that space is infinitely divisible and (2) that it is composed of ultimate physical points. Assuming that he has already demonstrated the absurdity of (1), he concludes that (2) is equally absurd because physical points must be extended (occupy space), so must be composed of lesser parts, therefore cannot themselves be ultimate parts. This leaves only the third alternative—his theory of mathematical points. These points represent a medium between (1) and (2); on the one hand they are indivisible and on the other unextended. But such points, he notes, have been rejected on the grounds that they are nonentities, so no combination of them could ever add up to a real object. Hume believes that he has an answer to this objection. Mathematical points, although they are extensionless—so nonentities in that sense—are nevertheless real because they are colored.[18] So he concludes: "The absurdity of both the extremes [infinite divisibility and physical points] is a demonstration of the truth and reality of this medium [mathematical points]" (40).

The second objection is based on the notion of penetration. Suppose, the argument runs, two unextended but colored mathematical points were to approach each other. They could not touch because neither has any parts, thus no surface capable of touching. The only alternative is that they penetrate each other, but nothing that occupies no space can penetrate something else that occupies no space either. Therefore mathematical points are impossible. Hume answers this objection first by noting that the penetration of one body by another must result in the annihilation of one or the other of the bodies and then argues that this is not what happens when two mathematical points come together. On the contrary, the two together form a union that results in a compound object, presumably occupying space: "From the *union* of these points there results an object, which is compounded and divisible, and may be distinguish'd into two parts, of which each preserves its existence distinct and separate, notwithstanding its contiguity to the other" (41—italics added).

Hume's argument raises problems. First, he does not successfully eliminate the possibility that the coalescence of the two points results in the annihilation of something. He tries to do this by asking several rhetorical questions. "Let [the objector] aid his fancy by conceiving these points to be of different colours, the better to prevent their coalition and confusion. A blue and a red point may surely lie contiguous without any penetration or annihilation. For if they cannot, what possibly can become of them? Whether will the red or the blue be annihilated? Or if these colours unite into one, what new colour will they produce by their union?" (41). What is surprising about this argument is that Hume failed to see that there is an obvious answer to his last question. If the blue and red points coalesce with each other, the result will be a colored point that is neither red nor blue but a shade somewhere between them.

The second problem is more serious. Let us suppose that we have two unextended mathematical points that approach more and more closely to each other. On Hume's theory they will finally join together and their "union" will result in an extended object. The question is: How is this possible? If we consider the approach of the two points to each other, we have to choose between two alternatives. Either (a) the points come together and touch each other or (b) they never actually touch but remain slightly separate from each other. Alternative (a) can be eliminated because mathematical points, being unextended, have no surfaces that can touch. There can be no real "union" of such points. Alternative (b) is equally unacceptable. What we are trying to do is to create a single object out of the two points. Since, on this alternative, the points are still separated, their approach obviously cannot result in the creation of one object. All we have are two distinct entities, the original mathematical points, standing slightly apart from each other. To sum up, Hume is trying to accomplish an impossibility. He begins with mathematical points, which he concedes to be nonentities in the specific sense that they are unextended. He then attempts, by putting these unextended items together, to create extended objects. But not even a million unextended items joined together can ever produce an extended object. It is impossible to create something from nothing.

The third objection Hume considers is actually several, arising from mathematics. Hume devotes more space to answering these, maintaining that his theory of indivisible mathematical points is more consonant with geometry than is the opposed theory of infinite divisibility. Most of his argument is critical, consisting of an attack on the notion of infinite divisibility. He contends that the definitions geometers give of a surface, a line, and a point require acceptance of his view because they are incompatible with the demonstrations, based on infinite divisibility, that the geometers try to derive from them. He criticizes two arguments given by geometers in defense of their view. According to the first, geometrical concepts exist only in the mind but cannot exist in the external physical world. Hume's answer is brief and pointed: Anything we can conceive is possible, therefore, if we really have an idea of infinite divisibility, then infinitely divisible objects must be possible.[19]

The second defense of the geometers is that, although we cannot form an idea of the kind they require—for example, of a line without breadth—we can, by a "distinction of reason" abstract the line from its breadth and base our mathematical reasoning on this abstraction.[20] In answer Hume argues, briefly, that this defense requires the mind to have an infinite capacity, a possibility he has already rejected, but, more fully, that it is incompatible with the definitions of a point, a line, and a surface. "A surface terminates a solid; a line terminates a surface; a point terminates a line; but I assert, that if the *ideas* of a point, line or surface were not indivisible, 'tis impossible we shou'd ever conceive these terminations" (43–44). Hume's case is clear. If we are to conceive a termination of a surface, line, or point, we must reach some final, irreducible end to our ideas to mark the termination. This is impossible on the theory of infinite divisibility; only if we assume ultimate, irreducible points, lines, and surfaces can it be done. The issues with which Hume is dealing in the first part of Section IV are, as his discussion reveals, difficult ones. Indeed, they have been contested from ancient times, being related to questions raised by the Eleatic philosophers and dramatically illustrated in the paradoxes of Zeno. They were also, as Hume points out, discussed by the scholastic philosophers as well as by geometers. It is beyond the scope of this book to pursue these problems (about which disagreement still exists) any further. Since our interest is in Hume's positive theory of space and time, I will concentrate on that. On this point one important conclusion emerges and it must be critical of Hume. He claims in Section IV to be presenting a viable theory of space and, by analogy, of time as well. But, as we have already seen, he cannot generate extension out of the multiplication of extensionless points. Thus, on his theory there can be no space. A similar conclusion can be reached about time. Time is composed of ultimate parts that, being indivisible, have no duration. From such durationless moments it is impossible to generate duration. Once again, no multiplication of nonentities can create an entity. So, on Hume's theory, time cannot exist.

Although I am critical of Hume, I am not objecting here to the conclusion to which his theory of space and time leads; namely, that neither has any existence in an external, independent world.[21] This is certainly a possible view and one that has been held by philosophers other than Hume. My point is a different one; Hume should have recognized this consequence of his theory and not continued to claim the reality of space and time.

We should pause to ask ourselves what led Hume to conclusions he was unable to support. I think his mistake lies at the very beginning of his argument in Section IV in which he claims that he has found, in mathematical points, an explanation of the ultimate parts of space that avoids the contradictions of infinite divisibility and the inadequacy of physical points. By filling these mathematical points with color he claims to give them reality without giving them extension. But does he succeed in doing so? Can we really picture a point of *color*—that is, have a visual image of it— that occupies *no space at all*? Hume tries to establish that this is possible by his spot of ink experiment.

Put a spot of ink upon paper, and retire to such a distance, that the spot becomes altogether invisible; you will find, that upon your return and nearer approach the spot first becomes visible by short intervals; and afterwards becomes always visible; and afterwards acquires only a new force in its colouring without augmenting its bulk; and afterwards, *when it has encreas'd to such a degree as to be really extended,* 'tis still difficult for the imagination to break it into its component parts. (42—italics added)

It seems clear, however, that the spot of ink, *whenever* we are able to see it, must occupy some space, however small. A colored point, if it is really visible to the eye, simply cannot be one of Hume's unextended mathematical points. He has based his theory of space on an untenable assumption.

A parallel problem besets his theory of time. The durationless moments out of which time is to be constructed, unlike the points of space that are filled with color, are filled with perceptions of every kind. If these perceptions are durationless, they cannot, however many of them there may be, add up to any duration. Since they constitute the content of our consciousness, our total experience collapses into a nontemporal instant. Finally, since time requires experienced succession, it can no more exist than can our experience of it.

7. Pure versus Applied Geometry (Section IV)

Although Hume refers to geometry in the early part of Section IV, his comments are largely critical in nature. However, in the latter part of the section he offers a positive account of geometry. This account has its foundations in his theory of ideas and the Empiricist Principle. Perhaps the best way to understand his view is to begin by distinguishing pure from applied geometry. Pure geometry is a deductive system beginning with definitions and axioms and deriving theorems from these. Its conclusions are precise; an equilateral triangle is always *exactly* equiangular and so on. Applied geometry, on the other hand, is the geometry of the surveyor or carpenter. Being based on sense observation and the employment of mechanical instruments, it is inherently imprecise. Unlike the pure geometer the applied geometer can say only that the equilateral triangles he observes or constructs are more-or-less equiangular. Turning to Hume it is easy to predict what his view about geometry will be. According to the Empiricist Principle the only ideas we can have of spatial objects are copies of the impressions we have experienced. Since these are always imprecise, Hume rejects pure geometry, as being beyond the range of our possible ideas. He writes: "As the ultimate standard of these [geometrical] figures is deriv'd from nothing but the senses and imagination, 'tis absurd to talk of any perfection beyond what these faculties can judge of" (51).

To illustrate his point about the imprecision of geometry, Hume begins with the notion of equality. He asks mathematicians: "[What do] they mean when they say one line or surface is EQUAL to, or GREATER, or LESS than another?" (45). Then, somewhat surprisingly, he concedes that these questions cannot be answered precisely even by one who accepts his own theory that extension is composed of indivisible points. Although it is theoretically possible to obtain exactness on his view—two lines are equal in length if they contain the same number of mathematical points—it is practically impossible to do so because we cannot accurately count the points. But the defender of infinite divisibility cannot gain precision even in principle, let alone in practice. Since, for him, any length contains an infinite number of parts, he cannot distinguish the length of an inch from that of a yard by counting their respective parts. Hume goes on to discuss a third theory, which he attributes to "Dr. *Barrow's* mathematical lectures" (46, n. 1), based on congruity.[22] We say that two figures are equal if, when we place one on the other, we find that all their parts correspond to and touch each other. However, Hume concludes, this view is reducible to his own theory of indivisible parts.[23]

Having undercut the possibility of providing any practically viable basis for geometrical precision, Hume offers a second surprise. Such a basis is unnecessary because we can, without any appeal to it, make infallible judgments about such matters. "'Tis evident, that the eye, or rather the mind is often able at one view to determine the proportions of bodies, and pronounce them equal to, or greater or less than each other, without examining or comparing the number of their minute parts. Such judgments are not only common, but in many cases certain and infallible" (47). In explanation Hume quickly substantiates this claim, which turns out to be a commonplace. The mind can, for example, directly discern that a line a yard in length is longer than one a foot in length. However, as he is quick to recognize, such discernment is possible only when we are dealing with gross differences; our infallibility dissipates when we have to make fine distinctions or judgments of equality and it is these with which geometry is primarily concerned. Our only recourse in such situations is to bring in instruments, such as calipers and microscopes, to make our observations as acute as possible. But, he cautions, "We are not possess'd of any instrument or art of measuring, which can secure us from all error and uncertainty" (48).

This conclusion leads Hume into a consideration of our use of standards in geometrical reasoning in general. Before pursuing this topic, however, he interjects some remarks about time. When we talk about the equality of two lengths of time, he notes, we must speak imprecisely because we have even less of a measure to make careful comparisons than we do in the case of extension. Returning to the realm of space, Hume considers the question of what we can appeal to as a standard to substantiate our judgments. Consider, for example, the distinction we make between a curved and a straight line. When the curve is exceedingly gradual, to what can we appeal to support our claim that the line is not straight? We have no standard that can guarantee precise judgments in such situations. All we have is a loose standard, based on observation aided by instruments. But this is sufficient.

> But tho' we can give no perfect definition of these lines, nor produce any very exact method of distinguishing the one from the other; yet this hinders us not from correcting the first appearance by a more accurate consideration, and by a comparison with some rule, of whose rectitude from repeated trials we have a greater assurance. And 'tis from these corrections . . . that we form the *loose idea* of a perfect standard to these figures, without being able to explain or comprehend it. (49—italics added)

A little later in the section (51) Hume criticizes pure geometry further. He offers two other examples, challenging the geometers' claims that two intersecting straight lines cannot have a common segment and that only one straight line can be drawn between any two points. Elaborating on the first example, although he agrees with the geometers when the lines intersect at, say, right angles, he disagrees when the lines intersect at very small angles. Suppose, he suggests, we have two straight lines approaching each other at the rate of an inch in every twenty leagues. These lines, when they intersect, will combine and become a single line for a considerable distance before they lose contact with each other again.

At this point Hume adds a note in his appendix. In it, after recapitulating his argument, he concludes with a statement in which he summarizes his theory of the foundations of geometry. Geometry is not, as most of its adherents maintain, a precise and unexceptionable science; rather it is coarse and inaccurate, being based on observation. "The first principles [of geometry] are founded on the imagination and senses: The conclusion, therefore, can never go beyond, much less contradict these faculties" (638).

After emphasizing that he disagrees with traditional geometers only on the question of the infinite divisibility of extension, Hume concludes Section IV by posing a dilemma for them. Consider, he says, the idea we have of the point of contact between a circle and a straight line. Granting that the two figures touch each other, they must do so either at a single point or over a considerable distance. If the geometer chooses the first alternative, he commits himself to Hume's theory of mathematical points, so must abandon his idea of infinite divisibility. If he chooses the second alternative—which, incidentally, Hume would accept if the circle were large enough—he contradicts one of his own demonstrations.

To sum up the controversy between Hume and the pure geometers, he contends that their systems, because they lead to absurdities and contradictions, must be rejected. Pure geometry is an impossible science. At the root of its difficulty, in Hume's judgment, is the geometers' assumption of the infinite divisibility of extension. But there is a more fundamental disagreement at issue here. Pure geometry, as an axiomatic, deductive system, must assume that we can reason with an exactness and precision that exceeds anything based on sense impressions. As Hume describes this view: "I know there is no mathematician, who will not refuse to be judg'd by the diagrams he describes upon paper, these being loose draughts, as he will tell us, and serving only to convey with greater facility certain ideas, which are the true foundations of all our reasoning" (53). This view Hume cannot accept because it is inconsistent with the Empiricist Principle. We can have no ideas that are not derived from impressions and, since the impressions are inexact, so, too, must the ideas that copy them be.[24]

8. The Rejection of the Idea of a Vacuum (Section V)

In Section V Hume explains and defends his views on the idea of empty space or a vacuum. The question of the existence of a vacuum had generated a long dispute among scientists and philosophers in the years just before the publication of the *Treatise*, with the Newtonians claiming that the universe is mostly empty space and the Cartesians that it is completely filled, or a plenum. Hume does not participate directly, except in a few ambivalent remarks, in this cosmological debate, confining himself to the question of whether we have an idea of a vacuum. His answer, which is negative, is hardly surprising; it follows from the Empiricist Principle. He begins the section by stating his position. "If the second part of my system be true, *that the idea of space or extension is nothing but the idea of visible or tangible points distributed in a certain order;* it follows, that we can form no idea of a vacuum, or space, where there is nothing visible or tangible" (53).

Hume begins the defense of his position by presenting three objections to it. (1) People have disputed endlessly about whether there are vacuums, but they could not do so unless they at least possessed the idea of a vacuum. (2) The ideas of rest and annihilation are both possible; we can imagine bodies remaining at rest just as we can imagine their being annihilated. What results if we combine these ideas? An illustration will help. Suppose a room with four walls, a floor, and a ceiling. From the very nature of their arrangement the walls, floor, and ceiling will surround a space. Now suppose that everything in the room, including the air it contains, is removed or annihilated. Will we not be left with empty space, or a vacuum? If we accept this line of reasoning, in which we have imagined the walls, floor, and ceiling to remain at rest and the contents of the room to be annihilated, we are imagining (having an idea of) a vacuum. (3) Motion is impossible without empty space because, if the universe were full (a plenum), there would be nowhere a moving body could go.

Hume limits himself to answering the first two objections, excusing himself from addressing the third on the grounds that it is a problem of natural philosophy, which is not within the scope of the *Treatise*. However, he does not respond to the objections immediately but instead concentrates on some related issues that will provide the basis for his answers, warning the reader at the outset about the difficulties of the argument. "In order to answer these objections, we must take the matter pretty deep" (55).

Hume launches his argument to establish that we have no idea of empty space by examining the idea of darkness. This idea cannot be identical with, or the source of, our idea of a vacuum because it is not a positive idea but merely the negation of light or visible objects. But the idea of a vacuum, if it really is to exist, must be a positive idea.[25] He next considers whether the idea might be generated from the idea of darkness mixed with visible objects. Suppose that, as we look up into an otherwise black night sky, we suddenly see two stars. Since we can perceive the distance separating the stars from each other, we may assume that we are actually perceiving empty space. But this is not correct.

> We may observe, that when two bodies present themselves, where there was formerly an entire darkness, the only change, that is discoverable, is in the appearance of these two objects, and that all the rest continues to be as before, a perfect negation of light. . . . This is not only true of what may be said to be remote from these bodies, but also of the very distance; which is interpos'd betwixt them. . . . Now since this distance causes no perception different from what a blind man receives from his eyes, or what is convey'd to us in the darkest night, it must partake of the same properties: And as blindness and darkness afford us no ideas of extension, 'tis impossible that the dark and undistinguishable distance betwixt two bodies can ever produce that idea. (57)

To sum up the argument, we can have no positive idea of empty space because we have no sense impression of it. But, Hume continues, we still "falsely imagine" (58) we have such an idea. He feels he needs to explain why we do so and offers a long and complex account of how this mistake occurs.

Hume's explanation of our error is based on two main constituents, (1) what he calls "fictitious distance" (62) and (2) the confusion of ideas, a result mainly of resemblance. He begins by giving an account of our falsely imagined or fictitious idea of distance, noting first that two visible objects separated by utter darkness (e.g., the two stars) affect the eye in the same way they would if the space separating them were filled with visible objects. Second, experience teaches us, through comparisons of the situation just described with one in which the space between the two objects is actually filled, that the empty space has the capacity to be filled, without any change in the two objects themselves. As Hume describes the change, "An invisible and intangible distance may be converted into a visible and tangible one, without any change on the distant objects."[26] Explaining the fictitious distance further, and emphasizing its importance, he writes: "This invisible and intangible distance is also found *by experience* to contain a capacity of receiving body, or of becoming visible and tangible. Here is the whole of my system" (63).

After making these preliminary points Hume is ready to explain how we mistakenly come to think we have an idea of empty space. To do so he appeals to the relation of resemblance. Because the two kinds of distance—empty, invisible distance and filled, visible distance—resemble each other so closely, we become confused and take one to be the other, believing, as a result, that we really have an idea of the first kind of distance because we have an idea of the second. He supports this analysis of our error by an appeal to psychology. "For we may establish it as a general maxim in this science of human nature, that wherever there is a close relation betwixt *two ideas,* the mind is very apt to mistake them, and in all its discourses and reasonings to use the one for the other" (60—italics added).

Hume then takes a further step, with considerable hesitancy, giving a physiological explanation of our mistaken identification of the two ideas of distance. When the mind wishes to survey an idea, he writes, it dispatches the animal spirits into the region of the brain in which the idea is stored. Unfortunately, however, the animal spirits sometimes wander from their paths and, instead of returning the desired idea, "rouze up" (60) one that is located nearby in the brain. The mind, blithely unaware of the substitution, continues to reason as though it were employing the idea it had summoned to appear. Hume concludes this explanation with the remark: "This is the cause of many mistakes and sophisms in philosophy" (61). Hume's appeal to brain physiology at this point seems to take him into natural philosophy, which he said at the outset he would avoid. Nevertheless, it has some bearing on a major problem in his philosophy. I will defer discussion of it until the next section.

Setting aside Hume's excursion into the brain, we have seen how he accounts for our error of thinking we have an idea of a vacuum; namely, that, because of the close resemblance between them, we confuse our idea of invisible distance with that of visible distance and then mistakenly conclude that we have an idea of empty space. However, this explanation, whatever its merits, does not seem to be one that Hume can put forward. He repeatedly claims that we have an idea of invisible distance and that this idea resembles our idea of visible distance. But we can have no such idea because we have no impression from which to derive it; the distance is *invisible*. Thus his claim violates the Empiricist Principle. If, putting aside this difficulty, we agreed with Hume that we have such an idea, his argument against our having an idea of a vacuum would collapse, because the unfilled, invisible distance that is the content of this idea is empty space. Hume apparently recognizes difficulties on these points, so labels the invisible distance "fictitious" distance and talks of our "falsely" imagining it. Nevertheless, he proceeds to use this falsely imagined idea as a central feature in his explanation of our belief in empty space. In doing this, however, he assumes that we can imagine, even if falsely, the invisible distance. But to imagine is to have an idea, and we can have no idea, false or otherwise, that we do not derive from an impression.

Toward the end of the section Hume responds directly to the objections to his denial of the idea of a vacuum with which he had begun, giving brief answers to the first two. To the first—that people dispute about the existence of a vacuum hence they must have the idea—he replies that they are just deceived. They think they have the idea of a vacuum but they really do not.[27] To the second, based on rest and annihilation and using the illustration of a room from which the air has been evacuated, he answers through an appeal to the notion of fictitious distance we have just examined. He ends the discussion on an ambiguous note, writing: "Thus I seem to have answer'd the three objections above-mention'd; tho' at the same time I am sensible, that few will be satisfy'd with these answers, but will immediately propose new objections and difficulties" (63).

After a short discussion in which he confesses that he cannot explain the "secret causes"[28] of the operations of bodies, Hume concludes Section V with some remarks on the subject of time. The purpose of his remarks is to explain why we think we have an idea of time in which no change occurs, an idea that he claims to be impossible. In response to the view that we must have such an idea, because we dispute about the existence of time without change, he replies with an appeal to the Empiricist Principle. "But that we really have no such idea, is certain. For whence shou'd it be deriv'd? Does it arise from an impression of sensation or of reflexion? . . . if you cannot point out *any such impression,* you may be certain you are mistaken, when you imagine you have *any such idea*" (65). He concludes by offering an explanation of why we mistakenly think we have an idea of time without any change. His account parallels his explanation of why we mistakenly think we have an idea of empty space and is subject to similar criticisms.

9. The Mind, the Brain, Animal Spirits, and Ideas (Section V)

As I noted briefly in the last section, Hume engages in an excursion into brain physiology in his attempt to explain why we mistakenly think we have an idea of empty space. His account of brain activities, however, has possible wider implications for his philosophy. I will examine these possible implications in this section.

In the passage in question in Section V, Hume is concerned with the general point of why we confuse ideas that resemble each other. His argument occupies a long paragraph; because of its possible importance I will reproduce a substantial portion of it:

> 'Twou'd have been easy to have made an imaginary dissection of the brain, and have shewn, why upon our conception of any idea, the animal spirits run into all the contiguous traces, and rouze up the other ideas, that are related to it. But tho' I have neglected any advantage, which I might have drawn from this topic in explaining the relations of ideas, I am afraid I must here have recourse to it, in order to account for the mistakes that arise from these relations. I shall therefore observe, that as *the mind is endow'd with a power of exciting any idea it pleases; whenever it dispatches the spirits into that region of the brain, in which the idea is plac'd;* these spirits always excite the idea, when they run precisely into the proper traces, and rummage that cell, which belongs to the idea. But as their motion is seldom direct, and naturally turns a little to the one side or the other; for this reason the animal spirits, falling into the contiguous traces, present other related ideas in lieu of that which the mind desir'd at first to survey. (60–61—italics added)

The crucial point of this paragraph is in the passage I have italicized. In it Hume lodges ideas in the brain. Although he does not mention impressions, it seems reasonable to assume that he would put them in the same place as well. If ideas occupy a place in a brain cell, which is a physical entity, they, too, must be physical entities. But, if our perceptions are physical entities existing in the brain, the concept of consciousness becomes redundant. Hume, thus, seems to be a materialist.

But does Hume really adopt materialism? Although his statement about ideas as physical entities in the brain supports this interpretation, there are sufficient reasons to reject it. (1) The denial of consciousness in favor of a materialistic ontology would mark a fundamental change in his philosophy, yet the paragraph in the text is introduced almost parenthetically. In addition, Hume concedes (in the paragraph preceding the one from which I have excerpted) that the explication he is about to offer may be "chimerical" (60). (2) Earlier in the paragraph itself he points out that "we must in the end rest contented with experience" (60). By experience Hume means the sum of our perceptions. From the very beginning of Book I he emphasizes that, whatever else they may be, perceptions are the content of consciousness. (3) If he were adopting a materialistic ontology, Hume would reduce the mind to the brain. But he clearly does not do so. On the contrary, he writes that the mind "dispatches the spirits into that region of the brain, in which the idea is plac'd." The mind, this statement implies, is an entity different from the brain and one that he has asserted, at the very outset of the *Treatise*, to possess consciousness. (4) From the context in which the passage appears, including the previous paragraph and the first sentence of the paragraph in question, it is apparent that Hume is concerned with the *causes* of our confused identification of ideas. The appeal to brain physiology, then, is to provide a physical, causal explanation of this confusion. Since a cause is different from its effect, the explanation he gives is consistent with the view that ideas are mental entities.

For these reasons it would be a mistake to conclude, on the basis of the passage I have reproduced, that Hume has suddenly become a materialist. But we are still left with the puzzling passage I have italicized. I offer two possible explanations of it. (1) It is just a loose use of language on Hume's part so need not be taken seriously, or (2) he is presenting a dual conception of ideas, as being (a) physical entities in the brain as well as (b) conscious entities in the mind. Further, ideas of type (a) are the causes of ideas of type (b). This interpretation leaves Hume in this passage supporting ontological dualism, rather than materialism. Whether he defends dualism elsewhere in Book I than here is, however, a question we cannot answer until we have completed our study.

If we accept interpretation (2), as out of deference to Hume we should, we are faced with a further problem. To support the theory of two kinds of ideas, physical and mental, we must have knowledge of external objects, in this case our brain. But such knowledge does not seem possible, given Hume's theory of ideas. He speaks to this point a bit later in Section V; I will discuss his comments in the next section.

10. KNOWLEDGE OF AN EXTERNAL BODY (SECTION V)

At the beginning of Part II Hume stated a correspondence theory of truth, which seems to commit him to the view that we can have knowledge of an external material world. Also, throughout the part he repeatedly refers to matter and bodies. Toward its end he inserts another discussion devoted to this important issue. He begins his remarks on a negative note. After explaining what he means by the invisible distance between bodies he goes on to write: "My intention never was to penetrate into the nature of bodies, or explain the secret causes of their operations. . . . I am afraid, that such an enterprize is beyond the reach of human understanding" (64). Nevertheless, although he disavows any possibility of our knowing the essential nature of the external world, he then adds that we can have some knowledge of that world. "But at present I content myself with knowing perfectly the manner in which objects affect my senses, and their connections with each other, *as far as experience informs me of them.* This suffices for the conduct of life; and this also suffices for my philosophy, which pretends only to explain the nature and causes of our perceptions, or impressions and ideas."[29] In this passage Hume claims to have knowledge both of the relations between objects and of the way in which they affect his senses. If this is so, he clearly seems to possess substantial knowledge of the external world. Yet the passage may not be so unequivocal as it appears. Two questions can be raised about it. (1) In the beginning of the paragraph (from which I excerpted a passage) Hume uses the term "bodies." But in the passage now under consideration, he replaces that term with the word "objects." Is it possible that this change in terminology indicates that he is no longer talking about material objects but about perceptions? From the context it seems he is not but that he is using the word "object" as the equivalent of "body." If so, his shift in terms has no theoretical significance. (2) The phrase "as far as experience informs me of them" (which I have italicized) raises problems. If experience is, as he has argued in Part I, made up of our perceptions, it would seem impossible for experience to extend beyond our perceptions to yield us knowledge of a nonperceptual object, or an external material world.

In summary, the passages I have just reviewed do not seem to offer any decisive answer to the question Does Hume think we can have any knowledge of external reality? Fortunately, he faces this question directly in the following section (VI) and, as we will see in chapter 5, answers it.

Summary

In my introductory remarks to Part II, I indicated that many commentators find this part an unfortunate anomaly that does not contribute positively to Hume's philosophy in the *Treatise.* There is sufficient truth in this judgment to raise the questions of why Hume inserted it and why he argued in it as he did. To understand Part II, we must assume that Hume was well acquainted with the developments in science and mathematics that had taken place in the years just preceding the *Treatise,* that he had become aware (largely through Bayle) of certain problems these posed and that he thought he could resolve the problems through the application of his theory of ideas to them. Thus, Part II offered him a welcome opportunity, both to solve problems that had led other leading intellectuals into contradictions and absurdities and to exhibit the power of his own philosophy. These reasons are sufficient to account for his attack on the theory of the infinite divisibility of space and time and his postulation of ultimate, indivisible mathematical points and moments, his rejection of pure geometry and his denial of an idea of empty space.

In their assessments of Part II, Hume commentators have in general been negative. Some have been harsh. The distinguished twentieth-century British philosopher C. D. Broad sums up his opinion in the following terms: "There seems to me to be nothing whatever in Hume's doctrine of Space except a great deal of ingenuity wasted in recommending and defending palpable nonsense."[30] The Hume scholar James Noxon, though less harsh, is equally definite in his appraisal: "Hume's unavailing struggles with space and time, his attempt to derive their ideas from experience conformably with his first principle that all ideas copy impressions and to elucidate geometry as the science of spatial extension yielded the least admired part of the *Treatise.*"[31]

I think we must agree with these appraisals, at least to the extent of acknowledging that Hume's arguments in Part II are neither clear nor convincing. Yet, in fairness to Hume, some qualifications need to be made. His criticisms of the theory of infinite divisibility have merit, revealing problems in the conception. The same is true of his denial of the idea of a vacuum, with its implied attack on Newtonian science. His own problems arise mainly out of his attempt to construct positive theories on the foundations of his epistemology. He thinks, for example, that he has a viable theory of space and time based on the composition of extensionless mathematical points and the succession of durationless moments, but it is obvious that he does not. Also, his rejection of pure geometry must raise the question: Have not Euclid and his long line of successors contributed anything to human knowledge? It is hard to escape the conclusion that, in this argument, Hume assumes his own epistemological position and, in doing so, begs the question against the geometers, who work from different assumptions. Finally, in his discussion of the idea of a vacuum he fails either to offer a plausible theory or to answer satisfactorily the objections he raises to his own view.

In addition to his long discussions reflecting his reactions to the science and mathematics of his day, Hume includes several statements concerning our possible knowledge of an external material world. In these he seems to be affirming that we have such knowledge. Yet at the same time he continues stoutly to adhere to the Empiricist Principle and his original theory of ideas, which seem incompatible with such a view. We can safely conclude at this point only that the issue is still open, and must wait to see what conclusion he reaches in the final section of Part II. This will be my main concern in chapter 5.

5

EXISTENCE AND EXTERNAL EXISTENCE

(Part II, Section VI)

Introduction

In the final section of Part II Hume shifts his focus sharply, from the ideas of space and time to the ideas of existence and external existence. He acknowledges that the two ideas "have their difficulties" (66) but adds that an understanding of the ideas will be helpful in the examination of knowledge and probability (topics to which he will turn in Part III). But both of these ideas are worthy of attention in their own right. The idea of existence has engendered many philosophical controversies, not the least being the question of whether "existence" is an authentic predicate, on the answer to which philosophers have continued to dispute the cogency of the ontological argument for the existence of God. For Hume's philosophy the idea of external existence is even more important because it bears directly on an issue he has raised in Parts I and II but has not resolved—the question of whether we can have any knowledge of an independent external world. If I understand him correctly he answers this question definitively in the section. But his argument, though brief, is convoluted and imprecise, even by Humean standards. As a result Hume scholars have disagreed about its conclusion, most maintaining that he concludes such knowledge to be impossible but a few disputing this interpretation.

Text

1. THE IDEA OF EXISTENCE (PARAGRAPHS 2–6)

Following an introductory paragraph Hume turns in Section VI to the question of whether we have an idea of existence (or of being). He begins by affirming that we do have such an idea, adding that we conceive every impression or idea we have to be existent. He next asks what kind of idea this is. Two possibilities suggest themselves: The idea of existence is (1) an idea derived from a distinct impression of existence that is conjoined with each of our other perceptions, or (2) it is identical with the idea derived from each perception. He rejects alternative (1) for two reasons: (a) Since every idea we have is derived from a similar impression, it follows that, if our idea of existence comes from a distinct impression of existence, that impression must be conjoined with each of our perceptions. But no two impressions are inseparably conjoined. (b) His second argument is a straightforward application of the Empiricist Principle. We can have no distinct idea of existence because we have no distinct impression of existence from which it can be derived. Hume sums up his reasons for rejecting alternative (1) in the following way: "Whoever opposes this, must necessarily point out that distinct impression, from which the idea of entity [existence] is deriv'd, and must prove, that this impression is inseparable from every perception we believe to be existent. This we may without hesitation conclude to be impossible" (67). Alternative (1) having been eliminated, we can turn to alternative (2)—that the idea of existence is not distinct from, but is identical with the idea of a perception. As Hume puts it, "The idea of existence . . . is the very same with the idea of what we conceive to be existent."[1]

Viewed in one way, Hume's position is unexceptionable. Whenever I have a perception, the perception necessarily exists. To say that I am entertaining an idea of a chimera but that my idea does not exist is to assert a contradiction. However, this is not exactly what Hume says in the statement I have just quoted. Instead he asserts that the idea of existence is the same as the idea of what we conceive to be existent. But this is not quite true. When I have an idea, say, of a chimera the content of my idea is an image of the mythological beast itself, not an image of its existence. To generate such an idea requires another, deliberate act of mind. If I make the effort I can concentrate my attention on the fact that my idea of the chimera exists. In doing so I am not having another idea, whose content is the "existence" of my idea of a chimera. On that point Hume is surely right. But this leaves a problem. To conceive of something, on Hume's theory, is to have an idea of it. Therefore, to perform the act of mind I have just described, it would seem necessary for Hume to argue that I have an idea whose content is the "existence" of the original idea. But this would leave him endorsing alternative (1), which he has already given good reason for rejecting. Hume seems to be making a legitimate point but he does not give an adequate explanation of that point in terms of his own epistemology.

Hume's argument raises another, terminological problem, centered on the word "object." The problem can be seen most clearly in a sentence that appears midway through his account and in a clause at its very end. He writes: "That idea [of existence], when conjoin'd with the idea of any *object*, makes no addition to it" and "every *object*, that is presented, must necessarily be existent" (67—italics added). The question arises over the meaning of the word "object" as it appears in these statements. Suppose I see a tree and derive from this impression an idea of a tree. We would normally say that the object of my idea is a tree. But we can mean two quite different things by such a statement. (1) The object of my idea may be the impression "tree" from which my idea is derived. That object, as we have already concluded, must exist. (2) But the object of my idea (as of my original impression) may be a physical tree standing in a meadow. That object, unlike the impression "tree," need not exist, for I may be mistaken in thinking I see a tree when I do not. To shift examples, suppose I am out walking on a hot summer day and "see" a lake on the path in front of me. Although my impression "lake" surely exists, my impression *of a lake* does not, because there is no lake to be seen. The problem with Hume's use of the word "object" is that he can be understood to mean that, when we have an impression, not only does the impression exist but so does the external object of the impression. But this claim, as my mirage example illustrates, is false.

Although Hume could have written more clearly than he did here, we can easily resolve this problem. We must understand him to be limiting himself to perceptions. When he talks about the "object" of an idea in these passages he is not referring to an external material object but to the impression of which the idea is a copy.[2]

2. THE IDEA OF EXTERNAL EXISTENCE (PARAGRAPHS 7–9)

If we conclude, as I think we must, that in the first part of Section VI Hume is concerned with our idea of existence only as it pertains to perceptions, he still has to answer the question of whether we have an idea of external existence or of an independent material world. He devotes the last three paragraphs of the section to this difficult issue.

Hume begins his discussion by saying, "A like reasoning [as that regarding existence] will account for the idea of *external existence*" (67). This statement raises problems. As we have just seen, Hume has argued that the idea of existence is (1) not a separate idea but (2) the same as the idea of what we conceive to be existent. If we attempt to transfer this reasoning to the concept of external existence, we seem to be on safe ground as far as (1) is concerned. We no more have a separate idea of external existence than we do of existence itself. But (2) is not so easy. Setting aside the difficulty I raised in the last section about this point as it concerns existence, we are faced with a further problem. To say that our idea of external existence is the same as the idea of what we conceive to be externally existent seems to imply that we have conceptions (or ideas) of external existents. But Hume has not shown how this is possible. The content of any idea we have is a perception and a perception is a mental phenomenon, not a material object in a world external to consciousness. In the next sentence (which I shall discuss in the next paragraph) Hume agrees with me in distinguishing between perceptions and external objects (67). If further confirmation were needed, it would be provided by the examples I have already used, of a chimera and a mirage. If we conceive of the external existent and it is identical to our idea of it, then we must populate the world with a whole host of dubious entities. Another possible interpretation of (2) is that it simply affirms that an idea like "chimera" is the same as the conception "chimera." But that is a tautology, which says only that an idea we have is identical to itself. It has no implications regarding the external world or our possible knowledge of it whatsoever.

But let us continue with Hume's argument. The next sentence gives important but ambiguous insights into his thought. He writes: "We may observe . . . that nothing is ever really present with the mind but its perceptions or impressions and ideas, and that external objects become known to us only by those perceptions they occasion" (67). Hume makes four points in this passage. (1) We are conscious (or aware) of perceptions only, (2) perceptions are different from external objects, (3) these objects "occasion"[3] our perceptions, and (4) the objects are known only through the perceptions they occasion. The crucial point is (4) and it is troublesome. The question it raises is obvious. If to know something one must have an idea of it and if perceptions are the only things of which we are conscious and they are different from external objects, it follows that we cannot know such objects, because we cannot be conscious of them. They are, in other words, inconceivable to us. According to this reasoning, Hume should at most have written only that external objects occasion our perceptions and not that they become known to us by these perceptions.

Perhaps Hume means what I have suggested he should mean but has stated his view in a misleading way. That this is correct seems indicated by what he writes in the next paragraph. He begins: "Now since nothing is ever present to the mind but perceptions, and since all ideas are deriv'd from something antecedently present to the mind; it follows, that 'tis impossible for us so much as to conceive or form an idea of any thing specifically different from ideas and impressions" (67). On the face of it this passage seems to confirm the conclusion I have reached. Because we can conceive only of what is present to the mind and perceptions are the only things so present, we can conceive of nothing but perceptions. Since ex-

ternal objects are different from perceptions, they must therefore be inconceivable to us. This is the conclusion most interpreters of the passage have
reached. The prominent twentieth-century critic of Hume, H. A. Prichard,
puts it this way: "[Hume] argued in Part II (on the idea of external existence) that we cannot even form the idea of *anything different from* impressions and ideas."[4]

Although Prichard is noted for the care and precision of his thought, a
close reading of the two statements reveals a discrepancy between what
Hume wrote and what Prichard attributes to him. Prichard has missed a
significant fact—that between the two paragraphs we are examining Hume
makes a shift in his language. Whereas in the first paragraph he implied
that we cannot have ideas of external objects because they are *different* from
perceptions, in the statement I have just reproduced he writes that we cannot have an idea of anything that is *specifically different* from a perception.
Why does he insert the adverb "specifically," which Prichard overlooks, into
his statement and what is its significance? In particular, are external objects specifically different from perceptions or are they not? If they are we
cannot conceive of them but if they are not perhaps we can. We must assume that Hume's insertion of the adverb was deliberate. But what does it
mean and how might it apply to external objects? This is a difficult question to answer, mainly because Hume does not define the phrase "specifically different," either here or, as far as I have been able to discover, anywhere else in Book I.[5]

We can, however, take a step toward resolving this issue by making an
inference from something Hume writes near the end of Book I. In Section VI of Part IV, in connection with his analysis of personal identity, we
find the following: "Tho' we commonly be able to distinguish pretty exactly betwixt numerical and *specific identity*, yet it sometimes happens, that
we confound them, and in our thinking and reasoning employ the one for
the other. Thus a man, who hears a noise, that is frequently interrupted
and renew'd, says, it is still the same noise; tho' 'tis evident the sounds have
only a specific identity *or resemblance*" (257–58—italics added). Assuming
that the phrase "specific identity" is equivalent to "specifically identical,"
we have in this passage Hume's explanation of what he means by the latter phrase. Anything A is specifically identical to something else B if it
resembles it. (How close the resemblance must be is not specified but
Hume's use of the word "identity" seems to indicate that it must be exact.)
In his example one's repeated perceptions of an interrupted noise are specifically identical (although not numerically identical) to each other. Ex-
trapolating from this account we can infer that anything A is specifically
different from something else B if it does not (exactly) resemble it but rather
differs from it in some other than just a numerical way. Continuing with

Hume's illustration we might reasonably conclude that the repeated sounds
we hear are specifically different from each other if, say, the first were a note
played on a flute and the second the note played on a cello. Although these
sounds resemble each other to some extent we should not say that they are
identical. Furthermore, we are able to make judgments about their resemblances and differences because we can compare our perception of one with
that of the other and recognize that these perceptions resemble yet differ
from each other.

Unfortunately, the explication I have just offered of the meaning Hume
gives to the phrase "specifically identical," and by extrapolation to the phrase
"specifically different," will not enable us to resolve our problem, because
the situation we are trying to understand differs from these examples in a
crucial way. In the "noise" examples we could reach a decision about specific identity or difference because, being able to hear the sounds, we could
compare them with each other. Generalizing, we can say that, if we are to
compare any two entities, A and B, with each other and then determine
whether they are specifically identical to or specifically different from each
other, we must be aware of both. They must, therefore, both be perceptions. As Hume says, "Nothing is ever present to the mind but perceptions"
(67). Suppose now that we wish to decide whether any entity in the external material world, say, a tree, is specifically identical to or specifically different from our perception "tree." To make the needed comparison we must
have a perception of the tree to compare with our perception "tree." But
then we would not be comparing the material object "tree" with our perception "tree" but instead would be comparing two perceptions with each
other. The external, material tree forever eludes us, so we can never reach
any conclusion whatsoever about whether it is specifically identical to or
specifically different from our perception "tree."

In a passage in Section II of Part IV Hume confirms the conclusion I
have just reached. "We suppose external objects to resemble internal perceptions. I have already shewn, that the relation of cause and effect can
never afford us any just conclusion from the existence or qualities of our
perceptions to the existence of external continu'd objects: And I shall farther add, that even tho' they cou'd afford such a conclusion, *we shou'd never have any reason to infer, that our objects resemble our perceptions.*"[6]

Hume's conclusion that we can never have any reason for thinking that
an external material object resembles a perception (is specifically identical
to it) should settle the issue, but we can carry the argument about the specifically different–specifically identical distinction a step further. If Hume
introduced this distinction to permit the possibility of our conceiving of
some external objects, which now it seems reasonably clear he did not, his
attempt necessarily failed. As we have just seen, the reason why we can-

not make any distinction between these two possible categories of objects is that objects of neither category are accessible to us because they are not perceptions. But if they are not perceptions we can conclude that they are inconceivable, hence unknowable. External objects, whether *supposed* to be specifically different from or specifically identical to perceptions, all fall outside the range of possible human cognition.[7]

Apparently unaware that his failure to explain what he meant by the phrase "specifically different" might confuse his readers, in the next sentence Hume states his conclusion about our possible knowledge of an external world in unequivocal terms. In language reminiscent of Berkeley he writes: "Let us fix our attention out of ourselves as much as possible: Let us chace our imagination to the heavens, or to the utmost limits of the universe; we never really advance a step beyond ourselves, nor can conceive any kind of existence, but those perceptions, which have appear'd in that narrow compass" (67–68). Although his language is metaphorical, Hume's conclusion could hardly be more definite. We can conceive of perceptions only and these perceptions are internal to us (or contents of our consciousness). Since a material world is, by definition, external to our consciousness and our internal perceptions are the only things of which we can be conscious, hence conceive, the conclusion follows that such a world is inconceivable, thus unknowable.

Having reached a definitive conclusion denying any possible knowledge of external existence, Hume ends Section VI by qualifying his denial. "The farthest we can go towards a conception of external objects, when suppos'd *specifically* different from our perceptions, is to form a relative idea of them, without pretending to comprehend the related objects."[8] For a second time in his argument Hume introduces a new concept, and one for which he offers no definition. What can he mean by a *relative* idea? It is impossible to answer this question with any degree of confidence. Nowhere in Book I does Hume define the concept; indeed, Section VI is the only place I have found in the text where the term "relative idea" appears. However, in a few scattered passages later in that book he makes statements that *may* bear on the question of what he might possibly have meant by a relative idea. It would be more confusing than helpful to analyze these statements in detail here. But one is sufficiently explicit to justify its being reproduced. In a paragraph in Section V of Part IV, in which he has returned to the subject of the specific differences between impressions and objects, Hume, without using the term "relative idea," nevertheless writes: "We are oblig'd either to conceive an external object *merely as a relation without a relative*, or to make it the very same with a perception or impression."[9] Noting that, in the passage from Section VI I have reproduced earlier in the paragraph, Hume says that we may be able to form a relative idea of certain external objects, "without pretending to comprehend the related objects," I think the statement I have just cited indicates what he means by a relative idea of such an external object. It is not an idea of an object; rather it is an idea of a relation in which we lack any idea of what is being related. But this explanation leaves us facing a problem. If the relative idea of an external object is an idea of "a relation without a relative," Hume seems to be affirming that we can have an idea of a relation without also having ideas of the objects the relation relates. But how is this possible? In another statement about relations in Part IV Hume says, "The very nature and essence of relation is to connect our ideas with each other" (204). But if we have no ideas of objects—as we do not, according to the explanation of a relative idea I am trying to reconstruct from Hume's account—we cannot have any relation either, because we have nothing to connect.[10]

But we need to pursue the point further. Suppose we accept the assumption under consideration that a relative idea of an object is not an idea of that object itself but just an idea of a relation between objects. Consider, for example, the fundamental relation of resemblance. Suppose we say that James resembles John. Let us assume for the moment that we can have an idea of the relation, resemblance, between two entities. Hume's account of "a relation without a relative" would be telling us that we can have such an idea even though we have no ideas of James and John themselves. But how could we possibly have an idea of the resemblance between the two people if we had no ideas of the people themselves? The supposition is simply unintelligible. Hume himself implies his agreement with this in his statement (that I reproduced in the previous paragraph) that the nature of a relation is "to connect our ideas with each other." To have a relative idea of any external object, on the only account Hume gives of what a relative idea might be, requires that we have an idea of the object (or objects) being related. But he has denied that we have any such idea. It follows, therefore, that a relative idea of an external object is an impossibility on Hume's epistemology. Such an oddity simply cannot exist.[11]

Hume never used the term "relative idea" again in Book I, which strongly suggests that he recognized its lack of intelligibility. This conclusion should be obvious. According to his epistemology, if we are to have an idea of any object, *whatever* it may be, we must have an impression of it, of which our idea is a copy. Either we have the required impression or we do not. If we have it, then it is an ordinary impression, coming to us in the ways Hume has listed in Part I. Its idea, which copies it, is also an ordinary idea. We need appeal neither to a "relative impression" nor to a "relative idea." If, on the other hand, we have no impression of the object, we can have no idea of it either. There simply is no place in Hume's epistemology for a "relative idea."[12]

Although Hume reaches a definitive conclusion about our possible knowledge of an external world, the issue is sufficiently important that it is worth noting something he says on the subject later in Book I. When he returns to the topic of the external world in Section II of Part IV, he refers back to his earlier account in Part II, Section VI, summing up the conclusion he had reached in that section in the following words: "For as to the notion of external existence, when taken for something specifically different from our perceptions, we have already shewn its absurdity."[13]

Summary

In the final section of Part II Hume discusses two related issues—our ideas of existence and of external existence. Although his discussions of both of these important topics are distressingly brief, conclusions of great philosophical importance follow from what he says and implies in the section. His claim that we have no separate idea of existence can be viewed as a precursor of Kant's criticism of the ontological argument in the *Critique of Pure Reason*. Of even greater importance for an understanding of his own philosophy is Hume's discussion of the idea of external existence. Although he attempts to qualify the conclusion he reaches by the appeal to undefined and unintelligible relative ideas, it is clear, from what he says in the section as well as later in Book I about the section, that he accepts the view that we can have no knowledge whatsoever of the external world. Material objects are simply inconceivable to us. That Hume should reach such a conclusion is understandable. Berkeley, starting from a similar set of epistemological assumptions, had already shown that, on those assumptions, the conclusion is inescapable.

Part 3

KNOWLEDGE
AND PROBABILITY

In Part III, the longest part of Book I, Hume returns to the central issues of epistemology and metaphysics, developing further the implications of his empiricist theory of ideas. Although he entitles this part "Of Knowledge and Probability," he concerns himself directly with the concept of knowledge only in the short first section. The rest of the part is devoted to what he calls probability. However, he uses this term in a way that is different and more broad than its later technical usage. The title Hume gives the part does not reveal its two most important contents: (1) His theory of causation, whose development occupies much of it, and (2) his account of belief, which is an integral element in that theory as well as vital to his general philosophy and his view of human nature.

In making probability central to the part, Hume is not concerned with the notion of statistical probability (although he devotes some attention to this topic). Instead, his interests are much wider. After having limited the range of our possible knowledge in Section I to what is intuitively or demonstratively certain, he concentrates his attention on the vast majority of our beliefs, which are about matters of fact, and so fall outside of this range. He speaks of such beliefs as constituting "probability" and maintains that, with only a few exceptions, they are based on an appeal to the relation of cause and effect. Because of its importance to our beliefs, this relation becomes the main topic of Part III. Following a tortuous path, Hume gradually develops his theory of causation, reaching a culmination in Section XIV, with his analysis of the idea of necessary connection.

Hume's theory of causation is arguably his most significant single contribution to philosophy. Certainly it is novel in its explanation of this fundamental concept. That he should challenge the standard conception of causation, which most philosophers to his time had accepted with little question, is an achievement of great historical note; that he should attempt to devise an entirely new and radical explanation of the concept attests to the power and originality of his mind.

Although it has had less influence on later thought, Hume's account of belief in Part III is of great importance to his own philosophy in the *Treatise*. Of special significance are his definition of belief, his conclusion about the rational justification of our beliefs about matters of fact, and his views concerning the amount of control we have over what we believe. The last point becomes increasingly important later in Book I, being a central feature of his argument in Part IV.

Part III is not easy to comprehend. Although Hume, once he embarks on his analysis of causation, pursues his goal relentlessly (and sometimes repetitively) to the end, it is often hard for the reader to understand just where he is heading. Part of the difficulty undoubtedly lies in the complexity of the subject as well as in Hume's need to articulate certain concepts and types of mental activity in novel and unexpected ways in order to develop his theory. But his exposition is made even more confusing because his argument for his conception of causation is far from sustained, being interrupted by major digressions in Section V (where he substantially revises his original analysis of memory) and in Sections XI through XIII (where he offers a psychological account of ordinary probability), as well as by frequent small forays into history, religion, and psychology that illustrate and illuminate some particular point he is making.

6

KNOWLEDGE
AND PROBABILITY

(Part III, Sections I–II)

Introduction

In the first two sections of Part III Hume makes an important distinction—between knowledge and what he calls probability—that will form the background for the theories he will develop in the remainder of the part. In this chapter I will limit my discussion to Section I and the first three paragraphs of Section II. My reason for stopping at that point is that Hume completes his general account of knowledge and probability there, turning for the remainder of Section II to an analysis of causation, which will be my subject in chapter 7.

Hume does not define either knowledge or probability explicitly in these sections. However, he gives some clues about the former from which it is possible to construct a fairly precise conception of what he means by it. "Probability," to which Hume devotes much more attention in the remainder of Part III than knowledge, can be a misleading term, particularly to readers after Hume's time. By "probability" Hume is not referring to the concept with which the word has come to be associated, with its technical connotations of mathematics and statistics. Rather he uses the term to denote any opinion we hold that falls short of fulfilling the conditions necessary to qualify it as knowledge. Although I will continue to use Hume's term "probability" on occasion, in what follows I will usually use the word "opinion" (or "belief"), because it conveys more accurately the epistemological concept with which Hume is concerned.

Text

1. KNOWLEDGE (SECTION I)

Hume begins his account of knowledge in Section I not with a definition of the concept but with a recapitulation of the seven kinds of philosophical relations he had distinguished and described in Section V of Part I.[1] His immediate purpose in doing this is to divide the seven into two groups: "[1] Such as depend entirely on the ideas, which we compare together, and [2] such as may be chang'd without any change in the ideas" (69). This division is important because it provides the basis for his distinction between knowledge and probability: the relations that depend entirely on the ideas we compare together alone yield knowledge; the others, which may be changed without any change in the ideas, yield only probability. In the remainder of Section I and the beginning of Section II he amplifies and explains this division.

Before we look further into Hume's distinction between knowledge and probability, we need to consider a preliminary point. The "objects" of knowledge or probability, Hume maintains, are the *relations* between ideas.[2] Although he does not say why he holds this to be true here, he does so a bit later. "All kinds of reasoning consist in nothing but a *comparison*, and a discovery of those relations . . . which two or more objects bear to each other."[3] To illustrate, when we say that someone knows something, or has an opinion about it, we are talking about his recognition not simply of the thing but of the thing in its relation to something else. We would not, for example, say that we know that a foot, because this is not a complete thought, but rather that we know that a foot is larger than an inch and smaller than a yard, and so on. These propositions all state relations between the lengths of the things in question. This point, whether it gives a full account of the nature of what we know or believe, is particularly true of our conception of causation. Here the *relation* between the object we call "cause" and the one we call "effect" is the focus of our attention.

After offering examples to illustrate the two classes of relations, Hume goes on to place each of the seven in its appropriate class, those capable of yielding knowledge being resemblance, contrariety, degrees in quality, and proportions in quantity or number. Those capable of yielding only probability or opinion are identity, relations of time and place, and causation. One point in his classification should be noted because it clarifies his account of the second class of relations, which he has described as those that "may be chang'd without any change in the ideas." Using cause and effect as an example, he describes it as a relation "of which we receive information from experience, and not from any abstract reasoning or reflexion" (69). This point is important because it explains why we cannot have knowledge about relations in the second class. When we compare ideas, as we do (to use his example) when we conclude that the three angles of a triangle equal two right angles, we are simply recognizing a relation in our mind that must hold about the idea "triangle," so we can legitimately claim knowledge about it. But when we conclude that an object is a cause of which another is the effect, we recognize that our experience might have been different and the relations, therefore, not hold. As a result we cannot have knowledge about such relations, but only opinion.

Having drawn his distinction between the two classes of relations and categorized each of the relations appropriately, Hume turns to a more detailed consideration of the various relations themselves, beginning with those about which we can attain knowledge. He begins by noting that three of these four relations "fall more properly under the province of intuition than demonstration" (70). Although Hume uses the term "intuition" to describe our recognition of these relations, it would be premature to assume that the statement itself implies that we have some new kind of apprehension, different from perception. Rather, as he indicates earlier in the same sentence—in his statement "Three of these relations are discoverable at first sight" (70)—all he is saying is that we apprehend the relations immediately, without the need for further examination or thought. But this account is not adequate, as he quickly realizes. In the next sentence, writing of our apprehension of the relation of resemblance, he adds a point of possible importance for an understanding of his philosophy. "When any objects *resemble* each other, the resemblance will at first strike the eye, *or rather the mind*" (70—last italics added).

The significant point of this statement appears in its final phrase. Why does Hume add this phrase? To answer this question it will be helpful to return to his original discussion of the idea of resemblance in Part I, Section VI. There he says that we have ideas of philosophical relations, the most basic of which is resemblance (14). But, if we are to have an idea of resemblance, which we *must* have in order to conceive of resemblance, this idea must, according to the Empiricist Principle, be a copy of an impression of resemblance. Do we have such an impression? In chapter 2 I discussed this matter at some length, arguing that we do not.[4] Hume, in the statement I have just reproduced, seems to be agreeing with me. He realizes that the resemblance between two objects is not something we sense with the eye but rather something we grasp with the mind. Three consequences can be drawn from this change in his thought. (1) It gives a second meaning to the notion of intuition that Hume had introduced in the preceding sentence. Not only does it mean "discoverable at first sight," hence requiring no further examination, but it also means not discoverable by sight (a sense impression) at all but rather by an act of mind, which is a different process. (2) In doing this it attributes a power to the mind, about which Hume had already made some remarks earlier in Book I.[5] This capacity, which Hume is attributing to the mind, is important because it may well include our recognition of other relations than resemblance and other things than relations as well. As far as relations are concerned, Hume seems to be on the right path in removing our recognition of them from the realm of perceptions and placing it in some active apprehension of which the mind is capable. The following points seem to be sound: (a) We do apprehend such relations as resemblance between things; (b) we do not apprehend these relations through our senses; (c) we must, then, apprehend them in some other way; therefore (d) Hume is reaching a reasonable conclusion when he argues that our apprehension of them is accomplished by an activity of the mind, to which he gives the term "intuition." (3) But this power of the mind to apprehend a relation directly, thus to have an idea of it, through a means different from sense perception, leaves Hume with a problem. It is inconsistent with the Empiricist Principle. Should we, therefore, conclude that, after making the Principle the foundation of his epistemology, Hume is now willing to make exceptions to it?

That we are not faced with an abandonment of Hume's basic philosophy, however, soon becomes apparent. Toward the end of Section I Hume launches an attack against mathematicians and traditional philosophers, in which he writes:

> 'Tis usual with mathematicians, to pretend, that those ideas, which are their objects, are of so refin'd and spiritual a nature, that they . . . must be comprehended by a pure and intellectual view, of which the superior faculties of the soul are alone capable. The same notion runs thro' most parts of philosophy. . . . 'Tis easy to see, why philosophers are so fond of this notion of some spiritual and refin'd perceptions; since by that means they cover many of their absurdities, and may refuse to submit to the decisions of clear ideas, by appealing to such as are obscure and uncertain. But to destroy this artifice, we need but reflect on that principle so oft insisted on, *that all our ideas are copy'd from our impressions.* (72)

It is evident from the conclusion of this statement that Hume is not willing to compromise the Empiricist Principle but holds to it as firmly as he did in Part I. So we are confronted with a problem. Hume has, as we have just seen, endowed the mind with the ability to apprehend directly and thus to have ideas of relations, through what he calls "intuition," even though we have no impressions of the relations. By parity of reasoning we must therefore conclude that such an apprehension is the result of "some spiritual and refin'd perceptions" employed to cover "absurdities." In attacking the mathematicians and philosophers Hume seems also to be attacking himself. This inconsistency in the foundations of Hume's epistemology is troublesome for a commentator. Although it may be dismissed as a minor lapse on Hume's part, it at least raises doubts about whether his empiricist theory of ideas will prove successful in providing a viable basis for his philosophy.[6]

Continuing his account of the four relations that can yield knowledge, Hume notes that, although the mind can directly intuit three of them, situations arise with the fourth (proportions of quantity or number) in which the exact difference between one figure or number and another can be discovered, if at all, only after repeated examination. To illustrate this point he turns to geometry and repeats a conclusion he had reached in Part II: That geometrical "demonstrations" are approximate only, and never exact. "I have already observ'd, that geometry, or the *art*, by which we fix the proportions of figures . . . never attains a perfect precision and exactness" (70–71). As a result we cannot include geometry among the disciplines capable of yielding knowledge. He continues his discussion of geometry at considerable length, repeating some of the arguments he had already employed earlier.[7]

Having explained that knowledge can be attained only about relations in which our conclusions are based solely on the comparison of ideas, Hume has at least two important questions left to answer: (1) In what disciplines can we attain knowledge? and (2) What is knowledge? Following his rejection of the knowledge pretensions of geometry, he immediately offers an answer to the first of these questions and, in the process of doing so, gives us some strong clues to his answer to the second. He writes: "There remain, therefore, algebra and arithmetic as the only sciences, in which we can carry on a chain of reasoning, to any degree of intricacy, and yet preserve a perfect exactness and certainty. We are possest of a precise standard, by which we can judge of the equality and proportion of numbers; and according as they correspond or not to that standard, we determine their relations, *without any possibility of error.*"[8] Algebra and arithmetic, thus, are for Hume the only disciplines capable of yielding knowledge. They can do so because we can carry on reasoning in them with "perfect exactness" and "certainty" and "without any possibility of error." Although the first two of these characteristics of knowledge are somewhat vague, the third is precise. In describing knowledge in terms of conclusions we reach "without any possibility of error," Hume seems to be accepting a historically important conception of knowledge; namely, that we can legitimately claim to know something if and only if we can demonstrate that our belief is true.[9]

Hume's criteria obviously circumscribe the realm of possible knowledge quite severely. Only algebra and arithmetic pass the test. So we have to concede that none of our everyday, commonsense beliefs or even the conclusions of the empirical sciences constitute things we can legitimately claim to know. Many philosophers would argue that Hume has made his knowledge-criteria far too restrictive, claiming instead that we can know much more than he allows us. This is clearly a disagreement in epistemology of a fundamental nature and one that we cannot pursue further here. Nevertheless, we should recognize two points. (1) Whether or not one agrees to draw the line between knowledge and opinion at the point Hume does, still he has made a legitimate and important distinction, between beliefs we have whose truth we can demonstrate and those whose truth we cannot demonstrate. (2) Because most of our beliefs, according to Hume, fall into the second category, their epistemological status becomes a matter of great importance. Since we cannot demonstrate their truth, we are led to ask: What kind of reasons can we give in their support? Or can we give any reasons to justify these beliefs at all? As we will soon discover, Hume devotes a good portion of Part III to answering these questions.

One final remark should be made about our arithmetical and algebraic knowledge. According to Hume, we can determine the relations of numbers without any possibility of error because we have a precise standard of the equality and proportion of numbers. To have such a standard means to have the capacity to recognize it, which requires that we possess ideas of the relations of equality and proportion of numbers. But, as in the case of the relation of resemblance, it can be questioned whether we can gain such ideas through having previously had their correspondent impressions. Who has ever seen "equality" or "proportions" of numbers? Once again, Hume must be appealing to some special power of the mind, like intuition, to apprehend these relations. So we have further reason to conclude that he recognizes that the mind has reasoning capacities, capable in the disciplines of algebra and arithmetic to lead it to conclusions we can legitimately claim as things we know. Unfortunately, his acknowledgment of these capacities seems to put him into conflict with the Empiricist Principle, which he has reiterated with special emphasis in Section I.

2. PROBABILITY (SECTION II, PARAGRAPHS 1–3)

Having circumscribed the area of possible knowledge in Section I, Hume turns to the realm of probability or opinion in Section II.[10] Here the three pertinent relations are identity, situations in time and place, and causation. Hume devotes the first three paragraphs of the section to a discussion of them, before commencing his long, complex, and revolutionary account of the one that is by far the most important—causation.

Hume's main aim in his brief discussion of these three relations seems to be to distinguish the last from the first two. To prepare the ground for making this distinction he writes: "All kinds of reasoning consist in nothing but a *comparison*, and a discovery of those relations, either constant or inconstant, which two or more objects bear to each other. This comparison we may make, either when both the objects are present to the senses, or when neither of them is present, or when only one" (73). When both of two objects we wish to compare, along with the relation between them, are present to the senses, Hume goes on to say, we directly perceive them and their relation, without any need for thought. In his words, "We call *this* perception rather than reasoning" (73). He then adds that such perception involves "a mere passive admission of the impressions thro' the organs of sensation" (73). He notes that this is the case with the two relations of identity and situations in time and place. With the exception of situations in time, it seems generally to be true of both relations. If I observe two billiard balls and declare them identical, both are present to my senses. If I say that one of them is to the left of the other, again they are both directly before me. However, with relations of time it would seem that one object of the relation must always be absent from the senses, for we cannot observe either the past or the future.

Hume is aware of the special case of temporal relations. Later in the same paragraph he points out that we call an object we are now observing and an object we observed earlier identical, even though we do not observe the two simultaneously. "We readily suppose an object may continue individually the same, tho' several times absent from and present to the senses; and ascribe to it an identity, notwithstanding the interruption of the perception, whenever we conclude, that if we had kept our eye or hand constantly upon it, it wou'd have convey'd an invariable and uninterrupted perception" (74). To account for our recognition of such relations Hume appeals to the third, or causation. Speaking directly to the relation of identity, he writes: "But this conclusion beyond the impressions of our senses can be founded only on the connexion of *cause and effect;* nor can we otherwise have any security, that the object is not chang'd upon us, however much the new object may resemble that which was formerly present to the senses" (74). In the next paragraph he generalizes, turning to the relation of causation to explain how we can perceive the other two relations that arise out of experience, when the objects related are not both present to the senses. "Here then it appears, that of those three relations, which depend not upon the mere ideas, the only one, that can be trac'd beyond our senses, and informs us of existences and objects, which we do not see or feel, is *causation*" (74).

Important conclusions can be drawn from Hume's brief discussion of the three relations in Section II. If, as he concluded in Section I, we can know nothing beyond algebra and arithmetic, almost everything we believe falls under probability. If, further, probability consists in the apprehension of one or more of these three relations and if the first two cannot yield probability beyond relations of objects immediately present to the senses, we are left with the vast bulk of what we believe based on our apprehension of the relation of causation. Thus Hume has set the stage for his examination of this fundamental relation, a task that will occupy him, either directly or indirectly, through much of the remainder of Part III.

Summary

Hume's main object in Section I and the first three paragraphs of Section II is twofold: To distinguish between knowledge and opinion (or probability) and to prepare the way for his new theory of causation. Making philosophical relations the objects of both knowledge and probability, he limits the former to the first four relations, the final three yielding only opinion. As a result he concludes that the only disciplines in which we can gain knowledge are algebra and arithmetic; for the rest of our beliefs we must be content with opinion. Finally, our opinions about anything not immediately present to the senses rest on an appeal to the relation of causation.

Hume's discussion in these sections reveals certain developing trends in his thought but it also gives rise to a problem in his philosophy. This results from his attribution of a special capacity to the mind, to intuit relations. Although he had spoken before of the power of the mind, in both Parts I and II, his account in Section I of Part III develops his conception of this kind of mental activity further. But this attribution creates a difficulty. The capacity of the mind to intuit relations, because it is incompatible with the Empiricist Principle, falls outside of the framework of his theory of ideas. So we must ask ourselves: Does Hume really still hold to his empiricist epistemology or is he in the process of abandoning it? If we accept the second alternative, we face at least two difficulties: (1) In Part I he described that epistemology as constituting "the elements" of his philosophy, therefore to abandon it would be to alter radically the basic foundations of his thought. (2) At the end of Section I of Part III he reiterates the Empiricist Principle, with emphasis. The developments in Hume's thought at the beginning of Part III, as a result, leave the commentator in a quandary. At this point in Book I Hume seems to be holding inconsistent positions on a point of fundamental importance to his philosophy. Can the inconsistency be eliminated? As I proceed with my analysis of Book I, I will keep this problem in mind.

7

THE RELATIONS OF
CAUSATION

(Part III, Sections II–IV)

Introduction

Hume begins his long and complex account of causation in the fourth paragraph of Section II. The first phase of his analysis occupies the remainder of that section, plus Sections III and IV, after which he breaks his argument briefly to discuss two other central issues of his philosophy, returning to causation in Section VI. In this chapter I will concern myself with his initial analysis, in which he explains that causation is a complex relation, composed of three other relations, all of which are essential to it. He says that the first two of these relations—contiguity and succession—are easily explicable but that the third—necessary connection—raises difficulties because we seem to possess no impression of any necessary connection between objects or events, therefore have no source from which we can derive an idea of it. So he views his main task to be the discovery of the required impression from which this idea can be derived, recognizing that at this stage of his inquiry he does not yet know where to look. So, abandoning any set methodology, he confesses: "We must . . . proceed like those, who being in search of any thing, that lies conceal'd from them, and not finding it in the place they expected, beat about all the neighbouring fields, without any certain view or design, in hopes their good fortune will at last guide them to what they search for" (77–78). Although Hume's search for the source of the idea of necessary connection eventually ends in success, it forces him to traverse many fields, some hardly neighboring, before he finally reaches his goal in Section XIV of Part III.

Text

1. The Relations of the Idea of Causation (Section II, Paragraphs 4–15)

Hume begins his inquiry by seeking the origin of our idea of causation. He does not ask whether we have such an idea but assumes, rightly, that we do. Since, according to the Empiricist Principle, all our ideas are copies of prior impressions, to discover the origin of the idea of causation we must find the impression from which it is derived. "'Tis impossible to reason justly, without understanding perfectly the idea concerning which we reason; and 'tis impossible perfectly to understand any idea, without tracing it up to its origin, and examining that primary impression, from which it arises" (74–75). To launch our search for this impression, Hume suggests, let us examine two objects we call cause and effect to see what we can find. Consider two billiard balls, one the cue ball and the other the object ball. The cue ball strikes the object ball, setting it in motion. We say that the moving cue ball, when it strikes the object ball, is a cause and the subsequent movement of the object ball an effect.[1]

Any search for the idea of causation in the billiard balls themselves proves hopeless. We might, Hume suggests, hope to find the source of our idea in some quality we perceive in the cause that produces the effect. He quickly destroys this hope, however, by pointing out that, no matter what quality we select as the causally productive one, we find that objects not possessing this quality also operate as causes. To return to our example, suppose we say that the quality of motion possessed by the cue ball is what makes it a cause; we soon realize that other objects, not possessing this quality—e.g., a hot ember that ignites a fire—are causes as well. So Hume generalizes, to conclude that "there is nothing existent, either externally or internally, which is not to be consider'd either as a cause or an effect; tho' 'tis plain there is no one quality, which universally belongs to all beings" (75). So we must look elsewhere than among the qualities of objects for the source of our idea of causation.

Having eliminated the qualities of objects as the source of the idea of causation, Hume concludes that the only alternative is to locate it in the relations among objects. "The idea . . . of causation must be deriv'd from some *relation* among objects" (75). In the remainder of Section II Hume argues that three such relations are required to account for the idea. The first is *contiguity*. The billiard balls offer a good example of this relation. If the two balls had not come into contact with each other we should hesitate to claim that the motion of the object ball was caused by that of the cue ball. This conclusion raises the question of the possibility of action at a distance, an issue that was debated well before Hume's time. In support of that possibility, one might argue that it is exemplified by the causal influence of the moon on the tides. Hume's claim that causes must be contiguous to their effects requires him to reject action at a distance; to answer possible counterexamples he argues that there must be a chain of causes and effects linking the two distant objects together. "Tho' distant objects may sometimes seem productive of each other, they are commonly found upon examination to be link'd by a chain of causes, which are contiguous among themselves, and to the distant objects; and when in any particular instance we cannot discover this connexion, we still presume it to exist."[2]

The second relation necessary to causation is that of the *temporal priority* of a cause to its effect or, as Hume later terms it, the *succession* of cause and effect. The motion of the cue ball comes first and that of the object ball succeeds or follows after it. Hume notes that some would dispute the necessity of this temporal relation of succession between cause and effect, maintaining instead that sometimes the two can be "co-temporary" (76). In response, he offers two rebuttals. (1) He appeals to experience. Almost always we observe the cause first, then the effect. (2) To be a cause is to act; that is, to produce an effect. We do not say of any event that it is the cause of another until the effect occurs as well. Now if the cause and effect were contemporary in any instance they always would be. They would always occur simultaneously. But, if this were true, *all* events (since they are linked together as causes and effects) would do the same and the history of the world would collapse into an instant. "The consequence of this wou'd be no less than the destruction of that succession of causes, which we observe in the world; and indeed, the utter annihilation of time."[3]

So we find two relations—contiguity and succession—to be essential components of the relation of causation. Granting them to be necessary conditions of causation Hume next raises the question of whether they are sufficient conditions as well. His answer to this question is negative. "An object may be contiguous and prior to another, without being consider'd as its cause" (77). He gives no examples to support this conclusion but they can easily be supplied. Consider the following: At a fire station near where I once lived whenever the alarm bell sounded the large vehicle doors adjacent to it would immediately open. I always assumed that the ringing of the bell was the cause that produced the opening of the doors as its effect. Both of Hume's conditions—contiguity and succession—were in evidence. I later learned that the situation was different from what I had assumed. What actually occurred was that, because it was his assigned duty, a fireman immediately pushed a switch to open the doors whenever the bell sounded. When I discovered this I no longer believed that the bell caused the doors to open, because I realized that the two events were not connected with each other. The ringing of the bell, without the subsequent activity of the fireman, would not be followed by any movement of the doors.

Hume agrees with the conclusion I have drawn from my illustration. "There is a NECESSARY CONNECTION to be taken into consideration; and that relation is of much greater importance, than any of the other two above-mention'd" (77). Hume's statement gives rise to two questions: (1) What does he mean by the concept of a necessary connection, which is of such importance to the cause-effect relation? and (2) Why must there be a necessary connection between a cause and its effect? Hume answers the second question in Section III (which I will discuss in my next section) but he delays his answer to the first, which constitutes the core of his theory of causation, until Section XIV. I will devote chapter 12 to that theory.

But Hume does begin in Section II to address the issue of the nature of the necessary connection between cause and effect, by raising the question of how we can apprehend the relation itself. Assuming that we have ideas of the two other necessary but less important relations of causation—contiguity and succession—in order to have an idea of the relation of necessary connection we must trace it to its source in some impression. "Here again I turn the object on all sides, in order to discover the nature of this necessary connexion, and find the impression, or impressions, from which its idea may be deriv'd" (77). But Hume is frustrated in his search. He can find no impression of a necessary connection either in the "*known qualities* of objects" or in their "*relations*" (77). This failure is critical because, according to the Empiricist Principle, to have any idea we must have an impression of which it is a copy; therefore, failing such an impression, we can have no idea of necessary connection and, as a consequence, no idea of causation. Hume is acutely aware of this difficulty, summing up his failure in the following statement: "Shall the despair of success make me assert, that I am here possest of an idea, which is not preceded by any similar impression? This wou'd be too strong a proof of levity and inconstancy; since the contrary principle has been already so firmly establish'd, as to admit of no farther doubt; at least, till we have more fully examin'd the present difficulty."[4]

Confronted with a problem for which there is no apparent solution Hume makes a tactical move. Instead of continuing to pursue his objective directly, he shifts his attention to other issues in the hope that their resolution will lead him to the goal he seeks. "'Tis necessary for us to leave the direct survey of this question concerning the nature of that *necessary connexion*, which enters into our idea of cause and effect; and endeavour to find some other questions, the examination of which will perhaps afford a hint, that may serve to clear up the present difficulty" (78). Hume finds two questions whose answers he believes will help lead him to the source of our idea of necessary connection: "First, For what reason we pronounce it *necessary*, that every thing whose existence has a beginning, shou'd also have a cause? Secondly, Why we conclude, that such particular causes must *necessarily* have such particular effects; and what is the nature of that *inference* we draw from the one to the other, and of the *belief* we repose in it?" (78). He turns immediately, in Section III, to an attempt to answer the first of these questions.

2. Why Is a Cause Always Necessary? (Section III)

Hume begins Section III with the assertion that "'Tis a general maxim in philosophy, that *whatever begins to exist, must have a cause of existence*" (78), adding that it is one of those maxims that, it is supposed, "tho' they may be deny'd with the lips, 'tis impossible for men in their hearts really to doubt of" (79). From the tone of these remarks it is apparent that Hume is dubious about this "maxim." In fact he immediately goes on to express his doubts and his reasons for them. To understand his arguments we must return to his account of knowledge in Section I, in which he concluded that knowledge results from the comparison of ideas and can be gained only through intuition and demonstration. But the causal maxim does not satisfy these conditions.

Against the claim that the causal maxim is intuitively certain, Hume argues that any relation, to be intuitively certain, must be one that is unalterable, as long as the related ideas remain the same, and this condition is not fulfilled by the causal maxim. Although he offers no reasons for his view, his conclusion not only seems correct but can, as he points out, be derived from his argument against the view that the maxim is demonstrably certain. A conclusion is demonstrable only if its denial involves a contradiction. But the proposition "Event X occurred but it had no cause" involves no contradiction. For example, I could say, with perfect consistency, "The fire station doors opened but nobody pushed the switch" or, even more flatly, "The fire station doors opened but nothing caused them to do so." My claim might be met with scepticism but it would not involve me in any contradiction. As Hume concludes: "The separation . . . of the idea of a cause from that of a beginning of existence, is plainly possible for the imagination; and consequently the actual separation of these objects is so far possible, that it implies no contradiction nor absurdity; and is therefore incapable of being refuted by any reasoning from mere ideas; without which 'tis impossible to demonstrate the necessity of a cause" (79–80).

Not content with having established through argument that it is impossible to gain certainty about the causal relation through intuition or demonstration, Hume turns in the remainder of Section III to refuting attempts made by earlier philosophers to do just that. In his words, "Every demonstration, which has been produc'd for the necessity of a cause, is fallacious and sophistical" (80). Looking at these pages (80–82) through the "wisdom" of historical hindsight, we can understand why Hume took the trouble to demolish arguments that to our eyes would hardly seem worth refutation. He was, in the early eighteenth century, setting out to destroy an assumption of science and philosophy considered to be axiomatic by many leading thinkers of his time, people such as Hobbes, Clarke, and Locke. He reviews three different arguments given by these writers and one by unidentified proponents (whom he treats with mischievous irony) in support of the causal maxim and points out, appropriately, that they all beg the question. It is not necessary to add anything to Hume's arguments here; in any case, nothing I could contribute would have the lucidity or persuasive force of his own remarks.

Having rejected intuition and demonstration as acceptable bases for our belief in causal necessity, Hume concludes Section III with the claim that this opinion must rest on observation and experience. "Since it is not from knowledge or any scientific reasoning, that we derive the opinion of the necessity of a cause to every new production, that opinion must necessarily arise from observation and experience" (82).

Here it would be worthwhile to assess Hume's general argument regarding the idea of causation. It marks a significant turning point in philosophical thought about this central concept of both science and ordinary life. Setting aside the weak arguments of the people whom Hume criticizes in Section III, it is fair to say that most previous writers in the modern tradition had assumed (usually without question) that there was a necessary connection between a cause and its effect and that we could (somehow) demonstrate this to be true. The genius of Hume lay in his recognition that this connection was not only nondemonstrable but was, on the contrary, an assumption for which no satisfactory justification had been given. Thus, by his argument Hume called into question an entire way of thinking about causation.

Having presented, but not yet elaborated, his own view of the source of our belief in causation, Hume realizes that the next task he should undertake is to explain how this belief arises. Rather than addressing the point directly, however, he notes that it will prove more convenient to consider the specific question: "*Why* [do] *we conclude, that such particular causes must necessarily have such particular effects, and why* [do] *we form an inference from one to another?*" (82). He ends the section by saying that he will make this last question the subject of his inquiry and suggests that his answer to it will prove to answer the question of how our belief in causation arises.

3. Impressions and Causal Reasoning (Section IV)

In Section IV Hume enlarges on the conclusion he had reached at the end of the previous section about the need to appeal to observation in our reasonings about causation. As he sums up his point, "All reasonings concerning causes and effects are originally deriv'd from some impression" (84). The central paragraph of the section consists of an example to support this conclusion. Suppose one reads in a book that Caesar was killed in the senate house on the Ides of March. Here a causal connection is being asserted between the action of a number of senators, like Brutus, and the death of Caesar. What kind of reasoning would one use to justify himself in believing this story? He would appeal, says Hume, to the authority of the historian who wrote the book, who would appeal to a previous historian, who in turn would appeal to a still earlier historian, and so on in a chain going back to that spring day in ancient Rome and to some contemporary of the actors involved who actually observed the fatal sword thrusts in the senate house. In this account, at each step of the way back into the remote past one builds one's reasoning on an appeal to a cause-effect relation. If, however, the long causal chain had no anchorage in someone's actual experience, it would, Hume concludes, be "chimerical and without foundation" (83).

4. An Impression of Memory? (Section IV)

I will conclude this chapter with a digression, which is occasioned by two remarks Hume makes in Section IV, in connection with his claim that all causal reasoning rests on experience. Although these remarks do not directly affect that claim they are important in their own right because they concern a concept central to Hume's philosophy in Book I; namely, memory. In the first paragraph of the section he writes (and I excerpt from the full passage):

> Tho' the mind in its reasonings from causes or effects carries its view beyond those objects, which it sees or remembers, it must never lose sight of them entirely, nor reason merely upon its own ideas, without some mixture of impressions, or at least of *ideas of the memory, which are equivalent to impressions.* . . . 'Tis impossible for us to carry on our inferences *in infinitum;* and the only thing, that can stop them, is *an impression of the memory or senses.* (82–83—italics added)

The point with which I will be concerned in this section is evident from the passages I have italicized in the quotation, in which Hume makes two similar, yet different, statements about the nature of memory, referring first to "ideas of the memory, which are equivalent to impressions" and then speaking of "an impression of the memory or senses." The importance of these passages rests on the importance of the concept of memory itself, which assumes an increasingly vital role in Hume's thought with the progress of his argument in Part III. Because memory is so central to Hume's philosophy it is important that we be clear about his conception of it.

What then is the problem? It is simply that, in two steps in this paragraph, Hume seems to be recategorizing memory, transferring it from the realm of ideas to that of impressions. In the first reference it is still an idea but is said to be "equivalent" to an impression and in the second reference it is directly labeled an impression.[5] If we conclude that Hume is indeed making a change in his categorization of memory, we must recognize the possibility that some of his subsequent arguments and conclusions may require an interpretation different from the one the reader would ordinarily give them.

In spite of the language he uses here, conclusive reasons can be given against the view that Hume is reclassifying memory, making it an impression rather than an idea. (1) In his statement of the elements of his philosophy in Part I, Hume is unequivocal about the status of memory. He entitles Section III of that part "Of the ideas of the memory and imagination." Throughout that section he repeatedly refers to the *ideas* of the memory. One passage, in particular, bears repeating. "Neither the ideas of the memory nor imagination . . . can make their appearance in the mind, unless their correspondent impressions have gone before to prepare the way for them" (9). (2) At the beginning of Part I, Hume tells us that impressions are of two kinds. First are sensations. Memory cannot be one of those because they are limited to our five senses. Second is a list including "heat or cold, thirst or hunger, pleasure or pain of some kind or other" (8). If Hume thought memory to be one of these he surely would have included it on his list. (3) Hume has a special reason in Section IV of Part III for overemphasizing the similarity between memory and impressions. He is concerned to distinguish causal reasoning from reasoning consisting only in the comparison of ideas. Since such reasoning often must appeal to memory (as in the Caesar example) and ultimately to sense observation, it is natural for Hume to concentrate on the similarity between the two. That this is his motivation is clearly suggested by the language he uses in the first sentence of the passage I have reproduced. (4) It must be acknowledged, however, that, from the beginning, there has been some ambiguity in Hume's characterization of memory. In his first introduction of the idea into his epistemology he writes:

> We find by experience, that when any impression has been present with the mind, it again makes its appearance there as an idea; and this it may do af-

ter two different ways: either when in its new appearance it retains a considerable degree of its first vivacity, and is somewhat intermediate betwixt an impression and an idea; or when it intirely loses that vivacity, and is a perfect idea. The faculty, by which we repeat our impressions in the first manner, is called the MEMORY. (8)

Although he labels memory perceptions "ideas" in this passage, he makes a special point of their vivacity (in contrast to imagination ideas), emphasizing this vivacity by describing them as being "somewhat intermediate betwixt an impression and an idea." Similar considerations may have influenced his language in Section IV, as well as elsewhere in Book I. (5) Nevertheless, it might be thought that Hume is changing his original view of memory in Section IV, reclassifying it as an impression. This assumption can easily be answered. In the next section of Part III, Hume returns to the subject of memory, revising his original theory from Part I. After repeating his identification of memory perceptions with impressions (84), he shifts over and throughout the remainder of his discussion refers to them as ideas. His statement, for example, that "both [memory and imagination] borrow their simple ideas from the impressions" (85) is unequivocal.

Since a reclassification of memory perceptions as impressions would not only require substantial change in his original theory of ideas but also could alter our understanding of his later philosophy and since it is clear that Hume did not contemplate such a revision of his views, the reasonable conclusion to draw is that, for Hume, memory perceptions remain ideas. Once again the commentator's task would have been easier if Hume had been more careful in the way he expressed his thoughts.

Summary

In the first phase of his analysis of the concept of causation Hume is concerned to make two foundational points: (1) To impress on his readers that the origin of our idea of causation cannot be found in the mere comparison of ideas but must have its basis in observation or experience. As a result our beliefs about the cause-effect relation cannot constitute knowledge but only opinion. (2) Since causation is not a quality of objects it must lie in relations between them. It is, he concludes, composed of three relations—contiguity, succession, and necessary connection. Assuming that we can have impressions from which we can derive our ideas of the first two relations,[6] we still have to account for our idea of necessary connection, which is by far the most important of the three, and yet cannot be traced to any sense impression. Hume does not resolve this issue in these sections but contents himself with setting the stage for its eventual resolution.

8

HUME'S REVISED
THEORY OF MEMORY

(Part III, Section V)

Introduction

Section V is a brief but important digression from the argument of Part III. In it Hume returns to two topics—the causes of our impressions and memory—which he had already discussed early in the *Treatise*, to elaborate his views further. His account of the first of these provides a welcome addition to his distressingly brief original statement; nevertheless, one wonders why he waited so long to provide it. Turning to memory, we find him revising his original theory, first stated in Section III of Part I, in a major way.

Although the issues to which it is devoted are of the utmost importance not only for Hume's argument in Book I but for epistemology and metaphysics in general, Section V is extraordinarily short, occupying only two pages of text. Probably because of its brevity, some Hume commentators seem not to have appreciated its significance and as a result have, I believe, failed to realize that in it Hume reexamines his original conception of memory and comes to the conclusion that that conception could not be supported by his empiricist theory of ideas so had to be substantially revised. The revised conception of memory Hume presents in Section V is philosophically important, so deserves our most careful attention.

Text

1. THE CAUSE OF OUR SENSE IMPRESSIONS (PARAGRAPH 2)

Hume begins Section V with some general remarks about the nature of causal reasoning, pointing out that the materials we employ in it are "of a mix'd and heterogeneous nature" (84). In particular, we make use of both impressions and ideas. As a result, he concludes, we have three things to explain: "*First,* The original impression. *Secondly,* The transition to the idea of the connected cause or effect. *Thirdly,* The nature and qualities of that idea" (84).

In the second paragraph Hume turns to the first of the three things that need explanation; namely, our sense impressions.[1] His object is to give an account of the causes of these impressions. He had addressed this point before in Book I, in at least three places. At the beginning of the *Treatise* he wrote cryptically: "[Impressions of sensation arise] in the soul originally, from unknown causes" (7). In Part II, however, he made two statements seemingly contrary to this.[2] In Section V he devotes a paragraph to the issue, suggesting three possible causes of our sense impressions. "As to those *impressions,* which arise from the *senses,* their ultimate cause is, in my opinion, perfectly inexplicable by human reason, and 'twill always be impossible to decide with certainty, whether they arise immediately from the object, or are produc'd by the creative power of the mind, or are deriv'd from the author of our being" (84). The first possible cause of our sense impressions Hume suggests is the commonsense view; we all assume that these perceptions are caused by objects in an independent external world. Hume, on occasion, seems to adopt this view. Later in the paragraph we are examining he writes: "We may draw inferences from the coherence of our perceptions . . . whether they represent nature justly, or be mere illusions of the senses" (84). Although he does not say that our perceptions are caused by nature but only that, when veridical, they represent nature, one might infer that the correspondence is a result of a causal connection between the two. Nevertheless, adoption of this view would create difficulties for Hume. As we found in chapter 5, Hume concluded in Part II, Section VI, that an independent, external world is inconceivable to us. If that be true, it is hard to conceive how he could then maintain that such a world causes our sense impressions.

The second cause of our impressions Hume suggests—that they are produced by the mind—certainly represents a possibility, but it is one that few philosophers in the Western tradition have adopted. Although Hume never pursues this possibility further in Book I, one can offer some speculation about it, in relation to his philosophy. Two points seem pertinent. (1) At this stage of his argument in Book I, Hume has cut the knower off from anything external to himself, because the only things of which he can be aware are perceptions and these exist within his own consciousness. If, therefore, these perceptions are to have knowable causes, their causes cannot be something outside of consciousness itself. The mind, it might be suggested, is an entity that does not suffer from such a disability. (2) The notion of the creative power of the mind extends further an element of some importance in Hume's thought, as we discovered in his account of "intu-

ition" in Section I of Part III.[3] If the mind has the power to intuit relations the senses cannot apprehend, perhaps it also has the power to create
the impressions that fill its consciousness. I do not know how Hume might
respond to this suggestion, since he never discusses it, but it would seem
congenial to certain things he has said, at least to this point.

The third possible cause of our impressions—God—although not one
widely held among philosophers, did have at least two vigorous defenders
in Hume's time, both of whose writings were well known to him—Berkeley and Malebranche. It is a view, however, that Hume would, we can assume, hardly find congenial.

One more comment might be made about these three accounts of the
possible causes of our impressions. Although Hume seems to prefer none
in the passage we have been examining, I have already suggested that he
might lean toward the first. Before leaving this point I would like to refer
to another statement he makes on the subject later in the *Treatise,* in a
passage that does not appear in Book I but in the first paragraph of Book
II. He writes: "Original impressions or impressions of sensation are such
as without any antecedent perception arise in the soul, from the constitution of the body, from the animal spirits, or from the application of objects to the external organs" (275). In this passage Hume gives two different causes of our impressions, both being external to our consciousness and
physical in nature. The second (in his final phrase) seems to be a form of
the first alternative presented in Section V. If, for example, a hot iron is
pressed to my skin, I feel pain. The first offers an explanation of our impressions different from independent, external objects. When I have an
impression of pain the cause of that impression is some activity in my own
body. Although this is a physical cause, it is not an external object, in the
same sense the iron is. My body could cause me to have the impression of
pain even though I was not being tortured by a hot iron. Nevertheless,
although they are different, both of these explanations refer to physical
causes of my impressions.[4]

Although Hume makes statements in Book II that appear to support
the view that he holds physical objects (including our bodies) to be the
causes of our impressions, a further question (besides that of the conceivability of such entities) arises. Is this a view he really wishes to defend? This
question leads us back to the opening remarks he makes in the passage from
Section V we are now considering. There are two of these; I will consider
them in reverse order. He writes, "'Twill always be impossible to decide
with certainty," and then proceeds to list the three possible causes. As we
have seen in chapter 6, Hume makes certainty a condition of knowledge
so we can conclude that he does not think we can ever *know* what causes

our perceptions. However, it may still be true that, although we cannot know what these causes are, we might have some reason to accept one explanation in preference to the others. That Hume would not agree with this is evident from the first of his opening remarks: "As to those *impressions*, which arise from the *senses*, their ultimate cause is, in my opinion, *perfectly inexplicable* by human reason." (84—last italics added). This is a decidedly more negative statement than the second. From it we can conclude that Hume holds that we can never offer any rational justification whatsoever for our opinions about the causes of our impressions. But why should we accept the statement? Why should Hume make it?

A partial answer can be given to my questions. If we are to say of any entity, A, that it is the cause of another entity, B, A must be an entity we can have an idea of or apprehend. If A is something of which we can have no awareness whatsoever, we can say nothing about it, so obviously cannot attribute causal power to it. As we concluded at the end of chapter 5, the only things of which Hume can be aware are perceptions. This limitation immediately rules out any appeal to external material objects or to God as the cause of our impressions. The question of whether it rules out the remaining alternative, our minds, is more difficult to answer. We can say tentatively that perceptions, as contents of consciousness, are different from the minds that entertain them, hence can conclude that minds are beyond possible human apprehension so cannot be designated as causes. But Hume has not yet discussed the relationship between minds and perceptions enough in Book I for us to draw any firm conclusions about his views on this point. It is one we will have to examine further later in our study.[5]

Nonetheless, let us suppose, for the moment, that Hume denies that minds cause impressions. Since he cannot say either that the material world or God causes them, we seem left with no explanation of their origin at all. This, of course, is what Hume implies in his opening statement. But I would speculate here about another resolution of the issue, one that, although Hume never mentions it himself, seems to me consonant with his epistemology. Why could Hume not say that our impressions have *no* causes? In the passage we have been examining, he assumes that they do have causes but gives no reasons why they must have them. Is it essential to assume a cause for everything that exists? As we saw in chapter 7, Hume says not. His argument bears repeating. "We can never demonstrate the necessity of a cause to every new existence . . . without shewing at the same time the impossibility there is, that any thing can ever begin to exist without some productive principle. . . . 'twill be easy for us to conceive any object to be non-existent this moment, and existent the next, without conjoining to it the distinct idea of a cause or productive principle."[6] My suggestion is that, since it is perfectly possible to think of some thing's coming into existence without having any cause, an obvious candidate for such honors would be sense impressions. They are, after all, basic ingredients in Hume's philosophy; he begins with them in the first sentence of the *Treatise.* Could he not say that they "just appear in the mind"? I do not know how Hume would respond to this suggestion; nevertheless, it seems to be one he might naturally adopt.

To sum up Hume's view about the causes of our sense impressions, we can consider the conclusion he reaches in the paragraph we have been examining to be definitive. He addresses the question deliberately and forthrightly, lists alternative possibilities, and gives a firm answer to the question of our possible knowledge of those causes. Because that answer reaffirms the original position he stated in Part I we can conclude that the contrary answers that appear in Part II do not represent his considered judgment so can be disregarded. This conclusion leads to a final point. In my discussion of Hume's view in Part I that the causes of our sense impressions are unknown, I remarked that it might still be possible for us to know that these impressions resemble other entities, including material objects in an external world.[7] That remark must now be retracted. Hume's conclusion in Section VI of Part II rules out the possibility I suggested. Because external material objects are inconceivable to us, we cannot have any notion as to whether they do or do not resemble our perceptions.

2. Hume's Revised Theory of Memory (Paragraph 3)

Although his brief statement about the causes of our impressions is important, even more important is the new conception of memory Hume presents in the paragraph that immediately follows. Although his account is very short it has consequences of considerable significance for his philosophy in Book I. Since it is a revised version of his original theory of memory, which appears in Section III of Part I, it might be helpful to pause briefly to recapitulate that view.[8] Hume there divides our ideas into two kinds—those of memory and those of imagination—and then goes on to cite the differences that distinguish them, noting two ways in which memory ideas differ from imagination ideas. (1) Memory ideas are "much more lively and strong than those of the imagination" (9) and (2) memory ideas must preserve "the original form, in which [their] objects were presented" (9), whereas imagination ideas are "not restrain'd to the same order and form with the original impressions" (9). In Section V Hume eliminates one of the two characteristics of memory ideas that distinguish them from imagination ideas. Let us turn to the text to see which of the two he drops and why he does so. Because the change has such important implications for his philosophy I will reproduce in full the paragraph in which he makes it.

> When we search for the characteristic, which distinguishes the *memory* from the imagination, we must immediately perceive, that it cannot lie in the simple ideas it presents to us; since both these faculties borrow their simple ideas from the impressions, and can never go beyond these original perceptions. These faculties are as little distinguish'd from each other by the arrangement of their complex ideas. For tho' it be a peculiar property of the memory to preserve the original order and position of its ideas, while the imagination transposes and changes them, as it pleases; yet *this difference is not sufficient to distinguish them in their operation, or make us know the one from the other; it being impossible to recal the past impressions, in order to compare them with our present ideas, and see whether their arrangement be exactly similar.* Since therefore the memory is known, neither by the order of its *complex* ideas, nor the nature of its *simple* ones; it follows, that *the difference betwixt it and the imagination lies in its superior force and vivacity.* A man may indulge his fancy in feigning any past scene of adventures; nor wou'd there be any possibility of distinguishing this from a remembrance of a like kind, were not the ideas of the imagination fainter and more obscure.[9]

The importance of this paragraph is apparent. In it Hume revises his original theory of memory, because he recognizes that its requirement (2) that an idea, to be a memory idea, must reproduce the order and position of the impressions from which it is derived, can never be applied in practice. To apply it we would have to compare the idea with the impression to determine whether the two coincide. But this we cannot do because the impression precedes the idea so that, by the time the idea exists to be compared, the impression is gone forever. Since we cannot distinguish memory ideas from imagination ideas by an appeal to characteristic (2), to differentiate between them we must instead rest content with an appeal to the other distinguishing characteristic (1). We can distinguish memory ideas from imagination ideas, Hume therefore concludes, *only* by their greater force and vivacity.

It is hardly necessary to emphasize the originality and novelty of this new theory of memory. Hume's conclusion that "the difference betwixt [the memory] and the imagination lies in [the memory's] superior force and vivacity" marks a dramatic departure from our ordinary way of thinking about the two. For most people, I think it fair to say, to distinguish memory from imagination without making any reference to a link between our memories and the past is to leave out the central characteristic of memory. Hume, one can reasonably surmise, was aware of this so did not revise his theory of memory without what he considered to be compelling reasons. I will explore those reasons further later in the chapter.

3. The Appendix Note (Appendix—Pages 627–28)

That Hume was well aware of the unusual, even paradoxical nature of his revised theory of memory and was concerned about it is evidenced by the fact that he added an appendix note to the long paragraph in Section V I have reproduced. Since this note represents his reconsidered judgment on the nature of memory and its difference from imagination, it merits our careful consideration. Hume begins the note with an illustration.

> It frequently happens, that when two men have been engag'd in any scene of action, the one shall remember it much better than the other, and shall have all the difficulty in the world to make his companion recollect it. He runs over several circumstances in vain; mentions the time, the place, the company, what was said, what was done on all sides; till at last he hits on some lucky circumstance, that revives the whole, and gives his friend a perfect memory of every thing. Here the person that forgets receives at first all the ideas from the discourse of the other, with the same circumstances of time and place; tho' he considers them as mere fictions of the imagination. But as soon as the circumstance is mention'd, that touches the memory, the very same ideas now appear in a new light, and have, in a manner, a different feeling from what they had before. Without any other alteration, beside that of the feeling, they become immediately ideas of the memory, and are assented to. (627–28)

The point Hume derives from his description of a situation that is familiar to us all appears at the end of the statement. The "forgetful" man first considers himself to be imagining the events described until suddenly they appear in "a new light" and he has a different feeling about them. This change in his feeling constitutes the transformation of his ideas from imagination ideas to memory ideas. To understand Hume's appendix explication of memory, therefore, we must grasp the nature of the feeling that makes an idea a memory idea and recognize how it differs from the feeling that makes an idea an imagination idea. Hume is quite explicit about what he means by these feelings and the difference between them. In the final paragraph of the note he writes: "Since, therefore, the imagination can represent all the same objects that the memory can offer to us, and since those faculties are *only* distinguish'd by the different *feeling* of the ideas they present, it may be proper to consider what is the nature of that feeling. And here I believe every one will readily agree with me, that the ideas of the memory are more *strong* and *lively* than those of the fancy" (628—first italics added).

So we find Hume in his appendix note reiterating the revised conception of memory he has presented in Section V. The difference in feeling between memory ideas and imagination ideas lies in the greater strength and liveliness of the former. And, as he has already concluded in Section V but repeats in the note, this is the *only* mark by which we can distinguish memory from imagination.

4. MEMORY AND HUME'S THEORY OF IDEAS (PARAGRAPH 3)

I return now to the main text of Section V. In the statement of his revised theory of memory there, Hume explains why he decided he had to make the revision he did, but he does so very briefly. I, too, have dealt with this point quite briefly in my commentary on the passage in section 2. It is time now to go back to this important change in Hume's thought and consider it at greater length. To begin we can say that Hume realized that his account of memory had to be revised because his original view was inconsistent with his empiricist theory of ideas. We must now try to see just where the inconsistency lay. Here an illustration may help. Suppose I look out my window and see a white house. Actually this visual impression, like almost all our impressions, is much more complex than that. I also see the windows of the house, its roof, its chimney, its garden, several trees, the hill behind it, the blue sky above it, and so on. Suppose, next, I close my eyes and try to remember the scene I have been observing. In my "mind's eye" I picture the white house (or really was it light cream in color?) with a red tile roof (or were they really tiles?). Did I see six trees, or seven? Was I, in fact, remembering what I actually saw or was I not, at least to some extent, misremembering? How can I answer these questions?

My illustration points up the difficulties inherent in determining whether any "memory" we have of a past scene or event is really an authentic memory or rather a mis-memory. This is the difficulty that gives rise to Hume's revision of his theory of memory in Section V. Let us see how this theory would analyze my illustration. My view of the white house was, in Hume's terminology, an impression. As such, it possessed three features: (1) It was acquired through one of my five senses, in this case sight, (2) it was quite strong or vivacious, and (3) it lasted only as long as I gazed at the scene; as soon as I closed my eyes it ceased to exist. Now let us suppose Hume first with his eyes open, viewing a scene like the one I have described, and then with them closed, with an idea of a scene he takes to be the same. He then asks himself: Am I really remembering what I saw? He begins his discussion in Section V by examining the way in which, according to his original theory of memory, he might answer his question. He would compare the "memory" idea with the impression itself to see if the two replicate each other. But this, he concludes, he simply cannot do. Since the impression no longer exists it is impossible for him to make the required comparison. And, if he cannot make the comparison, what reason does he have for supposing that his idea is anything like his original impression at all?

Because Hume's conclusions in the paragraph have such important implications, we must be sure we are interpreting his point correctly. So, even at the cost of repeating myself, I will examine his argument even more closely. It might seem that the conclusion I reached at the end of the last paragraph is an overstatement of anything Hume says in his argument. All he actually says, and all he intends, is that, because we cannot make the necessary comparison, we cannot guarantee that our memories of the past will *exactly* replicate that past. Nevertheless, these memories replicate the past sufficiently accurately in most instances to allow us to rely on them in our ordinary affairs. This conclusion is not radical; rather it is close to what most of us actually believe to be true about memory.

Such a moderate interpretation might be supported by three passages in the paragraph. Hume writes, in the first sentence, that "both [memory and imagination] borrow their simple ideas from the impressions." In this context the word "borrow," it can be argued, is a reference to the copy theory of ideas. Thus Hume is implying that our simple ideas, at least, replicate our impressions. Although he may be implying this, we must ask: *Can* he legitimately do so? How can he justify a claim that a simple idea is like "its" impression if, when it exists in our consciousness, the impression does not, so the two cannot be compared with each other? How can he justify the claim that the two are alike at all?

In the third sentence, after having shifted his attention from simple to complex ideas, Hume writes that "it [is] a peculiar property of the memory to preserve the original order and position of its ideas." If memory has this property or capacity, it might be concluded, it is, even if not always exact, at least reliable. However, such a conclusion overlooks the context in which the statement appears. Hume argues in the remainder of the sentence that we cannot appeal to this property in order to distinguish memory from imagination because we have no way of determining that any complex idea we have does in fact preserve the order and position of past impressions.

But, it could be argued, my gloss on the remainder of the sentence under examination itself overlooks a crucial word the sentence contains. Hume writes: "It [is] impossible to recal the past impressions, in order to compare them with our present ideas, and see whether their arrangement be *exactly* similar" (italics added). Might not Hume's use of the adverb "exactly" indicate that the change in his view is moderate rather than radical?

Admittedly, as he recognizes, we cannot justify the claim that our memory ideas are exact replicas of the past but this does not preclude their being reliable replicas of it. Two responses can be made to this interpretation. First, the function the term "exactly" performs in the argument can be interpreted in a different way. What Hume means, one could reasonably conclude, is that, because we cannot compare our present ideas with our past impressions, hence cannot say they are exact copies of those impressions, we cannot legitimately label any of them memory ideas rather than imagination ideas for the simple reason that, by definition, a memory idea *must exactly* replicate its impression. Second, if we cannot recall an impression to compare an idea with it to see if the two are exactly alike, no more can we recall it to see if they are somewhat alike or not alike at all, or even, for that matter, to see if any impression occurred in the first place.

Although Hume might have been a bit more clear in his argument defending his revision of his theory of memory, nothing in the paragraph in which it occurs can reasonably be interpreted to support the view that the theory presents only a modest alteration in his original position, leaving him with a theory compatible with our ordinary conception of memory. Instead, the paragraph presents a new conception of memory, quite different both from Hume's original view and from our ordinary thought. A closer look at some passages within the paragraph further support this conclusion. I call attention to three statements in the argument. Hume writes: "These faculties [memory and imagination] are as little distinguish'd from each other by the arrangement of their complex ideas."[10] The imagination, he also writes, "transposes and changes [its ideas], as it pleases." Since we cannot distinguish the memory from the imagination by the way in which they arrange their complex ideas, how do we know that the memory doesn't do exactly the same thing? We have no way, Hume is insisting, of checking our memory ideas against the original impressions to answer this question. The final sentence puts the issue beyond doubt. "A man may indulge his fancy in feigning any past scene of adventures; nor wou'd there be any possibility of distinguishing this from a remembrance of a like kind, were not the ideas of the imagination fainter and more obscure." Since we cannot distinguish between a memory idea and an imagination idea by checking the former against the past event it purports to replicate, we have only one recourse—to make our decision on the basis of the vivacity or faintness of the idea itself.

Before finishing my examination of the paragraph I need to consider a distinction that might be made. It could be argued that, although Hume concludes that the only way in which we can distinguish between memory ideas and imagination ideas *in practice*—or, as he puts it, "in their operation"—is by their relative vivacity, *in reality* they differ from each other in the fact that memory ideas must, and imagination ideas need not, exactly replicate the order and position of their antecedent impressions. Two responses can be made to this conjecture. (1) Hume's argument gives it no support. On the contrary (to repeat), he writes: "The difference betwixt [the memory] and the imagination lies in its superior force and vivacity." (2) More important, if we cannot appeal to the distinction in practice it becomes gratuitous. We may repeat the difference in a verbal definition but in fact we can never put it to use to distinguish the one from the other.

5. THE PAINTER AND THE LIAR (PARAGRAPHS 4 AND 5)

Following the paragraph in which he presents his revised theory of memory Hume adds two paragraphs to illustrate the new theory. His first illustration concerns a painter who wishes to portray an emotion. To make his idea of the emotion vivid the painter endeavors to see some person experiencing it. He also tries to paint his picture as soon as he can after he has actually observed the emotion, again in order to capture the emotion on canvas while his idea remains fresh.

This is sound psychology that would, I am sure, be confirmed by many painters. But Hume has a second reason for introducing the illustration. It appears in the last part of the paragraph, where he writes: "The more recent this memory is, the clearer is the idea; and when after a long interval [the painter] would return to the contemplation of his object, he always finds its idea to be much decay'd, if not wholly obliterated. We are frequently in doubt concerning the ideas of the memory, as they become very weak and feeble; and are at a loss to determine whether any image proceeds from the fancy [imagination] or the memory, when it is not drawn in such lively colours as distinguish that latter faculty" (85). Hume is here pointing out a problem arising from his revised theory of memory. Although we can, by an appeal to their relative vivacity, easily distinguish some of our ideas as memory ideas and others as imagination ideas, we cannot always do so. Some ideas, because they are neither lively nor faint but occupy a "gray area" in the middle, are hard to classify. Are they memory ideas or imagination ideas? We cannot be sure.

In the next paragraph Hume offers a second illustration—that of a liar—which is interesting, to say the least. (Some readers may find Hume's account of the liar outrageous; I find it a convincing confirmation of the remarkable novelty of his revised theory of memory.) Hume prefaces his illustration with some explanatory remarks, which themselves need explanation. He writes: "And as an idea of the memory, by losing its force and vivacity, may degenerate to such a degree, as *to be taken for* an idea of the imagination; so on the other hand an idea of the imagination may acquire such a force and vivacity, as *to pass for* an idea of the memory, and counterfeit its effects on the belief and judgment. This is noted in the case of liars; who by the frequent repetition of their lies, come at last to believe *and remember them,* as realities" (86—italics added).

In this quotation Hume writes that a memory idea may degenerate to such a degree as "to be taken for" an imagination idea and that an imagination idea may acquire such force and vivacity as "to pass for" a memory idea. Unless he is talking here about ideas in the "gray area" I discussed earlier, Hume seems to be implying that, even though an idea, once vivid, is now weak, it is still a memory idea and not an imagination idea and that, even though an idea, once weak, is now vivid, it is still an imagination idea and not a memory idea. If Hume is making anything more than a gratuitous verbal point, we must be able to distinguish the weak memory ideas that are taken for imagination ideas as still being memory ideas and the vivid imagination ideas that pass for memory ideas as still being imagination ideas. How are we to do this? The only way in which we can distinguish between the two kinds of ideas, Hume has just concluded, is by their relative vivacity. So, as far as we can determine, a memory idea, when it degenerates, *becomes* an imagination idea so it is misleading to say that it is "taken for" such an idea. In the reverse direction, an imagination idea, when it is enlivened, *becomes,* as far as we can determine, a memory idea, so it is misleading to say that it "passes for" such an idea.

We come now to the liar. Although Hume devotes only a sentence to him, we can reconstruct his picture of the liar from the context. He is a person who tells stories created from his imagination that he describes as events he remembers. His lying consists in his deliberate deception of his audience about this. He is not remembering these events, as he claims, but only imagining them. But now something happens. After frequent repetition the liar finds his ideas of the events he recounts becoming increasingly vivid until they are so forceful that they are transformed from ideas of his imagination into ideas of his memory. As Hume says, he comes "at last to believe and remember them, as realities." But if these ideas are now things the person remembers, he is no longer representing imagination ideas as memory ideas. In other words, he is no longer lying. To continue to call him a liar, Hume's argument implies, would be to slander him.[11]

6. A CRITICISM OF HUME'S LIAR ILLUSTRATION (PARAGRAPH 5)

I pause briefly to consider a criticism of Hume's liar illustration and, by extrapolation, of his revised theory of memory. Some readers would say that the repetitious liar is still a liar. Others, more generous, would say that, because he is no longer deliberately misleading his audience, he is not a liar but is simply self-deceived. However, very few would concede to Hume that he is now remembering the events he describes. Why not? Simply this. Memory, to be truly memory, must be the recollection of events in the past. Therefore, because the events the person is talking about never occurred, he cannot be remembering them.

Hume, I think, would be prepared to answer this objection. He could reply: I am well aware that most people think of memory as recollection of the past. But that is not the point. The question rather is: Can we ever say that such recollection occurs? To justify any claim that one is recollecting a past event three conditions must be met. (1) The event must have occurred. (2) One must have some form of mental awareness that one takes to be an awareness of that past event. (3) One must be able to offer reasons that establish that one's present awareness replicates the past event. Point (3), Hume could continue, is crucial and it cannot be satisfied, because, to make the necessary comparison between the two that would establish the replication, the past event would have to be brought into present consciousness and this cannot be done. Before anyone can legitimately raise such an objection against my revised theory of memory, Hume could then conclude, he must offer an epistemology capable of showing how the past can be recollected. And this no one can do.

I think the argument I have attributed to Hume is one he would himself have given to an objector. It is simply not enough to assert that recollection of the past is essential to memory; one must also show how such recollection is possible. It would take me too far from this commentary on Hume even to attempt to suggest how this might be accomplished. Suffice it to say that the task (as many philosophers have discovered) is an extraordinarily difficult one. But until it is successfully completed, to criticize Hume's revised theory of memory on the grounds that it omits any reference to recollection of the past is simply to beg the question against him.

Does this mean that we must accept Hume's revised theory? Before doing so we need to consider at least one problem to which it gives rise. The problem is internal to Hume's theory of ideas, raising a question about its consistency on a fundamental point. I will turn to it next.

7. HUME'S REVISED THEORY AND THE EMPIRICIST PRINCIPLE

According to the Empiricist Principle our ideas replicate their antecedent impressions, being exact copies of them. Hume's revised theory of memory raises a problem about this claim. Suppose any idea we have. If we are to say that it is an exact copy of some antecedent impression we must be able to compare the two. To do this we must recollect the impression, or bring it into consciousness. But this we cannot do because the impression, being past, no longer exists. Hume's revised theory of memory, with its elimination of recollection, seems, therefore, to be inconsistent with the Empiricist Principle. We must, however, be careful about how we state this inconsistency. It may still be true, as the Principle claims, that ideas are copies of antecedent impressions. But this we can never confirm, so Hume has no basis on which to claim that they are. Past impressions, like external objects, are simply inconceivable to us.

Could Hume resolve this difficulty and, if so, how? I will not attempt to answer these questions but only suggest two possible ways out of his dilemma. He might modify the Empiricist Principle, giving up the claim that ideas are copies of their antecedent impressions. This would leave him with a truncated version of the Principle that would read: All our simple ideas in their first appearance are derived from simple impressions.[12] But such an abbreviation of the Principle has some awkward consequences. If the copy component of the impression-idea relation is eliminated how are we to decide what particular idea is derived from what particular impression? Any impression, for all we could determine, might give rise to any idea. Further, what reason would we have for thinking that our ideas are derived from impressions at all? If we cannot say that they are copies of those impressions, may they not be quite independent of them? If this is possible, even the abbreviated form of the Principle I have just given becomes questionable.

The other alternative, of course, is to return to the original theory of memory. By doing this Hume could preserve the Empiricist Principle intact. But then he would be left with an equally formidable problem. He would have to embrace an account of memory in which memory is a recollection of the past. But that would require us to have an impression that, because it has ceased to exist, we cannot have.

I do not know how Hume might have resolved this dilemma. Here again it would have been helpful if he had pursued the implications of his thought further than he did. Since memory will play an important part in his theory of causation, Hume will have more to say about it in later sections of Part III. Perhaps there we will find a solution to the problems I have noted.[13]

Summary

Even though short, Section V of Part III is important for our understanding of Hume. In its few paragraphs he returns to two topics central to his philosophy that he had discussed at the very beginning of the *Trea-*

tise. His comments on the first—the causes of our impressions—though they amplify what he had said before, make little change in his view. These causes, which he had originally said to be unknown, he now concedes to be "perfectly inexplicable by human reason."

On the subject of memory, the change he makes in Section V is a substantive departure from his original account in Section III of Part I. His revision produces a conception of memory significantly different not only from his original view but also from common thought. Assuming that Hume was well aware of this we must conclude that he had a compelling reason to make the change. The reason, as we have seen, was his recognition that his original theory required us to have an impression we cannot have, because it does not exist. To avoid an inconsistency between his empiricist epistemology and his theory of memory, he therefore concluded, the latter must be revised. But, if my comments on it are sound, Hume's revised theory comes into conflict with the Empiricist Principle. To render the two consistent, the copy theory of ideas must be deleted from the Principle. But this deletion in turn raises serious questions about Hume's theory of ideas.

I think we must admire Hume for his discussion of memory in Section V. I am not now speaking about his revised theory of memory itself. That is debatable. Rather, I am referring to the fact that he displayed both intellectual integrity and candor in retracting a part of his original theory of memory when he realized that his epistemology required the retraction and going on to maintain a theory that few people would be ready to accept. It will be interesting to see how well this theory functions when Hume puts it to work in the sections ahead as he develops his theory of causation.

9

CONSTANT CONJUNCTION AND MENTAL CAUSATION

(Part III, Section VI)

Introduction

After his digression into the cause of our sense impressions and the nature of memory in Section V, Hume returns in Section VI to his main concern in Part III—the development of his theory of causation. In Section II he had begun a search for the impression from which we derive our idea of causation, arguing that we cannot find it in external objects themselves so must seek it in the relations among those objects. He identified two relations between objects that are necessary if the objects are to be causally related. (1) They must be contiguous to each other (relation of "contiguity") and (2) the cause must precede the effect (relation of "succession"). But these two relations, although necessary, are not sufficient to explain the idea of causation. A third relation, of much greater importance, has to be added. A cause and its effect must be necessarily connected with each other (relation of "necessary connection"). The relation of necessary connection, unlike those of contiguity and succession, generates a difficulty for Hume's philosophy. Whereas he believes we have impressions of contiguity and succession, from which we can derive our ideas of both, we seem not to have any impression of necessary connection. Whence then do we gain such an idea?

Rather than grappling directly with this problem, Hume suggested in Section II that we approach the issue by a circuitous route, in the hope that eventually we will find a solution for it.[1] In Section VI Hume discovers a feature of the causal relationship, to be added to the two relations of contiguity and succession, that he believes will carry him forward in his search for the impression of necessary connection, which will complete his theory of causation. In the first part of the section he describes this relation, explains how it is connected with contiguity and succession, and discusses the nature and extent of its contribution to his discovery of the idea of necessary connection.

If we agree that our experience of the relation between two objects leads us to believe that they are causally connected and, on each appearance of the first, to anticipate the appearance of the second, Hume asks in the latter portion of the section, how should we explain the mental transition we make from one to the other? In answer he offers an explanation of the way in which the imagination functions and the reasons why it does so. His theory combines an analysis of human mental activity with an account of the causes underlying it.

Text

1. The Inference from Cause to Effect (Title of Section)

Hume entitles Section VI "Of the inference from the impression to the idea." Just what does he mean by this phrase? The issue with which he is concerned is the relation between a cause and its effect. In many situations in which we assert a causal relationship both the cause and effect are present to us. We see a flame and feel its heat. Or we see the motion of the cue ball and then that of the object ball. We have, in these instances, direct sense impressions of both cause and effect. But this is far from always being true. Sometimes we see a flame at a distance and assume we will feel heat if we approach the blaze. Or we see the cue ball in motion toward the object ball and assume the latter will move when the cue ball collides with it. In these instances we have an impression of the cause but not yet one of its effect. Of that we have at the time only an idea. What we do is to make an inference from the impression of the cause (which is present to our senses) to the idea of the effect (which is not). The problem therefore becomes that of explaining this inference.

That the inference we make from an observed cause to an unobserved effect is important needs a brief comment. On it depend most of our practical actions. We believe that if we perform a certain act, say, light a fire, this will produce a certain effect, the experience of heat. We could not live long unless we assumed that a cause would be followed by its anticipated effect. Or, to put this in a different way, to live we must assume that the future will be like the past, and act accordingly. Turning from everyday life to theory, we find the same assumption essential to science. All scientific laws go beyond impressions, generalizing from phenomena that are directly observed to those that are not, asserting causal relations among these phenomena. To mention a classic example, Newton's law of gravitation is universal in its scope, applying to bodies beyond the range of observation, in both space and time, as exactly as it does to the bodies we observe. Because they believe such causal connections to be universal, scientists feel confident in basing predictions about the future on them.

2. CONTIGUITY, SUCCESSION, AND CONSTANT CONJUNCTION (PARAGRAPHS 1–3)

Hume begins Section VI on a negative note, arguing that we cannot base our inference from a cause to its effect on an examination of the objects we hold to be so related, because there is nothing in any object we call a cause that implies that some other object is its effect. "There is no object, which implies the existence of any other if we consider these objects in themselves, and never look beyond the ideas which we form of them" (86–87). Suppose we see a flame. There is nothing in the flame itself that implies that it will generate heat, because it is not impossible that it should generate cold, or not generate any feeling at all. Hume's argument is aimed at a form of *a prioristic* rationalism that claims that, given the essence of flame, it must be accompanied by heat. His argument seems clearly decisive against any such view. We simply cannot tell, even from the most minute examination of any flame, that it must generate heat. Generalizing, we must acknowledge that we lack the ability to predict the effects any objects will have merely from an examination of those objects themselves. Hume's argument on this point, although brief, is of great theoretical and historical importance. It eliminates the possibility of achieving a goal to which rationalistic philosophers had aspired—to provide a deductive interpretation of the causal relationship and thus produce a demonstrative science of nature.

To continue with Hume, we must next ask: On what, then, do we base our inference from an object we take to be a cause to another we take to be its effect? Hume's answer is simple in its expression but complex in its explanation. He begins by writing: "'Tis therefore by EXPERIENCE only, that we can infer the existence of one object from that of another" (87). The complexities arise when we attempt to explain the nature of the experience in question. In his explanation Hume lists four factors that must be taken into account: (1) contiguity, (2) succession, (3) constant conjunction, and (4) memory.

> We remember to have had frequent instances of the existence of one species of objects; and also remember, that the individuals of another species of objects have always attended them, and have existed in a regular order of contiguity and succession with regard to them. Thus we remember to have seen that species of object we call *flame,* and to have felt that species of sensation we call *heat.* We likewise call to mind their constant conjunction in all past instances. Without any farther ceremony, we call the one *cause* and the other *effect,* and infer the existence of the one from that of the other. (87)

All of the four factors I have listed as essential to the inference we make when we call some object a cause and another object its effect are included in the passage I have reproduced. We have already seen, from Hume's preliminary analysis of causation in Section II, that contiguity and succession are necessary to the causal relation. But, as he emphasized there, the presence of these two relations is not enough, in itself, to lead us to conclude that two objects are causally related. Something more in our experience is needed. So in Section VI he adds a third condition: "Contiguity and succession are not sufficient to make us pronounce any two objects to be cause and effect, unless we perceive, that these two relations are preserv'd in several instances" (87). This necessary additional perception is one of what Hume calls "constant conjunction." If, for example, we perceive for the first time a flame and feel heat contiguous to and succeeding it, we do not immediately infer that flame causes heat. But, if we perceive the same two repeatedly in the same relationship, we do make a causal inference from one to the other. Hume summarizes his account of the part played by constant conjunction in our idea of causation a bit later in the section, where he writes: "The idea of cause and effect is deriv'd from *experience,* which informs us, that such particular objects, in all past instances, have been constantly conjoin'd with each other: And as an object similar to one of these is suppos'd to be immediately present in its impression, we thence presume on the existence of one similar to its usual attendant" (89–90).

Two minor clarifications should be made in Hume's account of constant conjunction. (1) He calls it a "relation" (87), but it is not a direct relation between two objects in the way in which contiguity and succession are. Rather, it is a regular repetition of these two relations between objects, extending over many instances. So it might be called a second-order relation. (2) "Constant conjunction," though a euphonious phrase, is a slight misnomer. In most cases in which we believe two objects to be causally related, we do not do so because we perceive them to be *constantly* conjoined. There is no conjunction between flame and heat when no object is burning or between the motion of the cue ball and that of the object ball when no one is playing billiards. What Hume really means by the term "constant conjunction" is the regular repetition of a conjunction. Whenever flame appears, it is joined by heat; whenever the cue ball strikes the object ball, the object ball moves. These repeated conjunctions of the objects are constant only in the sense that they are regular or exceptionless. With this clarification, I will follow Hume in using the phrase "constant conjunction."

In constant conjunction Hume believes he has "insensibly discover'd a new relation betwixt cause and effect" (87). Recognizing that the addition of constant conjunction moves his analysis of causation substantially and importantly beyond the two relations of contiguity and succession, we must still remember that what Hume is seeking is the idea of necessary connection, which he holds to be necessary to the causal relationship. This recognition causes him to have second thoughts about the value of his new discovery. "We may now see the advantage of quitting the direct survey of this relation [causation], in order to discover the nature of that *necessary connection*, which makes so essential a part of it. There are hopes, that by this means we may at last arrive at our propos'd end; tho' to tell the truth, this new-discover'd relation of a constant conjunction seems to advance us but very little in our way" (87–88).

The reason for Hume's disappointment about constant conjunction lies in his realization that, even though we experience the constant conjunction of two objects on innumerable occasions, this experience will never generate a new idea, specifically the idea of necessary connection, in our minds. "From the mere repetition of any past impression, even to infinity, there never will arise any new original idea, such as that of a necessary connexion" (88). Nevertheless, Hume is not discouraged by this problem, concluding: "But tho' this reasoning seems just and obvious; yet as it wou'd be folly to despair too soon, we shall continue the thread of our discourse" (88). On the positive side, Hume has advanced his argument by establishing that, after having experienced the constant conjunction of two objects in the past, we do, on becoming aware of the one we have previously observed as cause, infer that it will be followed by the other, or the effect. He ends his discussion with an enigmatic remark: "Perhaps 'twill appear in the end, that the necessary connexion depends on the inference, instead of the inference's depending on the necessary connexion" (88). Before we finish our discussion of causation we will hope to understand what Hume means by this statement and why he makes it.

3. CONSTANT CONJUNCTION AND MEMORY (PARAGRAPHS 1–3)

In the long passage I reproduced in section 2, Hume lists four factors that lead us to make causal inferences. I have discussed the first three of these. In this section I will examine the fourth—memory—which functions in a different way from the other three.

Going back to the passage in question, we find that memory plays an essential part in Hume's argument. He writes that "we remember to have had frequent instances of the existence of one species of objects" and that we "remember, that the individuals of another species of objects have always attended them, and have existed in a regular order of contiguity and succession with regard to them." In the latter passage Hume introduces the concept of constant conjunction. We remember, to paraphrase, that in every instance in which we have experienced the first kind of object, we have also experienced the second kind in a relation of contiguity and succession to it. Continuing through the passage Hume reiterates the importance of memory to our perception of the constant conjunction of objects and, as a result, of the causal inferences we make.

We should agree with Hume that memory is an indispensable condition of our recognition of constant conjunction; we could not recognize that two objects were constantly conjoined unless we remembered them to have been so. But now we are faced with a serious problem. In the previous section (V) of Part III, to which I devoted chapter 8, Hume revised his original theory of memory from Part I. An important feature of this revision was his deletion of the requirement that memory include recollection of the past. On the revised theory a memory idea is simply a lively idea. If we attempt to apply Hume's revised theory of memory to his account of constant conjunction, we run into difficulties that seem insuperable. For what connection, we must ask, can we draw between a lively idea (i.e., a memory idea) we are experiencing now and our recollection of past constant conjunctions? If we cannot say that the idea involves such a recollection (as Hume has concluded in Section V we cannot), what can we mean when we refer to it as the memory of such past constant conjunctions?

After pondering over this question and trying vainly to understand how Hume might have explained our recognition of constant conjunction in terms of his revised theory of memory, I finally concluded that he would not do so at all—because, in his Section VI argument, he is not employing his revised theory but his original theory of memory. That this is a correct interpretation is confirmed by the way he writes about memory and constant conjunction there. In the long statement I reproduced in section 2 he says (to repeat): "We remember to have seen that species of object we call *flame*, and to have felt that species of sensation we call *heat*. We likewise call to mind their constant conjunction in all past instances."[2] This is surely the language one would use if he were conceiving of memory as the recollection of the past rather than simply as the possession of lively ideas.

This shift in the course of Hume's philosophy gives rise to several questions. First, why did he return to his original theory of memory in Section VI? Since he makes the shift without comment, one cannot be sure what his motives might have been. I can only suggest what may have happened in his thinking. In the first place, there is a break in Hume's focus of concern between the two sections. He is now concentrating on issues quite different from those that had occupied his attention in the previous section. It may be that, as a result, the ideas he had entertained about memory while writing that section were no longer vivid in his mind. Again, his concern in Section VI is with a new concept—constant conjunction—which he clearly thought could be put to use in furthering his quest for an idea of necessary connection and, thus, for completing his theory of causation. The achievement of this goal might well have appeared to him a sufficient justification for a return to the only conception of memory that would make it possible.

But Hume's resolution of one problem gives rise to others. If we agree that, in order to recollect past constant conjunctions, Hume must return to his original theory of memory, and if we also agree that the recollection of such past constant conjunctions is a necessary condition of his having an idea of causation,[3] we seem forced to conclude that Hume is caught in a contradiction in his philosophy. In Section V he revised his original theory of memory because he realized that, if one accepts his empiricist epistemology, it becomes impossible to recollect the past.[4] But in his account of constant conjunction in Section VI, which forms an essential part of his theory of causation, he must assume that we do recollect it. Therefore, Hume must either give up his empiricist theory of ideas or abandon any hope of developing a viable theory of causation. Since he continues to develop his theory of causation in Part III, employing the concept of constant conjunction in that development, I will follow him by doing the same in this commentary. But the argument that follows rests on a fundamental inconsistency in Hume's philosophy in Book I.

4. REASON AND CAUSAL INFERENCE (PARAGRAPHS 4–11)

Having introduced the concept of constant conjunction into his analysis of causation, Hume turns his attention to the question of why we make the inferences we do from causes to effects. He poses the question he will try to answer in the following way: "Since it appears, that the transition from an impression present to the memory or senses to the idea of an object, which we call cause or effect, is founded on past *experience*, and on our remembrance of their *constant conjunction*, the next question is, Whether experience produces the idea by means of the understanding or of the imagination; whether we are determin'd by reason to make the transition, or by a certain association and relation of perceptions" (88–89).

This passage calls for several comments. (1) Hume uses the neutral term "transition" to describe the "action of the mind" (89) when it moves from an impression to an idea. His main object in the argument to follow will be to give an account of this transition. (2) Although he speaks of an impression of the memory (as well as of the senses), I have already given reasons to conclude that he should not be read literally on this point.[5] (3) Although he formulates his problem in terms of the relation between causes and effects, his argument has a broader application, ranging over all the mental transitions we make that are based on experience rather than simply on the comparison of ideas. (4) In listing the alternatives he will explore—understanding and imagination—at the end of the passage, he equates the former with reason and the latter with the association of perceptions.

Hume begins his argument by asking whether these transitions are the work of reason. If they were, they would be based either on demonstration or on probability. He then sets about to eliminate both possibilities. He prefaces his arguments with an assumption that seems to be unexceptionable. "If reason determin'd us, it wou'd proceed upon that principle, *that instances, of which we have had no experience, must resemble those, of which we have had experience, and that the course of nature continues always uniformly the same*" (89).

In this passage Hume refers to two types of mental transition. First is the general one, from instances of which we have had experience to those of which we have not. The second is more specific but of great importance, from past to future instances. With it Hume introduces the concept of the uniformity of nature, raising the question, usually termed "the problem of induction" (with which generations of subsequent philosophers have wrestled), of how we justify inferences we make about future events on the basis of our experiences of past events. Why should we assume that flame will be accompanied by heat in the future just because we have always experienced it to be so in the past? What if nature changes?

Hume begins his critical comments by pointing out that, if the mental transitions we make are based on reason, they must be supported by arguments that are either demonstrative or probable. That they are not demonstrative, hence cannot represent instances of knowledge,[6] can easily be shown. If we could demonstrate that our experience will always remain the same and, in particular, that the future will be like the past, it would be impossible that it should be different. But we can *conceive* of its being different; for example, we can conceive of flame without heat. Since what is conceivable must be possible, the required demonstration cannot be accomplished. In Hume's words, "There can be no *demonstrative* arguments to prove, *that those instances, of which we have had no experience, resemble those, of which we have had experience*" (89).

Having eliminated the possibility of a demonstrative argument in support of our inferences from experience, Hume next considers whether these inferences are based on probability. Hume's use of the term "probability" here can again be misleading. What he means by it is a form of reasoning that is different from demonstration, because the conclusions of arguments based on it can be denied without contradiction. Thus, when he uses the word "probability" he is referring to any opinion or belief that falls short of knowledge, because its supporting reasons do not demonstrate its truth.[7] Nevertheless, it is important to recognize that in this argument Hume considers "probability" to be a form of reasoning, in the sense that we can give a rational, though not demonstrative, justification for the beliefs or opinions that are based on it. Hume begins by pointing out that our reasoning from probability is of a mixed nature, involving an appeal to impressions (because we are concerned with objects) and the relating of ideas (because it is a case of reasoning). In his words, " 'Tis . . . necessary, that in all probable reasonings there be something present to the mind, either seen or remember'd; and that from this we infer something connected with it, which is not seen nor remember'd" (89).

Hume offers several arguments against the view that our inferences from experience are based on reasoning from probability. His first is somewhat obscure as he states it but it can be restated to make it clearer. After pointing out that the only relation that can lead us to draw inferences beyond our experience is that of cause and effect, he writes: "Probability is founded on the presumption of a resemblance betwixt those objects, of which we have had experience, and those, of which we have had none; and therefore 'tis impossible this presumption can arise from probability. The same principle cannot be both the cause and effect of another" (90). An illustration might help to clarify Hume's argument; let us return to his example of flame and heat. Suppose someone were to see a flame in the distance and conclude that it is hot. Asked to justify his conclusion he might say, "All the flames I have experienced have been hot." Now suppose that it is pointed out to him that his answer presupposes that this particular flame will resemble all past flames in being hot. How would he go about justifying that presupposition? If he appeals to experience for his answer, the most he can reply is that all the flames he has experienced have resembled each other in being hot. But that leaves untouched the question: Will this flame, whose heat he has not experienced, resemble the others by being hot? The only way in which he can answer that question is by assuming that it will resemble the previously experienced flames in this respect. But, since that is the point at issue, to make such an assumption is to beg the crucial question.

Having stated his case, Hume turns to an objection to it, based on a line of argument common to our ordinary thought and to the views of many philosophers, particularly prior to his time. If in our past experience, we have observed that a certain event, C, is invariably followed by another event, E, we can legitimately conclude that C possesses some power to produce E, therefore that, when we observe an occurrence of C, we can legitimately infer that E will follow. Hume sums up the view in succinct terms. "The past production implies a power: The power implies a new production: And the new production is what we infer from the power and the past production" (90). Hume responds to this argument first by pointing out that, to say that an event, C, has the power to *produce* an event, E, is just another way of saying that C *causes* E and it is this causal connection itself that is under challenge. He then adds that, since such a response might be thought to rest too heavily on his own previous arguments, he will offer a different reply. So he continues by acknowledging, but only for purposes of the argument, that a cause does, in some given instance, possess a power that produces an effect. But then we must ask: How can we reason from this fact to the conclusion that the same power will manifest itself in the same way in other instances? Hume points out that in the original instance we never perceive this power because it is not among the sensible qualities of the object we label the cause, therefore, when we perceive the same sensible qualities in another instance, we have no reason to suppose the object will be possessed of a similar power. Hence no appeal to these experiences, even if it acknowledges that an object has had a power to produce another, gives us any justification for concluding that a similar object will possess such a power in the future. Any attempt to answer this question in the same way will give rise to another question of the same kind with the result that the attempted justification succumbs to an infinite vicious regress.

To summarize Hume's argument in these paragraphs, his object is to destroy the theory that our inferences from experience and, in particular, our causal inferences can be justified by reason. Since neither a demonstrable argument nor one based on experience can support such inferences we must conclude that they are rationally unsupportable. "Thus not only our reason fails us in the discovery of the *ultimate connexion* of causes and effects, but even after experience has inform'd us of their *constant conjunction,* 'tis impossible for us to satisfy ourselves by our reason, why we shou'd extend that experience beyond those particular instances, which have fallen under our observation" (91). But if we have no rational basis for the causal inferences we make, on what can we base them? This is the question Hume will be attempting to answer in the pages that follow, as he develops his theory of causation. However, he does give a clue to its answer at the beginning of the arguments he offers against reason that I have been reviewing in this section. As he put it in a passage at the outset of his argument (which I reproduced at the beginning of this section): "Since it appears, that the transition . . . which we call cause or effect, is founded on past *experience,* and on our remembrance of their *constant conjunction,* the next question is, Whether experience produces the idea by means of the understanding or of the imagination; whether we are determin'd by reason to make the transition, or by a certain association and relation of perceptions" (88–89). Having now seen that Hume eliminates the first alternative, understanding or reason, we can conclude that he will base his argument on an ap-

peal to the second, or imagination. How imagination functions in the production of our causal inferences must now be explored.

5. IMAGINATION AND CAUSAL "INFERENCE" (PARAGRAPHS 12–16)

Hume begins the final five paragraphs of Section VI by corroborating
the point about imagination and causal inference I just made. After reaffirming his previous conclusion, "Reason can never shew us the connexion of one object with another" (92), he continues with an affirmation of
his alternative. "When the mind, therefore, passes from the idea or impression of one object to the idea or belief of another, it is not determin'd by
reason, but by certain principles, which associate together the ideas of these
objects, and unite them in the imagination" (92). In this passage Hume
states that the mind, through the imagination, associates certain ideas together. It is determined to do so by "certain principles." Before we turn to
a review of these principles, we need to address a preliminary but important point. After beginning his discussion by asserting that "Reason can
never shew us the connexion of one object with another," Hume goes on
to conclude that certain principles "unite" the ideas of the objects "in the
imagination." Though flame may always have been accompanied by heat,
we can offer no reasons, either demonstrative or based on our past experience, to support our belief that it will continue to be accompanied by heat.
Nevertheless, the ideas of flame and heat are united in the imagination,
so that when we have an impression of the first, the idea of the second
naturally arises in the mind and we say that the flame causes heat. Why
does this union occur? What is the relationship between the "principles of
union" (92) among ideas and the fact that the ideas are united in the imagination? In the statement I have reproduced Hume is quite clear on this
point. The principles of union are *causes* and the union of ideas in the
imagination is their *effect*. In the next paragraph, in which he notes a qualification to this causal relationship, Hume nevertheless assumes his general causal thesis. "These principles I allow to be neither the *infallible* nor
the *sole* causes of an union among ideas" (92). I will return later in the section to the qualifications Hume introduces in this sentence; the essential
point now is his claim that the principles cause the union or association of
ideas.

In this account of the mental transitions we make, Hume has taken
another step forward in the development of his theory of causation. After
rejecting the standard view that the cause-effect relationship can be explained in "objective" terms, or through the theory that a given object, the
cause, possesses some productive power that brings about its effect, he
transfers the causal relationship into the mind, by locating it in the transi-

tion we make in our imagination from one impression or idea to another idea. He accounts for this transition by the view that certain principles of union or relations of ideas cause our imagination to move from one to the other. I will call this view Hume's theory of *mental causation;* the phrase seems appropriate to the account he gives in Section VI I have just been describing. Hume not only recognizes but emphasizes its importance to his explanation of cause and effect in general. Immediately after saying that the transition in our imagination from one idea or impression to another idea is determined by certain principles of association, he concludes: "Had ideas no more union in the fancy [imagination] than objects seem to have to the understanding, we cou'd never draw any inference from causes to effects, nor repose belief in any matter of fact. The inference [from cause to effect], therefore, depends *solely* on the union of ideas" (92—italics added). Or, to state the argument in a reverse way, the inferences (or transitions) we make from causes to effects depend solely on the union of ideas in the imagination, a union that is the effect of certain uniting principles, which are its causes.

We may now turn to those uniting principles or relations themselves. Part of Hume's account is simply a recapitulation of the theory he originally presented in Sections IV and V of Part I so it needs only a brief review.[8] There are three relations among ideas that cause their union in the imagination—resemblance, contiguity, and causation. In Part I Hume speaks of these as "natural relations" because they naturally cause the imagination to unite the ideas so related. At the present stage of his argument Hume is interested in the third of these—the relation of causation. Besides being a natural relation causation is also a "*philosophical* relation."[9] By this he means that it is a relation in terms of which we can compare ideas together. So considered, it has three bases; namely, contiguity, succession, and constant conjunction.

A bit earlier in this section, I noted a qualification Hume makes to his claim that the impression or idea of an object causes a transition in the imagination to the idea of another object related to it. Such an impression or idea, he acknowledges, is not the "infallible" or "sole" cause of a mental transition. His point rests on the vagaries of mental causation, which is simply not mechanical. Sometimes we may not make any mental transition at all, perhaps because our attention becomes fixated on the original impression or idea. Again, we may not make a transition to the related idea, because our mind may wander; in Hume's words, "The thought . . . may leap from the heavens to the earth, from one end of the creation to the other, without any certain method or order" (92). In these qualifications Hume is expanding on a point he had made in Section IV of Part I. There he had drawn an analogy between the association of ideas in the imagination and the gravitational attraction in Newtonian physics (12–13). But he recognized that, unlike the rigidity of gravitational attraction, mental association has a degree of looseness and flexibility about it. A cause that leads us to make a mental transition from an impression or idea to another idea, instead of being compelling, operates rather, to repeat Hume's felicitous phrase, "as a gentle force, which commonly prevails" (10).

Before concluding this section I should explain a notation I made in its title. I put the word "inference" in quotation marks there in order to emphasize that the action of the imagination when it makes a transition about a "matter of fact" (92) and, in particular, when it moves from a cause to an effect is not an inference, in the ordinary sense of that word. It is not an example of reasoning because it is neither demonstrative nor derivable from experience. So it is not a mental activity for which we can provide a rational justification. It is instead an effect, in the imagination, of the causal power of certain principles or relations of ideas. Throughout his discussion Hume himself uses the term "transition" to describe this mental action, writing, for example: "We have already taken notice of certain relations, which make us pass from one object to another, even tho' there be no reason to determine us to that transition" (92). The word "transition" more accurately describes Hume's theory than "inference" because it does not have the connotations of being a reasoning process that the latter word does.

One might conclude from Hume's view that the mental transitions we make are not the work of reason or understanding, hence cannot be rationally supported—that he is embracing irrationalism. Whether one should say this depends on what one means by irrationalism. If the simple conclusion that we can offer no reasons in support of these transitions is irrationalism, Hume must be labeled an irrationalist. On the other hand, we might conclude that, if we could offer reasons, they would be found to support the transitions. Since these would then not be in opposition to reason, to describe Hume's theory as "irrationalist" would seem too strong. Nevertheless, we can say without question that, since the transitions cannot be supported by reason, but occur "outside of reason," they are nonrational. Thus it seems fair to describe the position Hume reaches at the end of Section VI as nonrationalism, rather than as irrationalism.

Nevertheless Hume is lax about his terminology. He continues to talk about these transitions as inferences and describes the action of the imagination as reasoning. This terminology can seriously misrepresent his thought and cause confusion for the reader. To avoid such confusion, I will, though I continue to use Hume's terminology, make a point throughout my discussion of putting words like "reasoning" (other than demonstration) and "inference" in quotation marks. Both can be considered technical terms of Hume's philosophy.

Summary

In Section VI Hume continues the development of his theory of causation, still in search of the idea of a necessary connection to unite causes with effects. In the section he takes three steps toward his goal, two constructive and one critical. First, he discovers a new relation, constant conjunction, to add to those of contiguity and succession, which he concludes to be a necessary condition of our making causal "inferences" or transitions. Although he has misgivings about the extent to which this relation will forward his project of finding an idea of necessary connection, he is right, I believe, in emphasizing its importance to our ordinary thought about causes and effects. However, a serious question can be raised about whether the concept of constant conjunction is one Hume can legitimately employ. To be aware of past constant conjunctions one must be able to recollect them through memory. This means, for Hume, a return to his original theory of memory, which he found himself forced to revise in Section V because, according to his empiricist epistemology, recollection of the past is impossible. So Hume seems to be left facing two unpalatable alternatives: either to abandon the epistemological foundations on which Book I rests or to acknowledge that an essential element must be removed from the theory of causation he is developing.

The second contribution of Section VI is negative. Hume argues that the transition we make from causes to effects is not accomplished by reason; thus it is not an inference, in the ordinary sense of that term. To show this he maintains that we can neither demonstrate that a cause must produce a certain effect or even reach this conclusion through an appeal to experience. As a result, we can give no rational justification for the "inference." Finally, as an alternative to reason as the vehicle of our mental transitions from causes to effects Hume turns to imagination, concluding that the relations of contiguity, succession, and constant conjunction determine us to make a mental transition from an impression or idea to a related idea. Having rejected the theory that we can have any idea of a causal power in objects, whatever their nature might be, that produces effects, he substitutes, in place of "objective" causation what I have termed mental causation. Our next question, as we continue with Hume in pursuit of the idea of necessary connection, is to determine the relationship between that idea and his theory of mental causation. But our answer to this question will have to wait until chapter 12.

10

BELIEF

(Part III, Seĉtions VII–X)

Introduĉtion

Section VII of Part III, like Section V, may seem to be a digression from the main argument of Part III, for it, as well as the three sections that follow and elaborate it, is devoted largely to an explanation of the concept of *belief*. Although much of the discussion in these sections is digressive, this is not true of Hume's theory of belief itself, for he attempts to show that there is an essential connection between the mental transitions we make between causes and effects and what we believe. As he puts it, "Belief arises only from causation."[1] One object of this chapter will be to explain Hume's views concerning the relationship between causation and belief. Before this can be done, however, we need to understand just what Hume means by belief. I will devote Sections 1 and 2 to that question.

Hume makes a point of emphasizing the originality of his analysis of the nature of belief, writing, "This act of the mind [belief] has never yet been explain'd by any philosopher" (97 n. 1). But he has misgivings about his own explanation, because he finds no other words that can adequately convey what "belief" means. In an appendix note to Section VII he writes: "This operation of the mind, which forms the belief of any matter of fact, seems hitherto to have been one of the greatest mysteries of philosophy; tho' no one has so much as suspected, that there was any difficulty in explaining it. For my part I must own, that I find a considerable difficulty in the case; and that even when I think I understand the subject perfectly, I am at a loss for terms to express my meaning" (628).

After explaining the nature of belief in Section VII and three appendix notes, Hume turns in the subsequent sections to discussions of the causes of belief and its influence on our passions and actions. These sections, although they make several theoretical points, also contain long analyses of human psychology. They are perceptive and interesting in their own right but do not contribute greatly to Hume's philosophy. So I will not comment on them in detail but instead concentrate on points of philosophical significance. That Hume was less than sure of his conclusions on the subject of belief is evidenced by the fact that he adds four appendix notes to these sections. In the notes he elaborates and clarifies his original views.

Text

1. Hume's Definition of Belief (Section VII)

Hume begins Section VII by pointing out that, to believe something, we must have an idea or conception of it. The reason for this is obvious. If we had no idea of the thing, we would be unaware of it so could hardly possess any beliefs about it. Nevertheless, although possession of an idea is necessary, it is not sufficient for belief; we have many ideas about things we do not believe to exist. What, then, distinguishes belief ideas from non–belief ideas?

One answer to this question is to say that, when we believe in the existence of anything, we actually have two ideas, one of the thing itself and another of the thing's existence. Hume rejects this view, writing that "the belief of the existence joins no new ideas to those, which compose the idea of the object. When I think of God, when I think of him as existent, and when I believe him to be existent, my idea of him neither encreases nor diminishes."[2] We cannot distinguish the theist from the agnostic by arguing that, although they can both think of God and also think of him as existing, the theist possesses an additional idea, namely, the idea of God's "existence," that is distinct from his idea of God, an idea that the agnostic does not have. To support his view Hume points to the obvious fact that people disagree in their beliefs. To do so they must be thinking about the same things or be entertaining the same ideas. Otherwise there would be no disagreement. If a person believes that Caesar died in his bed and another person does not, their disagreement presupposes that they are thinking about the same thing—the place of Caesar's death. Furthermore, every idea the one can have about this historical event the other can have as well. Therefore, the disagreement cannot result from the fact that one possesses some additional idea the other lacks. This argument, Hume implies, can be generalized to cover all disagreements between our beliefs.[3]

If we cannot explain why we believe certain things by an appeal to a separate idea added to the ideas we have before our mind, the only alternative left, Hume concludes, is to examine the ideas we are contemplating themselves, to find some distinguishing mark that separates those we believe from those we do not. So Hume asks, "*Wherein consists the difference betwixt incredulity and belief?*" (95), a question he has already answered (but only in general terms) in the previous paragraph: "As this difference [between merely entertaining and believing an idea] lies not in the parts or composition of the idea, which we conceive; it follows, that it must lie in the *manner*, in which we conceive it" (95). Hume's object in the remainder of Section VII will be to explain what he means by the *manner* in which we conceive an idea when we believe it.

Hume's analysis is predictable. Since the only way in which our perceptions—and this includes our ideas—can differ from each other is in their relative force or vivacity, a belief idea must be one that is distinguished from other ideas in terms of this quality. "When you wou'd any way vary the idea of a particular object, you can only encrease or diminish its force and vivacity" (96). But a question still remains: Is a belief idea relatively forceful or relatively weak? Once again, Hume's answer is predictable: "As belief does nothing but vary the manner, in which we conceive any object, it can only bestow on our ideas an additional force and vivacity" (96). Hume then sums his argument up with a formal definition of belief. "An opinion, therefore, or belief may be most accurately defin'd, A LIVELY IDEA RELATED TO OR ASSOCIATED WITH A PRESENT IMPRESSION" (96). To make clear just what he means by the liveliness of a belief idea Hume uses an analogy. An idea, he argues, is like a color. A particular shade of a color may be either bright or dull. So, too, may an idea. When it is bright, it becomes a belief idea.[4]

Hume's definition of belief raises some problems. In the first place, his requirement that a belief idea be associated with a present impression seems too restrictive. Although this may be true of some of our beliefs, surely it is not true of all. For example, as I sit at my desk thinking about the meaning of "belief," I believe that I do not fully agree with Hume's definition of the concept. At the same time I am having numerous impressions—of my pencil, the paper I am writing on, the sound of the wind blowing in the trees, and so on. I find it hard to believe that my idea about Hume's definition of belief is associated with any of these impressions.

Hume can handle this problem. The definition of "belief" he gives in Section VII is deliberately restrictive. He is concerned at this point with beliefs we form about effects when we observe a cause. When, for instance, we see a flame we immediately have a lively idea of heat, which we associate with it. Although he maintains that most of our beliefs arise in this way, he is well aware that some do not. For that reason he describes belief elsewhere in Book I without any reference to a present impression. In Section X of Part III he writes: "Belief, therefore . . . is nothing but *a more vivid and intense conception of any idea*."[5] So we can conclude, in general, that Hume holds that, to say that we believe something, is to say that we have a lively or vivid idea of it.

But now we are faced with another problem. In chapter 8 we found that

Hume recognized his original account of memory in Part I to be inconsistent with his theory of ideas. So in Section V of Part III he revised it, concluding that, to remember something is simply to have a lively idea of it. But, if belief ideas and memory ideas are characterized only by the fact that they are lively, are all memory ideas belief ideas and vice versa? The first seems reasonable. If I remember that it rained yesterday I believe that it did. But what of the other? If I believe that the sun will shine tomorrow, do I remember that it will? This seems odd, to say the least.

To make his philosophy clear Hume needs to explain how beliefs differ from memories. Two possibilities suggest themselves. First, he might say that, although memory ideas and belief ideas are lively, they are not equally so. One kind is more lively than the other. Given his basic thesis that ideas differ from each other only in their relative vivacity, this would seem to be a natural way for him to distinguish between the two. But that raises a further question. Are memory ideas more lively than belief ideas or the reverse? Whether Hume would distinguish the two kinds of ideas in terms of their relative vivacity is an unanswerable question, because he never discusses the point anywhere in Book I.

Second, he might say that, although both kinds of ideas are equally vivid, memory ideas must—and belief ideas need not—involve a recollection of the past. This would, of course, mean a return to his original theory of memory. However, as we found in chapter 9, he has already made such a return in Section VI of Part III, in order to utilize the notion of constant conjunction in the development of his theory of causation. But now the question begins to press: How many times can his empiricist theory of ideas be violated and still remain the core of his philosophy?

I turn, finally, to Hume's claim that a belief idea is a lively idea. Is this necessarily true? Since the question is psychological, I will appeal to introspection to answer it. To sharpen the issue, we can ask: Are all my ideas when I believe vivid and all my ideas when I do not weak? I do not find this to be so. I would want to say, for example, that I believe I do not fully agree with Hume's definition of belief but I would certainly not claim that my ideas when I believe this are lively. On the other hand, when I look at El Greco's painting *The Burial of the Count of Orgaz*, I have a very lively mental picture (idea) of the count's soul ascending with the angels into heaven, but I do not for a moment believe that it did so.

Hume is not unaware of this problem. In the final paragraph of Section VII he addresses the kind of question I have just raised and concludes that I must be misdescribing my introspective evidence, writing, "This definition [of belief] will also be found to be entirely conformable to every one's feeling and experience" (97). In support of his conclusion he contrasts the strength of our ideas when we read something we believe with their weakness when we read something we do not believe. "If one person sits down to read a book as a romance, and another as a true history, they plainly receive the same ideas, and in the same order; nor does the incredulity of the one, and the belief of the other hinder them from putting the very same sense upon their author. His words produce the same ideas in both; tho' his testimony has not the same influence on them. The latter has a more lively conception of all the incidents" (97–98).

Although this example is hard to evaluate objectively, Hume seems to beg the question at issue by the way he formulates his illustration. When he writes, at the outset, that one person reads the book "as a romance" and the other "as a true history," he implies that the first reads it without believing its contents but the second reads it believing them. Under such circumstances it is plausible (but not necessary) to conclude with Hume that the ideas the second one has as he reads will be considerably more lively that those the first one has. But the existence of the second reader's lively ideas does not constitute his belief; rather it presupposes it. If he did not already believe what he was reading, he may very well, just like the first reader, have not had such lively ideas. To make his point Hume should have asked his two subjects to read the book *without* letting them know whether it was romance or history. Had he done so, he might very well have found one replying to him that he found it exciting but that he didn't believe it because the incidents it portrayed did not agree with the historical facts and the other replying that he found it dull but that he believed it because it agreed with the historical facts. Because a person's belief in what he reads can vary independently of the liveliness of his ideas as he reads, Hume seems to be mistaken in identifying the two.[6]

We can reasonably conclude from this illustration that the meaning Hume gives to the concept of belief differs substantially from our ordinary understanding of the term. Since he derives his notion of belief largely from his epistemological assumptions in Part I about the nature of our perceptions, we can fairly classify "belief" as yet another technical term of his philosophy.

Hume does not end Section VII with his definition of belief but adds some summary comments, including his book illustration as well as a lengthy footnote (96–97). The footnote needs some consideration because it seems to contradict the text. The point concerns causal "reasoning." After taking issue with the "logicians'" division of the acts of the understanding into conception, judgment, and reasoning, Hume makes a statement about causal "reasoning" that seems inconsistent not only with what he says on the same page in the text but with his analysis of causal "inference" in Section VI. The passage in question reads: "We infer a cause immediately from its effect; and this inference is not only a true species of reasoning, but the strongest of all others" (97 n. 1). But just above this statement he had written in the text: "Reason can never satisfy us that the existence of any one object does ever imply that of another; so that when we pass from the impression of one to the idea or belief of another, we are not determin'd by reason, but by custom or a principle of association" (97).

This apparent contradiction can be resolved. Hume is simply using the term "reason" in different senses in the two passages. The passage in the text is the theoretically important one; there he is reiterating his view that causal "reasoning" is not an activity of the reason but of the imagination, or the association of ideas. In the footnote statement he is using the term "reasoning" to indicate that the transition we make from a cause to an effect is not a direct perception but involves an action or movement of the mind. This is apparent from the context in which the statement occurs.[7]

2. The Appendix Elaborations (Pages 623–27, 628–29, and 636)

Hume adds three appendix notes to Section VII. All are concerned with the same point—his definition of belief and, in particular, the adjectives that should be used to describe best the special manner in which we conceive belief ideas.[8] Although he makes some refinements in his original description in the text, where, as we have seen, he uses the word "lively" to describe belief ideas, it is apparent that he is not fully satisfied with the adequacy of his refined description, for he writes, at the end of the second note, that "belief consists not in the nature and order of our ideas, but in the manner of their conception, and in their feeling to the mind. I confess, that 'tis impossible to explain perfectly this feeling or manner of conception. We may make use of words, that express something near it. But its true and proper name is *belief*" (629).

But let us examine in greater detail the additions Hume makes to his account of belief in his appendix notes. He begins the first note by suggesting that belief ideas might be explained by saying that they are complex, consisting not only of the simple conceptions of their object but of an additional idea as well, either (1) an idea of existence or reality or (2) an idea of reflection, or a passion. Hume rejects both of these suggestions, offering a number of arguments against each (623–26). I will not elaborate his arguments because they are clearly stated in the note and are largely repetitious of points he made in the text. Suffice it to repeat his conclusion: "These arguments . . . sufficiently prove, that belief only modifies the idea or conception; and renders it different to the feeling, without producing any distinct impression."[9]

Accepting with Hume that the "feeling" of our idea when we believe something consists in the special manner in which we conceive it, we can go on to see how he describes this feeling. Hume addresses this point in his second appendix note. "An idea assented to [believed] *feels* different from a fictitious idea, that the fancy alone presents to us: And this different feeling I endeavour to explain by calling it a superior *force*, or *vivacity*, or *solidity*, or *firmness*, or *steadiness*" (629). This list of somewhat vague terms illustrates why Hume was not fully satisfied with his explanation of belief. We should, I think, sympathize with him here. Although all of us would probably agree with him that when we believe something our state of mind is different from what it is when we do not believe, still, if we were asked to give adjectives to describe this special state, I doubt if we would find many that are less vague than those of Hume. We do, as he notes, readily recognize the state, but we cannot describe it precisely in words.

Nevertheless, Hume has expanded, and illuminated, his original definition of belief with these adjectives. The five can be divided into three groups. (1) "Force" and "vivacity." These two appear to express the same notion, both seeming to be synonymous with the adjective "lively" that he had used in his original definition in Section VII. (2) "Solidity" and "firmness." These two seem definitely to supplement the original definition, suggesting that our belief ideas have a special weight or gravity in our minds. (3) "Steadiness." This adjective also expands Hume's definition; belief ideas are not fluctuating but remain steady in our minds.[10]

Hume's amplified description of our states of belief merits some comment. I have already, in section 1, expressed some misgivings about characteristic (1) of belief ideas. Characteristic (3), besides being vague, is subject to the qualification that we often change our minds, disbelieving now what we had believed a short time ago. Characteristic (2) seems, at least to me, to be the most expressive of the characteristics Hume lists; our belief ideas do have a special feeling of solidity and firmness about them. However, we can express this feeling in other terms that describe it better. I would suggest that, when we believe something, we have an attitude of "assent" to it or "acquiescence" in it or even "conviction" about it. It might, however, be argued that these are not feelings. I would agree that the terms I have used express more than feelings (a point I will elaborate later), but I think that the mental states they describe have a special "feel" about them that we can directly experience when we believe something. To sum up, although Hume's descriptive terms help to give us a picture of the feeling we experience when we believe something, one can hardly fault his conclusion "that 'tis impossible to explain perfectly this feeling."[11]

The elaborations Hume gives in his appendix notes raise a further question: Why did he define "belief" in Section VII by describing it as a "lively" idea? This adjective is probably the least felicitous of those he might have used. The answer to this question surely lies in Hume's original theory of ideas in Part I. In the first paragraph of the *Treatise* he distinguishes impressions from ideas in terms of their relative force and liveliness and in Section III he distinguishes memory ideas from imagination ideas in the same way. Not only did Hume make their relative vivacity the mark by which to distinguish our various kinds of perceptions from each other but in Section VII he reiterates the point that it is the *only* change that can occur in an idea, writing that "as the same idea can only be vary'd by a variation of its degree of force and vivacity; it follows upon the whole, that belief is a lively idea" (97). However, in his appendix notes he recognizes that other adjectives than simple liveliness seem to offer a more adequate description of our state of mind when we believe something. In his final appendix note he writes: "The second error may be found in Book I. page 96. where I say, that two ideas of the same object can only be different by their different degrees of force and vivacity. I believe there are other differences among ideas, which cannot properly be comprehended under these terms. Had I said, that two ideas of the same object can only be different by their different *feeling*, I shou'd have been nearer the truth."[12]

Before leaving Hume's appendix notes we need to consider another point they contain, one of importance. In his attempt to explain the special feeling an idea we believe has, Hume makes a statement that runs counter to a central argument he has been developing in Part III. It concerns the role of imagination in our beliefs. He writes that "as it is impossible, that [imagination] can ever, of itself, reach belief, 'tis evident, that belief consists not in the nature and order of our ideas, but in the manner of their conception, and in their feeling to the mind. . . . [Belief] is something *felt* by the mind, which distinguishes the ideas of the judgment from the fictions of the imagination" (629). Hume seems to be saying here that, since the imagination cannot generate belief, this must be accomplished by something he calls "judgment," which apparently is a faculty different from the imagination.

This distinction raises two problems. (1) At the beginning of the *Treatise* Hume wrote: "When any impression has been present with the mind, it again makes its appearance there as an idea; and this it may do after two different ways. . . . The faculty, by which we repeat our impressions in the first manner, is called the MEMORY, and the other the IMAGINATION" (8–9). If a belief idea is not generated by the imagination but by the judgment, it would seem to follow that judgment is equivalent to memory. Is this what Hume means? He never indicates anything of the kind in the passage under consideration and a bit later in Part III he implies that it is not. Speaking of the different "systems" we construct by memory and through the relations of cause and effect, he concludes: "The first of these systems is the object of the memory and senses; the second of the judgment."[13] Since the judgment is different from the memory, we are forced back into identifying it with the imagination. But this is just what Hume denies in the appendix statement. Must we then introduce a new kind of idea into Hume's epistemology; namely, a judgment idea?

If we adopt the last suggestion, we face another problem. (2) Hume begins the appendix in which the puzzling statement appears by implying that the note is concerned with beliefs about any "matter of fact" (628). With certain exceptions (to be discussed later) our beliefs about matters of fact rest on the causal "inferences" we make. But one of Hume's major theses in the development of his theory of causation thus far in Part III has been that such "inferences" are the work of the imagination. As he summarized his view a bit earlier: "When the mind . . . passes from the idea or impression of one object to the idea or *belief* of another, it is not determin'd by reason, but by certain principles, which associate together the ideas of these objects, and unite them in the *imagination*."[14] According to this theory (for which Hume has argued in the preceding pages) our beliefs based on the causal "inferences" we make are generated in the imagination. So, if they are the work of the judgment, that faculty cannot be distinguished from the imagination, as Hume attempts to do in the appendix note. The statement in the note is perplexing because it suggests an activity of the mind called "judgment" that does not seem to have a place to fit into Hume's epistemology. I will say more on the subject later in this chapter.

3. Does Hume's Definition Define "Belief"? (Section VII)

In section 1 I raised several questions about specific points in Hume's definition of belief in Section VII. Here I will consider his definition as a whole, questioning whether it offers an illuminating explication of the concept. When we talk about our beliefs we use expressions that usually begin "I believe that . . ." We say, for example, "I believe that flame causes heat" or "I believe that Caesar died in the Roman Senate." Although Hume has contributed to our understanding of the psychology of belief, particularly in his appendix notes, his concentration on this point seems to leave the central meaning of belief untouched. Belief, as a state of mind, has a psychological component, but to understand the concept we must concentrate on its epistemological dimension. So conceived, belief is a conviction about some state of affairs. When I say, "I believe that Caesar died in the Roman Senate," I mean that I accept this event as a historical fact, or assent to the proposition "Caesar died in the Roman Senate" as true.

Why did Hume not give this ordinary—and obvious—definition of belief? This is not an easy question to answer but some of the following considerations are worth noting. It might be that he simply took the epistemological component for granted; but then it would seem curious that he should offer a formal definition of belief and not even mention that component.[15] More important to our understanding of why Hume proceeded as he did, however, is the context in which he offered his definition. Underlying his discussion is the assumption that belief arises only from causation. Having rejected an "objective" account of causation, because we have no experience of any power in a cause that produces its effect, he begins to elaborate his own alternative explanation of the cause-effect relationship. When, he argues, we have experienced two objects repeatedly appearing in the relations of contiguity and succession, we label the first "cause" and the second "effect" and on the appearance of the one immediately form an idea of the other. But we go further; we anticipate the appearance of the other or believe that we will experience it. After many exceptionless experiences of their connection, when we see a flame we immediately believe that we will feel heat. The idea we form of the effect, Hume concludes, must be different in some way from those ideas we form under circumstances in which we are not making cause-effect transitions; otherwise we should have no way to distinguish our causal "inferences" from noncausal ones. What more natural way could there be to set such ideas apart than by using his standard criterion of relative force or liveliness? So, given his concentration on developing his new theory of causation, it is understandable that Hume should define "belief" in the way he does.

Although we may differ with Hume about the importance of its psychological component to an adequate definition of belief, we can agree that such a component is necessary, whether we describe it as a lively idea, a firm idea, or a conviction about truth. We cannot believe anything unless we conceive of it or, in Hume's terms, have an idea of it. We cannot, for example, believe that heat is an effect of flame unless we have an idea of heat; no more can we believe that God exists unless we have an idea of God. I emphasize this requirement not only because it is necessary to belief but also because we will have occasion to return to it later.

4. The Causes of Belief (Section VIII)

Having defined "belief" as a "lively idea related to or associated with a present impression," Hume turns, in Section VIII, to the question: What causes belief ideas to possess the liveliness they do? Why is it that, when I see a flame, my imagination immediately generates a lively idea of heat and I believe that I will experience heat? Hume begins the section with an explanation of why this occurs, then devotes the rest of his discussion to an elaboration and defense of his view, appealing directly to experience for support and making use of a variety of illustrations. "I wou'd willingly establish it as a general maxim in the science of human nature, *that when any impression becomes present to us, it not only transports the mind to such ideas as are related to it, but likewise communicates to them a share of its force and vivacity*" (98).

This theory contains two theses. (1) It reasserts the view, which Hume had elaborated in Section VI, that our experience of an impression causes our imagination to generate an idea associated with it. When we see a flame we imagine heat. (2) Furthermore, the impression not only causes the related idea to appear; it transfers some of its own vivacity to the idea, thus making it a belief idea. When we see the flame we not only have an idea of heat but a lively idea of it, or, in other words, we believe that heat will follow.

Hume continues his argument by listing three relations between the original impression and the idea that cause the latter to be enlivened: (1) Resemblance. If I see a picture of an absent friend that resembles him, I find my idea of him "inliven'd" (99). (2) Contiguity. If I am away from my home, but still nearby, and see something that relates to it, the idea of home generated in my imagination is more lively than it would have been had I been far away.[16] (3) Causation. Hume gives the example of the clothes and furniture of a saint; when the devotee views them his experience causes him to have a lively idea of their maker and user. After referring specifically to the causal relation, Hume sums up his view in the following way:

> 'Tis certain we must have an idea of every matter of fact, which we believe. 'Tis certain, that this idea arises only from a relation to a present perception. 'Tis certain, that the belief super-adds nothing to the idea, but only changes our manner of conceiving it, and renders it more strong and lively. . . . There enters nothing into this operation of the mind but a present impression, a lively idea, and a relation or association in the fancy [imagination] betwixt the impression and idea. (101)

Continuing with his analysis of the causal relation as a source of belief, Hume points out, first, that our belief that a certain effect will follow from a given cause cannot be based on a power or quality in the object we call the cause because such powers and qualities are "entirely unknown" (102), and, second, that a single impression does not give rise to a belief in an effect to follow but that the belief arises only after we have experienced an exceptionless repetition or constant conjunction of two impressions in the past. Because of our past experience of constant conjunctions, he concludes, the lively idea of the effect, or our belief that it will follow the cause, arises immediately in our consciousness, "without any new operation of the reason or imagination" (102). He attributes our immediate mental transition from an impression of a cause to a belief in an effect to custom, or, to mention another term he uses later, to habit.

5. POETRY, MUSIC, AND PHILOSOPHY (SECTION VIII)

Hume concludes his account of the way in which the relations of resemblance, contiguity, and causation enliven our ideas to produce belief with a remarkable passage, but one that can easily be misunderstood. Because of its importance to his philosophy in Book I, I will examine it in detail. Hume writes: "Thus all probable reasoning is nothing but a species of sensation. 'Tis not solely in poetry and music, we must follow our taste and sentiment, but likewise in philosophy. When I am convinc'd of any principle, 'tis only an idea, which strikes more strongly upon me. When I give the preference to one set of arguments above another, I do nothing but decide from my feeling concerning the superiority of their influence" (103). The key to Hume's description of his philosophy lies in the first sentence. In Section VI of Part III he had concluded that "probable reasoning" or "reasoning" about matters of fact is not the work of reason but of imagination. It consists in mental "transitions" or "actions of the mind" for which no rational justification can be given. In my summary of his view in chapter 9, I concluded that it should be described as nonrationalism rather than irrationalism.[17] But why should such probable "reasoning" then become, as he now writes, "a species of sensation," and what does this phrase mean?

To answer the second question first, I think Hume has in mind here something like those sensations he listed at the beginning of the *Treatise*—"heat or cold, thirst or hunger, pleasure or pain" (8)—which we do not perceive through one of our five senses but, nevertheless, directly feel. This interpretation seems to be supported by his reference to "taste," "sentiment," and "feeling" in the sentences that follow. My first question is harder to answer. If probable "reasoning" involves a mental transition, usually from a cause to an effect, how can it be a sensation, which is a direct experience? I am not sure just how Hume would respond to this question. One possibility is that he is writing a bit loosely and means only to make the negative point that such "reasoning" is not an activity of reason. This suggestion is lent some support by his use of the words "nothing but" in the sentence. Another possibility is that, as he has pointed out a bit earlier, our beliefs are based on custom, so require no deliberate action of the mind. As he puts it, "The belief, which attends the present impression, and is produc'd by a number of past impressions and conjunctions ... arises immediately, without any new operation of the reason or imagination."[18] Nevertheless, one could wish that he had stated this important point more clearly than he did, in particular, that he had explained just what he meant by the term "sensation."

In the remainder of the passage Hume applies his conclusion about probable "reasoning" to his own philosophy. At this point we must note a distinction he does not himself make explicit. His statement that his preference for one set of arguments over another rests on his feelings applies only to probable "reasoning" about matters of fact and not to demonstration. Whenever in Book I he reaches a conclusion by an argument based solely on the relations of ideas, Hume is not engaging in probable "reasoning" so need not appeal to his feelings to determine what conclusion to accept. On such occasions reason is competent; the conclusion he reaches is capable of rational justification. It is only with "reasoning" about matters of fact that his decision must rest on taste.

This distinction gives rise to a question. What proportion of Hume's arguments in Book I to this point have consisted solely in the relations of ideas, hence are rationally defensible, and what proportion have dealt with matters of fact, and hence have been accepted by Hume simply because he has a sentimental preference for them? To answer this question adequately would require a careful review of every argument he has offered, in order to place it in the appropriate one of the two categories. Although such a task is one a scholar seeking a full understanding of Hume's mental processes ought to complete, it is far beyond the scope of this book. I can only offer a generalization here. Beginning with Section I, Hume has in Part III developed a distinction between knowledge and opinion. The former is based on the comparison of ideas and the latter is based on experience and concerns matters of fact. In Section I Hume concluded that only arithmetic and algebra qualify as knowledge, everything else we believe falling into the category of opinion. If we apply Hume's demarcation between knowledge and opinion to his philosophy in Book I—and even if we relax his standards to permit more than mathematics into the first category—we must acknowledge that most of Hume's arguments we have thus far encountered concern matters of fact and have rested on an appeal to experience. Indeed, Hume has often reiterated this point in reference to his arguments.[19] So we are led to agree with his conclusion in the passage I have reproduced that much of what he has written so far in Book I consists not in rational argumentation but rather in the expression of his personal preferences.

At this point some readers of the *Treatise* may feel cheated. They have been reading the *Treatise* in good faith, assuming that Hume was, like other philosophers, reaching conclusions through the use of arguments he considered to be cogent. Now they find that this is a misapprehension. He tells us that most of what he has written is not rational argumentation at all but simply the expression of his personal taste and sentiment. Book I is emotional autobiography. It may be of interest to the historian or psychologist, but is certainly of no concern to the philosopher.

Although one may sympathize with such a reaction, I believe it can and must, if we are in good conscience to continue our study of Hume, be avoided. And it can be, because the fact that Hume accepts arguments and conclusions simply because they appeal to him emotionally—even though he is incapable of supporting them through rational argument—is logically consistent with the possibility that the arguments he uses are cogent and the conclusions he reaches true. In the remainder of my commentary I will operate on that assumption, continuing to treat Hume's arguments as genuine philosophical arguments and evaluating the conclusions he reaches on the assessments I make of those arguments. Hume presumably would claim that I am deceiving myself in doing this, because my evaluations will be nothing more than the expression of *my* feelings. If he were to do so, however, he would be begging the question by assuming that all "philosophizing" about matters of fact is nonrational. But that is his assumption, not mine. So, although Hume realizes that he can offer no arguments to support his own philosophy, I—and anyone else who does not accept his characterization of philosophy—can.

However much one may disagree with Hume's construal of his own philosophy, we must admire his candor in stating his position with such forthrightness. That the passage I have been discussing is no momentary idiosyncrasy but a view Hume means to be taken seriously is plain from the fact that it is a consequence he believes to follow from his nonrationalism about opinion, or beliefs concerning matters of fact. Finally, it is a view about which he will have more to say in Part IV. So I will return to it again toward the end of this book.

6. Minor Modifications (Section VIII)

Although much of what Hume says in the remainder of his discussion of belief and related topics is anticlimactic, he makes several points of considerable interest and importance. In Section VIII he adds three modifications to the account he has given of our causal "inferences." He points out, first, that we often make such "inferences" without thinking about past conjunctions of cause and effect that we have experienced. For example, we refrain from attempting to ford a deep river without pausing to reflect. Our response is automatic; although memory is operative, it functions subconsciously. As Hume puts it, "Experience may produce a belief and a judgment of causes and effects by a secret operation, and without being once thought of."[20]

The second modification Hume makes concerns the necessity of constant conjunction or custom to causal "inference." He points out that it is possible to recognize a causal connection after a single experience of it. What he has mainly in mind here is a scientific experiment in which the investigator, after finding a cause to produce a given effect under carefully controlled conditions, without any further repetition of his experiment assumes that it will always do so under the same conditions. This assumption is explained, Hume concludes, by the fact that, although the scientist has had experience of only one case of this particular causal relation, he has had countless previous experiences of the second-order principle that, when like objects are placed in like situations, they will produce like effects. As he concludes: "The connexion of the ideas [of the cause and the effect] is not habitual after one experiment; but this connexion is comprehended under another principle, that is habitual" (105).

Hume's final alteration is more substantive. Throughout his earlier discussion he had emphasized the point that the lively ideas that constitute beliefs must gain their vivacity from their association with a present impression. Now, however, he recognizes the somewhat odd fact that a person may have an idea, which is, according to the Empiricist Principle, necessarily derived from a previous impression even though he has forgotten the impression from which it is derived. Nevertheless, he can not only conclude that he had had such an impression but also believe this. If he does, Hume asks, what is the source of his lively belief idea that he has had the impression? It must, he concludes, be the idea he now has, whose correspondent impression he has forgotten. In such a situation, as he puts it: "The idea here supplies the place of an impression" (106).

7. CAUSATION, CONTIGUITY, RESEMBLANCE, AND BELIEF (SECTION IX)

As I noted in the introduction to this chapter, Hume says that, of the three relations that determine us to associate ideas—contiguity, resemblance, and causation—only the last gives rise to belief. In Section IX, however, he goes on to modify this view, acknowledging that the other two relations can also produce the same effect, illustrating his arguments with several examples that reveal his acute perception of human psychology. Because the modifications he makes in his position are of relatively minor theoretical importance, I will be brief in my account of them. In addition, I will discuss some other points of interest he makes in the section.

Hume begins by pointing out what may seem to be an inconsistency in his theory. If, as he has argued, the relations of contiguity, resemblance, and causation (1) are derived from the same principles and (2) have the same effects in enforcing and enlivening our ideas, and that (3) belief is just a forcible and vivid idea, it would seem that all three relations can generate belief (107). Yet, he has concluded, "we find by experience, that belief arises only from causation" (107).

Instead of responding to this objection directly, Hume introduces a new topic whose relevance to the question seems opaque. The mind, he writes, forms two systems of perceptions. The first is composed of the ideas of things we remember; of it he writes, "Every particular of that system . . . we are pleas'd to call a *reality*" (108). The second system is based on custom or the relation of cause and effect. Because the mind finds itself determined to view the ideas arising from this relation without making any change in them, "it forms them into a new system, which it likewise dignifies with the title of *realities*."[21] Distinguishing the two systems from each other, he writes: "The first of these systems is the object of the memory and senses; the second of the judgment" (108). In the next sentences he makes it clear that judgment is part of the faculty of imagination.

Not only do these systems differ from each other in their sources but the second is by far the more important of the two. According to Hume: "'Tis this latter principle, which peoples the world, and brings us acquainted with such existences, as by their removal in time and place, lie beyond the reach of the senses and memory. By means of it I paint the universe in my *imagination*" (108—italics added). Continuing, Hume illustrates the second system by reference to our ideas of Rome (a city he had never visited). Generalizing, we can say that this system produces our ideas not only of places we have never been but of times we have never witnessed. Thus it is the source of our ideas of history and of our predictions about the future. Hume is not exaggerating when he says he paints the universe with it. Finally, and importantly, this system, or universe, is a construction of the imagination.

Having said this, however, we find ourselves confronted with a problem. Immediately after having given his imaginative description of Rome, Hume concludes by writing: "All this, and every thing else, which I believe, are nothing but ideas; tho' by their force and settled order . . . they distinguish themselves from the other ideas, which are merely the offspring of the *imagination*" (108—italics added). This statement is puzzling because it clearly contradicts the statement I reproduced just above it. Since both statements appear in the same paragraph one should assume that Hume is not denying what he has just written. The alternative is that he means something different by the term "imagination" in the second passage from what he means in the first. I will explore this difference further in section 8.

Hume, unfortunately, does not make clear the relevance of his discussion of systems to the issue before him but leaves the topic to return to the objection he had raised earlier. He offers a series of arguments and counterarguments, including illustrations, designed to determine whether, in psychological fact, the relations of contiguity and resemblance are capable of generating belief. His conclusion, with certain exceptions, is a compromise, marked by some ambivalence. Generally, he argues that contiguity and resemblance, operating alone, have little power to generate belief. "But tho' I cannot altogether exclude the relations of resemblance and contiguity from operating on the fancy in this manner [i.e., to produce belief], 'tis observable that, when single, their influence is very feeble and uncertain" (109). Later, however, he modifies this view. "Contiguity and resemblance have an effect much inferior to causation; but still have some effect, and augment the conviction of any opinion, and the vivacity of any conception" (110). To support this conclusion he introduces several interesting illustrations.

Toward the end of the section Hume makes a noteworthy point, claiming that a lack of resemblance can have the effect of destroying belief. "As resemblance, when conjoin'd with causation, fortifies our reasonings; so the want of it in any very great degree is able almost entirely to destroy them" (113). To support this view, he argues that religious people, though they profess a belief in immortality, do not really believe in it because such a life after death bears little resemblance to life on earth. He offers two graphic illustrations to confirm his point.

> The *Roman Catholicks* are certainly the most zealous of any sect in the christian world; and yet you'll find few among the more sensible people of that communion, who do not blame the *Gunpowder-treason,* and the massacre of St. *Bartholomew,* as cruel and barbarous, tho' projected or executed against those very people, whom without any scruple they condemn to eternal and infinite punishments. All we can say in excuse for this inconsistency is, that they really do not believe what they affirm concerning a future state.[22]

Hume concludes the section with a discussion of the effects of education in the formation and strengthening of belief. Just as the constant conjunction of two impressions in our experience leads us, by a customary transition, to believe that, when we experience the first, we will experience the second, so when an idea repeatedly strikes on the mind, it has a similar effect of generating our belief in it. "Education," as Hume uses the term here, consists in the repeated inculcation of ideas into the mind so is, in effect, the same as rote learning or indoctrination. Such inculcation Hume acknowledges to have an exceptionally strong but often deleterious influence on our beliefs.

Here I would add a brief comment to my earlier discussion of Hume's statements about "systems." Although he does not develop the argument explicitly one can glean from the tenor of his account of contiguity and resemblance later in Section IX that he is probably suggesting a coherence theory of belief. Our beliefs form some sort of coherent system. To the extent that an idea coheres with this system we believe it; to the extent that it does not, we disbelieve it. However, the connection between systemization and belief is far from secure, as Hume emphasizes in his discussion of education. The idea of a coherence theory of belief is of considerable interest; it is regrettable that Hume did not say more about it.

8. Probable "Reasoning" and Imagination (Section IX)

Hume adds a footnote at the end of Section IX; because of its importance I will reproduce it at length and comment on it in some detail.

> In general we may observe, that as our assent to all probable reasonings is founded on the vivacity of ideas, it resembles many of those whimsies and prejudices, which are rejected under the opprobrious character of being the offspring of the imagination. By this expression it appears that the word, imagination, is commonly us'd in two different senses; and tho' nothing be more contrary to true philosophy, than this inaccuracy, yet in the following reasonings I have often been oblig'd to fall into it. When I oppose the imagination to the memory, I mean the faculty, by which we form our fainter ideas. When I oppose it to reason, I mean the same faculty, excluding only our demonstrative and probable reasonings. (117–18 n. 1)

To understand Hume's point in this note, we can begin with his acknowledgment that he often uses the word "imagination" inaccurately, hence in a way contrary to true philosophy. In the note he "opposes" imagination to three things—memory, demonstration, and probable reasoning. Wherein does his inaccuracy lie? First, it is certainly accurate to oppose imagination to memory in the way he does. As he concluded in his revised theory of memory in Section V, imagination ideas are distinguished from memory ideas by being faint. Second, a main point of Section VI was to differentiate the transitions made by the imagination from demonstrative reasoning, so to "oppose" the two is also accurate. But, third, how can imagination "oppose" probable "reasoning" when the latter is a function of the imagination? As we have seen in the last two chapters, one of Hume's central theses in Part III is that the "transitions" or "actions of the mind" that occur when we engage in what he calls probable "reasoning," in distinction from demonstration, are the work of the imagination. So we can conclude that the inaccuracy of which he is speaking in this footnote lies in his distinguishing imagination from probable "reasoning." The distinction he wishes to make is not between imagination and something else but lies entirely *within* imagination itself.

What, then, is this distinction? Although Hume does not explicate it precisely, its nature is apparent from several remarks he makes. First, in the note he refers to the "whimsies and prejudices" of the imagination. Earlier in Section IX he spoke of such things as "the mere fictions of the imagination" (108) and a "loose floating image of the fancy" (116). On the other side he writes that the objects the relation of cause and effect presents are "fixt and unalterable" (110). Also, to repeat a passage I reproduced in the previous section, he writes: "All this, and every thing else, which I believe, are nothing but ideas; tho' by their force and settled order ... they distinguish themselves from the other ideas, which are merely the offspring of the imagination" (108). To generalize, we can say that the distinction Hume is making lies between ideas that are loose and those that are firm or between those that are the product of "whimsy" and those that are the product of "judgment."[23] Thus we can distinguish, say, between the scientist in his laboratory and the daydreamer building castles in the air. Nevertheless, the difference between the two is not one of kind but only of degree. Since the mental activities of both, being the work of imagination, lie outside of reason, they are equally nonrational.

9. BELIEF, ACTION, AND THE PASSIONS (SECTION X)

Hume completes his theory of belief in Section X with a discussion of the manner in which our beliefs influence our actions and our passions. This topic, at least, occupies him at the beginning of the section, but it is followed by a long, convoluted account of the way in which our passions and imagination influence our beliefs. The complexities of his argument in these latter passages, added to the fact that he pursues the issue at length in an appendix note, indicate that Hume was aware of problems in his philosophy. Although many of the things he says in both the section and the appendix note seem unexceptionable, it is difficult to reconcile them with the theories of probable "reasoning," imagination, and belief he has developed in Part III.

Hume begins the section with a reiteration of his nonrationalism: "The far greatest part of our reasonings, with all our actions and passions, can be deriv'd from nothing but custom and habit" (118). He then proceeds to explain the ways in which our beliefs move us to action, but he does so in an oblique manner. He points out that pleasure and pain are the chief moving principles of our actions. However, these perceptions can make their appearance in the mind in two different ways, either as impressions or as ideas. Impressions of pleasure and pain "always actuate the soul, and that in the highest degree" (118), but their ideas do not always have the same effect. Fortunately, Hume continues, we are not moved to act exclusively by either our impressions of pleasure and pain or by their ideas; thus we avoid the consequences of acting rashly and precipitately, on the one hand, or haphazardly, on the other. "Nature has . . . chosen a medium, and has neither bestow'd on every idea of good and evil the power of actuating the will, nor yet has entirely excluded them from this influence" (119). Specifically, he argues, the ideas that influence our passions—and, hence, our actions—are those that we believe. Because they are forceful and vivacious these ideas become equal (or almost equal) to our impressions (of pleasure and pain) in arousing our passions and moving us to act. "The effect . . . of belief is to raise up a simple idea to an equality with our impressions, and bestow on it a like influence on the passions. This effect it can only have by making an idea approach an impression in force and vivacity" (119).

It is hardly questionable that Hume is correct in concluding that ideas in which we believe have a much greater power of moving us to act than those in which we do not. That they have this power because of their greater vivacity, however, seems considerably less evident. What appears to be missing from his account is that we act on those things we believe because, in believing them, we accept them to be true.

In the fourth paragraph of Section X Hume reverses the direction of his argument, by pointing out that, although our beliefs arouse our passions, so too do our passions influence our beliefs. "As belief is almost absolutely requisite to the exciting our passions, so the passions in their turn are very favourable to belief" (120). As examples of this psychological phenomenon he cites the case of the coward who, because he lives in a state of fear, believes himself to be surrounded by dangers, and that of the melancholy person, who believes every event to be sad. Furthermore, Hume continues, other passions, such as admiration and surprise, enliven our ideas, thus create belief; "quacks and projectors [confidence men]," he notes, "meet with a more easy faith upon account of their magnificent pretensions" (120).

Hume completes the section with a complex discussion, to which he adds a long appendix note. The points he is trying to make in this discussion are diffuse and obscure, partly because he never states clearly what his objective is and partly because he uses the central terms, like "belief" and "imagination," loosely. The difficulties are also compounded by the facts (a) that he employs the "inaccurate" distinction he had made in the footnote at the end of Section IX, between probable "reasonings" and "whimsies" and (b) that he interweaves descriptive statements with normative ones, without seeming to recognize that he is doing so and, therefore, without providing any satisfactory justification for the latter. From the tenor of these passages it seems evident that Hume was aware that he was facing problems in his theory of belief—the long appendix note bears witness to this—but was not quite sure exactly what the problems were or how to solve them. I think, however, that we can bring his problems to light. There seem to be two main issues to be resolved. (1) Do we ordinarily believe things based on experience or causal "reasoning" (science and history) and do not believe things based on "whimsy" or "fancy" (poetry)? (2) Ought we to believe the former and not the latter?

Hume spends much of his time on question (1), which is one of descriptive psychology. His discussion is perceptive but inconclusive. He begins by arguing that probable "reasoning" or "judgment" is more effective in producing belief than fancy. He supports this conclusion by pointing out that poets give their poems historical settings "in order to procure a more easy reception for the whole" (122). But he adds, on the other hand, that poetry often has a stronger influence on belief than experience. "A vigorous and strong imagination is of all talents the most proper to procure belief and authority. 'Tis difficult for us to withhold our assent from what is painted out to us in all the colours of eloquence; and the vivacity produc'd by the fancy is in many cases greater than that which arises from custom and experience" (123). I think we can agree with Hume's conclusions about descriptive psychology. The reasons we have for believing things do vary from person to person and from time to time.[24]

The second question is much more difficult. Ought we to believe science and history but not poetry? Although Hume does not answer this question explicitly, he makes several remarks that strongly suggest an answer. One passage, in particular, bears repeating.

> As a lively imagination very often degenerates into madness or folly, and bears it a great resemblance in its operations; so they influence the judgment after the same manner, and produce belief. . . . When the imagination . . . acquires such a vivacity as disorders all its powers and faculties, there is no means of distinguishing betwixt *truth and falshood;* but every loose fiction or idea, having the same influence as the impressions of the memory, or *the conclusions of the judgment,* is receiv'd on the same footing. . . . A present impression and a customary transition are now no longer necessary to inliven our ideas. Every chimera of the brain is as vivid and intense as any of those inferences, which we formerly dignify'd with the name of conclusions concerning matters of fact . . .
> We may observe the same effect of poetry in a lesser degree.[25]

This Platonic passage may well strike a chord with philosophical readers. Yet it conceals a problem. Is the distinction one Hume can legitimately make? The implication that we should not believe poetry because it deals in fictions but should believe science and history because they represent truth assumes that we have some way of justifying the claim that the conclusions of our probable "reasonings" are true. But, by his nonrationalism regarding matters of fact Hume has long since foreclosed on this possibility. The scientist is in the same situation as the poet; although both may be speaking the truth, neither can give any reasons for believing he is.

Summary

In Sections VII through X of Part III Hume engages in a long and complex analysis of the nature of belief. His approach is primarily psychological although, particularly near the end, he attempts to draw normative conclusions about our beliefs. His concern in these sections is limited to beliefs about matters of fact, which rest on probable "reasoning" rather than on demonstration. In Section VII he provides a definition of belief—as a lively idea related to or associated with a present impression.

Because this definition is limited to beliefs based on causal "reasoning" Hume recognizes it to be too narrow. Not everything we believe is a result of the cause-effect relation. The relations of resemblance and contiguity also influence our beliefs. So, too, does education, or indoctrination. Our passions or emotions have their effects as well. Finally, many of our beliefs stem from our "imagination." (Since all of our beliefs, including those based on causal "reasoning," are the work of the imagination, Hume finds that he has to make a distinction between two senses of imagination, which he concedes to be inaccurate, in order to talk about this special group of beliefs.) Given all the sources of belief, Hume generalizes his definition, describing a belief idea as simply an idea that is lively. However, in his appendix notes he expresses his dissatisfaction with this account, stressing the special "feeling" of ideas we believe.

Hume's account of belief gives rise to three related problems, all of them serious. (1) Since all of our beliefs about matters of fact are based on probable "reasoning," which is the work of the imagination rather than of reason, they are nonrational. We cannot give any reasons to support their truth. This, he points out, applies to his own philosophy. Instead of being based on reason, it is based on feeling. He accepts his "conclusions" because they appeal to his taste. We are thus left with the question: Why should anyone else accept them? I have responded to this problem by arguing that, whatever Hume's motives for adopting his philosophy may be, that philosophy may still be true so must be examined on its own merits. (2) Having acknowledged that, because our beliefs rest on imagination rather than reason so cannot be supported rationally, Hume still attempts to draw a value distinction between them, arguing that we *ought* to base our beliefs on experience rather than "fiction." Although he is surely right about this, the question remains whether, on his theory, he can justify such an injunction. (3) Hume's whole account of belief is ambiguous, particularly in relation to his empiricist theory of ideas. Although he begins (96) with a definition of belief that seems demanded by his epistemological assumptions, it becomes apparent as he progresses that he does not really believe his own definition of belief. His misgivings are revealed in such things as his appendix notes and his distinction within the imagination between "whimsy" and "judgment." It seems apparent from these sections that Hume was aware of the inadequacy of his original epistemology, but was unwilling, on the one hand, to abandon it or, on the other, to modify it in any consistent manner.

11

PROBABILITY

(Part III, Sections XI–XIII)

Introduction

After completing his account of belief Hume turns to a discussion of probability. This inquiry grows directly out of what has immediately preceded it, for he is still concerned with the nature and causes of belief; but he now focuses his attention on the beliefs we hold that result from weak and conflicting past experience. These he describes as beliefs arising from probability. It is apparent that in these sections Hume is giving the term "probability" a different meaning from the one he had given it in Sections I and II of Part III, where he distinguished probability from knowledge. I will explain this difference in section 1.

These three sections on probability, filled with diverse and graphic illustrations, make interesting reading. They are also important in themselves, because they represent an early attempt that, though crude by later standards, was a forerunner of a vast historical development of the science of mathematical probability. Hume's significance as a pioneering figure in this field has been emphasized by several scholars. An example is D. G. C. Macnabb who, in his assessment of Hume's discussion of the probability of chances in Section XI, writes: "*Up to this point, the section is a masterly, non-technical introduction to the calculus of chances.*"[1] Nevertheless, the sections do not substantially contribute to Hume's theory of causation, being in large part a digression from that topic. For that reason, and also because much of the discussion is readily understandable, I will not consider the sections at length or in detail, but will concentrate my attention on points in them that are of philosophical rather than simply statistical significance.

Text

1. A Second Meaning of Probability (Section XI)

In chapter 6 we learned that in Sections I and II of Part III Hume distinguishes knowledge from probability on the grounds that the former is concerned with relations arising from the comparison of ideas, and the latter with those arising out of experience. Concluding that what we can know is limited to what we directly intuit or can demonstrate to be true (relations of ideas), he described the remainder of our beliefs, which concern matters of fact (based on experience), as "probability." By "probability" he meant any opinion or belief whose truth cannot be demonstrated. Another phrase he used in contrast to demonstration was "probable reasoning." In Sections VI and VIII he argued that beliefs resulting from probable reasoning are generated by the imagination. Probable reasoning is, thus, not really reasoning but rather transitions or associations of ideas in the imagination that, because no reasons can be given in their support, are nonrational.

Nevertheless, our beliefs are based on our experience so, to the extent that this experience varies, they will vary as well. And, in fact, our experience is not uniform but is often inconstant and conflicting. When such inconstancies occur, they weaken our beliefs. It is with such weakened beliefs that Hume is concerned in Sections XI through XIII. He explains them in terms of different levels of "probability," beginning in Section XI with what he calls "*the probability of chances*" (124). Thus the probability to which these sections are devoted falls within the broader "probability" with which he is concerned in Part III as a whole. He wants to understand why we believe certain things less firmly than we do others.

Hume begins his discussion in a way that, unless clearly understood, can be misleading. After noting the distinction he made in Section I, between knowledge and probability, he goes on to say that, although such a distinction is common to philosophy, it differs from our ordinary thinking. Whereas philosophers consider causal arguments to be only probable, "in common discourse we readily affirm, that many arguments from causation exceed probability" (124). To illustrate his point he adds: "One wou'd appear ridiculous, who wou'd say, that 'tis only probable the sun will rise tomorrow, or that all men must dye; tho' 'tis plain we have no further assurance of these facts, than what experience affords us" (124).

It is plain that Hume must be using the term "probable" in this illustration in a way different from his earlier use. One of his main points had been that a belief like "the sun will rise tomorrow" rests on nonrational transitions made by the imagination on the basis of custom or habit. He describes such transitions as probable "reasoning" or probability. In saying now that they exceed probability, he is shifting the meaning of the term. He goes on to justify his shift by pointing out that he is adapting his language to common discourse—and, it might be added, to commonsense opinion as well.

> 'Twould perhaps be more convenient, in order at once to preserve the common signification of words, and mark the several degrees of evidence, to distinguish human reason into three kinds, viz. *that from knowledge, from proofs, and from probabilities.* By knowledge, I mean the assurance arising from the comparison of ideas. By proofs, those arguments, which are deriv'd from the relation of cause and effect, and which are entirely free from doubt and uncertainty. By probability, that evidence, which is still attended with uncertainty. (124)

This passage calls for several comments. (1) Hume's talk of "several degrees of evidence" should not be taken literally. We have no "evidence" that the sun will rise tomorrow. (2) He is using the term "reason" in the passage in a way different from the way he has been earlier in Part III, in which he limited reason to beliefs whose truth can be demonstrated. A better term in the present context would be human "thought." Only the first subcategory, knowledge, can be attributed to reason; the other two, proofs and probabilities, are the offspring of imagination. (3) As a result, Hume is giving the term "proofs" a special meaning here. Proof is not, as it is normally conceived to be in philosophy, the equivalent of demonstration. No one can prove that the sun will rise tomorrow. (4) In his use of all three terms Hume is talking psychology. He differentiates among the three not on the basis of the strength of the reasons we can offer in their support but rather on the level of confidence we have in their truth. Knowledge means assurance; proofs mean entire freedom from doubt and uncertainty; probability means uncertainty. Hume is certainly right in regarding the psychological attitudes he describes as appropriate to the epistemological situations in question—although "assurance" may be a bit weak in connection with knowledge; "conviction" might have been better. The important thing to remember, however, is that Hume is making his distinctions in terms of our psychological responses, specifically in terms of the relative strength or weakness of our beliefs in different situations. In his discussion of probability that follows, his concern will, as a result, be with beliefs about which we are uncertain.

2. Chance and Belief (Section XI)

Hume entitles Section XI "Of the probability of chances." Since "probability," as he is using the term, means the same as strength of belief, the section is concerned with the effects of chance events on our beliefs. Hume begins by pointing out that a *pure* chance event would have no effect but would leave us in a state of indifference. (For Hume this statement should be a tautology, since a chance event just is one about which we have no beliefs regarding its cause.) If we are to engage in any "reasoning" that produces belief, the event must combine both causes and chance. To illustrate his point Hume asks us to consider the throw of a "dye" (127). If we throw a normal die, causal forces will result in its dropping from our hand to a flat surface where it will rest with one of its six sides facing up. But it is a chance matter which of these sides appears. In saying this Hume is not implying that no causes are at work determining the way in which the die will fall. He means only that, because we do not know what these causes are or how they will operate, we will not anticipate its falling in one way rather than another. We do not, as a result, form a lively idea of any one side as the favored side; we do not believe that any one side will be facing up, in preference to any other.

But now suppose the die we throw is marked with one spot on four of its sides and with two spots on the remaining two sides. Our reaction, Hume concludes, becomes more complex. Describing the mental condition of the die thrower, he writes: "'Tis plain, he must conclude the one figure to be more probable than the other, and give the preference to that which is inscrib'd on the greatest number of sides. He in a manner believes, that this will lie uppermost; tho' still with hesitation and doubt, in proportion to the number of chances, which are contrary" (127). Hume explains the hesitant or weak belief of the die thrower or, in other words, the probability of the differently inscribed sides' turning up by a kind of psychological arithmetic. Since the person believes that causal forces will result in the die's dropping from his hand and turning one side up, the appearance of any one side produces an idea in his imagination of equal liveliness to that of the appearance of any other. Since four sides have one dot on them, these ideas merge together in his mind to produce an idea of the appearance of a one-dotted side that is four times as lively as the idea of any given side. On the other hand, his idea of a two-dotted side's appearing is twice as lively as his idea of the appearance of any given side. These two ideas—of one- and two-dotted sides—come into conflict, the weaker idea subtracting its strength from that of the stronger, with the result that the liveliness of the stronger idea is cut in half. The die thrower's belief that the die face will show one dot is weakened by half. Since the probability that the die will land with a one-dotted rather than a two-dotted side facing up is the same as the vividness of his idea, we can conclude that, for this die, it is two-to-one.

3. The Probability of Causes (Section XII)

Hume begins his account of the probabilities of causes with the statement: "The probabilities of causes are of several kinds; but are all deriv'd
from the same origin, *viz. the association of ideas to a present impression*" (130).
By this he means that when we have an impression of what we call a cause,
the strength of belief we will have in the appearance of its effect—its probability—will depend on the past association of the two in our minds. He
develops this view with a short account of the way in which we reach our
beliefs about causal relationships through experience. After having had just
a single experience of a conjunction between two objects, we have only the
slightest expectation, when we observe the first, that the second will follow. Each additional experience of their conjunction increases our anticipation until, after repeated, exceptionless occurrences, our doubts dissolve.
We firmly believe the sun will rise tomorrow. Nevertheless, during the
accumulation of our evidence, and before we reach unquestioned belief, we
can speak only of the probability that the second object will follow the first.
Our belief is not yet firm. Summarizing he writes: "The gradation . . . from
probabilities to proofs is in many cases insensible" (131).

But sometimes, Hume continues, we never reach unquestioned belief.
We are left in a state of uncertainty when our past experience fails to yield
us evidence of constant conjunction but instead produces a general uniformity interspersed with contrary evidence. We have found, for example, that
a cold in the head is usually followed by a cough, but not always. In such
a situation we cannot talk of causal "proof" but only of probability. This is
what Hume means by the probability of causes. He devotes much of Section XII to a psychological account of the way in which we calculate such
probabilities.

Before turning to this discussion I will briefly comment on a point that
Hume makes, one that, while not directly relevant to his argument, is of
philosophical importance in its own right. He inserts a paragraph in which
he distinguishes between the response of the vulgar and of philosophers
to the uncertainty of events. The former believe that when an expected
effect does not follow from its normal cause the cause simply fails to operate; the latter, however, attribute the failure to the secret or unknown
operation of contrary causes. Going further, he maintains that philosophers
conclude that for every effect there must be a cause, even though we may
not know what that cause is. "From the observation of several parallel instances, philosophers form a maxim, that the connexion betwixt all causes
and effects is equally necessary, and that its seeming uncertainty in some
instances proceeds from the secret opposition of contrary causes" (132).
What Hume is asserting here is causal determinism, which he attributes

to "philosophers." This raises the question: Does Hume include himself among those philosophers? The paragraph itself yields no answer to this question. Although he points out that the philosophers' beliefs on the issue are much more sophisticated than those of the vulgar, he does not say whether or not he accepts their "maxim" of complete causal determinism.[2]

Returning to the probability of causes Hume offers two explanations to account for the relative weakness of our beliefs about the future, in situations in which our past experience has been irregular. He points out, first, that in such situations the habitual transition we make from cause to effect is "imperfect" (132). Although our mind is determined to pass from the cause to its most usual effect, the habit it forms of doing so is not so "entire" (132) as it is in situations in which the cause has always had the same effect. However, he turns to a second explanation to account for most of the beliefs we form on the basis of conflicting past experience. His argument (which occupies most of the remainder of Section XII) is complex in its detail but simple in its structure.

He begins with a reiteration of several points he has already made: (1) That we suppose the future will be like the past, (2) that this supposition is not based on reason or argument but on habit, and (3) that habit determines us to make a "full and perfect" (134) transfer of our past experience to the future. In the situation we are considering, our past experience of cause-and-effect relations has not been regular but conflicting. As a result our habitual determination is to expect in the future the same kind of irregularity we have experienced in the past. So, to determine the strength of our belief in the occurrence of any given future event, we unite our various past experiences of that event into one image or idea, then collect our past experiences of a contrary event into one image or idea and subtract the latter from the former. What remains of the liveliness of the first image after we have done this constitutes the strength of our belief or the probability that the event will occur.

To clarify this psychological arithmetic (which parallels what he had given before in Section XI) Hume uses an example. Suppose we observe twenty ships in a harbor, ready to put to sea. Our experience has informed us that, of every twenty ships that have sailed from the port in the past, nineteen have returned safely. So we unite the images of these nineteen different ships into one image that, as a result, becomes very lively. Against this lively image we put that of the one ship that has failed to return. The result is a strong but not perfect image or belief that a ship sailing from the port will safely return. We then say that it is highly probable that it will return.

This example capsulates Hume's theory of the probability of causes. A couple of comments might be made about it. It is an obvious consequence of his theory of belief, interpreting "probability" through the images we have in our mind, which we contrast in terms of their relative liveliness, reaching our conclusions about probability accordingly. A reasonable question to ask here is whether this is a satisfactory explanation of our probability judgments. I leave it to the reader to consider further.

Hume devotes most of the remainder of Section XII to elaborating and commenting on the view regarding the probability of causes I have just described. Since his discussion contains little that is new but is largely repetitious I will not pursue it further but will turn instead to consider a point he makes in the final paragraph of the section. This concerns analogy, or analogical "reasoning."

Hume begins by pointing out that all of our causal "inferences" are founded on two particulars—the constant conjunction of two objects in our past experience and the resemblance of a present object to one of the two. If (as he has just argued) the past conjunction of the objects has not been constant, our belief in their future conjunction will be weakened. But, he now adds, the same result will follow if the present object does not perfectly resemble either of two past objects. To the extent that the object before us is different from one of them, the habitual transition we make is less firm and, consequently, so is our belief that it will be accompanied by the other object. Since arguments from analogy are based on resemblance their success in producing belief is determined by the closeness of the resemblance experienced. So Hume concludes: "In the probability deriv'd from analogy, 'tis the resemblance only, which is affected. . . . An experiment loses its force, when transferr'd to instances, which are not exactly resembling; tho' 'tis evident it may still retain as much as may be the foundation of probability, as long as there is any resemblance remaining" (142).

4. Unphilosophical Probability (Section XIII)

Hume entitles Section XIII "Of unphilosophical probability." Although he never explains what he means by the term, one can infer what he has in mind by contrasting the contents of the section with those of Section XII. If our belief about something is different from what it would be if it were based strictly on our past experience, the result is unphilosophical probability. To use the example from the last section, if I believed that all twenty ships would return safely to port, this would be unphilosophical probability. In the first part of the section Hume describes types of situations in which our beliefs constitute unphilosophical probabilities; in the last part he argues that we ought not to accept such probabilities. Since the latter discussion is of some philosophical interest I will devote most of this section to it.

Hume begins by citing four different kinds of causes that do (or might) lead us to have ideas different in vivacity from what might be expected on the basis of our past experience. Since the relative vivacity of our ideas constitutes the strength of our beliefs, a vivacious idea means a strong belief and a faint idea a weak belief. Finally, since probability means the strength of our beliefs, it varies proportionately as well.

(1) Our belief in a recent fact is strong because our memory of it is fresh. However, as our memory fades with the passage of time, our belief in it wanes as well. The point Hume is making here is that, although the past fact we believe does not change with the passage of time, the strength of our belief in it does.

(2) This situation is hard to distinguish from the first because it also depends on the fading of our memory. Perhaps the point Hume wishes to add by it is revealed in his illustration of the drunkard (144). Not only does the waning of the drunkard's memory of his friend's untimely demise lead him to believe he can escape a like fate but results as well in his eventual return to a life of debauchery.

(3) The third reason Hume gives for diminished belief is somewhat different from the first two. If we have just experienced two objects in a causal relation, our observation of the first will lead us to believe strongly that the second will appear. But suppose that the object we now observe is not connected directly to the other object but that the connection is indirect, through a long series of intermediate causal relations. In this circumstance our belief in the appearance of the second object on our observation of the first, Hume concludes, will be substantially diminished: "When an inference is drawn immediately from an object, without any intermediate cause or effect, the conviction is much stronger, and the persuasion more lively, than when the imagination is carry'd thro' a long chain of connected arguments, however infallible the connexion of each link may be esteem'd" (144). Once again, although the connection between the first object and the final one is not diminished by the intervening causal links, our belief in the connection is.

This reason for diminished belief leads to a problem, which Hume discusses at some length. The problem is this: Since our ideas about historical events, particularly of the remote past, are based on long chains of causal connections, why do they not fade completely away and destroy our beliefs in these events? For instance, why do we continue to believe that there was ever such a person as Julius Caesar? Hume resolves this problem by a simple expedient. Although the links in the causal chain between those who actually knew Caesar and ourselves, who only read about him in history books, are almost innumerable, this fact does not diminish our belief in his reality because the links are all of the same kind. They consist in the repetition of accounts of his life handed down through printers and copyists through the millennia. So Hume concludes, "This circumstance alone preserves the evidence of history, and will perpetuate the memory of the present age to the latest posterity."[3]

(4) Hume sees the fourth source of qualified beliefs in our use of general rules. These strengthen rather than weaken our beliefs. He says we form such rules "rashly" (146), and that our doing so is the source of prejudice. We have observed a few Irishmen who are bores so make the sweeping generalization, which we then believe, that all Irishmen are bores, and so on. Rash generalizations, Hume claims, can get such a hold in our imagination that we continue to believe them in spite of direct evidence we have to the contrary. When we do so, however, we are making a mistake but it is one that commonly occurs. Hume reminds us that "human nature is very subject to errors of this kind" (147).

This explanation of beliefs formed through the rash application of general rules, leading us to embrace prejudices, introduces a new dimension into Hume's analysis of qualified beliefs. He had begun his discussion in a purely descriptive mode, his apparent intent being simply to explain the causes that lead us to acquire certain beliefs in the way we do, even though these beliefs vary from the facts of our past experience. But, with his claim that, when we base our beliefs on rash generalizations, we are committing an error, he shifts from the descriptive to a normative mode. His point clearly is that we ought not to do this. So he devotes much of the remainder of Section XIII to explaining why we should not hold such beliefs. In the next section I will examine his arguments.

5. DESCRIPTION AND EVALUATION OF OUR QUALIFIED BELIEFS (SECTION XIII)

The term "unphilosophical probability" itself has a normative coloring. It is not simply a description of beliefs that are held by people who are not philosophers, but one of the beliefs that no one ought to hold. In a complex argument toward the end of Section XIII, Hume attempts to justify this normative claim. His argument, which rests on a distinction between two types of general rules, parallels his argument in Section X, in which he concluded that we ought to believe history and science rather than poetry.[4] It is equally unsuccessful and for the same reason.[5]

To set the stage for his argument Hume uses an illustration.

Let us consider the case of a man, who being hung out from a high tower in a cage of iron cannot forbear trembling, when he surveys the precipice below him, tho' he *knows* himself to be perfectly secure from falling, by his *experience* of the solidity of the iron which supports him; and tho' the ideas of fall and descent, and harm and death, be deriv'd solely from custom and *experience*. . . . The circumstances of depth and descent strike so strongly upon him, that their influence cannot be destroy'd by the contrary circumstances of support and solidity, which *ought* to give him a perfect security. (148—italics added)

Although we can all agree with Hume that the person in the cage ought to feel secure, the question is: Why should he? His weighing of both possibilities—safety or death—rests on the application of general rules: (1) Iron cages in the past have been safe therefore this one will be, and (2) falls over precipices in the past have caused death so a fall now will have the same result. Why should a person believe general rule (1) rather than general rule (2)?

Although Hume's answer is far from clearly stated he seems to offer two reasons for preferring rule (1) to rule (2). Both rest on a value distinction between types of general rules. First, he says, some rules are based on "superfluous" (148) or "accidental" (149) circumstances. Rule (2), presumably, would be an example. Others are based on "essential" (148) or "efficacious" (149) causes. (Rule (1).) But can Hume make this distinction? Both (1) and (2) are based on past experience, on the one hand of the security of iron cages and on the other of the dangers of precipices. Both go beyond that experience to a new situation. Finally, the "inference" the man makes from his past experiences to his present situation is the work of his imagination, resulting from custom or habit. He can give no rational justification for it. So why ought he to conclude that he is secure rather than in danger? In the illustration, Hume says that the man "knows" himself to be secure. But he acknowledges that both beliefs have the same foundation; namely, his past experience. So what "supports" his "knowledge"?

If we consider the adjectives Hume uses to describe the two general rules, however, we must conclude that the account I have just given misses the point of his argument. Although it is the kind of account that, given the view about our "reasoning" concerning matters of fact he has developed in Part III, Hume ought to give, it is not, I believe, the account he does give here. The adjectives he uses (which I have reproduced in the previous paragraph) leave little doubt that Hume is distinguishing (1) from (2) on the grounds that the cause operating to keep people safe (an iron cage) is stronger than that endangering them (gravity) and that this cause will operate in the present situation as it has in the past. He is appealing to the concept of cause as power or efficacy.[6] But he has long since rejected that view.[7] So Hume bases his first reason for preferring (1) to (2) on a view of causation he does not accept.

Intermingled with his first reason Hume gives a second reason for preferring (1) to (2). He writes: "The general rule [iron cages are safe] is attributed to our judgment; as being more extensive and constant. The exception [falling over precipices] to the imagination; as being more capricious and uncertain" (149). Setting aside his distinction between the judgment and the imagination, which he has implied to be inaccurate,[8] the point Hume is making in this statement is that the man should prefer (1) to (2) because it is "extensive and constant" whereas (2) is "capricious and uncertain." This seems just another way of saying that our past experience has shown that people in iron cages hanging above precipices have more often been safe than sorry. If so, we have an example parallel to the ship illustration from Section XII (134). So the man's preference is the result of "philosophical" rather than "unphilosophical" probability. As a result, on this account of the man's situation and his thought processes, the example is inappropriate. In any event, because all "reasoning" about matters of fact is a nonrational process, resting simply on habit, he cannot give any argument to justify his belief either that he is safe or in danger. He just believes one or the other. To say, therefore, that he *ought* to believe one in preference to the other, meaning by this that he has a better rational basis for such belief, is illegitimate.[9]

Summary

The three sections on probability I have been reviewing in this chapter, although they are related to Hume's conception of causation, do not advance his analysis of that relation but represent a digression from his line of argument in Part III. Nevertheless, particularly because of their historical relationship to an important later intellectual development, they are of considerable interest in themselves. Hume's use of the term "probability" in these sections must be clearly understood for it can easily be misleading. His concern is not with probability as we ordinarily think of it. He is not, that is, writing about some feature of the objective world, describing situations in which causes fail to operate in a deterministic manner or in which different causes operate in opposition to each other. Rather, his concern is with the subjective realm and specifically with our beliefs. By "probability" he means the relative vividness with which an idea appears in our imagination under circumstances in which our past experience has been in conflict.

As a description of human psychology, Hume's account has much to recommend it. But he gets into trouble at the end of his account when he attempts to make value distinctions, arguing that we ought to be influenced in our beliefs by our past experience in certain ways rather than in others. He has already removed our causal "inferences" from the realm of reason, relocating them in the imagination as transitions we make as a result of habit but cannot support by rational argument. Therefore, he can offer no grounds to justify his conclusion that we ought to prefer one kind of transition to another.

12

NECESSARY
CONNECTION

(Part III, Section XIV)

Introduction

Hume begins the long development of his theory of causation in Section II of Part III. His concern is with the idea or concept of causation, his goal being to explain what we must mean when we talk about causation, or how the concept must be understood if it is to be intelligible to us. According to his epistemology, this requires that we discover the impression or impressions from which the idea of causation is derived: "We must consider the idea of *causation*, and see from what origin it is deriv'd. 'Tis impossible to reason justly, without understanding perfectly the idea concerning which we reason; and 'tis impossible perfectly to understand any idea, without tracing it up to its origin, and examining that primary impression, from which it arises" (74–75). Hume's argument through the remainder of Part III can best be described as a search for "that primary impression" from which our idea of causation arises. Actually he uncovers several essential impressions, all of them of relations. In Section II he concludes that the relations of contiguity and succession are necessary to generate the idea of causation but adds that they are not in themselves sufficient; much more important is the relation of necessary connection. But he then confesses that he can find no impression from which an idea of necessary connection can be derived. Undaunted, he launches his long search for such an impression. Along the way (in Section VI) he discovers the relation of constant conjunction, which he thinks to be of vital importance to his quest. Then, after his analysis of the notion of belief, which sets the stage for the last step in his theory, he finally (in Section XIV) unveils the impression from which the idea of necessary connection is derived.

Section XIV, in which Hume's argument is tightly reasoned but also excessively repetitive, can be divided (roughly) into three parts. The first consists of a series of criticisms of traditional "objective" theories of causation, or theories that attribute effects to the action of some power or efficacy possessed by causes, whether these be material objects or minds. Next comes his account of the idea of necessary connection and his explanation of its source. This, of course, is the heart of the section, which then concludes with definitions of "cause" and a brief survey of some consequences of his theory.

In this chapter I will concentrate on elucidating and then on assessing Hume's theory of causation. My assessment, however, will be limited. I will not attempt to evaluate the theory in itself; that would be far too large an undertaking for this book. In any case it has been done repeatedly and in detail by other writers.[1] Instead, I will be concerned only with the questions of how and how well the theory fits into Hume's total philosophy in Book I. But I might add, what hardly needs emphasis, that Hume's theory of causation is generally, and rightly, considered to be a major contribution to the history of modern philosophy. It is not a gross overstatement for J. L. Mackie to say: "The most significant and influential single contribution to the theory of causation is that which Hume developed in Book I, Part III, of the *Treatise*."[2]

Text

1. PRELIMINARY STATEMENT (PARAGRAPHS 1–2)

Hume begins Section XIV with a reiteration of the Empiricist Principle: "I repeat what I have often had occasion to observe, that as we have no idea, that is not deriv'd from an impression, we must find some impression, that gives rise to this idea of necessity [necessary connection], if we assert we have really such an idea" (155). This is the first of at least six appeals Hume makes to the Principle in Section XIV. He uses it both as the epistemological foundation for his own theory and, as we will see in the next section, as his basis for rejecting "objective" accounts of causation.

After a brief recapitulation of his preliminary discussions of causation in Part III, Hume concludes, as he had done in Section VI,[3] that the constant conjunction of objects in the relations of contiguity and succession cannot give rise to a new idea, and he needs the new idea of necessary connection to complete his theory. Immediately after reaching this conclusion, however, he reverses himself and adds that "upon farther enquiry" (155) he finds that the repetition does produce a new impression, from which an idea can be derived. "For after a frequent repetition, I find, that upon the appearance of one of the objects, the mind is *determin'd* by custom to consider its usual attendant, and to consider it in a stronger light upon account of its relation to the first object. 'Tis this impression, then, or *determination,* which affords me the idea of necessity" (156). Although this is only a preliminary, general statement, it reveals, in capsulated form, the essential point in Hume's concept of necessary connection. Because of its importance to his argument for causation I will discuss it in detail later in the chapter.

Hume concludes his preliminary remarks with a warning to his readers, not to be complacent. The theory he is developing, he points out, may seem obvious, given the arguments that have gone before. But it is of such fundamental importance to science—and, it might well be added, to everyday life and thought—that the reader should be prepared to give his fullest attention to what Hume is saying. "I have just now examin'd one of the most sublime questions in philosophy, *viz. that concerning the power and efficacy of causes;* where all the sciences seem so much interested" (156).

2. Hume's Critique of "Objective" Theories of Causation (Paragraphs 3–11 and Appendix Note)

Before turning to his own theory, Hume engages in a lengthy critique of other theories of causation current in his time.[4] He notes at the outset that attempts to define the idea of necessary connection in such terms as "*efficacy, agency, power, force, energy, necessity, connexion* and *productive quality*" (157) are fruitless because they provide no explanation of the concept but simply offer synonyms to put in its place. He then repeats the Empiricist Principle; if we are to explain this idea we must find the impression from which it is derived.

Using the Principle as his chief critical weapon, he then proceeds to demolish a variety of theories of what I call "objective" causation. By this I mean any theory that explains the cause-effect relation by claiming that the cause possesses some *power* or *force* that *produces* the effect. Such "objective" causal connections can take a variety of forms: (1) Body to body: The cue ball's collision with the object ball causes the object ball to move. (2) Body to mind: The cue ball's striking me on the head causes me to feel pain. (3) Mind to body: My will's volition causes my arm to move. (4) Mind to mind: My experience of pain causes me to fear fire.

Hume begins his critique of particular theories with an attack on the standard view of causation, which he attributes to Locke,[5] that bodies possess some power to produce effects. He has little new to say, contenting himself with repeating points he has urged before. The attempt to base the conclusion that a cause must possess some power to produce its effect on an appeal to reason cannot succeed because reason can neither generate any idea nor establish that every event must have a cause. After brushing aside any appeal to innate ideas, whose existence he denies, he then attempts, following Malebranche,[6] to find an intelligible account of the concept of power in the writings of those who defend this view. Naturally he fails. He concludes with a challenge to those who believe in a causal power embodied in material objects: "If any one think proper to refute [Hume's conclusion], he need not put himself to the trouble of inventing any long reasonings; but may at once shew us an instance of a cause, where we discover the power or operating principle" (159). The challenge is rhetorical. Convinced that we have no impression of such a power, Hume can conclude, with confidence, that we have no idea of it either. So the whole Lockean, commonsense notion of a causal power residing in material objects can be rejected because it is "entirely without foundation," the principles on which it rests being "perfectly unintelligible and inexplicable" (158).

Although Hume agrees with Malebranche's critique of this kind of causal theory, he disagrees equally with the type of theory Malebranche offered in its place.[7] Since matter contains no causal power but since we have experience of effects, Malebranche argued, we must find some entity that possesses the power to produce these. The next step for a philosopher, who was also a Catholic clergyman, was easy. All causal power resides in the will of God. Hume's critique of this theory is straightforward, consisting of an appeal to the Empiricist Principle. Since we have no impression of a causal power in God, we can have no idea of such a power. In his words: "For if every idea be deriv'd from an impression, the idea of a deity proceeds from the same origin; and if no impression, either of sensation or reflection, implies any force or efficacy, 'tis equally impossible to discover or even imagine any such active principle in the deity."[8]

Following a brief criticism of an argument that appeals to "second causes" (160), which he dismisses with another invocation of the Empiricist Principle, Hume adds an important appendix note (632–33). In this note he considers a different possible source of causal power—the human mind. He describes the theory as follows: "The motions of our body, and the thoughts and sentiments of our mind, (say [such theorists]) obey the will; nor do we seek any farther to acquire a just notion of force or power" (632). This theory covers two types of causation—mind to body and mind to mind. Hume's response to it is predictably negative. So, too, is his reason for rejecting it. Once more the Empiricist Principle decides the matter. If we are to have an idea of the power of the will, we must have some impression from which our idea can be derived; we have no such impression, therefore we can have no such idea: "The actions of the mind are, in this respect, the same with those of matter. We perceive only their constant conjunction; nor can we ever reason beyond it. No internal impression has an apparent energy, more than external objects have."[9]

Hume ends his critique of the various attempts philosophers have made to defend their versions of a theory of "objective" causation with a brief and, according to his epistemology, decisive refutation of all of them. "All ideas are deriv'd from, and represent impressions. We never have any impression, that contains any power or efficacy. We never therefore have any idea of power" (161).

3. The Source of the Idea of Necessary Connection (Paragraphs 12–19)

Hume does not doubt that we have an idea of necessary connection; the problem for him is simply to find its source. How can we get such an idea? In his attempt to trace the idea to its source he begins with a further scrutiny of the concept of power. In an argument that is partly repetitive of Section VI he points out that "power" is a general or abstract idea, and, since all such ideas are "nothing but individual ones taken in a certain light,"[10] in order to possess the general idea of power, we must have an idea of it derived from an impression of it in individual cases. But, when we look to the external world, hoping to find an impression of power in our survey of individual material objects, we are necessarily disappointed. We simply have no such impression. But now Hume makes an unexpected shift in his argument. Instead of concluding, as he had before, that we have no idea of power and that the concept is therefore unintelligible, he says only that the notion is "*wrong apply'd*" (162). Continuing this line of thought, he first points out that we cannot gain any idea of power from our observation of a single instance of two objects in a causal relation. But when we observe the same two objects repeatedly appearing in the same relation, we conceive a causal connection between them. So Hume reaches a crucial conclusion. "This multiplicity of resembling instances, therefore, constitutes the very essence of power or connexion, and is the source, from which the idea of it arises" (163).

At this point readers who remember Hume's account of constant conjunction in Section VI may demur. There, they will recollect, he had said quite unambiguously: "From the mere repetition of any past impression, even to infinity, there never will arise any new original idea, such as that of a necessary connexion" (88). Is Hume about to contradict himself? Not at all. He is well aware of what he had written in Section VI; his aim at the present point in his argument is to show how a new idea *can* arise, even though *apparently* it cannot. His argument is difficult; fortunately he has prepared the way for it by his earlier discussions of mental causation and belief.

Hume begins by acknowledging what I have just noted—that the observation of repeated instances cannot alone give rise to any new idea like that of necessary connection—appealing again to the Empiricist Principle to enforce his point. If a new idea is to be generated, therefore, constant conjunction must either "*discover*" or "*produce*" (163) something new that is the source of that idea. Or, to state the same point in a different way, the new idea must be an *effect* of the constant conjunction. "Every enlargement . . . (such as the idea of power or connexion) which arises from the multiplicity of similar instances, is copy'd from some effects of the multiplicity" (163). To discover how the idea of necessary connection is generated all we need to do now, continues Hume, is to understand the effects of constant conjunction. The important thing is to look for these effects in the right place. The error of "objective" theories of causation, as Hume points out once again (163–64), lies in their attempt to locate the effects of constant conjunction in the external world. Contrary to such views, the repetition of instances we observe, such as the results following the collision of billiard balls, cannot produce a new quality in the object from which an idea of necessary connection can be generated, because the instances are entirely independent of each other. Nevertheless, he contends, the resemblance between these several instances of constant conjunction does produce a new impression from which our idea of power is derived—but it is in the mind rather than in the external world. "Tho' the several resembling instances, which give rise to the idea of power, have no influence on each other, and can never produce any new quality *in the object*, which can be the model of that idea, yet the *observation* of this resemblance produces a new impression *in the mind*, which is its real model" (164–65). The new impression produced in the mind by our observation of the resemblance of past instances, Hume argues, is a feeling of "a determination of the mind to pass from one object to its usual attendant, and to conceive it in a stronger light upon account of that relation" (165). It is an impression of power, efficacy, or necessary connection; from it our idea of these is derived. "This determination is the only effect of the resemblance; and therefore must be the same with power or efficacy, whose idea is deriv'd from the resemblance" (165). In summation Hume writes, "Necessity . . . is nothing but an internal impression of the mind, or a determination to carry our thoughts from one object to another" (165).

Hume's conclusion seems puzzling. He claims to have found an impression from which the idea of necessary connection can be derived; namely, the determination of the mind, resulting from our observation of past constant conjunctions, to make a transition to an effect when we experience a cause. But how can a determination of the mind be an impression? Impressions, we learned at the very beginning of the *Treatise*, are either direct apprehensions gained through our five senses or immediate perceptions like pleasure and pain. A determination of the mind does not seem to be like either of these. Why, then, does Hume claim that it is an impression? His answer to this question constitutes the most ingenious as well as most important step in his theory of causation.

4. The Impression of Necessary Connection (Paragraphs 20–22)

Just as those philosophers who have attempted to discover a necessary connection between objects by searching in the objects themselves have been looking in the wrong place, so I too have looked in the wrong place for the source of our idea of necessary connection by trying to find it in an impression of *sensation*. The necessity, or determination of the mind, is an impression but it is an impression of *reflection*, not one of sensation. "The idea of necessity arises from some impression. There is no impression convey'd by our senses, which can give rise to that idea. It must, therefore, be deriv'd from some internal impression, or impression of reflexion" (165). That Hume's resolution of his problem—to find an impression from which our idea of necessary connection can be derived—is brilliant seems beyond question. After his long, complex quest through Part III he has achieved his goal with one masterstroke. He has discovered the needed impression in a place that no one could have expected. Instead of its being an impression we gain through our senses or immediately experience, it is an emotion we feel in our inner being. As such it must be, according to his epistemology, an impression of reflection. To repeat his original account of such impressions, they are, he says, "passions, desires, and emotions."[11]

At this point it might be well to pause and ask: Is Hume right in describing the determination of the mind to anticipate or expect an effect, after our experience of past constant conjunctions, as a feeling or emotion? First let us see what he says. He writes that "after we have observ'd the resemblance in a sufficient number of instances, we immediately *feel* a determination of the mind to pass from one object to its usual attendant" (165—italics added). Again, he writes later on the same page, "There is no internal impression [impression of reflection], which has any relation to the present business, but that *propensity*, which custom produces, to pass from an object to the idea of its usual attendant" (165—italics added). Although one could wish that Hume had developed this crucial step in fuller detail, his point seems clear. The emotion that renders the determination of the mind an impression of reflection is the *feeling* of determination or propensity we experience as we make the transition from a present cause to an anticipated effect, conceiving the latter "in a stronger light" (165). To put the point simply, we *believe* the effect will follow. We do not, Hume is arguing, simply make the transition from cause to effect; rather, our mental activity is accompanied by a special feeling or emotion that is introspectively observable. We directly feel a determination to anticipate the effect. This feeling is the impression of reflection from which our idea of necessary connection is derived.

Hume's analysis of human psychology, while not beyond dispute, seems quite convincing. The only way in which we can assess it is to consult our own mental life. Do we, when we observe the cue ball about to collide with the object ball, actually experience a *feeling* that the collision must result in a movement of the latter? If Hume is right, this feeling is stronger than and different from a mere intellectual expectation. I can speak only for myself on this question but I do find I have the kind of experience Hume describes. Generally speaking, this feeling of determination or propensity to anticipate the effect is not strong yet it is something of which I am (or can be) directly aware. I conclude, therefore, that I experience the impression of reflection that is the central ingredient in Hume's theory of causation. And I am inclined to think that most other people do so as well.

Hume concludes the statement of his theory of causation with a recapitulation of its main points (166). His recapitulation can be paraphrased as follows: (1) We can have no idea of a power in an object we call a cause to produce an effect in another object, or of a necessary connection between the two, because we have no impression of any such power or connection. (2) The idea we have of power or necessary connection arises from our observation of the constant conjunction or regular repetition of the relations of contiguity and succession between the objects. (3) The repetition or constant conjunction has no effect on the objects themselves; instead it influences the mind, producing in it through custom a transition from cause to effect. (4) This customary transition the mind makes is identical with causal power or necessary connection. (5) Causal power or necessary connection, therefore, is a feeling, or an impression of reflection, consisting in the determination of the mind to anticipate the customary effect when the cause is observed, or the mind's propensity to have a more vivid idea of this effect. (6) The idea of necessary connection is a copy of this impression of reflection [author's addition].[12]

5. Determinations of the Mind

Having tortuously, and sometimes repetitively, followed Hume's path as he has slowly developed his theory of causation, this seems an appropriate time to stop and assess it. As I indicated in the introduction to this chapter, to attempt an adequate assessment of the theory itself would be too great a task to accomplish in this book because it would require a review of a vast body of literature, usually complex and often conflicting, that has been written on the subject. All I can hope to do is to consider the theory's consistency with Hume's philosophy as a whole.

Concerns about consistency will almost surely have arisen in the mind of anyone who has followed the development of Hume's theory of causation carefully from its beginnings in Section II of Part III. But, partly because of the language Hume uses in the statement of his theory, the nature and locus of the problems are hard to discern and harder to articulate. Perhaps the best place to begin is with the Empiricist Principle. Throughout Part III Hume makes regular use of the Principle, primarily as a weapon to demolish "objective" theories of causation. All such theories, he contends, fail, the causal power they attribute to bodies or minds being unintelligible because we never have any impression, so can have no idea of it.

The concern that naturally arises from a close reading of Hume's own theory of causation is this: Can it itself succeed in escaping his criticism of such "objective" theories or does it not also succumb to the same objection? To answer this question we must concentrate on a particular relation it contains, that between our past experience of the constant conjunction of kinds of objects and our present feeling of anticipation, when we experience one of these objects, that the other will occur. Just what is the nature of this relation?

Hume talks about the relation in a number of places in Part III, describing it in a variety of ways. I select three of his statements. The first is from Section XI: "The mind is determin'd by custom to pass from any cause to its effect, and . . . upon the appearance of the one, 'tis almost impossible for it not to form an idea of the other. Their constant conjunction in past instances has *produc'd* such a habit in the mind, that it always conjoins them in its thought."[13] The other statements about this relation are from Section XIV: "Every enlargement . . . (such as the idea of power or connexion) which arises from the multiplicity of similar instances [constant conjunctions], is copy'd from some *effects* of the multiplicity" (163—italics added); "the repetition neither discovers nor causes any thing in the objects, but has an *influence* only on the mind, by that customary transition it *produces*" (166—italics added). In these passages Hume is describing a relation I discussed at some length in chapter 9 and there labeled "mental causation."[14] The relation is one between two kinds of experience, first, our past observation of the constant conjunction of two kinds of objects (like flame and heat) and, second, our present anticipation or belief that, on observing the first, we will experience the second. In the statements I have just reproduced Hume is affirming that the first kinds of experience are the cause of which the second is the effect. In saying this he is attributing a power or efficacy to the first that produces the second. But, even though both the cause and the effect are mental occurrences, the power by which the first "produces" the second is something of which we have no impression, hence can have no idea. It is an example of "objective" causation. Thus, like the philosophers he has criticized at the beginning of Section XIV, Hume, too, incorporates into his own theory a notion that is unintelligible. Or, put in another way, his theory of causation embodies a relation that not only violates the Empiricist Principle but also is inconsistent in a fundamental way with the theory of causation he originates in the *Treatise*.

Why did Hume appeal to an unintelligible mental causation in the formulation of his theory of causation? It is out of the question to reply that he incorporated an unintelligible relation into it deliberately. After his relentless attacks on standard theories and his repeated invocation of the Empiricist Principle, it would be incredible that he should knowingly make such a mistake. The alternative is that he did this inadvertently, that he failed to realize that the mental causation that formed a part of his theory is a case of "objective" causation.

What led Hume to make this mistake? This is, of course, a question to which no conclusive answer can now be given. The most one can do is to suggest what seems to be a plausible answer and then attempt to support it by an appeal to the text. My suggestion involves two points: (1) Hume failed to make a required distinction between (a) mental causation, or the power of our past experiences of constant conjunction to produce a feeling of anticipation in our mind, and (b) the feeling of anticipation itself, or the impression of reflection. (2) This failure was a result, in part, of the way in which he stated his theory.

In support of point (1) I reproduce a summary statement Hume makes of his theory: "The necessary connexion betwixt causes and effects is the foundation of our inference from one to the other. The foundation of our inference is the transition arising from the accustom'd union. These are, therefore, the same" (165). Although the exact antecedent of the word "these" in the last sentence is, perhaps, subject to question, it is clear from Hume's argument in the previous paragraph that he is identifying the necessary connection between causes and effects with the "inference" or transition we make from one to the other. But the statement I have just reproduced is obviously confused. From the passages I have reproduced earlier in the section we can easily identify Hume's confusion, which is contained in the second sentence. The "transition" cannot be the same as the "foundation" of our "inference," because the transition *is* the inference. Rather, as Hume adds at the end of the sentence, the foundation of the "inference" is the "accustom'd union," or, to describe it more accurately, our observation of past conjunctions, which gives rise to the inference or transition. So, if the foundation of our inference is the "necessary connexion," as Hume says in the first sentence, that connection cannot be the same as the transition. Instead it must be the same as the accustomed union. But to say that the accustomed union is the necessary connection that gives rise to the transition is to assume the notion of "objective" mental causation.

I turn next to point (2), an attempt to explain why Hume made this mistake. My explanation is centered on a phrase—"determination of the mind," or some variation thereof—that recurs repeatedly in Hume's development of his theory of causation. My special concern is with the central word "determination," which is ambiguous, having several meanings. Two of these are important here—(a) "Determination" as causal efficacy, as in the statement "Superior strength determined the outcome of the battle" and (b) "determination" as a mental disposition, as in "He felt a strong determination to succeed." My hypothesis is in two parts. The first is that Hume uses the concept "determination of the mind" in two ways, one in which "determination" has the meaning of (a) and the other the meaning of (b). A couple of examples will illustrate these two ways. To return to a passage I cited earlier, he writes that "*the mind is determin'd* by custom to pass from any cause to its effect."[15] Here Hume is using the notion of determination as (a) an expression of causal efficacy, specifically of mental causation. His other usage, (b), is exemplified in the statement, "after we have observ'd the resemblance in a sufficient number of instances, we immediately feel a *determination of the mind* to pass from one object to its usual attendant" (165—italics added). In this use Hume is talking of "determination" as a mental disposition or propensity we feel, to make the transition from cause to effect. A reading of Part III will corroborate the fact that Hume uses the concept "determination of the mind" in each of these ways repeatedly throughout the development of his theory.

The second part of my hypothesis is that Hume failed to keep these two meanings of the phrase distinct but treated them as though they meant the same thing. To support it I repeat the passage I reproduced at the beginning of the chapter: "For after a frequent repetition, I find, that upon the appearance of one of the objects, the mind is *determin'd* by custom to consider its usual attendant, and to consider it in a stronger light upon account of its relation to the first object. 'Tis this impression, then, or *determination*, which affords me the idea of necessity" (156). This statement is not easy to interpret. In it Hume says that the determination of the mind affords him the idea of necessity. But what determination? In the final sentence he refers to "this impression . . . or *determination*." From the way the sentence is written, it is clear that the word "this" modifies "determination" as well as "impression." So it seems reasonable to conclude that Hume believed himself to have referred to only one determination of the mind in the preceding sentence. That he is referring to (b), the feeling of determination he experiences, is obvious because it is that impression of reflection, of which he speaks at the end of the first sentence, from which his idea of necessity is directly derived. But he is also referring in the first sentence to (a), the causal efficacy of custom in determining the mind. He emphasizes the point by putting the concept of determination, understood as (a), in italics, to match the italics in the last sentence. We can conclude, therefore, that Hume meant the "determination" he speaks of in the last sentence to refer to everything he included in the first sentence. If he had intended to distinguish the two concepts of determination (a and b) from each other, he would not have referred to *this* determination in the final sentence but rather to *these* determinations.

To corroborate my view that Hume failed to distinguish the two meanings of "determination of the mind" I submit another passage, taken from near the end of Section XIV. He writes: "When any object is presented to us, it immediately conveys to the mind a lively idea of that object, which is usually found to attend it; and *this* determination of the mind forms the necessary connexion of these objects" (169—italics added). Although this statement is quite compressed, it includes both (a) and (b) forms of the determination of the mind. Yet Hume again speaks of "this" determination, making no distinction between the two.

Throughout this discussion of the two passages I have cited from Section XIV I have assumed that the notions—(a) mental determination and (b) the feeling of determination—must refer to two different kinds of determination of the mind in Hume's philosophy. If they did not, his use of the first in his theory of causation need not require him to embrace a second concept of power or necessity and, in particular, one that committed him to the unintelligible notion of mental causation. This assumption needs to be justified. Perhaps the best place to begin is with Hume's idea of necessity or power, which is an idea of reflection, or the idea of an emotion or feeling. The source of this idea is an impression of reflection, the feeling as directly experienced. This feeling is that of anticipation of an effect when we experience a cause, or a feeling of the determination of the mind (b), to do so. What is the source of this impression of reflection? We know, from Part I, that an impression of reflection is an emotion produced by an antecedent idea which, in turn, is derived from a direct impression, like that of "heat or cold, thirst or hunger, pleasure or pain" (8). Explaining the relation between the antecedent idea and the impression of reflection, Hume writes: "This idea of pleasure or pain, when it *returns* upon the soul, *produces* the new impressions of desire and aversion, hope and fear, which may properly be called impressions of reflexion, because derived from it" (8—italics added). The idea of pleasure or pain, in its turn, is derived from an antecedent impression of pleasure or pain.

In his account of the genesis of the impression of reflection, "power" or "necessity," Hume gives an explanation based on this original account from Part I. He writes, for example, that "*after* we have observ'd the resemblance in a sufficient number of instances, we immediately *feel* a determination of the mind" (165—italics added). Again, "the repetition neither discovers nor causes any thing in the objects, but has an influence only on the mind, by that customary transition it *produces*" (166—italics added). Putting these statements together, we can say that our observation of the repetition or constant conjunction of cause and effect in the past is the cause that produces (Hume should add "through the medium of an idea") the feeling of determination of the mind, or the impression of reflection, from which the idea of reflection in turn is derived. Finally, Hume equates this causal power with the determination of the mind. He writes that "the mind is determin'd by custom to pass from any cause to its effect" (128). So the determination of the mind (a) of which Hume writes in the final statement, since it is the same as the causal power exercised by our observation of the repetition of conjunctions, must (1) precede and (2) produce the impression of reflection, or the feeling of determination of the mind (b) to make the present transition. Therefore, the two determinations of the mind *cannot* be the same.

The hypotheses I have suggested offer a reasonable explanation of why Hume failed to recognize that he incorporated, in the determination of the mind (a), or mental determination, a notion of "objective" causation into his theory. It is, of course, impossible to be sure of this but the text seems to give my interpretation strong support. Whether I am right or wrong on this point, however, is not of great moment. The crucial fact is that Hume does appeal to "objective" causation. As a result, his theory violates both the Empiricist Principle and his own theory of causation in the same way that traditional theories, like those of Locke and Malebranche, do. Whatever its merits as a theory of causation may be, it is a theory that Hume cannot, in consistency, either put forward or accept.

Earlier I said that the inconsistency underlying Hume's theory of causation was inadvertent. Although I think this is true, there is at least a hint in Section XIV that he realized he was employing a notion of causal power in it that violated his theory of ideas. At the very end of the section he writes: "Such an influence on the mind is in itself perfectly extraordinary and incomprehensible; nor can we be certain of its reality, but from experience and observation" (172). This passage calls for three comments. (1) We need to know what Hume means by "such an influence on the mind." From the context of the full paragraph this statement concludes it is apparent that the influence on the mind of which he is speaking is a case of "objective" mental causation. (2) Hume's statement in the final clause of the sentence, which implies that we can be certain of this influence from experience and observation, is misleading. We do not have any impression of mental causation. The most he can mean by the statement is that we experience the constant conjunction of the objects and that, when such experiences occur, the mind has a feeling of determination to pass from cause to effect. (3) The important point in the passage is Hume's statement that the influence on the mind, or mental causation, is "incomprehensible."[16] His acknowledgment of this fact is tantamount to his recognition that he is appealing to a notion of causal power in his theory of causation that, on his epistemology, is illegitimate.

6. A PROPOSED REVISION

We have seen that Hume's theory of causation includes within it the very kind of "objective" causation it was specifically designed to avoid. Can this mistake be rectified and the theory be reformulated in a way consistent with his empiricist epistemology? I think it can and in this section I will suggest a way of doing so. Since the problem has been created by his incorporation of the notion of the determination of the mind, understood as mental causation, into the theory, the remedy lies in excising that notion. If this is done the theory could be reformulated along the following lines: After we have observed the constant conjunction of two kinds of objects over a period of time, when we now observe an object resembling the first kind, we have a feeling of determination to anticipate the appearance of one of the second, or we believe it will appear. There is, in this account, no appeal to a causal determination of the mind, to make the transition from one to the other. The feeling of anticipation simply arises in our minds under these circumstances. No explanation can be given of why it arises; *this just happens.*

Such a modified version of Hume's theory of causation would accomplish two goals. First, it would retain his idea of necessary connection or power, because it would continue to affirm the feeling of anticipation or expectation, which is the impression of reflection from which this idea is derived. Second, it would do so without any appeal to an illegitimate concept of "objective" power. Of course, it might prove awkward to fit it into his original account of the genesis of impressions of reflection as it appears in Part I. Whether Hume would be willing to accept such a modified version of his theory I cannot, of course, say. Also, whether such a theory is one that philosophers in general would find viable is another question I cannot answer.

7. ANOTHER PROBLEM

Before concluding my discussion of the question of Hume's consistency I need to refer to another problem in his theory of causation. Since I have already discussed this problem, which arises in Sections V and VI,[17] I will simply summarize it here. According to Hume, to generate both the impression and the idea of necessary connection we must have an idea of constant conjunction. To gain such an idea we must have had an impression of constant conjunction, or of many exceptionless past repetitions of two kinds of objects related to each other by contiguity and succession. In addition, we must remember these conjunctions, in the sense of recollecting them.[18] Such memory is necessary for us to be able, whenever we observe a conjunction between two objects, to compare it with our past impressions of conjunctions to determine if it resembles them. But we cannot recollect our previous impressions because, being things of the past, they are irretrievable. So we cannot make the required comparison. Without being able to appeal to past constant conjunctions, we cannot generate the idea of necessary connection.

As we saw in chapter 9,[19] Hume gets around this difficulty in Section VI by returning to a theory of memory he had abandoned in Section V, because he had concluded that it was inconsistent with his theory of ideas. So, to avoid a basic inconsistency in his philosophy in Book I he must either give up his empiricist epistemology or his theory of causation.

I have no suggestion to offer that would extricate Hume from this dilemma. We must acknowledge that, given the limitations of his epistemology on the one hand and the requirements of his theory of causation on the other, the two are intrinsically incompatible.

8. OUR BELIEF IN "OBJECTIVE" CAUSATION (PARAGRAPHS 23–27)

Hume completes his theory of causation with his identification of the impression of power or necessary connection with the feeling of the determination of the mind to pass from cause to effect, or to anticipate the effect when we observe the cause. But he still has much of interest to say about causation in the remainder of Section XIV. He begins by acknowledging the obvious fact that most people really believe in "objective" causation. They believe that objects in the external world possess a causal power that produces effects in other objects.[20] The motion of the cue ball, when it strikes the object ball, really does cause that ball to move. Hume explains this natural belief, which he calls a "biass of the mind" (167), by an appeal to psychology. "'Tis a common observation," he writes, "that the mind has a great propensity to spread itself on external objects" (167). Continuing, he points out that the situation here is analogous to that in which we "spread" sounds and smells on the external world. We believe, for example, that the tree falling in the forest makes a sound but, in fact, such a secondary quality has no existence outside of the mind.

Hume next inserts a passage in which his irony is obvious. Assuming the voice of a believer in "objective" causation reacting to Hume's theory he writes: "What! the efficacy of causes lie in the determination of the mind! As if causes did not operate entirely independent of the mind, and wou'd not continue their operation, even tho' there was no mind existent to contemplate them" (167). This is not irony simply for its own sake. Hume uses the paragraph to give additional emphasis to the striking difference between his account of causation and the view most people ordinarily hold regarding causes and effects.

Continuing in an ironical vein, Hume compares the "objective" believer's arguments to those of a blind man who thinks it absurd that the color of scarlet is different from the sound of a trumpet. But then he appears to make a concession to the "objectivist." "I am, indeed, ready to allow, that there may be several qualities both in material and immaterial objects, with which we are utterly unacquainted; and if we please to call these *power* or *efficacy*, 'twill be of little consequence to the world" (168). That Hume's concession has no real substance, however, is apparent, not only from the concluding clause of his remark, but also from what he writes immediately afterwards, where he says that, if we employ these "unknown qualities" in our theory of causation, "we are led astray by a false philosophy."[21]

9. The Two Definitions of "Cause" (Paragraphs 28–29)

Hume turns next to the task of defining "cause." He offers two definitions, the first of "cause" as a *philosophical* relation and the second of it as a *natural* relation or, as he elaborates, as we view causation as a comparison of two ideas or as an association between them.[22] He defines "cause" as a philosophical relation as follows: "'An object precedent and contiguous to another, and where all the objects resembling the former are plac'd in like relations of precedency and contiguity to those objects, that resemble the latter'"(170). In defining "cause" as a natural relation he writes: "'A CAUSE is an object precedent and contiguous to another, and so united with it, that the idea of the one determines the mind to form the idea of the other, and the impression of the one to form a more lively idea of the other'" (170).

These two definitions have been the subject of much discussion, as well as controversy, among Hume scholars. A number of questions can be raised about them. In the first place, why should he give *two* definitions of "cause"? The answer is apparent; Hume is in each one viewing the notion from a different perspective. In the first his concern is with the "objective" aspect of the relation, or with the fact of what he has called the constant conjunction of causally related objects. In the second he is concerned with the "subjective" side, with the effect that this constant conjunction has on our minds, or imaginations. But this distinction gives rise to a further problem. Hume calls both characterizations *definitions*. But, as many scholars have pointed out,[23] they are so different from each other that an object could satisfy one yet fail to satisfy the other. So they cannot both be definitions of the same concept. I do not think this problem is serious. Hume simply erred when he referred to the two as "definitions." Had he called them "characterizations" or "aspects" of "cause" the problem would never have arisen. So we can pass on to another question scholars have raised. Are the characterizations equally basic or is one primary and the other secondary? In response to this question, Terence Penelhum has written that "Hume's second definition is parasitic on the first."[24] This comment can be interpreted in the following way: The fact that we experience a constant conjunction between two objects leads us, on the occasion of our witnessing one, to anticipate the appearance of the other. The relationship between the two definitions is a causal one, from the first to the second.

Hume's account does, however, contain one point that has baffled scholars. He says, of both definitions, that they are "drawn from objects foreign to the cause" (170). The question, which Hume does not answer, is: What are these foreign objects? On this point there seems to be no scholarly agreement. To note here only two interpretations, John Wright says, "A cause is defined according to objects quite distinct from itself and its effect; namely, those objects whose observation stimulates the human organism to form the belief that it is the cause."[25] But Barry Stroud gives the following interpretation: "All that can be said is that we either have [the notion of causal necessity] or we don't, and that we get it only after having the appropriate kind of experience. I think that is what Hume is responding to when he acknowledges that any putative definition of causality will have to be 'drawn from something extraneous and foreign to it.'"[26]

After long efforts at trying to understand Hume's statement I have concluded that any interpretation I might give would be highly speculative, as likely wrong as right. So I forego any attempt to explain it, leaving it for the reader to interpret, as he or she thinks most fit.[27]

10. COROLLARIES (SECTIONS 30–34)

Hume concludes Section XIV by drawing several "corrollaries" (171) from his theory of causation. Although some of these are not peculiar to his theory, they are all of interest as examples of his views on a number of philosophical issues.

The first corollary Hume draws is the conclusion that all causes are efficient causes; he thus rejects the Aristotelian distinction between different types of causes. In his explanation of efficient causes he points out that they require our observation of the constant conjunction of two objects. Unless we observe this conjunction—and, presumably, have a feeling of anticipation as a result—he concludes, "there can never be a cause of any kind" (171). It follows from this conclusion that in a world without observers there would be no causes and effects.[28] He completes this corollary by adding that there is no distinction between a "*cause*" and an "*occasion*" (171). This conclusion is of some importance because he has used the term "occasion" several times in Part III. We can now assume that wherever it occurs it means the same as "cause."

The second corollary raises a question about an important metaphysical topic. Hume claims that his theory makes it "impossible to admit of any medium betwixt chance and an absolute necessity" (171), finally on the grounds that "the mind must either be determin'd or not to pass from one object to another" (171). He reaches no decision between the two here so one might ask whether Hume accepted complete mental determinism or, on the other hand, acknowledged that some of our mental transitions are gratuitous—not caused but matters of chance. At the very beginning of Book I he makes a statement that would indicate that he was willing to countenance the possibility of chance. In his original account of the association of ideas (of which our relating an effect to a cause is a prime example) he writes: "This uniting principle [association] among ideas is not to be consider'd as an inseparable connexion . . . but we are only to regard it as a gentle force, which commonly prevails."[29] Yet elsewhere in the *Treatise* he seems clearly to affirm mental determinism without qualification: "[In causal transitions] the thought is always determin'd to pass from the impression to the idea, and from that particular impression to that particular idea, without any choice or hesitation."[30]

The third corollary Hume draws follows directly from his two definitions of "cause"; namely, that we can provide no argument to establish that "every beginning of existence" (172) must have a cause. He concludes his remarks about this corollary with a statement, which I discussed in section 5, that the influence on the mind determining us to make a transition from cause to effect is "incomprehensible" (172).

Hume's final corollary is of considerable interest. He writes that "we can never have reason to believe that any object exists, of which we cannot form an idea" (172). He supports this conclusion by saying that "all our reasonings concerning causation are deriv'd from the experienc'd conjunction of objects, not from any reasoning or reflexion" (172). To what, we may ask, is Hume referring when he says that we can never have reason to believe that any *object* exists? What kind of object is in question here? We may, I think, definitely conclude that he is referring at least to external material objects. He says that, to have any reason to believe in the existence of an object, we must be able to form an idea of it. Since ideas are copies of impressions this means that we must have an impression of the object. But Hume has long since denied that we can have an impression of an external material object, writing that "nothing is ever present to the mind but perceptions" (67). Material objects are inconceivable to us because we cannot "conceive any kind of existence, but those perceptions, which have appeared in [the imagination]" (67–68). But he also adds another reason for endorsing the conclusion that we have no reason to believe in the existence of external objects, one based on his account of causation. Our causal "reasonings," he says, are derived from our experience of the conjunction of "objects." Since our experience consists in our perceptions, the objects we experience in such conjunctions will be those we perceive, or the content of our perceptions. As he puts it, "the same experience must give us a notion of these objects" (172). But we never perceive external material objects; therefore we can never have any reason to believe they exist.

Summary

Two quite different conclusions emerge from Hume's account of the idea of necessary connection and, as a result, from his entire theory of causation in Part III. On the one side, it is hardly necessary to reiterate that the theory represents one of his most original and brilliant accomplishments. In Section XIV Hume not only raised formidable objections to the established "objective" views of causation but offered a revolutionary new conception to put in their place. This conception has had a profound influence on the subsequent history of philosophy. Although it has had critics as well as supporters, its importance is attested by the fact that no one since Hume can write in an illuminating way about causation without taking his theory seriously into consideration.

As we have seen, in Section XIV Hume engages in irony against the defenders of "objective" causation. However, there is a deeper irony in the section. Hume rejected "objectivism" because it violated the Empiricist Principle. But, as we have found from our examination of his own theory, he is equally guilty of violating the Principle himself, in two ways. First, he included a notion of mental causation as part of his explanation of the idea of necessary connection. This notion is clearly a case of "objective" causation, hence is inconsistent with his epistemology. Although I have suggested a way of modifying his theory that would avoid this inconsistency, I can find no escape from the second—his appeal to past constant conjunctions of which, according to his epistemology, we can have no recollection. So we must conclude that Hume's theory of causation is one of his greatest contributions to philosophy but also one that he could not in consistency make.

13

CAUSAL RULES
AND ANIMAL "REASON"

(Part III, Sections XV–XVI)

Introduction

Although he completes his theory of causation in Section XIV, Hume does not end Part III there. Instead he adds two short sections to it. The first, entitled "Rules by which to judge of causes and effects," is clearly related to what has gone before. The second, "Of the reason of animals," while unrelated to what has gone immediately before, is, in addition to being interesting in itself, important for the light it sheds on Hume's views about reason and human nature.[1] My discussion of these sections in chapter 13 will be relatively brief. Since the two are quite different from each other I will divide my treatment of the text into two parts.

Text: Causal Rules

1. POSSIBLE CAUSAL RELATIONS (SECTION XV, PARAGRAPH 1)

Hume devotes most of Section XV to the statement of eight rules "*by which to judge of causes and effects*" (173). He prefaces his statement of these rules with a paragraph in which he begins by reminding readers that, according to his view, we cannot determine, prior to experience, what objects are causes and what objects their effects. He then goes a step further, writing: "Any thing may produce any thing. Creation, annihilation, motion, reason, volition; all these may arise from one another, or from any other object we can imagine" (173). Whatever one may think about the truth of this statement there are some questions about what it means. Four words in it—"may," "thing," "object," and "produce"—need interpretation. "May" can have two meanings; I think Hume intended both. To say that any thing may produce any thing means (a) that the statement involves no logical contradiction. That Hume intended at least this much seems clear from what he says in the final sentence of the paragraph. But he must have intended more because some relations between things may be logically possible and yet not be really possible because they are precluded by something other than logic. Specifically, if every object were necessarily connected with some other object, Hume's statement would be factually false. For example, if the collision of the cue ball with the object ball is necessarily connected with motion in the latter, it could not produce its annihilation instead, even though there is no logical contradiction in this supposition. So the statement must also mean at least (b) that there are no necessary connections between things. This is simply a reiteration of Hume's previous denial of "objective" causation. Turning to "thing" and "object" I believe Hume is using the two words synonymously here. But that leaves the question: Does he mean by them "external material object" or "perception"? Various arguments could be given in support of either interpretation but I will not pursue them because this question does not appear to affect the point he is making.[2] Finally, the word "produce" is equivalent to "cause," this being evident from the context.

But the entire passage contains a complication that is masked by its form and terminology. To understand it correctly we must distinguish between the point Hume is making verbally and the point that, according to his theory of causation, he should be making. Turning to the first, a straightforward reading of the passage has Hume concluding that any thing may produce any thing because there are no necessary connections between different things, therefore we have only their constant conjunctions to use as a basis for our causal "reasonings." However, it is obvious that, if this is what he means, he has not made his point well. One of the things we have learned from Hume's theory of causation is that necessary connection is essential to causation. If there are no necessary connections between things it is not possible for any thing to produce (cause) any thing. The only relations between things are those of constant conjunction and these, in themselves, are not causal relations. Strictly speaking, what Hume should have concluded is: *No thing* can produce any thing. I do not think this confusion in his language is serious because we can give his statement a different reading that will be consistent with his theory of causation and still convey the point he wants to make. The passage, thus, might be rephrased: Because there are no necessary connections between things, no thing may be said to produce any thing. Creation, annihilation, motion, reason, volition; all these may follow after [not "arise from"] one another.

But this is not enough. Hume certainly could have said more on the subject and, if he wished to illustrate the consequences of his theory of causation, should have done so. Since his statement is concerned with causal relations, what meaning should it be given if we interpret it according to his theory of causation? On this interpretation the picture changes substantially. In fact, Hume's statement can be given two interpretations, both of which are supported by the text. The first would take the following line: "When I [Hume] say that any thing may produce any thing, I must be understood to mean that, since the feeling of anticipation of an effect I have when I observe a cause results from my past experience of constant conjunctions of things and not on a perception of any necessary connection between those things, I cannot say, prior to experience, what cause may produce what effect. Rather, any thing may produce any thing." This interpretation seems to be implied by what he says in the first paragraph.

However, there are several passages in Part III that would support a slightly different interpretation. According to it Hume would mean: "Since, to say that any thing A causes any thing B is to say that when, after experiencing the past constant conjunctions of A's with B's, I observe an A, I have a feeling of anticipation that a B will occur, it follows that, when I say that any thing may produce any thing, I mean that, regardless of past constant conjunctions of A's with B's, when I observe an A, I may not anticipate the appearance of a B but may instead anticipate the appearance of something else." On this interpretation Hume is calling attention to the vagaries of human psychology. Although we generally, under the circumstances described, do anticipate a B when we observe an A, we may not do so. Thus "any thing may produce any thing" can be interpreted to read, "The observation of any thing may produce in our minds the anticipation of any thing."[3]

I do not think we need to choose between these two interpretations because both represent authentic aspects of Hume's views on causation. In the present context I would conclude that he had the first in mind when he said that any thing may produce any thing but he could well have had both. The important point in the passage is that he is reiterating his denial of any necessary connections between objects, whether these be understood as material bodies or as mental perceptions. Necessary connection, to the extent that it exists, exists solely in the feelings of the observer.[4]

2. THE EIGHT RULES (SECTION XV, PARAGRAPHS 3–10)

I will not discuss Hume's eight rules of causal reasoning in any detail. Although they are of considerable importance, both in themselves and historically, they do not contribute significantly to our understanding of his philosophy in Book I.

The first three rules are simply summaries of conclusions Hume had reached in developing his theory of causation.[5] Rule 4, however, goes beyond these and seems to be too strong. Hume says that we derive this rule "from experience" (173). What he means is that our experience is one of past constant conjunctions. But three questions might be raised on this issue. (1) Is our past experience really that of constant conjunctions? (2) Even if it is, what guarantee do we have that the same kind of conjunctions will hold in the future?[6] (3) The cause-effect relation requires necessary connection, which is the feeling of determination we experience to anticipate its customary effect when we observe a present cause. Since (as I have noted a bit earlier) we do not always feel such a determination, isn't the rule "same cause-same effect" a (slight) overstatement?[7]

Rules 5 and 6 need little comment. They are, as Hume points out, both derived from Rule 4. Assuming the rule "like cause—like effect," it follows that if several different objects produce the same effect there must be some quality in each of these objects that is identical and that is the true cause. On the other hand, if two resembling objects produce different effects, these objects must contain different qualities that cause the difference in the effects.

Rule 7 is also derivative from Rule 4, supplemented by Rules 5 and 6. It offers an explanation of a relation between causes and effects similar to the one John Stuart Mill was later, in his *System of Logic*, to label "concomitant variations."[8] Since it adds nothing of substance to the previous rules, it needs no comment. Nevertheless, Hume's warning about this rule, together with his illustration of heat and pleasure, is worthy of note.

Rule 8 needs little comment. It seems to provide a generally sound, if not unexceptionable, psychological generalization. The rule itself predates Hume, appearing, for example, in Hobbes, but accompanied by a quite different conception of causation.[9]

Hume concludes Section XV with some wise words on the difficulties of applying his rules of causal "reasoning" in practice, particularly when one is concerned with moral philosophy rather than with natural philosophy. Although one may take exception to his remark that these rules include "all the LOGIC I think proper to employ in my reasoning," and his perhaps too harsh judgment of "scholastic headpieces and logicians" (175), we must all agree with him that the application of rules, whether his or others, to guide our reasoning in the study of human nature is an extremely complex and difficult undertaking, fraught always with the possibility of error.[10]

Text: Animal "Reason"

1. KINDS OF ANIMAL "REASON" (SECTION XVI, PARAGRAPHS 1–8)

Section XVI probably comes as a surprise to most readers, considering what has gone before. Indeed, it is easy to view it as a delightful but still obvious digression from the argument of Book I. Such an appraisal, however, would miss the close relationship between Hume's views about the nature of "reasoning" in animals and in humans, as he expresses them here, and the general analysis of our "reasoning" about matters of fact that permeates his argument in Part III, and underlies his theory of causation.

After a rhetorical introductory paragraph Hume begins the argument of the section by emphasizing that, from our observation of animals, we must conclude that they engage in the same processes of "reasoning" that humans do. Thus, we can enlarge our understanding of human "reasoning" by observing the actions of animals. As he concludes: "When any hypothesis . . . is advanc'd to explain a mental operation, which is common to men and beasts, we must apply the same hypothesis to both" (177).

Proceeding to specifics, Hume points out that, from our observation of the actions of animals, we can conclude that they engage in two different kinds of reasoning: (1) "Reasoning" analogous to human "reasoning" from causes to effects and (2) a more sophisticated type of reasoning that adapts means to ends. He describes the first as "vulgar" and illustrates it by the case of a dog "that avoids fire and precipices, that shuns strangers, and caresses his master" (177). Speaking of these animal actions he writes: "I assert they proceed from a reasoning, that is not in itself different, nor founded on different principles, from that which appears in human nature" (177). In the remainder of Section XVI Hume develops this point, emphasizing the similarity between such animal "reasoning" and the transitions, based on past experience, we make in our imagination from causes to effects, and concluding that this similarity provides a proof of the account of human "reasoning" he has developed in Part III.

> Beasts certainly never perceive any real connexion among objects. 'Tis therefore by experience they infer one from another. They can never by any arguments form a general conclusion, that those objects, of which they have had no experience, resemble those of which they have. 'Tis therefore by means of custom alone, that experience operates upon them. All this was sufficiently evident with respect to man. But with respect to beasts there cannot be the least suspicion of mistake; which must be own'd to be a strong confirmation, or rather an invincible proof of my system. (178)

The second kind of animal reasoning Hume believes to constitute "more extraordinary instances of sagacity" and illustrates by a bird "that chooses with such care and nicety the place and materials of her nest, and sits upon her eggs for a due time, and in a suitable season" (177). He says nothing more about this type of animal reasoning in the section, probably because it is not directly analogous to the kind of human "reasoning" with which he has been concerned in Part III.[11]

2. "Reason" as an Unintelligible Instinct (Section XVI, Paragraph 9)

Hume concludes the section with a statement, based on his discussion of animals, about the nature of human "reason." From the context it is clear that the "reason" to which he is referring is "reason" as it engages in "reasoning" about matters of fact, in particular about causal relations.

> To consider the matter aright, reason is nothing but a wonderful and unintelligible instinct in our souls, which carries us along a certain train of ideas, and endows them with particular qualities, according to their particular situations and relations. This instinct, 'tis true, arises from past observation and experience; but can any one give the ultimate reason, why past experience and observation produces such an effect, any more than why nature alone shou'd produce it? (179)

This passage needs clarification. Since Hume is writing here about our causal "reasoning" and since a central point of Part III has been his thesis that such "reasoning" is the work of the imagination, we must conclude either that (a) he should have made imagination, not reason, the subject of both this passage and the entire section or (b) he is verbally conflating reason with imagination in them, as he has done before in Part III. Whatever his terminology, however, the important point he is making is that humans, like animals, do anticipate the appearance of a certain effect on observing a cause, after having experienced the constant conjunction of that cause with that effect in the past. No rational justification can be given for this mental propensity; it is simply the result of custom or habit. He describes it as a wonderful and unintelligible instinct. Certainly it is wonderful; without it we should probably perish. It is also, on Hume's epistemology, unintelligible. Whether it could be made intelligible on a different theory of causation is a question outside the scope of this inquiry.

Summary

The contents of the two final sections of Part III are quite disparate. In Section XV Hume concludes his theory of causation by setting down a list of rules to aid us in our causal "reasoning." The rules themselves are commendable and historically important. However, it is not clear how they relate to Hume's theory of causation. One is almost tempted to conclude that, when he wrote these rules, Hume was no longer aware of the revolutionary nature of the account of causation he had just completed but was rather, for the purpose of laying down rules, appealing to some form of causation in reality outside of human feelings that would give him a standard against which to judge the causal "inferences" we make. Unless he was doing this, it is difficult to understand how the rules (other than the first three) could serve any function.

Section XVI, although brief and subject to possible misinterpretation, should be viewed as a summation of Hume's theory of the nature of our "reasoning" about matters of fact, a part of his account of the human understanding that encompasses and goes beyond his analysis of causation. By concentrating on the "reason" in animals and drawing analogies between it and human "reasoning," Hume emphasizes the continuity between these forms of life and thus buttresses his naturalism, which is a basic principle underlying his effort to provide a science of human nature in the *Treatise*. Both animals and humans "reason" about matters of fact and they do so in similar ways. For such "reasoning," even at sophisticated levels, is accomplished through the imagination and is, thus, a nonrational process. Along with the animals we live and act largely through instinct.

Part 4

SCEPTICISM

Hume entitles Part IV "Of the sceptical and other systems of philosophy." This title, which suggests that the part will be devoted to an examination of various philosophical systems, both sceptical and nonsceptical, does not accurately describe its contents. With the exception of two short sections (III and IV) that include brief discussions of some views of the Aristotelians and the empiricists and one section (V) that pits theologians against materialists, the part is devoted to two main topics: (1) Hume's own original type of scepticism (in Sections I and VII) and (2) our knowledge of, but particularly our belief in bodies and minds (in Sections II and VI). The first of these two topics is primarily epistemological; Hume answers the question, What can we know? and then describes a way of life in which we can cope with the answer he has given. Although Sections I and VII are separated by about seventy-five pages of text, they are closely related to each other. To understand and appreciate Hume's scepticism fully, the reader should study each with the other in mind. With the second topic Hume goes beyond the range of epistemology, to face the ontological questions: Do bodies exist? and Do minds exist?

Some commentators have emphasized the sceptical character of Hume's philosophy throughout Book I. In doing so they have often focused their attention on the wrong places, pointing to various objects of ordinary belief of which Hume is alleged to be sceptical but virtually overlooking a much more sceptical dimension of his thought that he begins to develop in Part III and completes in Part IV. Although it is true that Hume concluded in Section VI of Part II that we can have no knowledge of an external material world, I believe that he would deny that many of his other putatively sceptical conclusions prior to Part IV are really sceptical.[1] To cite two examples: He came to the conclusion (in Part III, Section V) that we cannot recollect the past. But this does not mean that he was sceptical about memory; instead he redefined the concept. Also, although he rejected "objective" theories of "cause," he was not sceptical about causation itself; again he redefined the concept. Both it and "memory" became technical terms of his philosophy.

But at the beginning of Part III another, more subtle form of scepticism begins to take shape. It results from Hume's distinction between knowledge and "probability," and between reason and imagination. It leads to his conclusion that we can offer no rational justification for any of our beliefs about matters of fact, a view I have called Hume's nonrationalism.[2] This form of scepticism has close ties with the general scepticism of Part IV, ties I will try to illuminate in the chapters ahead.

Hume begins Part IV with an extreme form of scepticism that denies the distinction he had made at the beginning of Part III between knowledge and probability. Although he modifies this scepticism in an interesting and novel way before ending the book, the fact that he turns to scepticism in its final part enforces the conclusion that it constitutes the culmination of Hume's philosophy in Book I of the *Treatise*.[3]

14

HUME'S TOTAL
SCEPTICISM AND IRRATIONALISM

(Part IV, Section I)

Introduction

Hume entitles Section I of Part IV "Of scepticism with regard to reason." As we will find as we follow his argument in it, his point in using this title is to signal his intention to deny that reason can be a source of knowledge. But this raises a question: What *is* reason, that cannot produce knowledge? The term itself has several possible meanings and, as we have seen in earlier chapters, Hume has used it ambiguously throughout Part III, repeatedly talking about "reasoning" concerning matters of fact even after he had made it clear that this "reasoning" is the work not of reason but of imagination and is nonrational, in the sense of being something he cannot rationally justify. If we were to rely on Hume's common previous usage, consequently, we could easily be misled in our attempt to decide what he means by "reason" and "reasoning."

Fortunately, the first section of Part III (which Hume entitled "Of knowledge") contains an explicit discussion of the nature of reason in relation to the possible acquisition of knowledge. Since his account there is directly relevant to the argument he develops in Section I of Part IV, I will summarize it briefly here.[1] After beginning his discussion with the observation that the objects of possible knowledge are relations, Hume divides relations into two groups—those that depend entirely on the ideas we compare and those that may be changed without any change in the ideas. We can, he continues, have knowledge only of the first group, either through intuition or demonstration. Of the second group, which consists of our beliefs about matters of fact, we must content ourselves with "probability" or opinion. Limiting our discursive knowledge to demonstration he argues that we are able to carry on a "chain of reasoning" leading to conclusions whose truth we can know in only two sciences—algebra and arithmetic. "There remain, therefore, algebra and arithmetic as the *only* sciences, in which we can carry on a chain of reasoning, to any degree of intricacy, and yet preserve a perfect exactness and certainty. We are possest of a precise standard, by which we can judge of the equality and proportion of numbers; and according as they correspond or not to that standard, we determine their relations, *without any possibility of error*" (71—italics added). Although this conclusion narrowly circumscribes the realm of knowledge, it is clear that Hume is implying that in algebra and arithmetic we *can* attain it. We can do so because, by the use of our reason, we can demonstrate our conclusions to be true.

Although he does not refer back to this earlier view, in Section I of Part IV Hume returns to the question of mathematical knowledge, to reconsider the conclusion he had reached about the relationship between reason and knowledge in Section I of Part III. Starting from a reassessment of the possibility of knowledge in mathematics, he develops an unusual two-step argument that leads him to total scepticism or the complete destruction of reason. But he then draws back, appealing to his theory of natural belief to save him from the "Pyrrhonism" into which his argument has led him.

Text

1. Mathematical Knowledge Reconsidered (Paragraphs 1–2)

Hume begins Part IV with the statement: "In all demonstrative sciences the rules are certain and infallible; but when we apply them, our fallible and uncertain faculties are very apt to depart from them, and fall into error."[2] Because this is true, we do not have any adequate assurance that our results when we engage in such reasoning are correct. So he concludes, "*all knowledge* degenerates into probability" (180—italics added). Thus at the beginning of Part IV Hume is repudiating the view he held at the beginning of Part III that, in "demonstrative sciences" (mathematics), we can reason "without any possibility of error," hence attain knowledge. But, he immediately adds, we can enhance the probability by such devices as recalculation or by gauging the reaction of our peers to the results we have reached. Although we cannot claim knowledge in mathematics, we can claim an increasing probability. So Hume ends his introductory statement on an optimistic note.

Is Hume's optimism justified? Two preliminary points need to be emphasized. (1) In his discussion in Part III, Section I, although he had limited knowledge to the demonstrative sciences, he was emphatic in claiming that in them we can know things. By reducing these sciences to probability he is, as he states, reducing *all* knowledge to the same status.

We can, therefore, *know* nothing. Such a reduction produces scepticism, although in a possibly mitigated form. (2) Since the change Hume makes in this section constitutes the repudiation of a conclusion he had reached earlier on a central point of his epistemology, we can ask: Why this crucial change in his thought? He says he makes the change because of his recognition of human fallibility. Even if the rules in the demonstrative sciences are certain and infallible, we are apt to fall into error when we attempt to apply them. However, Hume had another reason for making the change. I will discuss it in my summary of the chapter.

Hume's argument in the first two paragraphs of the section hardly seems persuasive. Although no one would deny that we are fallible, such a fact in itself seems scarcely sufficient to support the unqualified claim that we can know nothing at all, if only for the reason that any argument to the effect that we are fallible about everything is self-referentially self-destructive. Nor does Hume attempt any such argument. On the contrary, he asserts only that we *sometimes* make mistakes. But if his point is qualified in this way, it might be asked, why does he conclude that *all* knowledge degenerates into probability? Can we not legitimately claim knowledge on those occasions on which "[our understanding's] testimony was just and true" (180)? Although he does not address this point explicitly, Hume might reply that, even though we sometimes reason correctly, we can never be sure on any given occasion that we are actually doing so, hence no claim we might make affirming the truth of any conclusion we reach is fully warranted. The *best* we can claim is that it is probably true.

But even the guarded optimism Hume expresses in his opening paragraphs does not last. In the four paragraphs that follow, the tone of his remarks changes completely, converting him from optimism to pessimism. This change is the result of a novel two-step argument, based on a recognition of human fallibility, that first confirms his "probabilistic" scepticism and then reduces it to total scepticism. I will devote the next two sections to this argument.

2. The First Step: From Knowledge to Probability (Paragraphs 3–4)

After some anecdotal remarks about the attitudes and activities of merchants concerning their accounts (181), Hume takes the first step of his two-step argument in the latter half of the third paragraph. Although, like many of his arguments, it is quite short, he manages within a few sentences to state it in two different ways. Suppose first, he says, we are attempting to add a long column of numbers. We cannot be sure the answer we reach is correct. The best we can claim is that it is probably so. But suppose that, to gain certainty, we break the column of numbers up, adding only two numbers at a time, until we have worked our way through the entire column. Could we not then be assured that our answer is correct? No, replies Hume, because we can never be sure just where to mark the dividing line between additions of whose results we can claim knowledge and those of which we can claim only probability. As he puts it, "We shall find it impracticable to shew the precise limits of knowledge and of probability, or discover that particular number, at which the one ends and the other begins" (181). But why should this pose a problem for knowledge? Hume's answer is that, because knowledge and probability are of "contrary and disagreeing natures" (181), we should be able to distinguish the one sharply from the other. That we are unable to do so makes it impossible for us ever to justify the claim that any addition we make is a case of knowledge rather than probability.

Hume's second formulation of the argument runs in the opposite direction from the first, from the simple to the complex. He writes: "Besides, if any single addition were certain, every one wou'd be so, and consequently the whole or total sum; unless the whole can be different from all its parts" (181). What Hume seems to mean is that, if we can add any two numbers together without any possibility of error, then we should be able to do so with any addition containing these numbers, no matter how long it might be. Since we cannot do the last without possibility of error, we cannot do the first either. On the basis of this two-directional argument Hume concludes: "Therefore all knowledge resolves itself into probability, and becomes at last of the same nature with that evidence, which we employ in common life" (181).

Although both of Hume's arguments rely to some degree on psychological considerations, hence are difficult to evaluate with precision, they seem far from coercive. Rather, they contain obvious logical flaws. To take the first, suppose we agree with him both that we cannot guarantee the truth of any long addition we do and that we cannot say at exactly what point knowledge ends and probability begins; does it follow that we can *never* say of any two numbers we add that we know we have done so correctly? How about 1 + 1 = 2? The second argument seems to be based on a confusion. It rests on the supposition that a whole cannot be different from its parts. So let us suppose we have a long column of numbers to add. Suppose also, as Hume does for the purposes of the argument, that we can add two simple numbers (like 1 + 1) correctly. There is no reason to conclude that, just because we can make this simple addition correctly, we must be able to do the same with the long, complicated addition. The claim that knowledge is possible in the first addition is quite compatible with the claim that it is not in the second. In such a situation the whole is, as far as knowledge is concerned, different from its parts.

Hume concludes his first-step argument with a remark of considerable importance to our understanding and evaluation of his scepticism. "I had almost said, that [my conclusion] was certain; but I reflect, that it must reduce *itself*, as well as every other reasoning, and from knowledge degenerate into probability" (181). This statement has two important implications. First, in it Hume *explicitly* broadens the scope of his scepticism. He began the section with an attack on the knowledge pretensions of demonstrative reasoning in mathematics. But in saying now that his argument can be applied to his own reasoning, which is clearly not itself mathematical, as well as to every other reasoning, he is making a much broader claim about his scepticism. He is implying that reasoning, of whatever type it might be, is subject to the same limitations as mathematical reasoning. It can never yield knowledge but only probability.[3] The second point concerns the limitations of his own argument. Since it is an example of reasoning and since reasoning results only in probability, Hume correctly and candidly draws the conclusion that his own thesis regarding the "probable" nature of demonstrative reasoning is itself not something he can legitimately claim to know. It, too, reduces to probability.

3. The Second Step: From Probability to Nothing (Paragraphs 5–6)

Assuming the correctness of the conclusion of the first step of Hume's argument—that all knowledge reduces to probability—we are ready to turn to the second, and crucial, step. Hume gives a preliminary statement of this step in the fifth paragraph, then states it in full in the sixth. As a summary of the relation between the two steps and of the course the second step will take he writes: "As demonstration is subject to the controul of probability [first step], so is probability liable to a new correction by a reflex act of the mind, wherein the nature of our understanding, and our reasoning from the first probability become our objects [second step]" (182). I will reproduce the second step in Hume's words at some length and then, because his way of formulating it is quite difficult to follow, restate it as I understand it.

> Having thus found in every probability, beside the original uncertainty inherent in the subject, a new uncertainty deriv'd from the weakness of that faculty, which judges, and having adjusted these two together, we are oblig'd by our reason to add a new doubt deriv'd from the possibility of error in the estimation we make of the truth and fidelity of our faculties. This is a doubt, which immediately occurs to us, and of which, if we wou'd closely pursue our reason, we cannot avoid giving a decision. But this decision, tho' it shou'd be favourable to our preceeding judgment, being founded only on probability, must weaken still further our first evidence, and must itself be weaken'd

by a fourth doubt of the same kind, and so on *in infinitum;* till at last there remain nothing of the original probability. (182)

Perhaps the best way to grasp the point of Hume's argument is through an example. Suppose I have just added a long column of numbers. Recognizing the difficulty of the computation, I realize I may have made a mistake. Although I am fairly confident of my conclusion, I would hesitate to claim I know it to be correct but would content myself with calling it probably so and perhaps then estimate this probability, giving it a figure, say, of 90 percent. But I cannot, Hume goes on, therefore conclude that the probability that my calculation is correct rests at 90 percent. My judgment that the calculation is 90 percent correct has resulted from my assessment of the relative fallibility of my reasoning process. But this judgment itself is made by an introspective examination of my original reasoning process, conducted by a process of reasoning. Since this second process of reasoning is itself fallible, its results are also only probable. So the original probability of 90 percent must be diluted by a second probability, leaving it at, say, 80 percent. As Hume puts it, "We are oblig'd by our reason to add a new doubt deriv'd from the possibility of error in the estimation we make of the truth and fidelity of our faculties." But then, in making this second probability estimate, since I am using the same fallible faculties, I must admit that this new estimate is no more than probable. Whatever probability assignment I give it, the result will be a further lowering of my original probability estimate, below the 80 percent at which it now stands. But, once again, I am employing fallible faculties in making this estimate of the fallibility of my faculties so must make a further reduction in my original probability estimate. And so on *"in infinitum,"* with the result, as Hume concludes, that "even the vastest quantity, which can enter into human imagination, must in this manner be reduc'd to nothing" (182).

This is an original, ingenious argument, well worthy of the subtle mind of Hume. But it gives rise to several questions. Three, in particular, seem serious.

1. It seems to involve a confusion. Hume is certainly correct in his initial contention—that we are not completely sure we have arrived at the correct conclusion when we first add a long column of numbers (or when we engage in any other complex reasoning); errors can creep in. So we must content ourselves with saying that our conclusion is only probably correct. Whether we can go further and stipulate a precise probability estimate of the correctness of our conclusion, although dubious, does not affect the argument because we can say that there is *some* statement of probability that is correct, just as there is some conclusion to our original addition that is correct. This is true whether we are able to state that probability correctly

or not. So we have two probability statements to consider: (a) the correct statement of probability, or the actual mathematical probability of the correctness of my answer and (b) my own estimate of that probability, which may well be different from (a). Which of these two is it that Hume's argument must claim to reduce to nothing? It cannot be (a); that cannot change any more than the correct sum of the original addition can change. So it must be (b). Let us try to see how Hume's argument attempts to effect a change in it. According to it, I have estimated the probability that I have added the column of numbers correctly at 90 percent. But when I examine my understanding, I must recognize that, because I am fallible, this examination itself is prone to error so can be only probable. I assess the probability of error here at, say, 10 percent, so reduce the probability of the correctness of my original estimate to 80 percent. And so on, into the infinite regress.

The crux of Hume's case rests on his move from my original probability estimate of 90 percent to a new probability estimate of 80 percent, which starts the regressive probability claim he then generates. This is, I believe, an illicit move. Suppose I do as Hume says. I examine the reasoning that led me to reach the 90 percent probability estimate but then recognize that this examination itself, because it was conducted by my fallible reason, can yield a conclusion that is also no more than probable. What would the probability in this examination be a probability about? If Hume's argument is to succeed, *whatever* the probability is about, it must have the effect of lowering the probability of my original estimate of probability (i.e., 90 percent) because that is what Hume attempts to reduce to nothing. At most there are only two points relevant to my original probability estimate that a probable conclusion resulting from my introspective examination of my reasoning process in reaching that estimate could be. I could reach a probable conclusion, first, that my original 90 percent probability estimate was mistaken or, second, that I had in fact originally estimated the probability at 90 percent. If I reached the first conclusion, the fact that I could say only that there is an element of probability in my judgment that the original probability estimate is mistaken would not alter that estimate in any way. The original estimate would still stand as I had made it; all I could now say is that I am unable to demonstrate it to be either correct or mistaken. On the second possible error in my examination of my original reasoning, I might be mistaken in concluding that I had made a probability estimate of 90 percent. But presumably I had made *some* estimate—90 percent, 89 percent . . . My present ability to state only with probability what that estimate was does not change, hence cannot lower the estimate I in fact made. Since these seem to be the only two points on which Hume could generate his regress, which requires a lowering of the original probability estimate, and since neither can succeed in setting the regress in motion, his second-step argument cannot produce the sceptical conclusion he draws from it.

2. The second problem with Hume's argument turns on a question of psychological fact; it concerns what he claims we do after we have engaged in a piece of complex reasoning, like adding a long column of numbers. Suppose we have just completed such an addition and realize we may have made an error. Do we do what Hume claims we do, or do we do something else? Speaking for myself, I cannot recollect ever having engaged in the kind of introspective examination of my reasoning Hume describes. Rather I do something quite different. If, after adding a long column of numbers, I am not sure my answer is correct, I simply add the numbers over again. If I get the same answer (and again the same answer after a third attempt) I conclude that I have added correctly. It is, of course, conceivable that I have mis-added each time but it is reasonable to conclude that the procedure I actually employ, instead of decreasing the probability that my answer is correct, increases it instead. Thus my claim to knowledge does not degenerate into a probability that reduces itself to nothing, but quite the opposite.[4]

Perhaps my description of what I do misses the point of Hume's argument. He is not concerned with what we in fact do but rather with what we ought to do. That, at least, is the message of the opening sentence of his preliminary statement of the second-step argument. "In every judgment, which we can form concerning probability, as well as concerning knowledge, we *ought* always to correct the first judgment, deriv'd from the nature of the object, by another judgment, deriv'd from the nature of the understanding" (181–82—italics added). What is the force of the "ought" Hume makes in this statement? Why ought we to correct our first judgment in his way, which, he then contends, leads to the conclusion that that judgment lacks any probability at all? This hardly seems to constitute a *correction* of the judgment in question. Is it not better to correct our first judgment in the way I do, which can lead us to a conclusion we can reasonably claim to be true?

3. To appreciate the third problem in Hume's second-step argument we must return briefly to the first step of his argument. There, as I noted in section 2, he concludes that all reasoning reduces to probability and then adds, as he should, that this point applies to the reasoning he has just used in his own argument. However, he makes no similar concession in regard to his second-step argument. But, since this argument is as much a case of reasoning as the first, the same kind of acknowledgment should follow it. So Hume should have concluded the second step with some such statement—parallel to his statement regarding his first-step argument—as: "I

had almost said, that this was probable; but I reflect, that it must reduce *itself,* as well as every other reasoning, and from probability degenerate into nothing." In other words, just as the first step of Hume's argument for total scepticism is self-destructive, so too is the second step, and in its case the destruction is total. On its own terms, the entire argument refutes itself.[5]

In this and the preceding section I have described the two steps of Hume's argument for total scepticism and then have raised objections to both. The conclusion we must reach is that, although his reasoning is subtle and ingenious, Hume does not make his case. This is not, of course, the conclusion he reaches. Just the opposite. At the very end of the sixth paragraph, after arguing that all reasoning reduces to nothing, he elaborates this point. In doing so he makes a distinction that is of considerable importance to his sceptical philosophy. I will discuss his conclusion and his distinction in the next section.

4. HUME'S TOTAL SCEPTICISM (PARAGRAPH 6)

The last sentence of the sixth paragraph of Section I reads as follows: "When I reflect on the natural fallibility of my judgment, I have less confidence in my opinions, than when I only consider the objects concerning which I reason; and when I proceed still farther, to turn the scrutiny against every successive estimation I make of my faculties, all the rules of logic require a continual diminution, and at last a total extinction of *belief* and *evidence.*"[6] That this sceptical conclusion is not one to be taken lightly but represents a view that Hume wishes to emphasize is made evident by the fact that he repeats it, in even stronger terms, a bit later in the section. "*I have here prov'd,* that the very same principles, which make us form a decision upon any subject . . . *I say, I have prov'd,* that these same principles, when carry'd farther, and apply'd to every new reflex judgment, must, *by continually diminishing the original evidence, at last reduce it to nothing,* and utterly subvert all belief and opinion" (183–84—italics added).

It is important to recognize that Hume's two-step argument has led him to two different conclusions, because this fact has significant consequences for his philosophy. He says that the argument results in the total extinction of (1) belief and (2) evidence. The first of these consequences is psychological; the second is epistemological. To believe something is to be in a certain mental state and to have evidence is to possess reasons capable of supporting or justifying what one believes.[7] Hume's conclusion is that his argument not only destroys our beliefs, but it equally destroys any reasons we might give for holding those beliefs. This conclusion Hume calls "*total* scepticism."[8]

Although Hume's scepticism encompasses most of our beliefs, since these are usually based on reasons, a question could be raised about whether it is *total*. Does his argument lead to the conclusion that we can know *nothing?* To answer this question we must go back to his discussion of knowledge in Section I of Part III. There he concluded that the only knowledge we can have is through intuition or through demonstration (70–71). But Hume's two-step argument is directed against the things we think we know through demonstration. He says nothing in it about the possibility of knowledge through intuition. Would his argument apply to such putative knowledge as well? It might be argued that intuitive knowledge escapes the argument because it does not involve reasoning. But it does involve judgment, against which the argument is addressed. In any case, since Hume states without qualification that his two-step argument applies to *all* knowledge, it is reasonable to conclude that this includes what he had termed intuitive knowledge in his earlier account in Part III.[9] So it seems fair to accept Hume's conclusion that the scepticism to which his two-step argument has led him is indeed total.

5. HUME'S RESPONSE TO TOTAL SCEPTICISM: TOTAL IRRATIONALISM (PARAGRAPHS 7–11)

Hume had an acute sense of the dramatic. Nowhere is it more vividly displayed than in Section I of Part IV. One would naturally expect that, after having reached the sceptical conclusion that any attempt he might make to give reasons in support of anything he believes must lead to the destruction of those reasons, Hume would, as a rational human being, abandon all his beliefs. But he does not. Quite the contrary. Immediately after destroying any possibility of his justifying his beliefs at the end of the sixth paragraph, he reverses himself by saying he does not sincerely assent to his own argument: "Shou'd it here be ask'd me, whether I sincerely assent to this argument, which I seem to take such pains to inculcate, and whether I be really one of those sceptics, who hold that all is uncertain, and that our judgment is not in *any* thing possest of *any* measures of truth and falshood; I shou'd reply, that this question is entirely superfluous, and that neither I, nor any other person was ever sincerely and constantly of that opinion" (183).

Anyone reading these passages carefully is bound to be taken aback. How can Hume refuse to accept a conclusion whose truth he claims to have proved? This is surely the height of irrationality. Such a reaction would, however, be premature, because at this point Hume introduces one of the central tenets of Book I—his theory of natural belief—to the resolution of what is arguably the fundamental question of epistemology; namely, whether we must accept total scepticism or whether we can find some way to avoid it. Hume gives his reason for his crucial reversal of stance in the sentence immediately following the one I have just reproduced. "Nature, by an absolute and uncontroulable necessity has determin'd us to judge as well as to breathe and feel" (183). To understand the significance of this abrupt turn in Hume's thought we must go back briefly to the sceptical conclusion he had reached at the end of the previous paragraph, in which he maintained that his two-step argument led to "a total extinction of belief and evidence." He is now retracting the first half of that conclusion. Although his sceptical argument succeeds in destroying the evidence, or reasons for our beliefs, it does not destroy our beliefs themselves, because it cannot do so. To judge is to believe, and we can no more stop judging than we can stop breathing and feeling. The fact that we can offer no reasons to support our beliefs is irrelevant; we continue to believe anyway. This is not a matter of choice for us because belief is "a faculty, which nature has antecedently implanted in the mind, and render'd unavoidable."[10]

Although Hume's view regarding belief raises some questions we will have to consider further, his point about the necessity of our believing seems well taken. First are our natural beliefs. It is hard to disagree with Hume's claim that we must believe in the existence of an external world or a causal power in objects. But there are other beliefs that seem equally hard to avoid. To function as living human beings it seems vital that we believe, for example, that some substances nourish our bodies and others poison them. The thesis that we should suspend our judgment about everything, which Hume attributes to "that fantastic sect"[11] (presumably the Pyrrhonists), would be difficult, indeed, to put into practice. Nevertheless, if it is impossible for us to offer reasons in support of any of our beliefs, why should we continue to believe anything? That this question raises a problem is evident from a comment I made earlier. If *all* of our reasoning in support of what we believe is in the end self-destructive it would seem to follow that, if we still continue to believe, our beliefs must be irrational.

Hume offers three responses to this charge. The first I have already given—that, whether it be irrational or not, we *must* continue to believe. We simply have no choice in the matter. If we grant the force of this argument, as I have just done, we still, however, face a problem. Although some of our beliefs seem forced on us by our nature, others do not. In fact, most of our beliefs are avoidable. Hume presumably believes mathematics; he also presumably believes his own philosophy. Since he is under no natural compulsion to believe either of these things and since his scepticism destroys any reasons he might have for believing them, if he nevertheless continues to do so, his beliefs are gratuitously irrational.

Hume's second response is more complex. In a long discussion occupying the next several paragraphs he argues that the sceptical conclusion he reached at the end of the second step of his argument is not one we often arrive at when we actually attempt to assess the probability of something we believe. His reason for saying this, as I understand him, is that, in order to reduce this probability to nothing, we would have to perform a large number of successive examinations of our thought processes, assessing the probability of each in turn. But we are simply not prepared to engage in such a taxing mental procedure, because it is beyond our ordinary psychological limits. Summing up his argument on this point, he writes that "after the first and second decision [assessment of our mental processes] . . . the action of the mind becomes forc'd and unnatural, and the ideas faint and obscure. . . . The attention is on the stretch: The posture of the mind is uneasy" (185). This argument does not deny that, if we were to continue our successive assessments of the probability of our mental processes in any given case, we should ultimately discover that we could give no rational justification for our original belief. What it claims, rather, is that we do not often continue the process that far; in fact we do not continue it very far at all. Whatever its truth as a psychological generalization, however, this conclusion does not affect the point at issue, which is epistemological.

Hume's third response to the charge of irrationality—which, for our purposes in understanding his philosophy, is the most important—is to explain our irrationality through his general theory of human nature. Immediately after having claimed that we are so constituted that we must believe, he describes the source from which our beliefs spring, explaining that "*belief is more properly an act of the sensitive, than of the cogitative part of our natures*" (183). I take Hume to mean by this that our beliefs are based on feeling rather than on reason, therefore to pose the question of their irrationality as a possible problem for him, as I did at the beginning of this discussion, is simply an irrelevancy.

Hume had taken the position early in Part III that our beliefs about matters of fact are based on feeling rather than on reason. In my interpretation of his view I argued that this position should be described as nonrationalism rather than irrationalism, because he is saying only that these beliefs "stand outside of" reason, not that they are opposed to reason. Reason, if it could be employed, might well support them.[12] In Section I of Part IV he enlarges on this position and alters it in two important ways. (1) He applies it not just to our beliefs about matters of fact but to *all* of our beliefs. (2) He no longer contents himself with his nonrationalistic position of Part III but embraces irrationalism. Our beliefs not only stand outside of reason but are in opposition to reason, because he has proved that any attempt to give reasons in their support is self-destructive. Hume's antidote for his total scepticism, thus, is total irrationalism.

Before leaving this difficult but crucial issue in Hume's philosophy, I should add one further point. As I mentioned earlier, I think Hume is right when he says that all of us (including himself) believe things. Some of these things we believe because we must. But a question arises. What support can he give for this claim he makes about human nature? To answer this question we must go back to his two-step argument. The claim under consideration—that people believe things because they must—concerns a matter of fact so is not a demonstrative but only a "probability" judgment. As such it falls under the second step of his argument. Without going through the details of that argument, we know what its outcome must be. The argument will reduce the evidence for his belief, as well as his belief itself, to nothing. Although Hume may still cling to the belief he will do so even though any attempt he might make to support it rationally must end in complete failure. Like all the rest of his beliefs, his theory of natural belief, which is a fundamental tenet of his philosophy of human nature, is itself irrational.

6. THE METAPHOR OF THE MONARCH (PARAGRAPH 12)

After his long psychological explanation of why we do not ordinarily reach the conclusion that our beliefs can have no rational support, Hume ends Section I with a general attack on reason. He does this through a picturesque metaphor I call "the metaphor of the *monarch*." It runs as follows:

> Reason first appears in possession of the throne, prescribing laws, and imposing maxims, with an absolute sway and authority. Her enemy, therefore, is oblig'd to take shelter under her protection, and by making use of rational arguments to prove the fallaciousness and imbecility of reason, produces, in a manner, a patent under her hand and seal. This patent has at first an authority, proportion'd to the present and immediate authority of reason, from which it is deriv'd. But as it is suppos'd to be contradictory to reason, it gradually diminishes the force of that governing power, and its own at the same time; till at last they both vanish away into nothing, by a regular and just diminution. (186–87)

Hume goes on to add that, fortunately, we rarely continue the dialectic between reason and scepticism to its final outcome because "nature breaks the force of all sceptical arguments in time" (187) or, in other words, we tire of pursuing them. But then he reiterates a further, crucial conclusion. "Were we to trust entirely to [the] self-destruction [of these sceptical arguments], that can never take place, 'till they have first subverted all conviction, and have totally destroy'd human reason" (187).

This sceptical conclusion does follow from Hume's argument—if that argument is cogent. But is it? Let us examine it more closely. Suppose, for example, a cognitivist were to say, "We are justified in believing certain things because we can establish them to be true," and a sceptic were to attack this claim, with the result that an argument between the two develops. It is not necessary to go into the details of this dialectical confrontation, with its series of arguments and counterarguments, in order to appreciate Hume's point. He concludes that *both* reason and scepticism are destroyed at the end of the process. But is this correct? Suppose that, after long debate, the cognitivist offers his final argument, which the sceptic then attempts to rebut. Now the sceptic's rebuttal must be either cogent or not cogent. We can ignore the second possibility because, if it were true, reason would remain viable. So let us assume that the sceptic's argument is cogent. If so, reason seems, as Hume contends, to be destroyed. But is scepticism, as he also contends, destroyed along with reason? Quite the contrary. If the sceptic has the last word, reason is destroyed and the sceptic has gained his end, so can apparently succeed to the throne.

But the sceptic would do well to hesitate before he takes his regal seat. His ascendancy to the throne, as we have just seen, rests on the supposition that his final argument against the cognitivist is cogent. It is an example of the use of reason to destroy reason. But this is a goal it is absolutely impossible for his argument to accomplish, for the claim that reason can be destroyed by a cogent argument is self-contradictory. In any argument between a cognitivist and a sceptic of the type Hume portrays in his metaphor of the monarch, the cognitivist—not the sceptic—*necessarily* emerges the victor. Thus the cognitivist need have no worries; his throne is *always* secure against any attempt by a sceptic, Hume included, to mount an argument capable of unseating him.[13]

Summary

It is clear from its title that Section I is concerned with a fundamental philosophical issue. What is not clear, but will become apparent only at the conclusion of this study, is that the section is essential to Hume's argument in Book I. In the section Hume broadens his scepticism in a significant way. At the beginning of Part III he had divided our ideas into those that yield knowledge (mathematics) and those that yield only "probability" or opinion (matters of fact). If we understand his denial that the second group constitute knowledge to imply scepticism about it, we can say that in Part III Hume had reached a position of broad but only partial scepticism. In Section I he turns his attention to mathematics again, but now to repudiate his earlier conclusion. Through his two-step argument he reduces mathematics, as well as everything else, not just to "probability" but finally to nothing. Because this argument destroys both our beliefs and any reasons we can offer for holding them, it results in *total* scepticism.

Why did Hume broaden his scepticism in such a significant way at the beginning of Part IV? He says he made the change because of his recognition of human fallibility but he had another, more important reason for doing so. As we will see before ending this study, the argument of Section I forms the foundation for that of the last section of Book I (Section VII). In Section I Hume is preparing the way for his final sceptical position, which is a variation of and, he believes, an improvement over classical Pyrrhonism. Although the full explanation of Hume's final form of scepticism must be deferred until chapter 18, two conclusions that emerge from Section I are directly relevant to that scepticism. (1) Hume believed that his ultimate position required the establishment of total theoretical or epistemological scepticism. Hence his two-step argument and his metaphor of the monarch, which he assumed to have successfully destroyed reason. (2) He was equally insistent, however, that his argument, although it destroys all rational basis for belief, does not destroy belief itself. The preservation of belief is essential to Hume's final form of scepticism, distinguishing it in his mind from the scepticism of the Pyrrhonists.

To repeat, it is essential that we do not lose sight of two important points about Hume's scepticism. First, his two-step argument, he contends, results in total scepticism because it destroys both belief and evidence. But in his refusal to accept his own sceptical conclusion Hume rescues only one of the two victims of his argument—belief. He says nothing later in the section about the revival of evidence for our beliefs; indeed, in his metaphor of the monarch he reiterates his total theoretical scepticism. Second, the fact that he continues to believe, even after destroying the rational basis for belief, commits him to total irrationalism. So we are left with a question: Does Hume later in Part IV offer any argument to resuscitate reason and, hence, rescue himself from irrationalism, or does reason remain, as he leaves it at the end of Section I, "totally destroy'd" (187)?

15

BELIEF IN AN
EXTERNAL MATERIAL WORLD

(Part IV, Section II)

Introduction

As we have seen, Hume talks about the external material world, raising questions concerning our possible knowledge of it, in a number of places throughout Book I. This is understandable. Not only is the issue important in itself but, as Berkeley had amply demonstrated and as Hume was well aware, it poses a particularly troublesome problem for anyone who accepts an empiricist theory of ideas. In Section II of Part IV Hume returns to the subject, but no longer to answer the question of whether such a world is conceivable to us. As far as he is now concerned, he has already answered that question—in Section VI of Part II. So he contents himself with a re-iteration of his conclusion there. At the beginning of the section he writes: "For as to the notion of external existence, when taken for something specifically different from our perceptions, we have already shewn its absurdity."[1] Going back to that earlier argument it would be worth our while to repeat what Hume had to say in it about our possible knowledge of external reality. There he had written: "Let us fix our attention out of ourselves as much as possible: Let us chace our imagination to the heavens, or to the utmost limits of the universe; we never really advance a step beyond ourselves, nor can conceive any kind of existence, but those perceptions, which have appeared in that narrow compass."[2]

Nevertheless, Hume is convinced that, even though we cannot conceive of an external material world, we still believe it exists. This is a natural belief we all share. In Section II his main object is to explain and account for this universal belief. Before he concludes the section he raises and discusses a related question of great ontological significance—Does such a world even exist?

Before turning to Section II itself I should make some preliminary remarks concerning my treatment of it. Section II is by far the longest section in Book I, occupying over thirty pages of text. It is also the most complex. As a result I cannot, in a limited space, discuss it in all its details. Fortunately, for philosophical purposes, this is not necessary. Much of Hume's argument in the section is psychological. Although his analyses of the operations of the mind are acute, as well as interesting in themselves, they are often only peripherally related to our central epistemological and metaphysical concerns. In what follows I will concentrate on Hume's philosophical views, limiting my discussion of his psychology to points that illuminate these.[3]

Another preliminary point concerns terminology, the now familiar ambiguity in Hume's use of the word "object." Although he often uses the word in this section in the ordinary way, to mean a physical body or a material entity in an external world, in some passages it is not clear whether he is doing so, particularly when he talks about such things as "objects of perception" and "sensible objects." To minimize confusion, in this chapter I will adopt the following terminology: When I am referring to the object or content of a perception, for example, the "sun" that is part of my conscious experience, I will use the simple term *perception* and when I am referring to an object in the external material world—the sun that exists in space—I will use either the term *material object* or the term *body*. If, on occasion, it is not clear what Hume means by "object" I will note that fact.

In Section II Hume devotes considerable attention to an unusual concept he may have derived from his study of Berkeley. This is a perception, but one that is not being perceived. An example would be the perception "sun"—in distinction from the sun in space—which is ordinarily a content of consciousness, during the time no one is conscious of it. I will call this an *unperceived perception*.

Finally, we should note that the title "Of scepticism with regard to the senses" (187), although suggestive of Hume's intent, does not accurately describe the contents of the section. I think Hume used this title to indicate that he was pursuing the path he had forged in Section I, which he had entitled "Of scepticism with regard to reason" (180).

Text

1. SCEPTICISM AND BELIEF ABOUT AN EXTERNAL MATERIAL WORLD (PARAGRAPHS 1 AND 2)

Hume begins Section II with an analogy. Just as he had shown in Section I that the sceptic, even though he cannot defend reason by reason, continues to reason and believe, so, too, he must believe in the existence of body, even though he cannot offer any arguments in support of this belief. He must believe because "Nature has not left this to his choice, and has doubtless esteem'd it an affair of too great importance to be trusted to our uncertain reasonings and speculations" (187).

Two conclusions emerge: (1) We cannot establish that an external material world exists. (2) Nevertheless, we all believe in its existence. As Hume puts it, "'Tis in vain to ask, *Whether there be body or not?* That is a point, which we must take for granted in all our reasonings" (187). This statement can be misunderstood. From the context in which it occurs (particularly the first sentence of the paragraph), it is apparent that Hume means by it only that we must assume the existence of body because we cannot help but believe it exists. He does not and could not, because of his previous conclusions, mean that we have any good reason for taking the existence of body for granted. So only one question remains: *Why* do we believe in the existence of body or of an external material world? Hume makes it clear that this is a *causal* question: "We may well ask, *What causes induce us to believe in the existence of body?*" (187). Most of Section II is an attempt to answer this question. "The subject, then, of our present enquiry is concerning the *causes* which induce us to believe in the existence of body" (187–88).

Hume begins his discussion of these causes by drawing a distinction between the continued existence of objects (or bodies) when they are not being sensed and their existence distinct from the mind and perception.[4] He does not elaborate on the meaning of continued existence but says he means by the distinct existence of material objects their external position and the independence of their existence and operation. He then goes on to point out that these two attributes entail each other. If a body continues to exist when not being perceived, its existence must be independent of the perception; if a body exists independently of the perception, it must continue to exist when not being perceived. Thus, for Hume, the two attributes of continued and distinct existence are necessary conditions for the existence of bodies, or of an external material world. With this elaboration he can reformulate his question. "What causes us to believe in the existence of body?" becomes "What causes us to believe in the continued and distinct existence of body?" He then suggests three possible sources for this belief—the senses, reason, and imagination—which he will proceed to examine in turn. Before starting his examination he reiterates a conclusion he had reached in Section VI of Part II; namely, that the notion of external existence, as something specifically different from our perceptions, is absurd (188). So it is clear that Hume takes it for granted at the beginning of Section II that he has already answered the question of our possible knowledge of an external material world in the negative. Nevertheless, he buttresses this conclusion with additional arguments during the course of the section.

2. The Senses and Belief in an External Material World (Paragraphs 3–13)

Hume spends several pages examining the question of whether the senses can be the source of our belief in the continued and distinct existence of material objects. He deals with continued existence first, in two sentences. "To begin with the SENSES, 'tis evident these faculties are incapable of giving rise to the notion of the *continu'd* existence of their objects, after they no longer appear to the senses. For that is a contradiction in terms, and supposes that the senses continue to operate, even after they have ceas'd all manner of operation" (188).

Hume next turns to the question of the distinct or independent existence of bodies, which he discusses at some length. He begins by recognizing two possibilities and then rules the senses out as the explanation of either. First is the view of a "double existence" (189), or the theory that our perceptions are images of external material objects. This is the theory that was advanced, among the empiricists, by Locke; it is generally called *representative realism.*[5] But, Hume argues, such a theory cannot be supported by an appeal to the senses because our perceptions do not point to anything beyond themselves. They simply are what they are. The sensation of "round," for example, is nothing more than the sensation of "round"; it does not contain in itself any reference to something independent of itself of which it is a copy. Therefore, when we make an inference from some perception to a reality beyond it in an external material world, we cannot be employing the sense itself to do so but rather some other faculty, either our reason or imagination.

The second possibility Hume considers is that our sense impressions are not images of distinct or independent material objects but are those very objects themselves. Describing this view as "a kind of fallacy and illusion" (189), he goes on to raise two main objections to it. If, he begins, our conclusion that our impressions are independent objects is to be based on our senses, we must be able to distinguish between those impressions and ourselves by use of our senses. To do this we must be able to make ourselves "the objects of our senses" (189). But this we cannot do. So he concludes: "'Tis absurd . . . to imagine the senses can ever distinguish betwixt ourselves and external objects" (190).

Hume's second argument is a bit difficult to follow. He begins by distinguishing between the "nature" of our impressions and their "situation and relations" (189, 190). Continuing, he argues that, as far as their nature is concerned, our impressions appear to our senses as contents of our consciousness and not as external existents. Our senses, he maintains, do not and cannot deceive us on this point. No more, however, can they deceive us about the situation and relations of our impressions. These also appear to the senses as contents of consciousness rather than as independent existents. As far as our senses inform us, he concludes, our impressions, both in their natures and in their situation and relations, must be just what they appear to be—contents of consciousness. To suppose otherwise would be "to suppose, that even where we are most intimately conscious, we might be mistaken" (190).

But Hume has additional reasons for rejecting the view that the continued and distinct existence of perceptions and material objects can be supported by an appeal to the senses. In a series of arguments strongly reminiscent of Berkeley, he first attacks the common opinion that our senses give us evidence of the existence of bodies external to our own, such as tables, buildings, and fields. This view, he points out, assumes that we perceive our own body itself as a material object existing in external space. But this assumption is false. "'Tis not our body we perceive . . . but certain impressions, which enter by the senses" (191).

After briefly summarizing his earlier arguments (191–92), Hume distinguishes three different kinds of sense impressions, the so-called primary, secondary, and tertiary qualities. He begins by noting that both philosophers and the vulgar suppose that impressions of primary qualities have an existence distinct from their being perceived, only the vulgar suppose this of impressions of secondary qualities and no one supposes it of impressions of tertiary qualities. However, he continues, these distinctions between kinds of impressions having different types of existence cannot be sustained by an appeal to the senses. Instead, as far as the senses inform us, all three kinds exist in the same way, as perceptions. So he concludes, "As far as the senses are judges, all perceptions are the same in the manner of their existence." (193)

Hume's argument about the relationship between our sense experience and our belief in the existence of an external material world can be summed up as follows: Our senses convey impressions. If our senses are to justify our belief in an external material world, their contents must either be copies of external objects or themselves such objects. But our senses can give no support to either possibility. Therefore our belief in an external material world cannot rest on any appeal to our senses. In Hume's words, "We may . . . conclude with certainty, that the opinion of a continu'd and of a distinct existence never arises from the senses" (192).

3. Reason and Belief in an External Material World (Paragraphs 14, 47)

If the belief in an external material world is based on reason, it must rest on some argument.[6] Although philosophers advance arguments whose aim is to establish the existence of material objects, ordinary people—"children, peasants, and the greatest part of mankind" (193)—certainly do not. They feel no need to give reasons to support their belief in a material world because they simply identify their impressions with external bodies. Although this identification is, Hume comments, "entirely unreasonable" (193), it describes the way in which the average mind works. So the factual question: Do we base our belief in an external material world on reason? must be answered in the negative.

Although Hume's description of the way in which the vulgar think makes it obvious that they do not base their belief in the existence of material objects on any process of reasoning, it may still remain true that others offer reasons that support this belief. Hume needs a different argument to eliminate that possibility. He provides this argument several pages later in Section II.[7] Hume's second argument (212) is based on his theory of causation. If we are to employ reason to justify our belief in an external material world, we must do so by establishing a causal connection between our perceptions and external objects. Hume begins by saying that we are aware of our perceptions and asks how we can draw an inference from their existence as contents of our consciousness to that of external material objects. Since we can do this only by establishing a causal connection between the two and since our idea of causality is derived from our past experience, we can conclude that two things are causally connected only if we consciously experience both. But the only entities of which we are conscious are perceptions. Therefore, we cannot employ any causal argument to justify an inference from them to entities that are not perceptions; i.e., material objects. In Hume's words: "We may observe a conjunction or a relation of cause and effect between different perceptions, but can never observe it between perceptions and [material] objects. 'Tis impossible, therefore, that from the existence or any of the qualities of the former, we can ever form any conclusion concerning the existence of the latter" (212). So we can conclude not only that it is false that people base their belief in an external material world on reason but also that, if they tried to do so, they would fail. We are left, then, only with the imagination as the source of this belief. In Hume's words, "That opinion must be entirely owing to the IMAGINATION" (193).

Before turning to Hume's investigation of the imagination, which occupies the central part of Section II, we should note an important shift in the nature of his argument at this point. In his examination of the senses and reason, his primary concern was epistemological—to determine whether either could *justify* our belief in the existence of an external material world. Although he still considers arguments concerned with justification, much of his discussion of the imagination is psychological, its aim being to *describe* how the imagination goes about generating this basic human belief. Such a shift is, of course, necessary for Hume because the imagination, being a non-rational faculty, is not capable of justifying the beliefs it generates.

4. THE EXISTENCE OF IMPRESSIONS AND OUR ATTRIBUTIONS OF THEIR EXISTENCE (PARAGRAPH 15)

Hume plunges into his account of the way in which the imagination gives rise to our belief in an external world by making an important onto-logical point and then noting two qualifying psychological facts: "All impressions are internal and perishing existences" (194). They exist only as contents of our consciousness and only for as long as we are conscious of them. Nevertheless, we believe some of them to have a distinct and continued existence, or to exist outside of our consciousness.[8] Our belief in such an existence, Hume maintains, arises "from a concurrence of some of their qualities with the qualities of the imagination" (194). To clarify this opaque phrase will be his task in the paragraphs that follow. Before describing Hume's account of why the imagination attributes a distinct and continued existence to certain impressions, it is important that we keep in mind one essential point. According to Hume such an attribution must be false because our impressions exist only as contents of our consciousness.[9]

5. CONSTANCY AND COHERENCE (PARAGRAPHS 16–24)

After brushing aside the theory that the reason we (falsely) attribute a distinct and continued existence to certain impressions lies in their invol-untariness and force (194), Hume finds the true cause in two qualities of these impressions—their constancy and coherence. His aim through much of the rest of Section II is to explain how these two attributes of the per-ceptions produce this result. His explanation, which is almost wholly psy-chological, is extraordinarily complex. I will not attempt to follow it through all its details but will concentrate on those parts of it that are of most philosophical interest.

Hume begins his discussion with the constancy of certain of the "ob-jects" (or contents) of our perceptions.[10] Although these objects are "per-ishing" (194), appearing and then disappearing when we shut our eyes or turn our head, some of them reappear repeatedly in the same form they had before. Mountains, houses, and trees do not change when we look away from them but remain constant. Because of their constancy we attribute an external existence to them, supposing them to be real entities in an in-dependent world. But, adds Hume, we attribute external existence to some objects of perception even when they are not constant. For example, if I leave a room in whose fireplace a fire is burning, when I return in an hour the fire looks quite different from when I left. Still I believe it has continued to burn while I was gone. In this case my belief is caused not by the constancy of my experience but by its coherence; I have had many similar experiences in the past.

Continuing his account Hume goes into considerable detail explaining why we attribute an external existence to the objects of certain of our constant and coherent perceptions. This argument appeals primarily to the coherence of our perceptions. Using a number of examples, he contends that the only way in which we can account for the coherence of our everyday experience is to suppose the existence of objects in an external world affecting our senses and continuing to exist even when we are not perceiving them. In his summary, "Here then I am naturally led to regard the world, as something real and durable, and as preserving its existence, even when it is no longer present to my perception" (197).

At this point in his discussion Hume raises a problem. When we attribute a continued existence to objects in an external world because this provides us with a way of explaining the coherence of our experience, we often go beyond anything warranted by our past experience. Specifically, we attribute a regularity (or coherence) to such objects much greater than any we have experienced. Since the regularity of our experience of an object of perception is broken every time we shut our eyes, when we attribute a continued existence to that object, as an external reality, we must be going beyond our experience, for the simple reason that we have no experience of an object during the time we are not experiencing it. Yet we all certainly make such attributions and, as he has just argued, must do so in order to give coherency to our experience.

To resolve this problem Hume returns to a point about human psychology he had made much earlier in Book I, in his discussion of mathematical equality.[11] The point turns on the tendency of the imagination to extend itself beyond our past experience. In his words, "The imagination, when set into any train of thinking, is apt to continue, even when its object fails it, and like a galley put in motion by the oars, carries on its course without any new impulse" (198). Applying his metaphor to the present issue, he argues that, having supposed the continued existence of objects in the past because of our experience of their coherence, our imagination extends this supposition to situations in which we do not actually experience the required coherence. In fact, the imagination extends the supposition to the point that we believe in the continued existence of all external bodies.[12] Here, however, Hume qualifies his conclusion. Coherence of experience, even when extended by the impetus of the imagination, is not in itself enough to account for our belief in the continued existence of an external material world. We must, he emphasizes, reinforce our belief by an appeal to the constancy of our perceptions.

Having identified the constancy and coherence of our perceptions as the characteristics causing the imagination to suppose that their objects have a continued existence independent of our perceiving them, Hume next turns his attention to the process by which the imagination accomplishes this transition. Before addressing his complex account of the psychological mechanisms involved, we need to pause briefly to raise a question prompted by a statement he makes early in the course of his discussion of coherence and constancy. He writes: "Having found that the opinion of the continu'd existence of body depends on the COHERENCE and CONSTANCY of certain impressions, I now proceed to examine after what manner these qualities give rise to *so extraordinary* an opinion" (195—italics added). What does Hume mean when he says that our opinion of (or belief in) the continued existence of body is "extraordinary"? Is he implying that our belief is false? If so he has reached an ontological conclusion; namely, that no external material world exists. If this is indeed what he intended to convey, his statement is obviously of great philosophical importance; it allies him ontologically with Berkeley. But we cannot be sure about Hume's intent here. Even though he concluded that our belief in an external world is extraordinary, we cannot assume that he held the belief to be false. For interpreters of Hume, the passage is frustrating; would that he had not left us to ponder an ambiguity.

6. The Mechanics of the Imagination (Paragraph 25)

Our experience is made up of a series of perceptions that are internal, perishing, and constantly interrupted. Yet our experience of these perceptions causes us to believe in the existence of an external world of enduring material objects. How is this belief generated? It is accomplished, according to Hume, by the imagination through a complex, four-step process. As he explains it:

> In order to justify this system [Hume's account], there are four things requisite. *First,* To explain the *principium individuationis,* or principle of identity. *Secondly,* Give a reason, why the resemblance of our broken and interrupted perceptions induces us to attribute an identity to them. *Thirdly,* Account for that propensity, which this illusion gives, to unite these broken appearances by a continu'd existence. *Fourthly* and lastly, Explain that force and vivacity of conception, which arises from the propensity. (199–200)

In the next four sections I will attempt to explain these four steps through which the imagination generates our belief in an external material world and then comment on them.

7. The Principle of Identity or Individuation (Paragraphs 26–30)

Before considering Hume's explanation of the *principium individuationis,* or principle of identity, we need to understand why he begins his account with it. We believe that material objects in the external world persist through time. The sun we see today is the same sun we saw yesterday. Our evidence for this belief, of course, is only a series of successive and interrupted perceptions. But we could not have such a belief, or even any evidence for it, unless we possessed a concept of identity. Without this concept we would be unable to say that today's sun is the *same* sun as yesterday's sun. To have a concept, for Hume, is to possess an idea. Therefore his task in the first of his four steps is to explain how we acquire the idea of identity.

Suppose we look at the sun.[13] The object or content of our visual perception is bright, yellow, round, and blurry. Because it is the perception of a single object it is the source of our idea of unity. We say that the sun is the same with itself. But suppose we continue to gaze fixedly at the sun. Then we have a number of successive perceptions the content or object of which is invariable.[14] Such perceptions, because their content is a succession of objects, are the source of our idea of number or multiplicity. But neither of these ideas—unity or number—is an idea of identity. Furthermore, it seems impossible to generate any such idea from either or both of them. Hume writes: "Since then both number and unity are incompatible with the relation of identity, it must lie in something that is neither of them. But to tell the truth, at first sight this seems utterly impossible. Betwixt unity and number there can be no medium; no more than betwixt existence and non-existence. After one object is suppos'd to exist, we must either suppose another also to exist; in which case we have the idea of number: Or we must suppose it not to exist; in which case the first object remains at unity" (200).

Hume resolves his problem by an appeal to the idea of time. The argument is subtle but his point can be explained in the following way: Suppose we look at the sun for several seconds. We can break this period of time into a number of different moments that succeed each other. Having done this we can select two different moments from the time span during which we are looking at the sun, and can then view these moments in either of two ways. (1) We can survey them at the same instant. If we do this the result is an idea of number, because the object we are looking at is actually being perceived at two different moments, so, Hume says, "must be multiply'd, in order to be conceiv'd at once, as existent in these two different points of time" (201). In other words, Hume seems to be saying that we can imaginatively take two moments of time during which we are looking at an object, stand off from them, and view them as a single moment.

But in order to do this, we must presuppose our awareness of both separate moments and hence of two distinct objects of awareness, one at each of these moments. This awareness constitutes our idea of number or multiplicity. (2) We can survey the moments as they actually appear to us; namely, as successive. During each of these successive moments both the object we are looking at and our perception of it remain unchanged. From this point of view the only thing that changes is time; each moment succeeds the one preceding it. This view, Hume argues, gives us the idea of unity. So, when we look at an object like the sun over a period of time, we can do so in such ways as to generate either the idea of number or the idea of unity. This ability, in turn, gives rise to a new idea that is neither unity or number but is either of them, depending on which of the two views we take. The new idea is identity. "Here then is an idea, which is a medium betwixt unity and number; or more properly speaking, is either of them, according to the view, in which we take it: And this idea we call that of identity" (201).

Ingenious as it is, this argument does not succeed. As we saw at the outset, Hume recognized that his problem, in generating an idea of identity, lies in the fact that this idea is incompatible with the ideas of both unity and number. Now, in his solution to the problem, he equates it first with one and then with the other. But clearly it can be neither. The mere fact that the two ideas—unity and number—are incompatible with each other forces the conclusion that any alleged idea that is both of them constitutes an impossibility. Nor has Hume generated any idea that is neither of them, but lies somewhere between them. Indeed he acknowledged this to be impossible at the beginning of his argument when he wrote, "Betwixt unity and number there can be no medium; no more than betwixt existence and non-existence." Since the mechanism of the imagination by which he is attempting to account for our belief in an external world requires that we have an idea of identity and since his attempt to generate such an idea fails, we must conclude that, without its first step, his four-step process cannot successfully be completed. Although it may be an exercise in futility, we will, nevertheless, continue to follow Hume through the remaining three steps in his progress of the imagination.

8. Why We Attribute an Identity to Interrupted Perceptions (Paragraphs 31–36)

Assuming that he has generated an idea of identity, Hume proceeds to the second step of his imaginative process. In this step his object is to explain the way in which we come to believe that constant or invariable perceptions, even though they are interrupted, are numerically identical. For example, we look at the sun, then look away. When we look back we believe we are having the same sense impression as we had had before. This belief, of course, is false because the two impressions, being separated by a gap in time, cannot be the same. Hume describes the belief as an "error and deception" (202). Nevertheless, it is one we all share.

Before proceeding to explain why we make this error Hume pauses to note a change in his terminology. Heretofore he has recognized the distinction philosophers make between the terms "object" (when this is used to refer to a material body) and "perception," but now he warns the reader that, for the next several pages, he will no longer make this distinction but will use the two terms interchangeably. His reason for doing so is to conform his "speaking and thinking" (202) to that of the vulgar, who use the two terms indiscriminately to mean the same thing. As he puts it: "Those very sensations, which enter by the eye or ear, are with [the vulgar] the true [external] objects. . . . In order, therefore, to accommodate myself to their notions, I shall at first suppose; that there is only a single existence, which I shall call indifferently *object* or *perception,* according as it shall seem best to suit my purpose, understanding by both of them what any common man means by a hat, or shoe, or stone."[15]

Having altered his way of speaking and thinking, Hume is ready to address the second step in the process. Why do we make the error of believing that perceptions (or material objects) that resemble each other, but are interrupted, are identical with each other? Why do we believe the sun we perceive today is the same sun we perceived yesterday? Hume answers this question with a dual psychological account based on our mental lethargy. The key to his account is the relation of resemblance. In a situation in which we make the mistake of identifying interrupted perceptions or material objects, two resemblances are involved. First is the resemblance of the objects themselves. Today's sun looks like yesterday's sun. Second is the resemblance between the dispositions of the mind when we perceive the two objects. Hume maintains that the act by which the mind surveys a series of interrupted objects closely resembles the act by which it surveys an uninterrupted or identical object. Because of these two resemblances, of objects and mental dispositions, the imagination moves from one object to the next so smoothly and with such little effort that we come to believe we are viewing a single, identical object, not a succession of different objects. "The thought slides along the succession [of objects] with equal facility, as if it consider'd only one object; and therefore confounds the succession with the identity."[16]

After completing his explanation of this second psychological step, Hume draws back momentarily. Although we do believe interrupted perceptions to be identical ones, we still recognize that this belief is mistaken, because we are also aware that they are interrupted so must be different from each other. This awareness gives rise to mental perplexity. Hume writes: "The very image, which is present to the senses, is with us the real body; and 'tis to these interrupted images we ascribe a perfect identity. But as the interruption of the appearance seems contrary to the identity, and naturally leads us to regard these resembling perceptions as different from each other, we here find ourselves at a loss how to reconcile such opposite opinions" (205). To resolve this psychological dilemma Hume turns to the third step of our mental processes. "The perplexity arising from this contradiction produces a propension to unite these broken appearances by the fiction of a continu'd existence" (205).

9. The Fiction of a Continued Existence (Paragraphs 37–40)

In the third step Hume explains how, through the fiction of a continued existence, we come to believe in the "illusion" (200) of the identity of interrupted perceptions or objects. He begins by arguing that, to do this, we must give up one or other of the two opposed opinions—that interrupted perceptions are identical and that they are different. But which one? Hume is momentarily at a loss; both tendencies to believe seem equally strong. But then he notices a distinction that is relevant to our tendency to ascribe an interruption to our perceptions and hence deny their continued existence when we are not perceiving them. This tendency assumes that a perception, to exist, must be perceived, or that there are no unperceived perceptions (perceptions that continue to exist even while not being perceived). But this is not necessarily so. As Hume writes, "the interruption in the appearance of a perception implies not *necessarily* an interruption in its existence."[17] If this be true it becomes possible for us to sacrifice our second tendency to our first, thus permitting us to believe that our interrupted perceptions are actually the same.

Having reached the conclusion that we all, the vulgar and philosophers alike, suppose not only that our perceptions continue to exist even when not perceived but also that these perceptions are identical with material objects, Hume turns next to the question of how this supposition can be explained. Two questions need to be answered: (1) What reason can we give for supposing that unperceived perceptions exist? and (2) How do we conceive of an object's being perceived without the creation of a new perception?

To answer his first question Hume introduces a novel and somewhat startling theory of the nature of the mind. The mind, he writes, "is nothing but a heap or collection of different perceptions."[18] Since perceptions are distinguishable from each other, they can exist in independence of each other. It follows, therefore, that any given perception can be separated from all the rest that make up the mind and exist in isolation from them. Such an independently existing perception would be an unperceived perception. The existence of such perceptions, Hume insists, involves "no absurdity" (207).

Hume's answer to his second question follows quickly from his answer to the first. If a perception can exist without being perceived and an object (body) is the same thing as a perception, it follows not only that such an object can exist without being perceived but that it can become, through being perceived, "present to the mind" (207). Therefore it is not necessary to create anything new in order to perceive the object. As Hume puts it: "The same continu'd and uninterrupted Being [perception or material object] *may*, therefore, be sometimes present to the mind, and sometimes absent from it, without any real or essential change in the Being itself" (207—italics added). But he immediately adds an important qualification to this point. All he is saying is that perceptions or material objects *may* continue to exist when not being perceived. He is not implying that they do *in fact* continue to exist but only that the supposition that they do does not involve a contradiction. "The supposition of the continu'd existence of sensible objects or perceptions involves no contradiction. We may easily indulge our inclination to that supposition."[19] And, it might be added, we all routinely indulge this inclination.

It is easy to misread Hume's argument here. As I have just indicated, it would be a mistake to conclude that he is implying that perceptions or material objects continue to exist when they are not being perceived. All he has said is that to suppose this to be true is not self-contradictory.[20] Another point that may be overlooked is that Hume is here describing the view of the vulgar. When he equates perceptions with material objects, he is not saying that the two are the same, but only that the vulgar assume them to be the same. Also, at this point Hume introduces a new kind of possible entity into his philosophy; namely, unperceived perceptions. An example would be our conscious experience (perception) of the sun when we are not in fact having the experience. The introduction of this concept raises an interesting question: How are unperceived perceptions related to material objects? How is the unperceived perception "sun" related to the sun in space? We know that the vulgar identify perceptions with material objects and, since unperceived perceptions are identical with perceptions, we can conclude that the vulgar must identify unperceived perceptions with material objects. That is, they must identify the unperceived perception "sun" with the sun in the sky. If they are correct in this identification, it follows that, if unperceived perceptions exist, so, too, must material objects exist. But are they correct in the identification? Hume gives no answer to this ontological question here. Since I will have to raise the point later in the chapter, when I consider unperceived perceptions from a different perspective, I will defer further discussion of it for now.

A final point that needs to be mentioned in connection with step three concerns a problem of interpretation. At the very beginning of his discussion Hume writes of "the fiction of a continu'd existence" (205) of perceptions or material objects and at the end he writes of our "feigning a continu'd being" (208). What does he mean by these expressions? A natural interpretation would be that he means that our supposition that perceptions and, in particular, material objects continue to exist when not being perceived is false. On this interpretation Hume would be denying the independent existence of an external material world. He would, thus, be a Berkeleyan. Although this may be the correct interpretation of his statements, another interpretation is possible. He might mean only that, because we cannot justify the beliefs, they are "fictions" in the sense that they are ungrounded postulations or suppositions we make. Interpreted in this way, the beliefs in question might still be true. Which of these two interpretations should we accept? This is a question we cannot answer definitively at this point, mainly because Hume does not make clear just what he means either by a fiction or by the act of feigning. The natural assumption, of course, is to conclude that he knew what the word "fiction" meant and that he was using it deliberately, to contrast it with "fact." However, because of the implications of his meaning for his conclusion regarding the existence of an external material world, we must be careful not to introduce interpretations that may fail to convey his intent. Fortunately for the interpreter, Hume gives us a clue to his thought a bit later in the section. In a paragraph summing up the four steps in the process by which the imagination leads us to believe in the existence of body, he writes: "This propension to bestow an identity on our resembling perceptions, produces the fiction of a continu'd existence; since *that fiction, as well as the identity, is really false.*"[21]

10. Belief in a Continued Existence (Paragraphs 41–42)

The third step in the imaginative process has led us to feign the continued existence of perceptions or material objects. But to feign, Hume points out, is not the same as to believe. "But as we here not only *feign* but *believe* this continu'd existence, the question is, *from whence arises such a belief;* and this question leads us to the *fourth* member of this system" (208).

Hume begins his account by briefly reviewing his theory of belief, which he had presented in Part III, Section VII. There he had defined belief as a lively idea related to or associated with a present impression.[22] Recapitulating that view, he repeats that impressions are the most vivid (or lively) perceptions we have. Furthermore, the mind transfers their vivacity to any idea related to them. The related idea thus gains in vivacity and, since belief consists in the vivacity of an idea, we come to believe it. "[The mind] is excited by the lively impression; and this vivacity is convey'd to the related idea" (208).

Applying his general theory of belief to the issue before him, Hume makes a minor modification in his account. Just as an impression conveys vivacity to an idea related to it, it also conveys vivacity to an idea resembling it. Now, Hume continues, our memory presents us with a large number of perceptions that, though interrupted, perfectly resemble each other. Because of the resemblance between these perceptions, we have a propensity to consider them the same and connect them together by a continued existence and thus to feign their continued existence and that of material objects. Finally, since the perceptions of the memory are lively, this liveliness is conveyed to our ideas, which means that we come not just to feign the continued existence but to believe in it as well. Hume's argument bears repeating in his own words:

> Our memory presents us with a vast number of instances of perceptions perfectly resembling each other, that return at different distances of time, and after considerable interruptions. This resemblance gives us a propension to consider these interrupted perceptions as the same; and also *a propension to connect them by a continu'd existence.* . . . Here then we have a propensity to feign the continu'd existence of all sensible objects; and as this propensity arises from some lively impressions of the memory, it bestows a vivacity on that fiction; or in other words, makes us believe the continu'd existence of body. (208–9—italics added)

The logic of this argument raises a question. Hume must accomplish two goals in his fourth step. (1) He must explain the mechanism by which the act of feigning, which presumably lacks vivacity, becomes the act of believing, which possesses it. This is, in fact, the issue he addresses in the step. (2) He must explain how the act of feigning creates an idea in the mind, specifically the idea of an object that continues to exist even while not being perceived. This he must do if he is to believe, because a necessary condition of belief is the possession of a lively idea.

The problem with Hume's reasoning in this step lies in the second requirement. To see just what the difficulty is we must review his theory of belief in some detail. We know from his definition that, to believe something, we must have an idea. But an idea of what? To apply our question to the issue before us, let us begin by supposing that Hume believes that some X exists. To be able to believe this he must possess some (lively) idea. But need it be an idea of X? More precisely, need it be an idea whose content is the entity X? To find Hume's answer to this question we must return briefly to his account of belief in Part III. At the beginning of the section on the idea of belief (VII), he discusses the content of the idea we have when we believe that something exists, using God as his example. He writes: "*The idea of an object is an essential part of the belief of it.* . . . When I think of God, when I think of him as existent, and when I believe him to be existent, *my idea of him* neither encreases nor diminishes."[23] As this passage makes clear, to believe in the existence of an entity it is necessary, according to Hume, that the idea we have be an idea whose content is the entity in question. This view is understandable because, for him, an entity of which we had no idea would be inconceivable, hence could hardly be anything about which we could possess beliefs. We can say, therefore, that to believe that any X exists we must have an idea whose content is X. Applying this conclusion to the present case we can say that to believe that an external material object exists we must have an idea whose content is an external material object. Finally, to believe in the *continued* existence of such an object, it follows *a fortiori* that we must have an idea of it.

So we must ask: How does Hume come to have an idea whose content is an external material object? Although I have discussed this question at considerable length earlier, the point merits a brief recapitulation. As a result of my analysis of Hume's argument regarding our possible knowledge of an external world in Part II, Section VI, I concluded that he denied that we can have any idea of external material objects.[24] To repeat a portion of a statement taken from this earlier part of the *Treatise,* Hume writes: "Nothing is ever really present with the mind but its perceptions or impressions and ideas" (67).

We can now return to Hume's step four to see how his reasoning in it is related to his position that we can be aware only of perceptions, either impressions or ideas. He begins his account by saying that we feign the existence of continuing material objects. If we accept the line of reasoning that follows we should conclude that, because of the resemblance of our interrupted perceptions, our act of feigning—or, perhaps more accurately, the fiction that is the content of this act—becomes lively. And this is, indeed, the way in which Hume argues. "[Our] propensity to feign the continu'd existence of all sensible objects [bodies] . . . bestows a vivacity on that fiction."[25]

Let us grant for purposes of argument that Hume has generated a lively fiction by his act of feigning and that this is a fiction of a material object that continues to exist unperceived. Does he have any idea of such an object? He does only if the fiction in question is an idea. But it clearly is not. If it were, he would not have found it necessary to introduce the unusual concepts of "feigning" and of a "fiction" at all; he could have used his ordinary terminology of "impressions" and "ideas."

The reason why Hume must introduce the notion of feigning, and thus to distinguish a fiction from an idea, is made clear in the course of his argument (which I described earlier). He begins by summarizing his original theory of belief from Part III, Section VII, writing: "It has been prov'd already, that belief in general consists in nothing, but the vivacity of an idea; and that an idea may acquire this vivacity by its relation to some present impression" (208). Applying this theory of belief to the question of our belief in the continued existence of body, he notes that our memory, here presenting us with innumerable "impressions" that resemble each other, gives our idea the vivacity required to render it something we believe.

This argument would be viable if the two processes were analogous, but they are not. In Hume's original account of belief we can have an idea of that in which we believe because we have had previous impressions of *it*. We can believe that the flame of a fire will produce heat because we have had repeated past experiences of flames and have found that they have always been accompanied by the experience of heat. So when we experience flame again we will have a lively idea of its accompanying heat, or will believe the flame will be hot. But in the present case we have had no previous experience of bodies that continue to exist while unperceived. All that we have had are repeated perceptions that resemble each other. The previous impressions (e.g., of heat) that can be the source of the idea in his original theory do not occur in the present case. Therefore, we have no source in our impressions to generate any idea of such a body. We can, as a result, have no such idea. To fill in the gap, Hume creates "fictions," which, because they are not ideas so are by definition inconceivable, are clearly entities that can have no legitimate place in his philosophy.[26]

This conclusion has consequences of some importance for Hume's epistemology. If to believe that an object X exists Hume must possess a (lively) idea of that object and if he can have no idea of the continuing existence of bodies, Hume cannot, on his theory of belief, believe in their continuing existence. Further, we must remember that this conclusion is a specification of a broader consequence of his theory. Without any ideas of bodies Hume cannot, according to his theory of belief, believe that they exist at all. Thus the fourth step in his psychological account cannot occur.

But this leaves us with a further problem. Hume obviously *does* believe in the existence of an external material world. He begins Section II with the words: "Thus the sceptic . . . must assent to the principle concerning the existence of body, tho' he cannot pretend by any arguments of philosophy to maintain its veracity. Nature has not left this to his choice" (187). We must conclude, therefore, that Hume believes something that, according to his theory, he cannot believe. How are we to resolve this contradiction between Hume's philosophy and his beliefs? More to the point, what, if anything, can be done to allow him to believe in the existence of an external world, something he undoubtedly did?

A couple of responses to this dilemma seem possible. First, in his fourth step Hume is still thinking with the vulgar. The conclusion I have just reached implies only that he cannot believe in the existence of material objects but certainly does not deny him the capacity to believe in the existence of perceptions. But the vulgar identify the two. Therefore, Hume's ability to believe that perceptions exist is, by definition, an ability to believe that external material objects exist as well. But this response does not resolve the problem. We need not question Hume's claim that, in the thought of the vulgar, perceptions and material objects are the same. The question, rather, is: Can Hume think with the vulgar on this point? That question must be answered in the negative; his epistemology precludes him from doing so. When he has an idea by definition he is aware of a perception, so he can believe in the existence of perceptions but, because he has no ideas giving him an awareness of external material objects, he cannot believe in their existence.

We might come to Hume's aid by attacking his theory of belief, arguing that, to believe that some X exists, it is not necessary to possess an idea of X. But the consequences of such a move are problematic. For Hume, to conceive of something is to have an idea of it. Therefore, the suggestion I have just made would require him to believe in the existence of something that is inconceivable to him. It would ask him to believe in something when all that occupies his consciousness is a void.[27] However, I do not think a criticism of Hume's theory of belief gets to the root of his problem; instead his epistemology must be questioned at a more fundamental level. Hume derives his definition of belief from his general theory of ideas. Consequently, if he has argued consistently, any deficiency in the former is a result of a deficiency in the latter. The reason why Hume cannot believe in the existence of an external material world lies finally in his original epistemological assumptions. So, if he is to succeed in accounting for that belief, he must give up his empiricist theory of ideas. This would, of course, require a fundamental change in his philosophy in Book I.

11. Do Our Perceptions Have an Independent Existence? (Paragraphs 44–45)

Earlier in Section II (207–8) Hume argued, in opposition to Berkeley's view, that the supposition of the independent and continued existence of perceptions or objects involves no contradiction. It does not follow, however, that they do in fact have such an existence. Hume now turns to the factual question.[28] Before beginning he makes it plain that, although his four-step account explains the way in which the imagination leads us to believe in the continued existence of objects even when they are not being perceived, such a belief is fallacious. "But tho' we are led after this manner, by the natural propensity of the imagination, to ascribe a continu'd existence to those sensible objects or perceptions, which we find to resemble each other in their interrupted appearance; yet a very little reflection and philosophy is sufficient to make us perceive the fallacy of that opinion."[29] Continuing, Hume repeats a point he had made early in the section—that continued existence entails distinct or independent existence and vice versa. Furthermore, the denial of either one entails the denial of the other. Focusing his attention on independent existence, he writes: "The doctrine of the independent existence of our sensible perceptions is contrary to the plainest experience. This leads us backward upon our footsteps to perceive our error in attributing a continu'd existence to our perceptions."[30]

In support of his conclusion that our perceptions have no independent and continued existence Hume appeals to a variety of "experiments" (210). Although his discussion of these experiments is very brief, the examples he uses can be separated into three types: (1) perceptual errors, (2) variability in primary qualities, (3) variability in secondary qualities. To illustrate (1) he points out that, when we press our eye with our finger, the objects we see are doubled, but we do not attribute a continued existence to both of these perceptions. To illustrate (2) he points out that the sizes and shapes of objects change with their distance from us. To illustrate (3) he points out that the colors of objects change when we are sick. He concludes: "Our sensible perceptions are not possest of any distinct or independent existence" (211).

Clearly, Hume is claiming that our belief in the independent and, hence, continued existence of our perceptions is false because they have no such existence and that the experiments he cites establish this. But he does not develop any argument in support of the second of these claims. So we must ask: How do the illustrations he gives establish that our perceptions have no continued and independent existence? We know already that he does not deny the logical possibility of their having such an existence. So what is it that prevents this existence? Let us look more closely at the illustrations themselves.

Hume is certainly correct in saying that our perceptions change under the differing conditions he describes. We do perceive two objects when we press our eye, and so on. If our perceptions were to exist independently of our consciousness they would be unperceived perceptions. But an unperceived perception, though it might be a very unusual ontological entity, presumably would be identical in its characteristics or qualities to a perceived perception. The mere fact that it is not being perceived would not alter its descriptive nature. If this is correct (as I think Hume would agree), it would seem to follow that, if variable perceived perceptions admittedly exist, variable unperceived perceptions can exist just as well. The double-objects I see can remain double-objects (unperceived perceptions) when I am not perceiving them and the variable sizes and shapes I see can do the same, as can the changed colors. There seems to be no reason why this should not happen, if Hume is here talking about nothing more than unperceived perceptions. Why then does he say that none of these things exists?

Perhaps the best way to grasp Hume's reasoning is to use one of the examples he gives. He notes that objects change their apparent sizes as we view them from different distances. In other words, our perceptions of these objects change. And, as I have just argued, there is nothing to prevent these perceptions from changing when they are unperceived. Only one thing remains that cannot change—the material object itself. The house I am looking at does not grow larger as I approach it and smaller as I move away from it. On this account we can explain why Hume denies the existence of unperceived perceptions. The impossibility in question is not logical but physical. If perceptions and material objects are the same thing (as the vulgar believe), unperceived perceptions cannot be a third kind of entity, distinguishable from material objects. Since the two must be the same and since material objects cannot exist with variable characteristics, neither can unperceived perceptions. But since unperceived perceptions have the same characteristics as perceptions, they must, if they exist, have variable characteristics. Since they cannot have such characteristics, unperceived perceptions do not exist.

This conclusion has a disturbing implication. Hume is, in his experiments, offering a criticism of the vulgar view, which identifies perceptions and material objects. If his argument leads him to conclude that perceptions have no independent and continued existence it follows that the same must be said of material objects. The vulgar view results in the denial of an external material world.[31] Small wonder, then, that in the next paragraph Hume moves from the world of the vulgar to that of philosophers. Before I follow him in this move, however, I need to repair an omission in my account of the argument I have been reviewing in this section.

12. The Other Side (Paragraph 45)

In my discussion in the previous section I omitted to mention part of a sentence that appears in the second paragraph of Hume's argument. In speaking of double vision he points out that we do not attribute a continued existence to both perceptions and then goes on to add that "all our perceptions are dependent on our organs, and the disposition of our nerves and animal spirits" (211). This statement seems unquestionably to assert the existence of material objects—at least of our own bodies. Besides being a rejection of the Berkeleyan implications of the vulgar view, the statement puts Hume on record as affirming the existence of body.

Before we accept this conclusion as definite, however, we need to understand just what Hume means by the statement I have quoted. In particular, we must examine the relationship between it and his theory of ideas. To do this we must return to an argument he uses earlier in Section II. In the course of his criticism of the view that we can establish the existence of body by an appeal to the senses he offers the following argument: "To begin with the question concerning *external* existence, it may perhaps be said, that . . . our own body evidently belongs to us. . . . properly speaking, 'tis not our body we perceive, when we regard our limbs and members, but certain impressions, which enter by the senses; so that the ascribing a real and corporeal existence to these impressions, or to their objects, is an act of the mind as difficult to explain, as that which we examine at present."[32] Although the point Hume is making in this passage is epistemological, it has ontological overtones. When we look at our body, or its parts, strictly speaking we cannot be seeing a material object. Instead all we are aware of are certain impressions. Therefore, talk of our "body" is misleading; what we are really talking about is our impressions, because those are the only things of which we can be conscious. If we transfer this conclusion to the passage we are now examining, we can interpret Hume's statement as follows: When he says that all of our perceptions are dependent on our organs, he is talking in the ordinary way but, nevertheless, in a way that, on his epistemology, requires reformulation. What he must mean is something like this: All of our perceptions are dependent on a certain subset of perceptions; namely, the impressions of shape, color, and so on we have when we look in a certain direction—into what, in ordinary talk, we call our body. Therefore, Hume's language in the passage under question does not, as at first sight it seems to, assume that we possess a body with physical organs. It is, on the contrary, quite consistent with the view that we have no material body at all.[33]

13. THE PHILOSOPHICAL SYSTEM OF DOUBLE EXISTENCE (PARAGRAPHS 46–50)

The conclusion resulting from Hume's experiments—that our perceptions have neither a continued nor an independent existence—lays bare the deficiency of the vulgar view. Because that view identifies perceptions with material objects, the fact that the former have no independent existence entails that the latter have none either. But we all, and above all the vulgar, believe in the existence of an independent external world. Philosophers, recognizing this problem, have come to the theory of "double existence."[34] They distinguish, as the vulgar do not, between perceptions and material objects. Although, they acknowledge, perceptions are interrupted, perishing, and nonidentical, material objects (which are different from perceptions) continue to exist and preserve their identity even when they are not being perceived. Unfortunately, Hume immediately adds, this philosophical system does not remedy the defect of the vulgar one; rather it compounds the difficulties. "But however philosophical this new system may be esteem'd, I assert that 'tis only a palliative remedy, and that *it contains all the difficulties of the vulgar system*, with some others, that are peculiar to itself."[35]

Hume's acknowledgment that the philosophical system of the double existence of perceptions and material objects contains *all* the difficulties of the vulgar system is hardly an advertisement for it. One's pessimism concerning its viability is increased when we recollect that in section 11 we found that the vulgar system leads to the conclusion that no external world exists yet that we all believe in such a world. If the philosophical system contains all the difficulties of the vulgar, it includes this one. But let us continue with Hume's argument to see if he does, in fact, agree with this conclusion.

Hume begins his discussion with the statement: "There are no principles either of the understanding [reason] or fancy [imagination], which lead us directly to embrace this opinion of the double existence of perceptions and objects."[36] In his defense of this statement he goes on to examine both reason and imagination, showing that neither can directly support the double existence hypothesis. His main goal in his arguments is to show that this hypothesis cannot succeed in providing any basis for our belief in an external material world.

Hume's case against reason is based on his theory of causation.[37] The only basis, he argues, on which we can infer the existence of one thing from that of another is by means of the cause-effect relation. The idea of this relation arises out of our past experiences of having perceived the two things constantly conjoined. But we perceive only perceptions, never material objects. So, although we can make causal connections between different perceptions we cannot do so between perceptions and objects. Hume concludes: "'Tis impossible, therefore, that from the existence or any of the qualities of [perceptions], we can ever form any conclusion concerning the existence of [material objects]" (212).

Hume does not offer any argument to support his conclusion that the double-existence hypothesis "has no primary recommendation to the *imagination*" (212), mainly because he thinks no argument is necessary. He simply challenges anyone who disagrees with him to offer an explanation of why it has such a recommendation so that he can examine it. If we remember that the imagination, in order to function, must have some idea before it and we never have an idea of a material object, it is difficult to see how anyone could meet Hume's challenge on this point.

Hume continues by arguing that the double-existence hypothesis acquires its influence on the imagination from the vulgar view in which perceptions and material objects are supposed to be the same. He then gives a brief psychological account of how the imagination leads us to the vulgar view, according to which "our sensible perceptions have . . . a continu'd and uninterrupted existence" (213–14). But, since our perceptions are dependent—and interrupted—"a little reflection" (214) makes us realize that the vulgar identification of perceptions with material objects must be abandoned. He then adds that, once we abandon that view, " 'twou'd naturally be expected, that we must altogether reject the opinion, that there is such a thing in nature as a continu'd existence, which is preserv'd even when it no longer appears to the senses" (214). If a little reflection would lead us to reject the vulgar view and therefore to accept the conclusion that nothing in nature has a continued and independent existence, one would expect that philosophers (who presumably reflect) would all agree in denying the existence of independent material objects. But this is not what has happened. "Philosophers are so far from rejecting the opinion of a continu'd existence upon rejecting that of the independence and continuance of our sensible perceptions, that tho' all sects agree in the latter sentiment, the former, *which is, in a manner, its necessary consequence,* has been peculiar to a few extravagant sceptics."[38]

Hume is certainly correct in pointing out that most philosophers had embraced the double-existence hypothesis.[39] But he is doing more here than simply stating a historical fact. He is also indicting the double-existence theorists for defending an indefensible view. Although they accept what is incontestable—that our perceptions exist only as perishable contents of our consciousness—they refuse to accept its necessary consequence—that nothing else has any other existence. Rather they illogically and, hence, indefensibly claim the existence of an independent material world. Thus Hume comes to the same conclusion as Berkeley. The philosophical hypothesis of double-existence leads necessarily to the conclusion that material objects do not exist.

14. The Conflict between Reason and Imagination and Its Resolution (Paragraphs 51–55)

Why do philosophers, even though the consequence of their hypothesis is the conclusion that no material world exists, continue to believe that it

does? Hume devotes the next several paragraphs to this question. Much of
what he says in his argument, which is throughout psychological, repeats
points he has already made, but these bear repeating. The controlling thesis
of his argument is his conviction that all of us, vulgar and philosopher alike,
must believe in the existence of an external material world, whatever conclusions we reach on the question after we have reflected on it.

> There is a great difference betwixt such opinions as we form after a calm
> and profound reflection, and such as we embrace by a kind of instinct. . . . If
> these opinions become contrary, 'tis not difficult to foresee which of them
> will have the advantage. As long as our attention is bent upon the subject,
> the philosophical and study'd principle may prevail; but the moment we relax
> our thoughts, nature will display herself, and draw us back to our former
> opinion. Nay she has sometimes such an influence, that she can stop our
> progress, even in the midst of our most profound reflections, and keep us
> from running on with all the consequences of any philosophical opinion.
> Thus tho' we clearly perceive the dependence and interruption of our per-
> ceptions, we stop short in our career, and never upon that account reject the
> notion of an independent and continu'd existence. (214)

As an analysis of the psychology of philosophers this passage is both
disturbing and humbling. Even if, when we pursue our reflections to the
end, we come to a Berkeleyan conclusion, few of us can accept that conclusion because we are also human beings who share with the vulgar a belief
in the existence of an external material world, a belief "'tis impossible ever
to eradicate" (214). Even more, this belief is so strong that it prevents us
from pursuing our philosophical reflections to their ultimate conclusions.
We become, with a few exceptions like Berkeley, intellectual cowards.

But philosophers, though they share the vulgar belief, are disturbed by
it. The vulgar identify perceptions and material objects and at the same time
believe material objects to be independent and continuing. This causes no
concern to them but it does to philosophers, who are acutely aware of the
dependent and perishing nature of perceptions. To resolve the contradiction philosophers "contrive" (215) the double-existence hypothesis, in which
perceptions perish but material objects persist. This hypothesis, with its
fictitious claim that objects exist in a continuing, independent world, both
"pleases our reason" (215) by affirming the perishing nature of our perceptions and "at the same time is agreeable to the imagination, in attributing
a continu'd existence to something else, which we call *objects*" (215). Repeating his point, Hume writes: "The imagination tells us, that our resembling
perceptions have a continu'd and uninterrupted existence, and are not annihilated by their absence. Reflection tells us, that even our resembling
perceptions are interrupted in their existence, and different from each other.
The contradiction betwixt these opinions we elude by a new fiction" (215).

15. Hume's Sceptical Doubt and Its Resolution (Paragraphs 56–57)

Hume devotes the final two paragraphs of Section II to a summary of the sceptical conclusion about the external material world to which his argument has led him. He begins with an expression of distrust about the mechanics of the imagination he has so laboriously described in the section, in particular of the falsity of the suppositions the imagination makes. "I cannot conceive how such trivial qualities of the fancy [imagination], conducted by such false suppositions, can ever lead to any solid and rational system" (217). Going on, he returns to the vulgar view that our perceptions continue to exist when not perceived. Of it he writes: " 'Tis a gross illusion to suppose, that our resembling perceptions are numerically the same; and 'tis this illusion, which leads us into the opinion, that these perceptions are uninterrupted, and are still existent, even when they are not present to the senses" (217). Thus Hume reiterates his earlier conclusion that there are no unperceived perceptions.

Turning next to the philosophical view, he makes a puzzling statement, writing: "And as to our philosophical [system], 'tis liable to the same difficulties; and is over-and-above loaded with this absurdity, that it at once denies and establishes the vulgar supposition" (217–18). This seems, at least on the surface, to be a partial misstatement of the philosophical double-existence theory. Clearly that hypothesis does not *establish* the vulgar position affirming the existence of unperceived perceptions, because one of its main objectives is to find a theory that can avoid such a "gross illusion." Why, then, does Hume say it establishes the vulgar position? His answer is as follows: "Philosophers deny our resembling perceptions to be identically the same, and uninterrupted; and yet have so great a propensity to believe them such, that they arbitrarily invent a new set of perceptions, to which they attribute these qualities. I say, a new set of perceptions: For we may well suppose in general, but 'tis impossible for us distinctly to conceive, objects to be in their nature any thing but exactly the same with perceptions" (218).

This passage forces us to reconsider Hume's version of the double-existence theory. An assumption of that theory, as he had described it earlier in the section, is that perceptions and material objects are different from each other.[40] He now gives a revised account of the theory, claiming that philosophers do not suppose the existence of material objects different from perceptions but rather "arbitrarily invent a new set of perceptions." His reason for saying this is that we cannot conceive of material objects as anything different from perceptions.

This passage calls for several comments. (1) If philosophers do not invent material objects by the double-existence hypothesis but only a new set of perceptions, it follows that the "material objects" of which double-existence philosophers have written must be reduced to perceptions. (2) If this "establishes" the vulgar view, it follows that that view, in identifying perceptions and material objects, also reduces the latter to the former and is correct in doing so. (3) The vulgar view that perceptions continue to exist even when not perceived is false; Hume has already denied the existence of unperceived perceptions. Therefore, (4) material objects do not exist when they are not perceived. There is no independent material world. Finally, (5) philosophers generally do not have the courage to draw the last conclusion because they *must* believe in the existence of an external world.

Returning to his indictment of philosophers, Hume asks: "And how can we justify to ourselves any belief we repose in . . . this confusion of groundless and extraordinary opinions?"[41] The belief he and other philosophers, as well as the vulgar, have in the existence of an external material world, Hume is implying, is not only unavoidable, but irrational as well. We believe in its existence but we can offer no justification to support our belief. On the contrary, the inescapable conclusion of philosophical investigation is that no such world exists.

Hume is understandably distressed by his conclusions, particularly because he can see no way to avoid them. "This sceptical doubt, both with respect to reason and the senses, is a malady, which can never be radically cur'd. . . . As the sceptical doubt arises naturally from a profound and intense reflection on those subjects, *it always encreases, the farther we carry our reflections*" (218—italics added). Yet there is a way out of the sceptical doubt—but it is not a philosophical way. The solution is not further reflection; that just magnifies the scepticism. On the contrary, the only cure to the sceptical doubt lies in abandoning philosophical reflection. "Carelessness and in-attention alone can afford us any remedy. For this reason I rely entirely upon them" (218). Hume is not content with describing his remedy for his own sceptical doubt but concludes Section II with a remark that all of us who consider ourselves philosophers should ponder. "Whatever may be the reader's opinion at this present moment, . . . an hour hence he will be persuaded there is both an external and internal world" (218). However philosophical we may be, we cannot, Hume is telling us, really accept the sceptical conclusion about the existence of an external material world to which our philosophizing must lead us; human nature steps in and forces us to believe.[42]

Summary

The argument of Section II is extraordinarily subtle and complex. Perhaps the most important point to remember about it is that Hume's main aim in it is to give an explanation of our belief in an external material world. Although this belief is false and irrational, the fact remains that we all accept it—because we must.

Early in the section he argues that we cannot justify our belief through appeal either to the senses or to reason. So we must turn to the imagination, not to justify the belief (which it cannot do), but only to explain the psychological mechanisms that cause us to have it. This psychological explanation covers the central part of the section. Like most of Hume's discussions of psychology it is convoluted, ingenious, and brilliant. Nevertheless, questions can be raised about it, particularly concerning his account of the first and fourth steps.

From the very beginning Hume assumes that external material objects are inconceivable to us, taking it for granted that he had established this conclusion by his argument in Section VI of Part II. However, during the course of the section he buttresses that conclusion with some additional arguments.

Finally, but with circumspection, he approaches the ontological question of the existence of a material world. Although he never mentions him by name it seems fair to assume that Hume is haunted throughout the section by the philosophical presence of Berkeley, about whom he appears ambivalent. Although he seems reluctant to associate himself with Berkeley, he recognizes that the conclusion he had drawn about the existence of matter is unavoidable.

So one might well ask what was Hume's own position on the question of the existence of an external material world. Many Hume scholars have debated this question and have given different answers to it. My reading of Section II leads me to conclude that he does not offer a single, unequivocal answer but is still wrestling with the problem in the section. I believe he is torn between three incompatible views—the naive realism of the vulgar, the representative realism of philosophers like Locke (the double-existence hypothesis), and the subjective idealism of Berkeley.[43] At this point in Book I the conclusion Hume emphasizes is not any philosophical theory but the ineradicable belief we all have that there is an external world. But, unfortunately, such a belief is not one he can share. Although Hume undoubtedly believed that he believed in an external material world, he was mistaken in doing so because, lacking any idea of this world, he could have no such belief.

After the long and arduous arguments in Section II, as well as those in Section VI of Part II, one might think that Hume has laid the issues of the existence of an external world and our possible knowledge of it finally to rest. Such an expectation would, however, be premature. As we will find in the next chapter, he has more of interest to say on the subject. In particular, he faces the ontological question squarely, giving his answer to it as well as the reasons on which that answer rests.

16

CRITIQUE
OF PHILOSOPHERS AND
THEOLOGIANS

(Part IV, Sections III–V)

Introduction

In Sections III through V of Part IV Hume breaks the continuity of his argument to examine a variety of views held by other philosophers and by theologians. Thus the sections are, to some degree, a digression. But in them he continues to discuss the topic of an external material world. Although some of the content is repetitive of Section II, he amplifies certain arguments and reaches an important additional conclusion. So, in part, the sections (particularly III and IV) consist of addenda to Section II. In my survey of all three sections I will concentrate on those passages that illuminate Hume's own thought, treating his criticisms of other writers quite briefly.

My procedure does, however, involve me in a problem. It is not always clear just when Hume is expressing a view of someone else and when he is expressing one of his own. Attempting to distinguish between these situations is, on occasion, difficult and requires a close reading of the text. In particular one must be careful not to attribute a position to Hume unless evidence can be given that makes it reasonably clear, either from the language he uses or from the context, that he is speaking for himself.

A special comment should be made about Section V. Certainly it is relevant to Hume's philosophy in Book I because he uses it to establish the conclusion that all metaphysical speculation about substance, whether it be mental or material, is absurd. Yet much of its content is digressive, consisting not of an elaboration of his own philosophy but of a polemical attack on both theologians and materialists. Perhaps Hume inserted it into the book because controversies about substance were a topic of debate at his time.

Text

1. ARISTOTELIAN ERRORS (SECTION III)

Hume entitles Section III "Of the antient philosophy" (219). This title is much too general to describe the contents of the section, which consist mainly of a critique of the Aristotelian doctrine of material substance. The value of the section for our understanding of Hume does not, however, lie in this critique but in Hume's development of points about our belief in an external material world and the causes that lead us to hold such a belief.

Hume's main object in the section is twofold: (1) To offer a psychological account, based on his theory of imagination, explaining why we (and the Aristotelians) believe in the existence of matter and (2) to reiterate his conclusion that no theoretical justification can be given for that belief. After a charming prelude on the significance of dreams, Hume begins his argument in a way repetitious in form, although not in detail, of his beginning in Section II. His aim is to give a psychological explanation of our ordinary, natural belief that we perceive individual material objects that persist through time, even though our perceptions themselves lack both simplicity and identity. Starting with identity, he points out that, even though a perceptual object changes through time, if we observe its changes as they gradually occur, we consider the object to be the same. We do so because our imagination makes the transition from one idea of the object to the next, related but different idea without effort. But suppose we perceive this changing object at a certain time and then do not perceive it until much later, after it has changed considerably. Our imagination is unable to make the transition without great effort so we question whether the object we perceive is the same object we perceived before. "When we gradually follow an object in its successive changes, the smooth progress of the thought makes us ascribe an identity to the succession; because 'tis by a similar act of the mind we consider an unchangeable object. When we compare its situation after a considerable change the progress of the thought is broke; and consequently we are presented with the idea of diversity."[1]

This disparity causes a conflict within the imagination. Why should the mere fact that we do not perceive an object for a long period of time cause us to believe we are not perceiving the same object at all? To avoid this result the imagination, Hume says, takes a further step. "In order to reconcile which contradictions the imagination is apt to feign something *unknown* and invisible, which it supposes to continue the same under all these variations; and this *unintelligible* something it calls a *substance, or original and first matter*."[2]

Turning to the question of simplicity Hume gives a parallel psychological explanation. If we observe a compound object like a peach we can join its various qualities together by an easy act of the imagination, almost as though we were observing an uncompounded or simple object. But we can observe the peach in a different way, by becoming aware of the diversity of its various parts. When we concentrate on the compound object in this way we find it difficult to say that it is one simple thing. To overcome this difficulty the imagination again must "feign an unknown something, or *original* substance and matter . . . as what may give the compound object a title to be call'd one thing, notwithstanding its diversity and composition" (221).

Hume next uses these acts of the imagination as a way of explaining the peripatetic philosophy. He shows how this natural process of feigning gives rise in that philosophy to further concepts like substantial forms, accidents, and occult qualities. After labeling the material substance of the Aristotelians an "unintelligible chimera" (222), he concludes by emphasizing that it is based on the psychological processes he described at the beginning of the section. "The whole [peripatetic] system . . . is entirely incomprehensible, and yet is deriv'd from principles as natural as any of these above-explain'd" (222). So Section III might be described as a psychoanalysis of the peripatetic philosophy.

Before completing his critique of ancient philosophy Hume turns his attention to the notion of "cause." Here he makes an important advance in his views about causation, beyond the conclusions he had reached in Part III. There he had contented himself with the claim that causal connections in the material world are inconceivable and unintelligible to us, but he still acknowledged that they may nevertheless actually exist.[3] Now he faces the ontological question directly and answers it negatively. Speaking of the quest of philosophers seeking to find causes in matter, he remarks (with some irony): "What can be imagin'd more tormenting, than to seek with eagerness, what for ever flies us; and seek for it in a place, *where 'tis impossible it can ever exist?*"[4]

Hume concludes his brief survey of the ancients with some unflattering remarks about the peripatetics' introduction of such things as "*sympathies, antipathies, and horrors of a vacuum*" (224) into their philosophy. His final remarks in the section are heavily ironical, and clearly exhibit his contempt for Aristotelianism.

2. The "Justification" of Imagination (Section IV)

In Section IV Hume turns his attention to "modern philosophy" (225). Although he mentions no names in the section it is apparent from the subject matter that he has his empiricist predecessors, Locke and Berkeley, prominently in mind. He discusses the epistemological conclusions of the modern philosophers, assessing some of their arguments and adding arguments and conclusions of his own. The argument is not only epistemological but ontological as well. In it Hume addresses both the questions, Can we have any perception of an external material world? and Does such a world exist? Before beginning this task, however, he makes some comments about the imagination that arise from his critique of the ancient philosophers in Section III. He begins by offering an objection to that critique. "But here it may be objected, that the imagination, according to my own confession, being the ultimate judge of all systems of philosophy, I am unjust in blaming the antient philosophers for makeing use of that faculty" (225). On the surface this may seem a trivial objection but Hume is aware that, in the context of his own philosophy, it assumes unusual significance. Two of his earlier conclusions are pertinent. (1) All "inferences" we make are the work of the imagination. (2) Because this is true, no rational justification can be given for these "inferences"; indeed, according to his total scepticism, they are in opposition to reason. Since Hume, by his theory of the imagination, his scepticism, and his doctrine of natural belief, has destroyed any basis he might have for giving rational arguments against the opinions of the ancients, why should he criticize them for holding these opinions without rational support?

Hume answers the objection he has raised by drawing a distinction within the imagination. Some imaginative inferences are better than others; namely, those that are "permanent, irresistable, and universal; such as the customary transition from causes to effects" (225). Poor imaginative inferences, on the other hand, are "changeable, weak, and irregular" (225). They are exemplified by the reasoning of the peripatetic philosophers. But his distinction does not in itself resolve Hume's problem for we can ask: Why are inferences of the first type better than those of the second? His answer is that we must make inferences of the first type in order both to live and to live well, whereas we can easily get along without the second type. "The former are the foundation of all our thoughts and actions, so that upon their removal human nature must immediately perish and go to ruin. The latter are neither unavoidable to mankind, nor necessary, or so much as useful in the conduct of life."[5]

Although Hume does not develop his protopragmatic "justification" of certain types of imaginative "inference" further, we have evidence in these passages of at least some concern he felt about the irrationality of his own philosophical beliefs. Nevertheless, questions must be raised about the distinction he makes between different principles of reasoning. Is his indictment of the Aristotelians factually correct? Did they appeal to "changeable, weak, and irregular" principles in their philosophy? To make his case Hume would have to provide more documentation than he does. Also, Hume contends that the Aristotelians based their philosophy on imagination. I think Aristotle, at least, might dispute that claim, arguing instead that he tried to support his conclusions by reason. He would probably go further and find Hume's view that we "reason" with our imagination less than credible and certainly he would reject Hume's irrationalism.

3. Implications of the Modern Philosophy (Section IV)

Turning to the modern philosophers Hume asks whether their imaginative inferences are, as they claim them to be, better than those of the ancients. To answer this question he renews his analysis of the double-existence theory, or representational realism, basing his examination on the standard distinction philosophers like Locke had made between primary and secondary qualities. His argument is complex, repetitive, and hard to follow. I will not attempt to cover every point he makes in it but will concentrate on the conclusions he reaches.

Hume begins his account with what he calls "sensible qualities" (227), or what are usually called secondary qualities. According to the modern philosophers these are "nothing but impressions in the mind, deriv'd from the operation of external objects, and without any resemblance to the qualities of the objects" (226). After reciting several reasons in support of this view, all "deriv'd from the variations of those impressions" (226), Hume concludes that the modern philosophers are right. "'Tis certain, that when different impressions of the same sense arise from any object, every one of these impressions has not a resembling quality existent in the object. . . . [I]t evidently follows, that *many* of our impressions have no external model or archetype" (227—italics added). Hume says here only that *many* of our impressions have no external model. He immediately supplements this conclusion with a further argument that leads him to generalize. "Now from like effects we presume like causes. Many of the impressions of colour, sound, &c. are confest to be nothing but internal existences, and to arise from causes, which no ways resemble them. These impressions are in appearance nothing different from the other impressions of colour, sound, &c. We conclude, therefore, that they are, *all of them*, deriv'd from a like origin" (227—italics added).

Agreeing that secondary qualities are only "internal existences" (227), Hume follows the modern philosophers to the second point in their epistemology. "For upon the removal of sounds, colours, heat, cold, and other sensible qualities, from the rank of continu'd independent existences, we are reduc'd merely to what are called primary qualities, as the only *real* ones, of which we have any adequate notion. These primary qualities are extension and solidity."[6] In attributing to modern philosophers the view that primary qualities are *real* Hume means that, according to them, these qualities exist outside of the mind, as attributes of bodies in the external world. Hume, however, rejects this view, saying that it is subject to many objections, but that he will limit himself to one of them "which is in [his] opinion very decisive" (227). Continuing, he writes: "I assert, that instead of explaining the operations of external objects by its means, *we utterly annihilate all these objects*. . . . If colours, sounds, tastes, and smells be merely perceptions, nothing we can conceive is possest of a real, continu'd, and independent existence; not even motion, extension and solidity, which are the primary qualities chiefly insisted on" (227–28—italics added).

This is a conclusion of great importance ontologically. Hume begins by making the dramatic claim that the system of secondary and primary qualities annihilates external objects. He elaborates more fully at the end of the statement, saying that it leaves the primary qualities of motion, extension, and solidity without any real, continued, and independent existence. If this be true and if these qualities are claimed to be attributes of bodies, bodies have no existence either. Material objects do not exist, and the external world is annihilated. Finally, he claims that this consequence follows from the view that colors, sounds, tastes, and smells (the secondary qualities) are perceptions, hence "subjective." Since this last view is one he has said he accepts, the conclusion we must draw is that Hume is allying himself with Berkeley ontologically. He is agreeing that no external material world exists.

But on this crucial point Hume has stated his conclusion before completing his argument. He has not yet shown why his acceptance of the "subjective" nature of secondary qualities leads him to conclude that no external world exists. He explains his reasoning in an argument (which he repeats in somewhat different terms) extending over the next several paragraphs. I will not follow this complex argument in all its details here but simply summarize it.

The argument can be separated into two main parts. In the first part, Hume begins with the three primary qualities of motion, extension, and solidity. He then argues that motion depends on extension and extension on solidity. Focusing his attention on solidity, he argues that it "is perfectly incomprehensible alone" (228), but instead depends on the conception of solid bodies. He then asks what idea we have of bodies. Secondary qualities, he has already concluded, can give us no such idea. This leaves only the primary qualities of motion and extension. But these, he has just shown, depend on that of solidity. So any attempt to base solidity on them would involve a circular argument. He concludes: "Our modern philosophy, therefore, leaves us no just nor satisfactory idea of solidity; nor consequently of matter."[7] The attempt made by modern philosophers to give an account of an external material world through an appeal to primary qualities, after acknowledging the "subjective" nature of secondary qualities, Hume is saying, ends in failure. He makes this point explicitly in the next paragraph: "After the exclusion of colours, sounds, heat and cold from the rank of external existences, there remains nothing, which can afford us a just and consistent idea of body" (229).

In the second part of his argument Hume concentrates on the idea of solidity itself, which, he points out, we think we derive from the sense of "feeling" or of "touch" (230). The question he then poses is whether this sense can give us any idea either of solidity or of bodies. His answer, which he supports with several illustrations, is that it cannot. "The impressions of touch . . . neither represent solidity, nor any real [material] object" (230–31).

Hume concludes Section IV with an important summary of his views, both epistemological and ontological, about an external material world. "Thus there is a direct and total opposition betwixt our reason and our senses; or more properly speaking, betwixt those conclusions we form from cause and effect, and those that persuade us of the continu'd and independent existence of body. When we reason from cause and effect, we conclude, that neither colour, sound, taste, nor smell have a continu'd and independent existence. When we exclude these sensible qualities there remains nothing in the universe, which has such an existence" (231). This passage calls for a number of comments. (1) Hume, in the first sentence, makes a statement and then corrects it. To say that there is a "total opposition" between our "reason" and our "senses" is not accurate. The opposition is, instead, within the imagination, between our causal "reasoning" and our natural belief in the existence of body. (2) The conclusion Hume reaches from cause and effect follows from the "subjective" nature of secondary qualities, specifically color, sound, taste, and smell. He says nothing about the sense of touch here but he has just completed an argument showing that it cannot fill the gap left by the other four senses. (3) The conclusion he reaches is that "nothing in the universe" has a "continu'd and independent existence." As Hume states it, this conclusion is, at this point, too broad. What he should have said, and undoubtedly meant, is that nothing in the *material* universe has such an existence or, in other words, that no external material world exists. Thus, he is reiterating the conclusion he stated earlier in the section and reaffirming his agreement with Berkeley on this central issue of ontology. (4) But a final point, of significance, must always be remembered. Although his *philosophy* leads him to a Berkeleyan conclusion, Hume implies in the passage, he does not accept that conclusion but continues to believe in the existence of an external material world.[8]

He does so because he must. Some readers may find Hume's irrationalism on this central question of metaphysics repugnant. But, whether or not it is excusable, the fact remains that many intellectuals have followed a similar path. This is particularly true of theologians, some of whom have concluded, on theoretical grounds, that God does not exist but continue to believe in his existence because they believe they must.

4. MATERIAL AND MENTAL SUBSTANCE (SECTION V, PARAGRAPHS 1–4)

With Section V, which he entitles "Of the immateriality of the soul," Hume seems to be turning to a new subject. This is only partly true. The title itself is somewhat misleading. What Hume is concerned with in the section is the notion of mental substance, not in isolation, but in contrast with the notion of material substance, to which the three previous sections had been devoted. The argument takes place in the context of a dispute between theologians and materialists, or atheists.[9] In his partial shift of emphasis from material to mental substance Hume is laying the groundwork for his full discussion of the mind in Section VI. For the student concerned with Hume's own philosophy Section V is to a considerable degree digressive. Much of it consists in arguments and counterarguments between theologians and materialists, in which Hume sometimes takes positions that clearly do not represent his own thought and which are only of peripheral relevance to his philosophical views. For that reason I will give them only a brief survey, concentrating my attention on those passages that can further our understanding of Hume.

He begins the section by noting a difference between theories regarding matter and those regarding mind. The former, he concludes, lead to contradictions but the latter need not. But, he then adds, certain philosophers have immersed discussions of mind in the same difficulties as those of body.[10] They have done so by attempting to develop theories of material and mental substance and then explaining how perceptions inhere in one or the other of these. What both sides (mistakenly) assume is that they understand the meaning of the notion of substance and of the inhesion of perceptions in a substance. "These philosophers are the curious reasoners concerning the material or immaterial substances, in which they suppose our perceptions to inhere. In order to put a stop to these endless cavils on both sides, I know no better method, than to ask these philosophers in a few words, *What they mean by substance and inhesion?*" (232). Obviously Hume believes his question cannot be satisfactorily answered. He writes: "This question we have found impossible to be answer'd with regard to matter and body... in the case of the mind, it labours under all the same difficulties" (232). Elaborating briefly on the last point, he invokes the

Empiricist Principle. To have an idea of anything we must first have an impression of it. But we have no impression of mental substance so can have no idea of it. Therefore it is inconceivable to us.

Hume's main object in Section V is to show that we can give no meaning to either of the two opposed philosophical hypotheses. He does this by alternately taking the side of theologians, who suppose mental substances in which perceptions inhere, in order to refute materialists and then of materialists, who suppose material substance in which perceptions inhere, to refute theologians. Both sides, he concludes, are successful in their refutations, with the result that they mutually destroy each other.

5. Are Perceptions Substances? (Section V, Paragraphs 5–6)

After having used the Empiricist Principle to refute anyone who claims to have an idea of mental substance, Hume turns his attention to those who base their theories of substance on their definition of the term itself, as "*something which may exist by itself.*"[11] Hume's argument is of special interest because of his use of "perceptions" in it. A reader might easily be led to conclude that Hume is making the claim that perceptions are substances. This would, however, be a misunderstanding. The passage that can be misunderstood reads: "Since all our perceptions are different from each other, and from every thing else in the universe, they are also distinct and separable, and *may* be consider'd as separately existent, and *may* exist separately, and have no need of any thing else to support their existence. They are, therefore, substances, *as far as this definition explains a substance.*"[12] Despite what he appears to say in the final sentence Hume is not claiming that perceptions are substances. Two points make this clear. First, one must note the qualification in the final clause of the last sentence (which I have italicized). Hume does not accept the definition of substance that implies that perceptions are substances; just before the passage I have reproduced he wrote that "this definition agrees to every thing, that can possibly be conceived; and never will serve to distinguish substance from accident."[13] Second, he does not say that perceptions *do* have an independent existence but only that they *may* have one. This is a point about perceptions he had discussed at some length in Section II, in which he concluded that, although the supposition that perceptions have an independent existence involves no contradiction, nevertheless his "experiments" establish that they in fact have none.[14] Hume's use of "perceptions" in this argument about substances is almost surely ironical. He has chosen as his example of a substance, according to the definition in question, something that everyone would agree to be not remotely like a substance.

Hume makes his denial of the substantival nature of perceptions explicit in the paragraph that follows. Adding to this the fact that we can find no support for the notion of a substance or for the idea of inhesion either by an appeal to our sense impressions or through a definition, he concludes that the dispute between theologians and materialists is meaningless to us.

> We have no perfect idea of any thing but of a perception. *A substance is entirely different from a perception.* We have, therefore, no idea of a substance. Inhesion in something is suppos'd to be requisite to support the existence of our perceptions. Nothing appears requisite to support the existence of a perception. We have, therefore, no idea of inhesion. What possibility then of answering that question, *Whether perceptions inhere in a material or immaterial substance,* when we do not so much as understand the meaning of the question? (234—first italics added)

To buttress this conclusion Hume launches into a lengthy discussion of the arguments of both theologians and materialists.

6. Objects That Exist Nowhere (Section V, Paragraphs 7–14)

Hume begins his discussion on the side of the theologians, summarizing one of their arguments against the materialists' view that perceptions inhere in bodies. If this were possible, perceptions (e.g., thoughts and feelings) would have spatial dimensions, which is "utterly absurd and contradictory" (234). This argument leads Hume into an extended discussion of a related issue that is of some interest. What kind of objects, he asks, are capable of local, or spatial conjunction? Certainly this is not true of the objects of hearing, taste, or smell, any more than it is of emotions. None of these is extended so none can be conjoined with anything in space. From this Hume concludes: "'Twill not be surprizing after this, if I deliver a maxim, which is condemn'd by several metaphysicians, and is esteem'd contrary to the most certain principles of human reason. . . . *that an object may exist, and yet be no where;* and I assert, that this is not only possible, but that the greatest part of beings do and must exist after this manner" (235). Turning to specifics Hume claims that the objects to which his maxim applies include those we perceive through the senses of hearing, taste, and smell as well as the objects of our feelings and thoughts, but not to the objects of sight and touch. His reasoning in support of the maxim is compelling. "A moral reflection cannot be plac'd on the right or on the left hand of a passion, nor can a smell or sound be either of a circular or a square figure. These objects and perceptions, so far from requiring any particular place, are absolutely incompatible with it" (236). It is hard to disagree with Hume on this point. We certainly do not give spatial properties to the objects of the kinds of perceptions in question. We do not—except figuratively—say that a sound we hear is round or square. Yet we do use these spatial adjectives to describe the objects of our sense perceptions of sight and touch. For example, we see an object we are looking at as occupying space.

Having made this distinction between the objects of different kinds of perception, Hume goes on to note that we often give spatial characteristics to objects, like those of taste, that do not have them.[15] He explains this "illusion" (237) by an appeal to the psychology of the imagination, using much the same kind of analysis he has given many times before. He concludes his discussion of this point by adding that the results of our tendency, which is completely natural, are "unintelligible and contradictory" (238). The entire discussion confirms the charge made by the theologians: That the materialists' claim that our perceptions inhere in extended bodies is an "absurdity" (238).

7. Theologians as Atheists (Section V, Paragraphs 15–28)

Hume does not leave the theologians long to savor their victory. The materialists, he argues, can easily turn the tables on them. Objects or contents of perceptions that are extended (e.g., things we see) can no more inhere in an unextended mind than those of perceptions that are unextended (e.g., things we hear) can inhere in extended bodies. As Hume puts it: "The free-thinker may now triumph in his turn; and having found there are impressions and ideas really extended, may ask his antagonists, how they can incorporate a simple and indivisible subject with an extended perception?" (240).

Having made this point Hume launches a general attack against the theologians. After repeating that the question of the immateriality of the soul is "utterly unintelligible" (240), he continues: "I assert, that the doctrine of the immateriality, simplicity, and indivisibility of a thinking substance is a true atheism, and will serve to justify all those sentiments, for which *Spinoza* is so universally infamous" (240). To substantiate this charge Hume offers a long, complex but basically *ad hominem* argument. After summarizing the metaphysics of Spinoza in a paragraph he claims that "this hideous hypothesis is almost the same with that of the immateriality of the soul" (241). To substantiate this claim he illustrates in detail the parallels between the two metaphysical systems. His arguments, although they contribute little to our understanding of his own philosophy, are of interest in their own right, revealing as they do the acuteness of his mind.

I will not review Hume's arguments in detail here but, in summary, note two points. First, his thesis that, because the theologians' notion of the indivisibility and simplicity of the soul parallels Spinoza's theory of a single, simple substance, it must be atheistic, assumes Spinoza to be an atheist. Whether Hume himself thought this to be true is difficult to tell. For the purposes of his argument itself his appeal to the pejorative term "atheist," although it may have had some effect on his contemporaries, is really gratuitous. His decisive philosophical point lies in the arguments he offers to demonstrate the conceptual difficulties inherent in both systems of thought. This leads to the second point—that Hume considered his critique of both theologians and Spinoza to be decisive. The conclusion on which he insisted is not simply that the theories are mistaken but that the whole enterprise that generated them is a traffic in absurdity. "I turn my attention to these hypotheses [of theologians and of Spinoza] . . . and find that they have the same fault of being unintelligible, and that as far as we can understand them, they are so much alike, that 'tis impossible to discover any absurdity in one, which is not common to both of them."16

8. MATTER, MIND, AND CAUSE AND EFFECT (SECTION V, PARAGRAPHS 29–33)

Hume completes Section V with a further criticism of the theologians. His argument concerns their claim that matter can never be a cause producing effects in the mind. The basis for their contention, he points out, is quite straightforward. A body, through its motion, can cause motion in another body but it cannot cause a thought or an emotion in a nonmaterial substance, or a mind. Although this argument may seem persuasive, Hume maintains, it is not cogent. "Few have been able to withstand the seeming evidence of this argument; and yet nothing in the world is more easy than to refute it."17

To one who has read Book I it should be equally easy to predict how Hume will refute the theologians' argument. He immediately points out that they rest their case on a mistaken view of the cause-and-effect relation. They assume, that is, that a cause possesses some power that produces the effect. But he has already destroyed that assumption and given an alternative analysis of causation, one that, instead of appealing to "objective" causal power, rests on our past experiences of the constant conjunction of objects. It follows from his theory that anything X can become the cause of any other thing Y, if the two are constantly conjoined. Therefore bodies in motion can be the cause of mental events.

Having established that bodies can cause thoughts Hume goes on to show that they do in fact do so. His argument rests on a simple appeal to experience. We have found by experience that the activities of bodies are constantly conjoined with activities in the mind. Since the causal relation results from constant conjunction, these experiences warrant the conclusion that bodily events are causes of which mental events are effects. "We find by the comparing their ideas, that thought and motion are different from each other, and by experience, that they are constantly united; which being all the circumstances, that enter into the idea of cause and effect, when apply'd to the operations of matter, we may certainly conclude, that motion may be, and actually is, the cause of thought and perception."[18] Theologians might not be convinced by Hume's argument, replying that, by assuming his own analysis of causation, which they reject, it begs the question against them. Such a reply, however, would not be decisive but would simply shift the controversy into a different arena; namely, that of the proper understanding of causation.

Although Hume ends Section V with some flattering remarks about religion, the conclusion we should draw from it is quite different. He is defending neither the theologians nor the materialists in this section. No more is he criticizing them in the sense that he is simply finding deficiencies in their arguments. Rather he is condemning the entire enterprise in which both sides are engaged. All talk about substance, whether it be mental or material, is unintelligible and absurd.[19]

Summary

Although they contain a number of new and interesting arguments, Sections III through V add little to Hume's epistemology and metaphysics. Most of the conclusions he draws from these arguments repeat those he has drawn earlier in Book I. For this reason the sections can be viewed largely as addenda. One exception, of great importance, must, however, be made to this appraisal. In Section IV Hume reaches the conclusion that no external material world exists. Although he agrees with Berkeley as a philosopher, it is apparent that he does so reluctantly because, as a man, he simply finds himself unable to believe his own philosophical conclusion.

These sections have another kind of value because they give us a glimpse of Hume's assessment of other thinkers. His low opinion of Aristotelianism is evident from Section III; what he might have said about Platonism is a matter of conjecture. Although he does not mention them by name, it is evident that he has his two empiricist predecessors in mind in Section IV. His agreement with Berkeley against Locke is of great significance both ontologically and historically.

Section V is something of an anomaly. With the exception of his argument near the end concerning body-mind causation, most of the section is a digression from Hume's own philosophy. But it is a fascinating digression because it reveals Hume at his critical and polemical best. Laden with irony, it exhibits the contradictions and absurdities metaphysicians can get entangled in when they attempt to talk about the notion of substance— whether this be mental *or* material.

17

HUME'S MIND

(Part IV, Section VI)

Introduction

Section VI of Part IV is of unique importance to the argument of the *Treatise*. In it Hume concentrates directly on the human mind, which is the general subject of the entire *Treatise* and, as the faculty of thought or understanding, the special subject of Book I. Nevertheless, despite its importance, the section totals only a dozen pages, of which several are devoted mainly to a repetition and embellishment of arguments he had already given in Section III about our belief in the identity of material objects through time.[1] The contents of these pages, although interesting in themselves, seem largely to digress from the subject matter of Section VI, although Hume, to justify the digression, writes: "[Personal identity] is our present subject; and to explain it perfectly we must . . . account for that identity, which we attribute to plants and animals; there being a great analogy betwixt it, and the identity of a self or person" (253). Since I have examined Hume's discussions of bodily identity in earlier chapters,[2] I will limit myself here to any additional points he makes on these pages that bear on his views regarding our belief in personal identity.

In its structure Section VI is patterned roughly after Section II. Hume begins with a short epistemological discussion, designed to answer the question: Can we know that we have a mind? His discussion leads him not only to an epistemological conclusion about our knowledge of mind but to an ontological conclusion about its existence as well. Having resolved these issues, he turns, for the remainder of the section, to the psychological question: What causes us to believe we have a mind? The argument, as usual, is complex and Hume's conclusions both novel and radical. Beyond that, however, they are clearly disturbing to their author. Hume added a substantial appendix note to the section, beginning it by saying that "upon a more strict review of the section concerning *personal identity*, I find myself involv'd in such a labyrinth, that, I must confess, I neither know how to correct my former opinions, nor how to render them consistent" (633).

One of my tasks in reviewing the section will be to understand Hume's reasons for being so deeply disturbed by his theory of mind. I will also refer to additional comments he makes in the appendix note in my exposition of the section itself, whenever these add to an understanding of a particular point under discussion.

The title I have given to this chapter needs some explanation. First, I use the word "mind" rather than "self" in it. Nothing is implied in this usage. Hume himself uses both terms, as well as "personal identity," synonymously in Section VI and I will do the same throughout this chapter. By referring to *Hume's* mind I am also following him. In his arguments (particularly at the beginning of the section) he uses the method of introspection to discover the nature of his own mind, but notes that, although his conclusions apply to himself, it is possible that they do not apply to others (252).

Finally, I will, as Hume himself does, repeat myself on occasion, as I examine issues from different perspectives. I believe the subject matter of the chapter, and Hume's Section VI itself, to be more than important enough to justify such repetition.[3]

Text

1. The Self and the Empiricist Principle (Paragraphs 1–2)

Hume begins Section VI with the remark: "There are some philosophers, who imagine we are every moment intimately conscious of what we call our SELF" (251). According to these philosophers, "[We] are certain . . . both of [the self's] perfect identity and simplicity" (251). The important characteristic of this conception of the self is "identity." By this Hume means the view that each one of us is an enduring self possessing an identity sufficient to justify us in saying that we remain the same self or person through time. Most of his argument in the section is directed toward this concept of self-identity.[4]

Hume begins his argument with an invocation of the Empiricist Principle. To say we are conscious of our self, he points out, is to imply that we have an idea of that self and, since all our ideas are copies of impressions, that we have an impression of it. He then denies the existence of any such impression. "It must be some one impression, that gives rise to every real idea. But self or person is not any one impression" (251). Lacking any impression of our self, we necessarily lack any idea of it. After enumerating a variety of impressions we can have he concludes: "It cannot . . . be from any of these impressions, or from any other, that the idea of self is deriv'd; and consequently there is no such idea" (252). Since, to be conscious of something is to have an idea of it, it follows that those philosophers who claim we are conscious of ourselves must be mistaken.

In these opening paragraphs Hume answers the epistemological question: Can we have any knowledge of our self or mind? in the negative. Since we have no impression, hence no idea of it, our self or mind must be inconceivable. Hume bases this sceptical epistemological conclusion, as we have just seen, on an appeal to the Empiricist Principle.

2. HUME AND HIS PERCEPTIONS (PARAGRAPH 3)

Hume begins his positive theory of the mind and its relation to perceptions with a series of statements about perceptions themselves. "All [our particular perceptions] are different, and distinguishable, and separable from each other, and may be separately consider'd, and may exist separately, and have no need of any thing to support their existence."[5] The central point these statements convey is that of the independence of perceptions. They are independent in two ways. (1) They are different, distinguishable, and separable from each other and (2) they do not need anything to support their existence. Both of these characteristics of perceptions are important to our understanding and appreciation of Hume's theory of mind but they are important in different ways. In chapters 15 and 16 I discussed the independence of perceptions from other things at some length, concluding that, for Hume, perceptions can exist in independence of any "substance" supporting them but do not exist unless there is some perceiver perceiving them.[6] In this chapter I will be concerned mainly with their independence from each other.

Hume continues his positive analysis of mind by concentrating on himself, conducting an introspective thought-experiment.

> For my part, when I enter most intimately into what I call *myself*, I always stumble on some particular perception or other, of heat or cold, light or shade, love or hatred, pain or pleasure. I never can catch *myself* at any time without a perception, and never can observe any thing but the perception. When my perceptions are remov'd for any time, as by sound sleep; so long am I insensible of *myself*, and may truly be said not to exist. And were all my perceptions remov'd by death . . . I shou'd be entirely annihilated, nor do I conceive what is farther requisite to make me a perfect non-entity. (252)

This interesting passage calls for a number of comments. Hume is describing a thought-experiment we can all perform. When he performs it he finds that all his conscious states consist of perceptions. Nothing he can discover when he observes his own consciousness is different in nature from a perception. I will not pursue here the issue of whether this analysis is correct. Some readers may claim that the result of Hume's inspection, whether it gives a complete catalog of the contents of *his* consciousness, certainly does not give one of *theirs*. If this is so, Hume would simply reply that such readers are different from him. "If any one upon serious and unprejudic'd reflexion, thinks he has a different notion of *himself*, I must confess I can reason no longer with him. All I can allow him is, that he may be in the right as well as I, and that we are essentially different in this particular" (252).

Hume's introspective experiment raises a second question. In using the phrase "when I enter most intimately into what I call *myself*," he presents through his sentence-structure and terminology a picture of a perceiver examining some object, in this case his own consciousness. It is analogous to what a scientist might say: "When I examine this tissue through a microscope . . ." So we can ask: Who, or what, is the observer that is perceiving "myself," or my perceptions, and that Hume identifies by the pronoun "I"? This question is important because Hume makes it plain that his awareness of anything requires a subject-object relationship. The objects are the perceptions perceived and the subject is the "I" that perceives these perceptions. Without such a dual relationship perception could not occur. Can this "I," this perceiving observer, be identified with the conscious state it is observing or is it an entity external to that conscious state? These are difficult questions to answer but questions Hume must and will attempt to deal with in the paragraphs that follow.

Hume draws two immediate inferences from his introspective experiment—that when he dies he will cease to exist and that when he is in a dreamless sleep he also ceases to exist. Although some would certainly agree with his denial of immortality, most of us would have serious misgivings about his claim that we stop existing when we are unconscious. When Hume says he ceases to exist when he is asleep, his point can be interpreted in either of two ways. The existence of perceptions is either (1) a necessary condition of his existence or (2) is identical with his existence. Although on both interpretations he would cease to exist while asleep, the first makes a distinction between Hume's perceptions and himself, which the second does not. Hume accepts the second interpretation. Although he does not make the point explicitly in the text, he adds a statement about death in the appendix note that affirms this interpretation and that seems equally applicable to the sleep state. "The annihilation, which some people suppose to follow upon death, and which entirely destroys this self, is nothing but an extinction of all particular perceptions. . . . These therefore must be the same with self; since the one cannot survive the other."[7]

Hume's claim that he ceases to exist while sleeping has some interesting consequences. One might say that during those periods he is temporarily in the same condition as he will be in after his death. And when he awakens he is resurrected. I do not think this way of describing the situation would cause Hume any concern; sleep, for him, is, in fact, a "little death." But another point is involved here. Since a gap occurs in Hume's existence whenever he sleeps, we can ask how the self that comes into existence when he awakens is related to the self that existed before he went to sleep. Specifically, are the two selves the same self or are they different selves? Hume is unequivocal in his answer to this question. "There is properly no *simplicity* in [the self or mind] at one time, nor *identity* in different [times]" (253). The important point here is Hume's denial of identity to himself. What are we to make of this denial? Certainly it seems to be shocking. If Hume is not the same self after sleeping as he was before and if it took him three years to write the *Treatise*, must we conclude that the book was multiauthored? I think, however, that this feeling of shock can be assuaged. The issue with which we should concern ourselves, as philosophers, is not that of how many minds contributed to the writing of the *Treatise* but rather that of whether the theory of mind its authors present in it is viable. This, however, is an issue we cannot yet resolve because we do not know what that theory is.

But perhaps I am misinterpreting Hume here. Is it not possible that he is anticipating a distinction he will make a few pages later (257–58), between numerical and specific identity, and implying only that, although after sleep he is not numerically identical to himself before sleep, he is still specifically identical to himself? To evaluate this interpretation we need to understand the distinction. He writes: "Tho' we commonly be able to distinguish pretty exactly betwixt numerical and specific identity, yet it sometimes happens, that we confound them. . . . Thus a man, who hears a noise, that is frequently interrupted and renew'd, says, it is still the same noise; tho' 'tis evident the sounds have only a specific identity or resemblance" (257–58). That Hume cannot claim even specific identity to himself across gaps in consciousness, however, is apparent, for at least two reasons. To be able to say that his present conscious state resembles his conscious state before sleep he would have to be able to recollect that previous state in order to compare the two. But this he cannot do. As he wrote in Section V of Part III, "it [is] impossible to recal the past impressions, in order to compare them with our present ideas" (85). No more is it possible to recall and thus to compare past perceptions or conscious states in general with present ones. This point is important because, as we have just seen, Hume identifies himself with his perceptions. The second reason rests on a factual point. Hume's perceptions after sleeping would, with, at most, rare exceptions, be different in their nature from his perceptions before sleeping. Therefore they would not satisfy the condition of specific identity he requires as, for example, in his illustration of the repeated noises. Since he is his perceptions, it follows from the fact that these differ on the two occasions that he differs as well. He is not the same Hume after sleep that he was before sleep.

Continuing with Hume's thought-experiment itself we recall that he set it up by speaking of "when I enter most intimately into what I call *myself.*" From the form of the clause it is clear that he is describing a "perceiver-perceived" situation, the perceiver being "I" and the object perceived being "myself." But in this situation the perceiver and the perceived are the same; by the act of introspection Hume is perceiving himself. Finally, he concludes that the perceived ("himself"), understood as something that continues through time, does not exist. Therefore, the "I," or Hume himself as perceiver, does not continue to exist through time either.

This conclusion raises a problem. If there is no entity external to the contents of consciousness corresponding to the "I," there seems to be nothing to conduct Hume's introspective experiment. So how can the experiment take place? Here we must be careful not to reach too hasty a conclusion. Hume has not yet completed his argument. He has only implied that anyone who thinks the introspective experiment he has conducted includes an introspector, in the sense of an entity external to consciousness perceiving the contents of consciousness, must be mistaken. No such external entity exists. So Hume has a problem still to resolve. What does perceive his conscious states? Or, to put the question in somewhat different terms, What does the term "I" refer to if it does not refer to some entity? This is the problem of the nature of Hume's self or his mind. He turns his attention to it in the next paragraph, resolving it through the introduction of two metaphors.

3. HUME'S TWO METAPHORS (PARAGRAPH 4)

Hume describes the nature of the mind through two metaphors, which I will call, respectively, the *metaphor of the bundle* and the *metaphor of the actors*. He does not say why he offers two metaphors but a close examination of them makes it clear that they must be distinguished because they differ from each other in an essential respect.

Hume begins with the metaphor of the bundle. "But setting aside some metaphysicians [who claim to perceive themselves], I may venture to affirm of the rest of mankind, that they are nothing but a bundle or collection of different perceptions, which succeed each other with an inconceivable rapidity, and are in a perpetual flux and movement" (252). Four comments can be made about Hume's metaphor of the bundle. (1) He uses the word "collection" in it as well as "bundle." I do not think he means anything by this word different from the word "bundle." (2) Individual minds are distinguished from each other by being different bundles of perceptions; there is the bundle that is Hume's mind, the bundle that is my mind, and so on. (This interpretation may be questioned from the text but I believe it states what Hume meant.) (3) It is a basic principle of Hume's philosophy that individual perceptions are distinct existences, independent of each other.[8] (4) Since these distinct, independent existences appear in bundles, something must bundle them together. So we are left with a question. How do the perceptions get bundled or collected together to form different individual minds? This is an important question to which I will return in sections 4 and 6.

Hume follows his metaphor of the bundle with a second, more colorful metaphor—that of the actors.

> The mind is a kind of theatre, where several perceptions successively make their appearance; pass, re-pass, glide away, and mingle in an infinite variety of postures and situations. There is properly no *simplicity* in it at one time, nor *identity* in different; whatever natural propension we may have to imagine that simplicity and identity. *The comparison of the theatre must not mislead us. They are the successive perceptions only, that constitute the mind;* nor have we the most distant notion of the place, where these scenes are represented, or of the materials, of which it is compos'd. (253—final italics added)

The metaphor of the actors would be easy to interpret, if it were not for the fact that midway through it Hume makes a vital correction in it. He begins the metaphor by comparing the mind to a theater, in which perceptions are portrayed as actors playing their parts. It is clear from the way in which he states the metaphor that the theater, as the mind, performs the same function the bundle does in the first metaphor. The mind or theater is pictured as an entity different from the perceptions or actors themselves, which contains them or gives them a stage on which to perform. It is the tie that binds them together. But in the middle of the metaphor Hume makes a crucial retraction, removing the theater, or external mind. To speak of a theater (mind) containing actors (perceptions) is misleading, Hume now insists, because there is no such thing. The only things that exist are the actors or perceptions themselves. Nothing whatsoever holds them together; they simply follow after each other in time. As Hume says, "They are the successive perceptions only that constitute the mind." In the concluding clause of the metaphor he emphasizes the absence of any theater or mind, writing "nor have we the most distant notion of the place, where these scenes are represented."

It is apparent that the metaphor of the actors is essentially different from that of the bundle. There are no bundles because there is no device outside of the perceptions themselves to collect and bind them together. They are left totally on their own, in their own separateness. The importance of this change in Hume's theory of mind can be seen from one of its consequences. The point concerns the principle of individuation. If we think of a given mind, A, as a bundle of perceptions, we can distinguish it from another mind, B, which is a different bundle of perceptions. As long as the bundles exist and are separate bundles, we can speak of a plurality of minds, individually different from each other. With the metaphor of the actors, however, we lose any principle of individuation. Since perceptions are not contents of any mind and have nothing to bundle them together—there is no theater in which the actors are performing—we have no way of distinguishing any succession of perceptions from any other. Instead, all perceptions are equally homeless. So Hume could not distinguish "himself" from "anyone" else. No more can "anyone" do so. "We" are all indistinguishable contents of a succession of perceptions and nothing more. Because of the difference between them, the two metaphors leave us with a question: Which of the two must Hume, on the basis of his philosophy, consider to give the more accurate picture of the mind? I will return to this question in section 6, only noting here that, whichever of the two metaphors we adopt, it is apparent that the word "mind" is yet another technical term of Hume's philosophy.

4. BELIEF IN MIND (PARAGRAPHS 5–22)

Following his two metaphors Hume shifts his attention, from an account of the nature of mind to an explanation of the causes leading us to believe in its existence. His object is to explain how the imagination leads us to believe there is some real entity, which we call our mind, that continues to exist and maintain its identity through time. As in the case of body, he thinks we all share this belief. "What then gives us so great a propension to ascribe an identity to these successive perceptions, and to suppose ourselves possest of an invariable and uninterrupted existence thro' the whole course of our lives?" (253). Hume's argument, which covers several pages, is curious. He begins by saying that he will account for the "identity, which we attribute to plants and animals," because there is a "great analogy" (253) between it and self-identity. He then goes into lengthy detail explaining why we attribute an identity to such things. The discussion, although interesting in itself, being full of illuminating illustrations, is largely digressive. It would have been better placed in either Section II or Section III,[9] where he was directly concerned with our belief in the continued existence of body, than in Section VI. Because the discussion does not contribute, except by analogy, to an understanding of our belief in self-identity and also because Hume addresses this question directly toward the end of the section, I will not devote a great deal of space here to these paragraphs, but limit myself to the main points Hume makes in them. Early in his discussion he emphasizes that when we attribute an identity to a succession of related objects, we are making a "mistake" (254). Calling this mistake an "absurdity" (254) resulting from a "biass" (254) of the imagination, he applies this conclusion to our propension to believe in the existence of the self as an enduring entity. "Thus we feign the continu'd existence of the perceptions of our senses, to remove the interruption [in them]; and run into the notion of a *soul,* and *self,* and *substance,* to disguise the variation" (254). A bit later he describes his task in the remainder of the section in the following terms: "Our chief business, then, must be to prove, that all objects, to which we ascribe identity, without observing their invariableness and uninterruptedness, are such as consist of a succession of related objects" (255). Applying this statement to minds or selves, Hume is confirming that, although we believe in self-identity, we are mistaken in doing so. We are really only a succession of related objects or perceptions. But this leaves a question: If perceptions are independent of each other, what relates them?

Before attempting to answer this question directly Hume develops his argument concerning bodily identity, which he will then transfer by analogy to the realm of mind. Making use of a variety of illustrations, he draws a distinction between what he calls "numerical" and "specific" identity (257). Consider a noise that continues unchanged for a period of time; this has a numerical identity. Then consider a similar noise that is interrupted and then repeated. This (or these) has a specific (but not a numerical) identity. However—and this is Hume's point—because of the similarities in our experiences of these two kinds of noises, we often confuse them, attributing a numerical identity to the noise that has only a specific identity. This is the mistake or absurdity to which he has referred, which is a result of a bias of the imagination. The next step in his argument will be to transfer the same line of reasoning analogically to the mind, making use of the distinction between numerical and specific identity, as well as our propensity to confuse the two.

It would take me too far afield to pursue in detail the distinction that Hume has drawn between the numerical and specific identities of material objects, so I will limit myself to two comments. First, he claims "a great analogy" on this point between bodies and minds. But is the analogy so great? In the first part of his metaphor of the actors, he describes the mind as "a kind of theatre where several perceptions successively make their appearance; pass, re-pass, glide away, and mingle in an infinite variety of postures and situations. There is properly no *simplicity* in it at one time, nor *identity* in different" (253). This hardly seems analogous to the same noise that is intermittent rather than steady, or even to a plant that grows into an oak tree (257) or a river that is constantly flowing by (258).

My second comment is of a different and more important kind. To draw the distinction he does between numerical and specific identity Hume must be able to recognize both of these, whether they be in a noise, a tree, a river, or whatever. He says that we have a "distinct idea" (253) of these things, but this is just after he has concluded that the mind is nothing more than a succession of perceptions. But no mere succession of perceptions could hear a continuing noise, let alone distinguish between one that is uninterrupted and one that is interrupted. Indeed, no such succession of perceptions could perceive anything. For Hume even to introduce the bodily analogies he employs in Section VI he must abandon the account of the nature of his mind that he has just given, substituting in its place some unspecified form of a theory of mind that he is determined to repudiate.

At the beginning of paragraph 15 Hume returns to the topic with which he had begun several pages earlier. He writes: "We now proceed to explain the nature of *personal identity*" (259). This statement is misleading. Hume will not explain the nature of personal identity, because, as he has already made clear, no such identity exists. He adds later in the paragraph: "The identity, which we ascribe to the mind of man, is only a fictitious one" (259). Hume's concern is, instead, with the question: What causes us to believe in the fiction of personal identity, or the fiction that we possess a mind that continues to maintain its identity through time?

Hume's analysis is, as expected, psychological. As he has indicated, it is analogous to the account he has just given of our belief in the continued and independent existence of body. Before we begin with it, however, we need to be reminded that we already have a conclusive reason for rejecting it, because we know that Hume cannot believe that he, or anyone else, has a mind, as a real entity that persists through time. Since the argument leading to this conclusion parallels the one I gave in chapter 15, which showed that Hume could not consistently believe in the existence of an external material world,[10] I will not pursue it in detail now but only repeat its main points. To believe in the existence of any entity one must have an idea of that entity. Hume has no idea of mind as an enduring entity. Therefore, Hume cannot believe in the existence of such a mind.

I return now to Hume's psychological explanation of how we come to believe in the existence of an enduring mind. Instead of assuming the conclusions he has already reached about body as a basis for his argument, he begins by stating two alternative accounts of mind: Either the distinct perceptions that compose the mind are united together to form a real identity, which is the mind, or these perceptions are only associated together by the imagination. In his words: "As, notwithstanding this distinction and separability [of perceptions], we suppose the whole train of perceptions to be united by identity, a question naturally arises concerning this relation of identity; whether it be something that really binds our several perceptions together, or only associates their ideas in the imagination" (259). Hume does not waste any time in answering the question he has raised, but immediately rejects the first alternative in favor of the second. "This question we might easily decide, if we wou'd recollect what has been already prov'd at large, that the understanding never observes any real connexion among objects. . . . For from thence it evidently follows, that *identity is nothing really belonging to these different perceptions*, and uniting them together; but is merely a quality, which we attribute to them, because of the union of their ideas in the imagination" (259–60). Having made definite the point that the association of ideas by the imagination is all that can constitute what we call personal identity, Hume next offers an explanation of how the imagination accomplishes the task of uniting distinct perceptions. He begins his account with the two relations among perceptions—resemblance and causation—on which "identity depends."[11] Describing the two relations as the "uniting principles in the ideal world" (260), he goes on to explain how they contribute to our joining perceptions together. "The very essence of these relations consists in their producing an easy transition of ideas" (260). This statement is important for an understanding of Hume's argument. He is not saying that the relations themselves associate perceptions together but rather that they cause the easy transition of ideas in the mind, which is the association. The actual task of association is accomplished by two faculties of the mind—imagination and memory—and results in the fiction of personal identity. As Hume puts it in the remainder of the sentence from which I have just excerpted, "our notions of personal identity, proceed entirely from the smooth and uninterrupted progress of the thought along a train of connected ideas, according to the principles above-explain'd [the two relations]."[12]

Continuing his account Hume explains how the two relations cause us to make an easy transition of ideas, thus connecting them together. He begins with the relation of resemblance. Although the faculty of imagination is involved in the transition, that of memory plays the central role. Hume writes: "Suppose we cou'd see clearly into the breast of another, and observe that succession of perceptions, which constitutes his mind or thinking principle, and suppose that he always preserves the memory of a considerable part of past perceptions; 'tis evident that nothing cou'd more contribute to the bestowing a relation on this succession amidst all its variations."[13] Psychologically, what happens is this: We experience a succession of perceptions and remember that many of these resemble each other.[14] When we gather these resembling perceptions together, it becomes easy for the imagination to make a transition from one to another and hence to suppose the continuance of a single object, or perception. Although in fact there is only a succession of distinct perceptions we imagine that these perceptions are linked together to form one continuing perception, which we call our mind. "Must not the frequent placing of these resembling perceptions in the chain of thought, convey the imagination more easily from one link to another, and make the whole seem like the continuance of one object?" (261).

Hume concludes his discussion of resemblance by emphasizing the essential role played by memory in the process. "The memory not only discovers the identity, but also contributes to its production, by *producing the relation of resemblance* among the perceptions" (261—italics added). This statement is not quite accurate. The memory does not actually produce the resemblance among the perceptions; the fact that they resemble each other depends on their own nature. What the memory produces is our recognition of this resemblance and it is only because we recognize that they resemble each other that we are led by our imagination to join the perceptions together.

Hume's account of the way in which memory and imagination join forces to connect successive perceptions that resemble each other is not complete. He clearly grants crucial powers to both in the accomplishment of this result but he does not explain how they bring it about. Let us see how they might do so. In his account he asks the rhetorical question, "For what is the memory but a *faculty*, by which we raise up the images of past perceptions?" (260—italics added). This characterization of memory repeats his description of it, as well as of imagination, in Part I. When he originally introduced the two, he wrote of them, "The faculty, by which we repeat our impressions in the first manner [with vivacity], is called the MEMORY, and the other the IMAGINATION" (8–9). The two are faculties the mind employs to derive ideas from impressions. But what exactly is their nature *as faculties of the mind?* To answer this question we must understand the nature of the mind itself. At the outset of his argument Hume identifies the mind with a "succession of perceptions" (260). This identification repeats the description he had given of the mind in his metaphor of the actors. If the mind itself consists in a succession of perceptions, no faculty of the mind can consist in anything more than such a succession. So we can conclude that both memory and imagination consist *at most* in a succession of perceptions. At the beginning of Section VI Hume said that when he entered most intimately into what he called himself, he always stumbled on some perception, and could never observe anything but the perception (252). This is what led him to the conclusion that his mind consisted only in a succession of perceptions. Obviously, if he had pursued his introspective search further, into his memory and imagination, he would have made the same discovery and therefore have reached the same conclusion about them. If the mind is not a real entity enduring through time, no more can they, as "faculties" of the mind, be such entities.

So the question, How does memory raise up the images of past perceptions? must be reformulated to read, How does a succession of (vivacious) perceptions raise up past perceptions? And the question, How does imagination make an easy transition from one resembling perception to another? becomes, How does a succession of (faint) perceptions make an easy transition from one resembling perception to another? This leads to a further question. Can successions of perceptions accomplish the tasks Hume has now given to them? To answer this question we must recall just what perceptions are; namely, impressions and ideas. Impressions are of two kinds—direct sensations of color, sound, touch, taste, and smell and direct feelings like "heat or cold, thirst or hunger, pleasure or pain" (8). Ideas are exact copies of these impressions, differing from them only in being less vivid or lively. Such perceptions can be simple, like the color "red," or complex, like a scene in which several different colors occur. Therefore, to ask the questions, How can a succession of perceptions remember the past or associate perceptions together? must, for Hume, be to ask, How can a succession of such things as the color "red" or the feeling "pain" or any complex of these perceptions succeeding each other through time accomplish these tasks? Hume does not address this question, let alone answer it. The only conclusion we can reach is that it cannot be satisfactorily answered. The perception "red" (whether in the form of an impression or an idea) cannot raise up the past. It has no power of memory. No more can it connect perceptions together. It has no power of imagination. Furthermore, no succession of perceptions can accomplish these results. However much two perceptions, independent of each other, may resemble each other, they cannot be associated together on the basis of their resemblance because nothing capable of accomplishing the task of association exists.

Before leaving this point it might be helpful to see how and where Hume has gone astray. In his appeal to memory and imagination as the agencies that associate perceptions, he has viewed both, as he says, as faculties of the mind. This is to reify them, or to make them both real entities that are parts of a more inclusive real entity, the mind. It is only because he has reified them that he can claim that they are able to accomplish the tasks he has assigned them. But the reification is illegitimate. Memory and imagination cannot be faculties of the mind in the way Hume needs because there is no mind, as a real, enduring entity, of which they can be parts. Rather, there is only a succession of perceptions. And a succession of perceptions can neither recognize that resembling perceptions resemble each other or unite perceptions together. Hume has first repudiated a conception of the mind, then, to account for our belief in the existence of minds of the kind he has rejected, he has turned to the relation of resemblance, which he then explains by appealing to the conception of mind (through the "faculties" of memory and imagination) he has just repudiated. Needless to say, his argument is self-refuting.

I turn now to Hume's explanation of the way in which the cause-effect relation leads us to believe in personal identity, or the continuing existence of our mind. He begins it with a statement that needs careful analysis. "As to *causation;* we may observe that the true idea of the human mind, is to consider it as a system of different perceptions or different existences, which are link'd together by the relation of cause and effect, and mutually produce, destroy, influence, and modify each other. Our impressions give rise to their correspondent ideas; and these ideas in their turn produce other impressions. One thought chaces another, and draws after it a third, by which it is expell'd in its turn."[15] Hume's statement that he is offering "the true idea" of the mind here may be important. It seems to indicate that the metaphor of the bundle, in which perceptions are linked or collected together, gives a more accurate picture of the mind than the metaphor of the actors, in which perceptions are independent of each other. Hume says that the cause-effect relation succeeds in linking perceptions together. So let us look closely at this linkage to see just how it is accomplished.

Although his language is partly figurative, Hume's point is reasonably clear. The mind is a "system" that is "link'd together by the relation of cause and effect" in which "one thought [idea] chaces another, and draws after it a third, by which it is expell'd in its turn." To put this more prosaically, Hume seems to be saying that the different perceptions have the capacity to link themselves together. They not only "chace" but catch each other. When they do so they form collections of perceptions. Each of these collections, or bundles, is an individual human mind.

But Hume's appeal to a cause-effect relation among perceptions, linking them together to form individual minds, is not free of problems. In the first place, it seems to assume an "objective" theory of causation, as far as perceptions are concerned. He says that different perceptions "produce, destroy, influence, and modify each other." Here Hume seems to be speaking literally, rather than figuratively. So we can ask: How can these things occur? Let us take his most explicit causal concept—"produce." How can a perception produce another perception? To take a simple example, consider two notes (or sounds) in a song. We say the second note follows naturally after the first. But would we ever say that the second note is *produced* by the first—that the first possesses some power that causes the second to follow after it? What could we, or Hume, mean by this?

Hume does not explain how perceptions can cause each other but simply asserts that they do. This claim is too important to be accepted as it stands but requires full explanation. And one may well suspect that no explanation can be given because the account Hume offers of how perceptions relate themselves together is inexplicable. That perceptions succeed each other in time he may be able to say; that they exercise "objective" causal influences on each other he cannot. Later in the paragraph he makes a statement that throws some light on what the correct account of the connection between different perceptions must be. He writes that "the same person may vary . . . his impressions and ideas" (261). In other words, it is not his perceptions themselves that cause the variations among his impressions and ideas (the notes of the song) but an entity, his mind, different from those perceptions, which possesses the perceptions, that accomplishes the task. The difficulty with this explanation—which is one most of us would accept—is that Hume has denied that any such independent entity exists.

Hume continues his account of the cause-effect relation as the source of personal identity in the paragraph following the one I have been examining, writing: "As memory alone acquaints us with the continuance and extent of this *succession of perceptions* [our mind], 'tis to be consider'd . . . as the source of personal identity. Had we no memory, we never shou'd have any notion of causation, nor consequently of that chain of causes and effects, which constitute our self or person."[16] In his statement that memory alone is the source of personal identity Hume seems to be making two points. First, if we had no memory of the past, we would have no awareness of ourselves as the same beings who persist through time. Second, memory is a necessary condition for our recognition of causal relationships, hence for our realization that we consist of a chain of perceptions, causally connected. This point is presumably based on his theory that the idea of necessary connection, hence of causation, requires the *remembered* past experience of constant conjunctions. Although both of these theses about the essential part played by memory in our recognition of ourselves as enduring individual persons would probably be generally accepted, they do not, in themselves, fully explain the relationship between memory and personal identity. Still to be answered is the question: How does memory accomplish the task it must perform if such identity is to be a reality? To answer this question we must consider further the nature of memory, on Hume's theory of mind.

We have seen earlier in this chapter, as well as in chapter 2, that Hume considers memory to be a faculty of the mind. We must now acknowledge that this characterization, as it is ordinarily understood, is erroneous. The picture of the mind as a real, enduring entity possessing faculties must be abandoned as a misdescription. As Hume once again says in the passage we are examining, the mind is a "succession of perceptions" (261). So, if memory is to be a faculty, it must be a faculty of a succession of perceptions. This mode of expression, however, seems, at best, puzzling and, at worst, bizarre. So we must rephrase the conception of memory Hume is using here in a way that is more easily understood. Then we can assess its viability. What Hume presumably would mean when he implies that memory is a faculty of a succession of perceptions is simply that this succession remembers the past. With this interpretation clear, we can return to our original question: How can a succession of perceptions remember? To answer the question we need to return to Hume's theory of memory. Here we are (momentarily) halted by the fact that he holds two theories, the original one of Part I and the revised one of Part III.[17] However, this fact need not deter us long because both theories share a common feature: To remember any thing or event one must possess a lively idea of that thing or event.

Our problem with memory should now be apparent. A succession of perceptions must be made up of individual perceptions following each other in time. To say, then, that at any given time we remember something we must mean that some perception has a lively idea of that thing. Once again, we are faced with a problem we have already encountered. How can a perception—an impression or an idea—possess a lively idea? Hume does not explain how this is possible. My conclusion is that he could not do so because the entire conception is unintelligible. So we are forced to conclude that, (1) if the cause-effect relation is to be the basis of personal identity, (2) if memory is essential to that relation, and (3) if memory is an impossibility on his theory of mind, it follows that Hume cannot successfully appeal to the causal relation as an explanation of our existence as a "system" in which perceptions are somehow linked together.

Although I have dealt with this point in detail, my lengthy discussion seems hardly to have been necessary. Hume himself has already reached conclusions in Section VI that obviate his argument about causation and personal identity that I have just examined. As I pointed out at the beginning of this section, Hume's discussion of personal identity, which occupies the latter part of Section VI, is not about a *factual* personal identity but about a *fictitious* one. It is about a belief we have, based on imagination, that we are enduring selves even though we are only successions of perceptions. His argument leading to this conclusion appears in paragraph 16. I have excerpted from it before but, because of its importance, I reproduce it here in fuller detail.

> 'Tis evident, that the identity, which we attribute to the human mind . . . is not able to run the several perceptions into one, and make them lose their

characters of distinction and difference, which are essential to them. 'Tis still true, that every distinct perception, which enters into the composition of the mind, is a distinct existence, and is different, and distinguishable, and separable from every other perception, either contemporary or successive. But, as . . . we suppose the whole train of perceptions to be united by identity, a question naturally arises concerning this relation of identity; whether it be something that really binds our several perceptions together, or only associates their ideas in the imagination. . . . This question we might easily decide, if we wou'd recollect what has already been prov'd at large, that *the understanding never observes any real connexion among objects,* and that even the union of cause and effect . . . resolves itself into a customary association of ideas. For from thence it evidently follows, that *identity is nothing really belonging to these different perceptions, and uniting them together.* (259–60— italics added)

Given this statement, particularly its final two sentences, Hume's assertion that "the true idea of the human mind, is to consider it as a system of different perceptions . . . link'd together by the relation of cause and effect" (261) clearly cannot represent his own description of the true nature of mind. Furthermore, his attempts to explain how our imagination, with the aid of memory, leads us to believe in the fictitious existence of an enduring mind all end in failure.

5. Hume's Misgivings (Appendix Note)

In the introduction to this chapter I reproduced a statement from Hume's appendix note to Section VI in which he confessed that he did not know "how to render [his opinions] consistent" (633). The note itself is important, not only because in it Hume recognizes that his account of mind in Section VI is "very defective" (635) but also because "mind" is the central concept of his philosophy in Book I. Without a satisfactory theory of mind, Hume realizes, his epistemology and metaphysics stand in jeopardy. The note itself is devoted mainly to a reiteration of points he had made in Section VI, but it is clear that Hume's attitude has changed to one of intellectual defeat. He concludes the note by posing a difficulty in his theory of mind (which I will review in the following paragraphs) and then writes, in final resignation: "For my part, I must plead the privilege of a sceptic, and confess, that this difficulty is too hard for my understanding" (636).

To appreciate the difficulty Hume is unable to resolve we need to begin with a statement that appears a bit earlier in the note. He writes:

Having . . . loosen'd all our particular perceptions, when I proceed to explain the principle of connexion, which binds them together, and makes us attribute to them a real simplicity and identity; I am sensible, that my account is very defective. . . . If perceptions are distinct existences, they form a whole only by being connected together. But no connexions among distinct existences are ever discoverable by human understanding. We only *feel* a connexion or a determination of the thought, to pass from one object to another.[18]

As I have shown in the previous section, Hume's attempt to explain how we can "feel" a connection between different, distinct perceptions cannot succeed. But the reason for his final scepticism goes deeper. The problem, which he cannot resolve, is that he cannot give a satisfactory explanation of how there can be any connection between independent perceptions.

> All my hopes vanish, when I come to explain the principles, that unite our successive perceptions in our thought or consciousness. I cannot discover any theory, which gives me satisfaction on this head.
>
> In short there are two principles, which I cannot render consistent; nor is it in my power to renounce either of them, viz. *that all our distinct perceptions are distinct existences,* and *that the mind never perceives any real connexion among distinct existences.* Did our perceptions either inhere in something simple and individual, or did the mind perceive some real connexion among them, there wou'd be no difficulty in the case. (635–36)

This passage raises several points. First, the terms "thought" and "consciousness" Hume uses in it are important. He is not limiting himself here to his "understanding" but is employing general terms. Thus, he is implying that he cannot offer any theory even of the imagination capable of uniting successive perceptions. If the individual perceptions that constitute the mind are independent of each other, there is *no way* they can be connected together. Continuing, he makes the point explicitly in his statement of the two principles he italicizes in the passage. His admission that he cannot render these principles consistent, however, is somewhat puzzling. As many Hume commentators have pointed out, there is no inconsistency between the two principles themselves; both can be true together.[19] With a bit of ingenuity we can gain a reasonable understanding of the problem Hume is really grappling with here. Despite what he says, he does not mean that the two principles are inconsistent *with each other.* Rather the two together are inconsistent with something else. What this "something else" is can be gleaned from the passage I have reproduced, plus the argument that immediately precedes it.

To begin, Hume assumes that we believe in the existence of minds. Although he does not claim (as he had about body) that we *must* believe in their existence, he says that we have a "great . . . propension" (253) to do so. This psychological point, however, is not an argument; the belief is, in fact, irrational. But that, in itself, should pose no difficulty for Hume because, from the beginning of Part IV, he has maintained that *all* of our beliefs are irrational. The difficulty results, rather, from the fact that it leaves him without a viable theory of mind, and he must have such a theory for his philosophy in Book I. That this problem constitutes the inconsistency he is referring to in the passage is confirmed by the final sentence, in which he concludes that, if our perceptions were those of an enduring mind or if these perceptions could be connected together, there would be no difficulty.

6. A RETURN TO HUME'S TWO METAPHORS

At the end of section 3, after pointing out the crucial difference between Hume's metaphor of the bundle and his metaphor of the actors, I asked which of these two metaphors more accurately describes his concept of mind. Is the mind, for Hume, a *bundle* of perceptions or simply a *succession* of perceptions? I will attempt to answer that question in this section.

To begin with what Hume says later in Section VI, we have found one occasion on which he seems to be employing the bundle metaphor. This is in his account of the relation of causation, where he writes that "the true idea of the human mind, is to consider it as a system of different perceptions or different existences, which are link'd together by the relation of cause and effect" (261). This account, however, is an exception, which, as we have already seen, Hume repudiates elsewhere in the section. Generally he talks of the mind as a "succession of perceptions" (253, 260, 261).

But this evidence is not conclusive, in part because Hume does not always write with full precision. To decide the issue between the two metaphors we must ask: Which is more consistent with his philosophy as he applies it to "mind" in Section VI? One way of stating the difference between the metaphors is to note that in the bundle metaphor the mind has some kind of identity through time. It is a *bundle*. Although the mind's identity in this metaphor is probably considerably less than we ordinarily attribute to it, nevertheless it is sufficient to differentiate individual minds from each other. They are different bundles. On the actors metaphor no such identity exists. There are no individual minds, bundled together and capable of being differentiated, but only individual perceptions succeeding each other through time.

Let us look again at some things Hume says that relate to this difference between the metaphors. First, he interrupts his metaphor of the actors midway through with the statement "There is properly no *simplicity* in [the mind] at one time, nor *identity* in different" (253). A sentence later he adds, "They are the successive perceptions only, that constitute the mind" (253). Later in the section he writes: "The identity, which we ascribe to the mind of man, is only a fictitious one" (259). In the next paragraph he elaborates the point, writing: "'Tis evident, that the identity, which we attribute to the human mind . . . is not able to run the several different perceptions into one, and make them lose their characters of distinction and difference, which are essential to them" (259). Again, "Identity is nothing really belonging to these different perceptions, and uniting them together" (260).

Special weight should, I think, be given to the conclusions Hume reaches in his appendix note, because they reflect his final, considered position. In it we find him writing: "If perceptions are distinct existences, they form a whole only by being connected together. But no connexions among distinct existences are ever discoverable by human understanding" (635). This statement, which seems to be an unequivocal rejection of the metaphor of the bundle, is followed by another that is equally definitive. "There are two principles [I must accept] . . . *that all our distinct perceptions are distinct existences,* and *that the mind never perceives any real connexion among distinct existences*" (636). These statements make it abundantly clear that Hume recognizes that he cannot support the metaphor of the bundle, which collects or unites perceptions together to produce an enduring mind or self, whether with a numerical or specific identity, that can be individuated from other minds, or bundles. The metaphor of the actors, with its distinct or independent perceptions simply succeeding each other in time, must, therefore, be Hume's considered description of the nature of mind.

Nevertheless, as I have already pointed out, Hume does say things in Section VI that support the view that he attributes some form of identity to the mind, and, thus, that favor the bundle metaphor. For that reason we need to give the metaphor some independent examination. Although it is a metaphor, the description of the mind as a bundle it gives is one of some kind of real, enduring entity. A bundle is more than a plurality of items. It is a plurality of items bundled or bound together to form a whole. The items—or perceptions—are independent of each other. Hume constantly reiterates this point. To form a bundle, they must therefore be bundled. What, then, bundles them? There seem to be only two possibilities. (1) They are bundled by something different from them or (2) they bundle themselves. Alternative (1) can be quickly discarded. The only entity external to perceptions that could bundle them together would be the mind that possesses them. But, Hume insists, no such external entity exists. So we turn to (2), the alternative that perceptions bind themselves together. Here the question becomes: How do they do this? This alternative could be pursued at some length but it is not necessary to do so because it has already been effectively eliminated. To recapitulate, the question to which Hume devotes much of Section VI, and which I examined in the previous section, is: How does the imagination lead us to believe in our existence as a mind enduring through time? The same question could be asked about our belief in our mind as a bundle of perceptions, because the metaphor of the bundle requires some form of self-identity. As we have seen, Hume's argument appeals to two kinds of things—(a) the relations of resemblance and causation among the perceptions and (b) the faculties of the mind—imagination and memory—that unite the perceptions on the basis of these relations. On the alternative we are now considering, we must eliminate (b) because we cannot appeal to the "faculties" of a nonexistent mind. That leaves only the two relations. I have already (in section 4) examined Hume's claim that different perceptions act causally on each other, and I have given reason to reject it. So we are left with "resemblance." Hume's assumption that perceptions resemble each other is certainly correct; the color "red" does resemble the color "orange" and so on. But that is not enough here. For the color "red" to join itself with the color "orange," *because of their resemblance,* so that the two become united together as part of a "bundle of perceptions," it is necessary that the color "red" recognize the fact that it resembles the color "orange."[20] This, I conclude, is simply beyond its powers, or the powers of any perception.

I have examined the metaphor of the bundle in detail because it is easy for a reader to assume that, since it appears first in Section VI, it must be Hume's authentic and authoritative account of the nature of the self, or even to assume that the metaphor of the actors is a mere repetition of it. We can now conclude that neither of these assumptions is correct. The two metaphors, as I demonstrated in section 3, differ from each other in a crucial way, and the metaphor of the bundle—which has beguiled many students of Hume—is not, as I have just shown, one that Hume can legitimately offer as a description of the mind or self.

We are left, then, with the metaphor of the actors, which must be taken—as Hume himself does generally take it later in Section VI—as the best description he can give of the mind. The mind must be conceived as a "succession [not a bundle] of perceptions." This metaphor, however, is not without problems. I have already (in section 3) discussed the problem of individuation so will not return to it here. But there are others. Consider the term "succession," which is a temporal concept. For Hume to be able to say that his mind is a succession of perceptions, the perceptions that constitute his mind must be aware of their preceding and succeeding each other in time. But this they cannot do. Perceptions do not possess concepts, let alone the concept of time or succession. So we must modify the metaphor. What can we say? Perhaps we might describe the mind not as a succession but simply as a plurality of perceptions. But Hume is in no position to accept such a description. "Plurality" is a numerical concept. So, for a perception to be aware of its existence as one of a plurality of perceptions it would have to be able to count. It is hard to know where to go from here, except to identify the "mind" with a perception. Interestingly enough,

Hume comes close to suggesting just such a possibility, writing in the appendix note: "Suppose the mind to be reduc'd even below the life of an oyster. Suppose it to have only one perception, as of thirst or hunger. Consider it in that situation. *Do you conceive any thing but merely that perception?*" (634—italics added).

7. HUME'S MIND AND HIS PHILOSOPHY

"Mind" is the central concept in Book I of the *Treatise*. The word itself appears nearly four hundred times in the text, beginning with the first sentence of Section I, Part I. The mind possesses perceptions; through its faculties of memory and imagination it repeats impressions as ideas and associates them together; it is determined to anticipate a perception after its repeated experience of the constant conjunction of that perception with another; it generates lively ideas and thus believes; it feigns and thus creates fictions; and so on. Altogether the mind performs a multitude of diverse, complex, and essential activities. Without a viable concept of mind, Hume's philosophy in Book I would disintegrate. In Section VI Hume directly addresses the question of what the mind is and how it can perform its tasks. It is apparent, however, that the mind, reduced to a succession of perceptions, can perform none of these tasks. Thus, Hume's account of the nature of mind vitiates most of the argument of Book I.

In a note at the beginning of this book, I quoted the Hume scholar Norman Kemp Smith as saying that the root causes of the difficulty of the *Treatise* lie "in the arrangement of the work as a whole."[21] Although Smith was concerned about a different problem of arrangement than I am, we must recognize that Hume's deferral of his explanation of the nature of mind until its end raises a serious question about his organization of Book I. I do not believe that Hume deliberately led his readers astray by the way in which he used "mind" throughout Book I. Yet this much I must say. The first time I read the *Treatise* I assumed that where Hume used the word "mind" he was talking about a real entity that persisted and retained some form of identity through time. I am also sure that most readers make the same assumption. It is only when we reach Section VI of Part IV that we must accept the fact that we have been radically mistaken and realize that we must, as a result, reassess the meaning of much that we have read.

Why, then, did Hume defer his analysis of this central concept until the very end of Book I? I do not know but I am inclined to think that he did not fully realize at the outset that his epistemological assumptions would lead him to the conclusions he finally reached about mind. Some support is given to this suggestion by the fact that it was only after he had completed Book I that he recognized fully the inconsistencies in his account of mind, so added the appendix note to Section VI. Perhaps also, as a literary stylist, he was aware of the syntactical infelicities his description of mind would have introduced into the text. Regardless of these and of Hume's possible sensitivity to them, however, Section VI lays a heavy burden on Hume scholars. If they are to understand and evaluate Book I adequately they must return to Part I, Section I, and, wherever the term "mind" appears thereafter in the text, substitute for it "succession of perceptions."

8. ADDENDUM: HUME'S ONTOLOGY

I add this section to chapter 17 as an addendum because the point I will be concerned with in it does not arise solely from Hume's conclusions about the nature of mind in Section VI but is instead a consequence of several successive conclusions he has reached in Part IV, beginning with Section II. The question I will address is: What, according to Hume's philosophy, actually exists?[22]

We can begin by listing three different kinds of entities whose existence, Hume has said, might be affirmed: (1) Bodies, (2) minds, and (3) perceptions. Perceptions, further, can be subdivided into two types: (a) Unperceived perceptions and (b) perceived perceptions.[23] The distinguishing feature of this putative ontology is its addition to Cartesian dualism. Several Hume scholars have commented on the addition, usually critically. Jonathan Bennett, referring to it as the "reification"[24] of sense-data, traces it back to Hume's empiricist predecessors. John Bricke, following Bennett, devotes a good portion of his book *Hume's Philosophy of Mind* to what he calls Hume's "reification of perceptions."[25] According to his interpretation Hume held perceptions to be substances. Although I believe that Bricke is correct in emphasizing the great importance of perceptions in Hume's ontology, he goes beyond Hume in according them the status of substance. It is true that, in Section V of Part IV, Hume, after offering a standard definition of substance, continues, "[Perceptions] are, therefore, substances, as far as this definition explains a substance" (233). But this is not his own view. As he emphasizes immediately afterward, "A substance is entirely different from a perception."[26]

To return to the kinds of entities that might exist, we begin with bodies. We have found that in Sections II and IV of Part IV Hume was driven reluctantly to the philosophical conclusion that no external material world exists.[27] This eliminates bodies. At the end of his second metaphor in Section VI he explicitly denies the existence of minds, as real, enduring entities, reducing them to successions of perceptions. This leaves perceptions as the sole contents of his ontology. Turning to these we have found that in Section II of Part IV he devoted considerable attention to unperceived perceptions, to reach the conclusion that, although their existence involves no contradiction, they do not in fact exist.[28] This leaves perceived perceptions. Hume explicitly reaches conclusions in Book I that leave such perceptions as the only kinds of entities that exist.

But let us consider this somewhat attenuated ontology further. A perceived perception is one that is perceived. For it to be perceived requires the existence of something that perceives it. So we can ask: What perceives perceptions? Hume's general answer seems to be clear. In the first sentence of Book I he writes: "All the perceptions *of the human mind* resolve themselves into two distinct kinds, which I shall call IMPRESSIONS and IDEAS. The difference betwixt these consists in the degrees of force and liveliness, *with which they strike upon the mind*" (1—italics added). What Hume is saying here is that the perceiver of perceptions is the mind. He reiterates a similar view in the section we have just been examining when he describes his act of introspection, writing that "when I enter most intimately into what I call *myself*, I always stumble on some particular perception or other" (252). In other words, "I" (in this case Hume), conceived as a perceiver, perceive perceptions when "I" introspect.

What is the point of dwelling on something we would all grant to be obvious? Simply this; perceived perceptions do not exist alone but require something that perceives them. This something Hume identifies as the mind. But if the mind, as Hume conceives it, does not or cannot perceive perceptions, such perceptions do not exist. And if they do not exist Hume's ontology loses all content and, as a result, his universe collapses into nothingness.

If Hume is to avoid this consequence of his own arguments he must offer some viable explanation of how minds can perceive perceptions. The problem facing him should now be clear. He has denied the existence of minds as real, enduring entities distinct from their perceptions, reducing them to successions of perceptions. Therefore, if perceptions are to be perceived, they must be perceived by other perceptions. Is this a real, viable possibility? Can perceptions perceive perceptions? To answer the question we need to remember what a perception is; namely, either an impression or an idea. Since ideas are exact copies of impressions we can concentrate on the latter. These are, first, the objects or contents of our five senses—colors, sounds, and so on—and, second, direct perceptions of heat or cold, thirst or hunger, pleasure or pain. If perceptions are to be perceived, then these are the kinds of things that must perceive them. I will not attempt to explain how this could be done—how the color "red" could perceive the sound "B-flat" or the feeling of thirst perceive that of heat—because I do not think it can be done. The conception is simply ludicrous. I am sure that Hume would agree with me in this. He always speaks of perceptions as the *ob-*

jects we perceive or the contents of our conscious experience when we are perceiving and never as themselves perceivers. Perceptions, as a result, require for their existence some subject other than perceptions that perceive. They are not and cannot themselves be subjects that perceive. I have found nothing in Book I that would suggest that Hume ever entertained any other view about the nature and capacities of perceptions. But if minds are nothing but perceptions and perceptions do not perceive, perceived perceptions do not exist. With their exit the universe vanishes.

I do not want to be misunderstood here. I am *not* suggesting that Hume was an ontological nihilist. Such a suggestion would be presumptuous. Hume was without question a radical thinker but can we seriously believe he was that radical? Yet we are left with a disturbing question: How can we explain what led Hume to develop an ontology whose logical outcome was nihilism? I cannot answer this question in a way satisfactory even to myself but I would like to offer two suggestions for consideration. First, we should not forget that Hume was a great ironist. Could this be the greatest irony of Book I? I hesitate to offer this suggestion, because it is, to put it mildly, speculative; however there are some indications of ontological irony in certain of the remarks Hume makes earlier in Part IV. My second suggestion is, I believe, much more probably correct. I do not think that Hume realized the implications of his own arguments, because he did not pursue their consequences to their ultimate ends. If Hume were alive today he would, I believe, be as astonished to learn that Book I ends in ontological nihilism as, I am sure, at least some of his contemporary commentators will be.

Summary

What Hume says in Section VI, and the implications that can be drawn from what he says, can be summarized in the following main points: (1) The mind (or self), conceived as a real entity possessing some identity that continues through time, does not exist. The same can be said of all the "faculties" of the mind. (2) This denial of our enduring selfhood is a consequence of the Empiricist Principle. (3) The mind must be described instead as simply a succession of perceptions. (4) This account of mind is not viable. It is, as Hume concludes in his appendix note, "very defective." (5) If Hume's mind were what he concluded it to be, it could not even begin to perform the functions he has attributed to it, including that of writing the *Treatise*. (6) We can conclude, therefore, that the *Treatise* itself is a sufficient refutation of the theory of mind it contains.

Although Hume reaches the first four of these conclusions himself, I do not know if he was aware that the last two follow from them. Had he been so, it is hard to believe that he would have allowed Book I to be published without a radical revision of Section VI. If he had attempted such a revision, however, he would have found himself faced with an almost insurmountable obstacle. As he makes clear at the outset of the section, he is convinced that acceptance of the Empiricist Principle requires his adoption of the conception of mind he then gives. So, to abandon this conception in favor of one that is both viable in itself and capable of supporting his argument throughout Book I, he would have to repudiate the Principle. It is far beyond the scope of this study to speculate about the changes Hume would have to make in Book I if he were to give up the Empiricist Principle but this much can at least safely be said: It would be a quite different book from the one we now have.

With characteristic candor Hume acknowledged the grave defects in his theory of mind, as well as his inability to correct them. Whether or not he recognized the fact, these defects not only have their original source in the empiricist theory of ideas with which he began the *Treatise* but also complete the destruction of that epistemology.

18

HUME'S
"TRUE" SCEPTICISM

(Part IV, Section VII)

Introduction

Toward the end of Section VII Hume, in an obvious reference to himself, speaks of a "true sceptic" (273). Such a sceptic is to be distinguished from a Pyrrhonist, whose version of scepticism, Hume maintains, dictates a form of life that no one can live. Hume devotes a substantial portion of the final section of Book I to an explanation of what he means by "true" scepticism. This theory is, it is fair to say, a major contribution to the history of scepticism as well as the summation of much that Hume has written about human nature in Book I. The "true sceptic" combines a self-description—of a person who, although a philosopher, was preeminently a human being—with a portrait of the ideal philosopher.

Hume probably had two thoughts in mind in introducing the term "true sceptic." First, he clearly had concluded that scepticism itself is the true answer to the question, Is knowledge possible? That is the central thesis of Section I of Part IV. Second, to distinguish the theory he presents in Section VII from other forms of scepticism, which he believes to be unacceptable, he refers to it as "true," that is, "real" or "viable" scepticism. In recognition both of the historical significance of the theory and of its importance to Hume's philosophy in Book I, I have adopted the term as my title for chapter 18.

Section VII serves another important purpose for Hume. In it he summarizes many of the main conclusions he has reached in Book I, repeating them and in some instances enlarging on them. It is reasonable to regard the statements he makes in this section as his considered and definitive position on the issues in question.

Text

1. HUME'S DESPAIR (PARAGRAPHS 1–2)

Hume begins the final section of Book I on a note of despair, comparing himself to a sailor who has come close to shipwreck: "Methinks I am like a man, who having struck on many shoals, and having narrowly escap'd ship-wreck in passing a small frith, has yet the temerity to put out to sea in the same leaky weather-beaten vessel. . . . My memory of past errors and perplexities, makes me diffident for the future. The wretched condition, weakness, and disorder of the faculties, I must employ in my enquiries, encrease my apprehensions. And the impossibility of amending or correcting these faculties, reduces me almost to despair" (263–64). Although Hume writes here in a highly metaphorical way, there seems little doubt that the despair he evinces is real. And, if the conclusions we have reached so far in this book are sound, he had good reason to despair.

In the passage I have quoted, Hume speaks of the weakness and disorder of his faculties, and, more important, of the impossibility of amending or correcting them. In the next paragraph he writes, "When I turn my eye inward, I find nothing but doubt and ignorance" (264), and again, "Every step I take is with hesitation, and every new reflection makes me dread an error and absurdity in my reasoning" (265). But Hume has another reason for his despair as well. It is social. He foresees that the conclusions he has reached will not be favorably received and that, as a result, he will be ostracized by society. "When I look abroad," he writes, "I foresee on every side, dispute, contradiction, anger, calumny and detraction" (264). In particular, he is apprehensive of the negative reception both he and his philosophy will receive at the hands of the learned. "I have expos'd myself to the enmity of all metaphysicians, logicians, mathematicians, and even theologians; and can I wonder at the insults I must suffer? I have declar'd my dis-approbation of their systems; and can I be surpriz'd, if they shou'd express a hatred of mine and of my person?" (264). That Hume was prescient in his judgment about the reception the *Treatise* would be given is evidenced by the way in which most of his contemporaries responded to it. Particularly in Scotland the most eminent eighteenth-century philosophers attacked it harshly and, too often, unfairly.[1] Only a German philosopher, Immanuel Kant, while not agreeing with Hume, proved sufficiently perceptive to recognize the importance of his thought.

Following his melancholy recital of his plight, Hume devotes several paragraphs of Section VII to a recapitulation of a number of the main conclusions he has reached in Book I. He deals with some topics quite briefly but spends considerable time on others. Since these summaries constitute his final judgments on the issues involved, we need to consider them with care. I will devote the next section to them, discussing each in (roughly) the same order Hume does.

2. MAJOR CONCLUSIONS OF BOOK I SUMMARIZED (PARAGRAPHS 3–7)

Body In chapter 16, section 3, I concluded that Hume, as a philosopher, found himself forced to agree with Berkeley that no external material world exists but that, as a man, he continued to believe in its existence. He has little to add in Section VII on this subject but what he says is significant. "Without [imagination], by which the mind enlivens some ideas beyond others (which seemingly is so trivial, and so little founded on reason) we cou'd never assent to any argument, nor carry our view beyond those few objects, which are present to our senses. Nay, even to these objects we cou'd never attribute any existence, but what was dependent on the senses; and must comprehend them entirely in that succession of perceptions" (265). In this statement Hume makes two points. (1) He reiterates the view he had developed, particularly in Section II of Part IV, that our belief in the existence of objects in an external world independent of perceptions is a result of the activity of the imagination. However, (2) this belief cannot be supported rationally. If we base our belief on argument we are forced to concede that the only things whose existence we can legitimately affirm are perceptions, which have no existence outside of the mind. Continuing his argument in the following paragraph he points out that "it [is not] possible for us to reason justly and regularly from causes and effects, and at the same time believe the continu'd existence of matter" (266). Yet we do both and thus "embrace a manifest contradiction" (266). Although we believe in the existence of matter, philosophical reasoning leads to the conclusion that such a belief is false.[2]

Mind Hume's summary of his account of mind, although very short, is also significant. He writes of "that succession of perceptions, which constitutes our self or person" (265). The important point to note here is that he does not describe the self as a "bundle" but only as a "succession" of perceptions. This confirms the conclusion I reached in section 6 of chapter 17 that the metaphor of the "actors" rather than that of the "bundle" constitutes Hume's definitive characterization of the mind. It also confirms the implications I drew from that characterization. If there is no entity "mind" separate from successive perceptions, "it" can have no "faculties," such as "memory" and "imagination," either.

Memory Hume's account of memory in Book I raises problems beyond the one I have just mentioned. In Part I, Section III, he distinguished memory from imagination in two ways. First, memory ideas are more lively than imagination ideas and, second, the order and form of memory ideas must copy those of their precedent impressions while imagination ideas can rearrange these. But in Section V of Part III he realized that the second distinction could not be maintained because we have no way of ascertaining whether or not an idea copies the order and form of something that no longer exists so cannot be compared with it. As a result he gave up this way of distinguishing between memory and imagination and in his revised theory of memory held that it differs from imagination only in the greater liveliness of its ideas. But now a problem arises. Memory plays a crucial part in Hume's later philosophy in Book I, particularly in his theory of causation and in his analysis of mind. In both of these theories the concept of memory to which Hume appeals is not his revised theory but his original theory, with its reference to the past. How can we explain such a reversion, which occurs *after* he has reached the conclusion that such an account of memory cannot be defended, so must be abandoned? I have been unable to find anything in the text that provides an answer to this question.

The uncertainty caused by Hume's failure to clarify this discrepancy leaves us with the question: Did he have any theory of memory that he considered to be definitive? Although he does not answer this question completely in Section VII, he explicitly repudiates his original theory of memory, with its reference to the past. "Nay farther, even with relation to that succession [of perceptions], we cou'd only admit of those perceptions, which are immediately present to our consciousness, nor cou'd those lively images, with which the memory presents us, be ever receiv'd as true pictures of past perceptions."[3] Since the only alternative to Hume's original theory of memory is his revised theory, which distinguishes memory from imagination only in terms of the greater liveliness of its ideas, giving up all reference to the past, we can fairly conclude that this theory remains, despite what he wrote in the meanwhile in Book I, Hume's definitive theory of memory.

Causation   Hume reiterates the theory of causation he had developed in Part III without change. Causes are not powers that produce their effects. Rather, causation consists only in the determination of the mind, after our past experience of constant conjunctions, to anticipate the "effect" when we observe the "cause." "This connexion, tie, or energy [causation] lies merely in ourselves, and is nothing but that determination of the mind, which is acquir'd by custom, and causes us to make a transition from an object to its usual attendant, and from the impression of one to the lively idea of the other" (266). To leave no doubt about his denial of a causal power operating in an external world he concludes: "When we say we desire to know the ultimate and operating principle, as something, which resides in the external object, we either contradict ourselves, or talk without a meaning" (267).

Total Scepticism In Section I of Part IV Hume presented a two-step argument leading him to reach the following conclusion: "When I reflect on the natural fallibility of my judgment, I have less confidence in my opinions, than when I only consider the objects concerning which I reason; and when I proceed still farther, to turn the scrutiny against every successive estimation I make of my faculties, all the rules of logic require a continual diminution, and at last a total extinction of belief and evidence."[4] This conclusion, which he claims to have "prov'd" (183), Hume calls total scepticism. But although he has proved it, he nevertheless refuses to give up believing, because "Nature, by an absolute and uncontroulable necessity has determin'd us to judge as well as to breathe and feel" (183). Thus, his response to his total scepticism is total irrationalism.[5]

In Section VII Hume returns to the subject of total scepticism, making some further, illuminating remarks about it. He begins his discussion by reaffirming his earlier total scepticism. "For I have already shewn, that the understanding, when it acts alone, and according to its most general principles, entirely subverts itself, and leaves not the lowest degree of evidence in any proposition, *either in philosophy or common life*."[6] But, although he reaffirms his total scepticism, Hume is now much more aware than he was in Section I of its destructive consequences. He writes, first: "Shall we, then, establish it for a general maxim, that no refin'd or elaborate reasoning is ever to be receiv'd? Consider well the consequences of such a principle. By this means *you cut off entirely all science and philosophy*" (268—italics added). These are serious consequences, as Hume well realizes. First, he acknowledges that his total scepticism precludes the possibility of science. For one who was undoubtedly an admirer of Newton it must have been difficult for Hume to accept the fact that his philosophy was incompatible not just with the content of the new science but with its very existence. It is to his great credit that he did not try to evade this consequence but accepted it openly. In addition, his conclusion has direct consequences for himself. What becomes of his own project in the *Treatise*—to produce a "science of man," which he had described in the introduction as "the only solid foundation for the other sciences" (xvi)? All those bright hopes with which he began Hume now recognizes as having been vain.

Also, as Hume points out in the passage I have reproduced, his total scepticism makes philosophy impossible as well. If this is true, what are we to conclude of the contents of Book I of the *Treatise*, which are obviously philosophical? All this, too, must be "cut off." Insofar as the *Treatise* is a philosophical document, nothing Hume writes in it can be given any rational support. But, Hume then notes, the same judgment must be applied to the argument he has used to establish his sceptical conclusion. Since *all* reasoning is subverted by his sceptical argument, this argument, because it employs reason, must itself be subverted. He writes: "You expresly contradict yourself; since this maxim [to reject reason] must be built on the preceding reasoning, which will be allow'd to be sufficiently refin'd and metaphysical" (268).

Hume is well aware of the accumulation of difficulties into which his total scepticism has led him. He goes on to add: "What party, then, shall we choose among these difficulties? If we embrace this principle, and condemn all refin'd reasoning, we run into the most manifest absurdities. If we reject it in favour of these reasonings, we subvert entirely the human understanding. We have, therefore, no choice left but betwixt a false reason and none at all" (268). In the final sentence of this statement Hume reveals his appreciation of the intellectual impasse into which his total scepticism has led him. His choice must literally be between "a false reason" and "none at all." Is there any escape from this impasse? Hume sees none. "For my part, I know not what ought to be done in the present case."[7]

The conclusions Hume reaches about the disastrous consequences of his total scepticism leave the commentator with a problem. Why did Hume reaffirm his total scepticism in Section VII? More to the point, why did he ever offer the argument in Section I leading him to total scepticism in the first place? That section cannot be passed over as an aberration on Hume's part. His reaffirmation in Section VII of the sceptical conclusion he reached there makes it clear that its inclusion was deliberate and important. Hume must have had powerful reasons for including Section I in Part IV. To appreciate just what these reasons were we must understand Hume's final sceptical stand, or his "true" scepticism, as well as the relationship between that stand and his total scepticism. This will be our topic in sections 5 and 6.

To sum up the results of this section we find Hume reaffirming, either directly or by implication, many of the major conclusions he had reached in Book I, including his denial of the existence of an external material world; his description of the mind as a succession of perceptions (the metaphor of the actors); his revised theory of memory from Part III, Section V; his "subjective" theory of causation; and his total scepticism.

3. IMAGINATION (PARAGRAPHS 3, 6–7)

In addition to the summary conclusions I have just surveyed, Hume discusses a variety of other topics in Section VII. Two are of special interest—his conclusions concerning the functions of imagination in human mental processes and his conception of natural belief. Both have become increasingly important features of Hume's thought with the development of his philosophy in Book I. So I will review them at some length before turning to his "true" scepticism—imagination in this section and natural belief in the next.

Toward the end of his summary of the major conclusions I have just reviewed Hume makes an important but enigmatic pronouncement. "The memory, senses, and understanding are . . . all of them *founded on* the imagination, or the vivacity of our ideas" (265—italics added). Undoubtedly this statement is significant, but what does it mean?

Hume's use of the phrase "founded on" is far from clear. Presumably he means that, in some sense, the imagination is more basic than the other three "faculties." But it is hard to understand what this sense precisely is or, in connection with memory and the senses, how the imagination can be more basic than they are. But let us see if we can elucidate Hume's statement, examining each of the "faculties" mentioned in turn.

Beginning with the memory, it is difficult to understand how it can be founded on the imagination. The two are distinct "faculties," distinguished from each other by the relative vivacity of their ideas. If an idea possesses a certain level of vivacity it is by definition a memory idea; if it possesses a lesser vivacity it is by definition an imagination idea.[8] How can the one be founded on the other? Possibly Hume meant something like this: Imagination ideas precede memory ideas temporally, the latter growing out of the former as these acquire vivacity. This explanation is dubious, however, since ideas do not always seem to acquire vivacity with the passage of time but, on the contrary, often lose it. So on my explanation we might equally well say that the imagination is (often) founded on the memory. Perhaps, however, Hume meant this: According to his original theory, memory is different from imagination because it must preserve the order and form of the original impressions but in his revised theory of memory he eliminates this distinction. Memory ideas and imagination ideas differ from each other only in that the former are more lively than the latter. Could this be what Hume meant when he said that the memory is founded on the imagination? I do not know, and have no further suggestions to offer.

Hume's claim that the senses are founded on the imagination is also troublesome because it seems to conflict with his epistemology. In Section III of Part I Hume argued that the imagination is a faculty by which the mind repeats impressions in the form of ideas. Although these ideas are copies of the original impressions, the imagination can put them together however it wishes. Nevertheless, no idea can exist for the imagination unless it is preceded by its correspondent impression. As Hume puts it, "neither the ideas of the memory nor imagination . . . can make their appearance in the mind, unless their correspondent impressions have gone before to prepare the way for them" (9). What, then, can Hume mean by his statement that the senses are founded on the imagination? Perhaps he was thinking along the following lines: We believe in the existence of an external world that is revealed to us by our senses. This is a mistake because our senses yield only perceptions (impressions), which are internal to the mind. However, our imagination, through the elaborate psychological process described in Section II of Part IV, leads us to believe in an external world and mistakenly to attribute this belief to sense perception. Thus one might argue, somewhat obliquely, that the senses are founded on the imagination. I do not know if this is what Hume meant by his claim. Would that he had not been so terse in his statement.

Hume's conclusion that the understanding is founded on the imagination is easier to explain. In fact, if we assume the understanding to be the "faculty" with which we "reason," we can put Hume's claim in even stronger terms. The understanding is not only founded on the imagination but is reducible to it. This was one of the important conclusions Hume began to develop in his argument in the early sections of Part III.[9] That it represents Hume's definitive view in Book I is confirmed by a statement he makes a bit later in Section VII, in connection with a distinction he has just drawn within the imagination. He describes the understanding in the following way: "The understanding, that is, . . . the general and more establish'd properties of the imagination."[10] So we can say that, for Hume, there are not two "faculties"—the understanding and the imagination—but only one: the imagination.[11]

The passage we are examining raises further problems of interpretation. These arise from its concluding phrase "or the vivacity of our ideas." Hume appears in the phrase to be attributing vivacious ideas to the imagination. This seems odd, because he has distinguished the imagination from the memory on the grounds that the ideas of the former are weak and those of the latter strong. "'Tis evident at first sight, that the ideas of the memory are much more lively and strong than those of the imagination. . . . When we remember any past event, the idea of it flows in upon the mind in a forcible manner; whereas in the imagination the perception is faint and languid."[12] However, in the paragraph that leads up to his statement about the imagination we are now considering, Hume argues that experience and habit "conspiring to operate upon the imagination, make me form certain ideas in a more intense and lively manner, than others" (265). This seems clearly to imply that imagination ideas are lively, or at least more lively than others. But what kind of ideas could be *less* lively than imagination ideas? Perhaps Hume had another distinction among ideas in mind here, one within the imagination itself. Some imagination ideas, he may be saying, are more lively than other imagination ideas. If this is indeed what he means he has not expressed himself very clearly.

Another question can be raised about the phrase "the vivacity of our ideas." Is Hume *identifying* the imagination with the vivacious ideas or is he merely describing the nature of ideas joined together by the "faculty" of imagination? Although it is difficult to tell from the way the sentence in question is written, we know already how it must be interpreted. In the previous chapter I concluded that, since mind is, for Hume, not a real entity but only a succession of perceptions, "it" cannot possess "faculties" like imagination, conceived of as real entities, either. "Imagination" must also be viewed as a succession of perceptions.[13] Although Hume's account forces us to alter our conceptual framework in a radical way, this in itself does not constitute a problem for his philosophy. The problems arise later, when we pursue the implications of his theory. As we have seen throughout our study, the imagination plays a central role in Hume's epistemology, performing a wide variety of activities. But if "imagination" is just a succession of perceptions, we have to conclude that these activities are beyond "its" powers.

Setting aside the negative consequences of Hume's theory of imagination, we must recognize both the importance of the concept to his philosophy and its originality as a way of explaining human "thought." Three points are worth noting. (1) "Imagination" is a nonrational "faculty"; we cannot justify the conclusions we reach through its employment by means of argument. (2) "Imagination" is the foundation on which all of our beliefs rest. (3) "Imagination" is natural. We must, because we are the kind of beings we are, believe certain things our "imagination" delivers to us. Thus, Hume's theory of imagination is directly and closely related to his theory of natural belief.

4. Natural Belief

Although Hume does not engage in any specific discussion of natural belief in Section VII, limiting himself to a few remarks, the theory has become a basic feature of his philosophy, as he sums it up in his conclusion to Book I. For this reason it merits both a general review and an evaluation.

The theory itself seems to have developed gradually in Hume's thought in Book I. It does not form a prominent feature of his argument (at least explicitly) in the first three parts.[14] But it permeates Part IV, receiving its first formulation in Section I. There, after presenting his two-step argument leading to total scepticism, Hume immediately repudiates his own conclusion, at least in part. Although he continues to maintain that any attempt to justify our beliefs necessarily leads to the destruction of the reasons we give, he refuses to accept the consequences of this conclusion. On the contrary, he argues, we continue to believe, because we must. The theory of natural belief makes its next major appearance at the beginning of Section II where Hume, even as he denies that we can give any reason for our belief in the existence of body, emphasizes that "the sceptic . . . must assent to the principle concerning the existence of body. . . . Nature has not left this to his choice" (187). Finally, after coming to the conclusion in Section VI that the mind is a succession of perceptions, he immediately asks the question, "What then gives us so great a propension to ascribe an identity to these successive perceptions, and to suppose ourselves possest of an invariable and uninterrupted existence thro' the whole course of our lives?" (253). This propension, Hume implies, is another natural belief.

So we find that on major issues of his philosophy Hume appeals to the theory of natural belief as an explanatory principle. But just what does he mean by a natural belief? To believe, we know from his definition, is to possess a lively idea (96). But not all of our beliefs are natural beliefs; to qualify, a belief must be one we must accept because we are the kind of beings we are.[15] Thus Hume is, in his theory of natural belief, making an important statement about human nature. He is saying that we are believing creatures, at least to the extent that we necessarily believe in such things as an external material world, our own existence as enduring entities, and so on.

Many scholars have emphasized the importance of Hume's theory of natural belief. Norman Kemp Smith, for example, writes, "Hume's manner of regarding the 'natural beliefs' has . . . been all-important in determining his attitude to the problems dealt with in Book I."[16] In this theory Hume reveals his deep understanding of human nature. Personally, I would find it next to impossible to believe that there is no external material world or that I do not persist through time as a single self. I think most people would agree with me in these, and other fundamental beliefs. Hume scholars are right in considering his theory of natural belief to be one of Hume's most significant contributions to the history of thought.

Nevertheless, this theory gives rise to some problems. Three seem worthy of mention. (1) As a result of his two-step argument in Section I Hume arrived at the conclusion of total scepticism. Any attempt we make to provide a rational justification for anything we believe must end in failure. Yet we continue to believe anyway. Presumably, Hume believed his theory of natural belief. But, according to his own sceptical argument, he could not defend this belief rationally. Many scholars agree with Hume in believing his theory of natural belief and would be prepared to offer arguments in support of their doing so. In this endeavor, unfortunately, the originator of the theory could not join them.

(2) To believe in the existence of anything one must have an idea of the thing in which he believes.[17] Hume claims that we have a natural belief in the existence of an external material world, of our own minds as enduring entities and of other things. But he also maintains that we have ideas of none of these things. It follows, therefore, that we cannot have a belief, natural or otherwise, in their existence either.

(3) A question can be raised about the existence of natural beliefs themselves. We know, from Hume's definition, that a belief is a lively idea. If we go back and reexamine Hume's views on belief, particularly in Section VII of Part III, we recognize another important point—that belief requires a believer. This requirement is almost too obvious to mention; nevertheless, because of its importance, it needs to be documented. At the beginning of Section VII Hume writes: "The idea of an object is an essential part of the belief of it, but not the whole. We conceive many things, which we do not believe. In order then to discover more fully the nature of belief, or the qualities of those ideas *we* assent to, let us weigh the following considerations" (94—italics added). Near the end of the same section he adds that "as belief does nothing but vary the manner, in which *we* conceive any object, it can only bestow on *our* ideas an additional force and vivacity" (96—italics added).

The problem should now be apparent. By his use of the pronouns "we" and "our" in the passages I have quoted, Hume is assuming that, for a belief to exist, some believer—person or mind—must believe. But we now know that a mind or person is simply a succession of perceptions. For a belief to exist, therefore, Hume must say that a succession of perceptions assents to an idea. In order to assent to an idea it is first necessary to possess the idea. So, if beliefs are to exist on Hume's philosophy, a succession of perceptions must possess ideas. I will not repeat the reasons I have given before to show that this is impossible;[18] I would simply say that, if we accept Hume's account of mind, we must conclude that no beliefs of any kind, natural or other, can exist. Nevertheless, even though the theory of natural belief is not a view that Hume could consistently have put forward, it remains a significant contribution to the history of thought.

5. "True" Scepticism (Paragraphs 8–15)

Hume's most important positive contribution to philosophy in Section VII is his "true" scepticism.[19] The view is not easy to explicate,[20] mainly because it consists largely of a description of sets of dispositions and a way of life, derived from a theory of human nature. We can understand and appreciate it best if we place it in the context of two other forms of scepticism—(1) classical Pyrrhonism and (2) Hume's total scepticism of Section I, Part IV. I will discuss its relationship to the former in this section and to the latter in section 6.

Hume's attitude to the classical Pyrrhonists, as he understood them, is ambivalent.[21] He supported their idea of a suspension of judgment, but only up to a point, disagreeing with them vehemently about their (purported) recommendation that we should suspend judgment on everything. We have already seen his reason for this disagreement; the total suspension of judgment is not humanly possible. So his problem is to find a theory that will allow for a partial suspension of judgment but will not go all the way with the Pyrrhonists to a total suspension. "True" scepticism is Hume's novel and ingenious solution to this problem.

Hume develops his theory autobiographically, by describing a way of life he follows himself—a way that consists in shifts in disposition or mood, and consequently of activity, following a cyclical pattern. In describing the theory one can enter the cycle at any point; I will do so at the point at which Hume seems most clearly to be introducing it (268). He has apparently been engaged in philosophizing, with the following consequences: "The *intense* view of these manifold contradictions and imperfections in human reason has so wrought upon me, and heated my brain, that I am ready to reject all belief and reasoning, and can look upon no opinion even as more probable or likely than another" (268–69). Faced with the sceptical results to which his reasoning has led him he finds his mood becoming one of despair. "I am confounded with all these questions, and begin to fancy myself in the most deplorable condition imaginable, inviron'd with the deepest darkness, and utterly depriv'd of the use of every member and faculty" (269). At this point, however, nature comes to Hume's rescue. "Most fortunately it happens, that since reason is incapable of dispelling these clouds, nature herself suffices to that purpose, and cures me of this philosophical melancholy and delirium, either by relaxing this bent of mind, or by some avocation, and lively impression of my senses, which obliterate all these chimeras. I dine, I play a game of back-gammon, I converse, and am merry with my friends" (269).

Two points in these passages need comment. First, Hume makes it clear that "reason is incapable of dispelling these clouds." No rational resolution can be found for the problems either of philosophy or ordinary life.[22] As he puts it, "I am ready to reject all belief and reasoning" (268). This is a reiteration of the conclusion of total scepticism he had reached in Section I. Second, "nature" effects a cure for his "philosophical melancholy and delirium," not by resolving the problems but by shifting his mood and activities.

But this is only one phase of the full cycle. Although Hume's clouds of doubt are dispelled by a shift in mood and activity, in which he gives up philosophy in favor of amusement, his is not a temperament to find permanent satisfaction in backgammon. After a suitable interlude devoted to the pastimes of everyday life he becomes bored, so welcomes a return to the pursuit of intellectual matters.

> At the time, therefore, that I am tir'd with amusement and company, and have indulg'd a *reverie* in my chamber, or in a solitary walk by a river-side, I feel my mind all collected within itself, and am naturally *inclin'd* to carry my view into all those subjects, about which I have met with so many disputes in the course of my reading and conversation. . . . I am concern'd for the condition of the learned world, which lies under such a deplorable ignorance in all these particulars. I feel an ambition to arise in me of contributing to the instruction of mankind, and of acquiring a name by my inventions and discoveries. *These sentiments spring up naturally in my present disposition.* (270–71—final italics added)

So we have traced an episode in Hume's life, consisting in a cycle beginning with his application to philosophy, which leads him into "the deepest darkness"; followed by a turn to amusement and indolence, leading him to backgammon, which in turn results finally in boredom; then, again, a return to philosophy. Presumably this return initiates a new cycle, and the pattern is repeated. Buried in this account of his style of life is Hume's "true" scepticism. It will take considerable further effort to extricate it.

It is important to note that Hume is describing his own psychological career. That he should shift from philosophical concerns to amusement and then back again is, as he makes clear, a perfectly natural sequence that results from the state of his disposition at the time he makes the shift. But, the question can be asked: What has this psychological account of Hume's dispositions and the activities they produce to do with scepticism? Scepticism is not a psychological view or theory but an epistemological position that denies the possibility of knowledge. To explain the connection between the two we must pursue our analysis further.

Perhaps the best way to begin is to distinguish Hume's view from classical Pyrrhonism. The Pyrrhonists refused to develop any philosophical theories, suspending their judgment on all such matters. On this point Hume broke with them. When his mood was right (as it must have been when he was engaged in writing the *Treatise*), he was not only willing to theorize but, I think it safe to say, delighted in doing so. His suspension of philosophical judgment was episodic, coming only when he turned away from his studies to devote himself to the pastimes of ordinary life.[23] Thus Hume's account of his way of living represents a significant improvement over that of the Pyrrhonists because it permits him to engage in philosophical theorizing, an activity they forswore. This difference marks the essential distinction between his "true" scepticism and Pyrrhonism. (I do not include Hume's own belief that his "true" scepticism is superior to Pyrrhonism because it allows him to make judgments about practical matters as well, because his assumption that the Pyrrhonists denied us the ability to do this is not correct.) But, one might well ask, why is it better to be able to philosophize than not to be able to do so? We will see Hume's answer in a moment.

As we have found, Hume turns away from philosophy when his philosophizing leads him to an impasse. But this in itself is not a sufficient explanation of his abandonment of his studies. Why does he not continue to butt his head against the wall? Or, perhaps more pertinently, why does he ever engage in philosophizing in the first place? Hume's answer to the last question—and, hence, his response to Pyrrhonism—is hedonistic. Speaking of his return to philosophy after a period devoted to amusement, he writes: "These sentiments [the urge to philosophize] spring up naturally in my present disposition; and shou'd I endeavour to banish them, by attaching myself to any other business or diversion, I *feel* I shou'd be a loser in point of pleasure; and this is the origin of my philosophy" (271). Hume's reasons for later abandoning philosophy in favor of amusement are also hedonistic, but partly in a negative sense. As he puts it (in a passage I quoted earlier): "Nature . . . cures me of this philosophical melancholy and delirium . . . by some avocation. . . . I dine, I play a game of back-gammon." One can well empathize with Hume here. There *is* pleasure to be found in the activities of the intellect—pleasures that the Pyrrhonists (presumably) never enjoyed—just as there is in innocent pastimes. Indeed, one might go beyond Hume and argue that the two kinds of activity not only supplement but actually invigorate each other. After a bout of philosophizing one can turn to game-playing with zest and, after this pastime becomes boring, return to philosophy with positive pleasure. Whether such a hedonistic account provides a sufficient justification for engaging in philosophy is, of course, open to dispute. Some who have given their lives to philosophy will undoubtedly reject it as inadequate, claiming that they have better reasons for what they do. I will leave this issue to the reader, adding only the modest comment that there seems to me to be some truth in what Hume says.[24]

In the passage in which Hume justifies his philosophizing hedonistically, he speaks of pleasure in connection with the *origin* of his philosophy. It is clear from the context that Hume is using the term "origin" here in a temporal sense. He begins to philosophize, after a period of indolence, because doing so again will bring him pleasure. But there is another sense of "origin" that needs to be taken into account as well. This concerns the origin of the specific theories that result from his philosophical activities. Why does Hume, in addition to philosophizing, philosophize in the way he does and, in particular, reach the conclusions he does? This is a point he addressed in a remarkable paragraph much earlier in Book I. Because of its importance to our understanding of Hume's thought, the passage bears repeating. "'Tis not solely in poetry and music, we must follow our taste and sentiment, but likewise in philosophy. When I am convinc'd of any principle, 'tis only an idea, which strikes more strongly upon me. When I give the preference to one set of arguments above another, I do nothing but decide from my feeling concerning the superiority of their influence" (103). Although Hume does not use the word "pleasure" itself in this passage, the way in which he "justifies" his philosophical conclusions seems clearly hedonistic. Like poetry and music, philosophy is simply a matter of taste. Thus this passage fits nicely into Hume's hedonistic account of the "origin" of his philosophy in Section VII. That it is a view he still accepts is clear from the fact that he reiterates it in the section. "After the most accurate and exact of my reasonings, I can give no reason why I shou'd assent to it; and feel nothing but a *strong* propensity to consider objects *strongly* in that view, under which they appear to me" (265).

Another feature must be added to Hume's account of his cyclic shift from philosophy to amusement, then back to philosophy again. We have seen that this cycle is a result of his psychological dispositions or moods and is based on hedonistic motivations. In addition, Hume maintains, he has no choice in the matter; the shifts are a necessary product of his nature. He writes: "I may, nay I must yield to the current of nature, in submitting to my senses and understanding; and in this blind submission I shew most perfectly my sceptical disposition and principles" (269).

This statement calls for several comments. When Hume talks about submitting to his "senses" and "understanding" presumably he is referring to those periods in his psychological cycle in which he alternates between an indulgence in amusement and a concentration on study. But why *must* he submit to each of these in turn? He simply asserts this requirement of his nature but never gives an explanation of it. Perhaps he found it was just a brute fact about himself. Nevertheless, we can recognize an element of truth about human nature in what he says. There is a natural rhythm in the lives of even those who devote themselves most strenuously to the life of the intellect; they need occasional relaxation. Whether others are, like Hume, so rigidly determined that this cyclic alternation constitutes a "blind submission" to nature is, however, open to question.

Hume's final comment in the statement is somewhat puzzling. How does his blind submission to the cyclic movement of his life "shew most perfectly [his] sceptical disposition and principles"? To return to a point I raised earlier, scepticism is an epistemological theory, but Hume's submission is simply a psychological response he, of necessity, makes at certain times. Perhaps his willingness to abandon philosophy and turn to back-gammon when he runs into difficulties might be said to exhibit a "scepti-cal disposition" but his description of such a shift, and the reverse shift back to philosophy later, seems hardly in itself to state any sceptical "principles" or theory. This is an important point to which I will return in the next section.

One final comment about Hume's "true" scepticism. Throughout his discussion he expresses a general attitude toward his activity of philoso-phizing that can be distinguished both from his enthusiasm for it when the disposition to philosophize seizes him and his antipathy toward it when that enthusiasm is extinguished. Philosophy, Hume cautions, is not an activity we should pursue intensely. Instead our attitude toward it should be carefree. This is the attitude of the "true" sceptic. In his words: "In all the incidents of life we ought still to preserve our scepticism. If we believe, that fire warms, or water refreshes, 'tis only because it costs us too much pains to think otherwise. Nay if we are philosophers, it ought only to be upon sceptical principles, and from an inclination, which we feel to the employing ourselves after that manner."[25] In a statement in which he sums up his "true" scepticism Hume adds: "The conduct of a man, who studies philosophy in this careless [carefree?] manner, is more truly sceptical than that of one, who feeling in himself an inclination to it, is yet so over-whelm'd with doubts and scruples, as totally to reject it. A true sceptic will be diffident of his philosophical doubts, as well as of his philosophical conviction; and will never refuse any innocent satisfaction, which offers itself, upon account of either of them."[26]

6. "True" Scepticism and Total Scepticism

I suggested in the last section that Hume's "true" scepticism, as he de-scribes it in Section VII, seems hardly to be a form of scepticism at all. As an account of a way of life that simply describes a person's fluctuating dis-positions and activities, even with the view it presents of human nature it still implies nothing about the possibility or impossibility of knowledge. If one examines what Hume says about the "true" sceptic in the section it seems hard to find anything in it that cognitivists would have to reject. On the contrary. Cognitivists could well agree with Hume that philosophers should not devote all of their time to thought but should alternate between study and leisure. They could also accept Hume's view that they ought to pursue philosophy only to the extent that doing so gave them pleasure and that they should not involve themselves too intensely in the activity. They might even concede Hume's psychological determinism that mandates the cyclic alternation between philosophy and amusement.

A problem with Hume's "true" scepticism arises for cognitivists only when we recollect the reason Hume gives for his periodic flights from philosophy to backgammon. As we saw earlier, his pursuit of philosophy leads him to "the deepest darkness," from which he is fortuitously rescued by nature. Whether cognitivists could accept this aspect of the account depends on what *exactly* Hume means by the passage. If the impasses into which Hume is led when he philosophizes are contingent, the view could be accepted by cognitivists. They could argue that, although they often find problems in their philosophizing that they cannot resolve, so turn away from philosophy in temporary despair, they nevertheless also reach other conclusions whose truth they can justify. Thus they can claim to know something so can defend their cognitivism against the attacks of the sceptics. But if, when Hume talks of "the deepest darkness," he means that his philosophizing necessarily leads him to an impasse in which he must concede that he can know nothing, cognitivists cannot follow him, for such a concession is total scepticism. Without the presupposition of total scepticism, Hume's "true" scepticism could be described with equal accuracy as "true" cognitivism. It is incompatible with cognitivism, hence truly a form of scepticism rather than simply an essay in human psychology, *only* if it is part of a complete epistemology that includes total scepticism as a part as well. Hume's "true" sceptic, to be truly a *sceptic,* must be a total sceptic as well, but one who lives the kind of cyclic life Hume describes in Section VII.

This conclusion is sufficiently important to merit elaboration. In section 2 of this chapter we found that in Section VII Hume reiterates his total scepticism of Section I. We can now understand his reason for doing so. He recognized that total scepticism is a necessary part of the full theory that makes his "true" scepticism an authentic form of scepticism. The logic of his argument can be formulated in the following way: All of our attempts to justify our theories and beliefs by an appeal to reasons necessarily end in failure, therefore we must conclude that we can know nothing. Yet we still have a desire to philosophize. But how can we justify such an activity if we have already proved that it cannot succeed? Here Hume's subtle genius comes into play. We do not expect any success from our philosophizing.[27] Although our necessary failure may throw us temporarily into despair, we can quickly recover our spirits with a game of backgammon. Not only that but we have had the pleasure (up to a point) of philosophizing and can anticipate a similar pleasure in the future when our mood encourages us to return to our study. Hume's "true" scepticism is, thus, a combination of his total scepticism of Section I and the way of life he describes in Section VII. So we can offer the following character portrait of the "true" sceptic, or self-portrait of David Hume.[28] Although he can

offer no rational support for his philosophical theories, he enjoys philosophy. His pleasure in intellectual activity leads him back to his study after
periods of amusement to resume again his fruitless quest. But in this very
activity he enjoys a great advantage over the Pyrrhonist, who can never
experience the pleasures of philosophy at all.

But a problem remains. We can understand why Hume found it necessary to put his psychological account of Section VII together with his total scepticism of Section I to create his "true" scepticism. Yet we need to
ask: Can the views Hume states in these two sections be consistently put
together? As an account of human dispositions, motivations, and activities, the "true" scepticism of Section VII belongs to psychology. It is a part
of the science of human nature, which, Hume writes, "is the only science
of man" (273). But how can Hume make any contribution to the science
of human nature? In a passage from Section VII that I have already discussed, he acknowledges that his total scepticism cuts off "entirely all science and philosophy" (268). The implication is plain. If total scepticism
precludes the possibility of science, *a fortiori* it precludes the possibility of
any science of human nature, and thus of the psychological theory Hume
presents in Section VII. Although this theory probably represents the high
point in historical statements of scepticism, it is, unfortunately, a theory
that Hume could not consistently put forward. His "true" scepticism of
Section VII both requires his total scepticism of Section I and is rendered
impossible by that scepticism.

7. Hume's Humility (Paragraph 15)

Some critics of Hume, including his first reviewer, have charged him
with egotism.[29] Whatever the merits of this charge, it seems belied by the
words with which Hume concludes Book I. He writes: "We are apt not
only to forget our scepticism, but even our modesty too; and make use of
such terms as these, *'tis evident, 'tis certain, 'tis undeniable. . . .* I may have
fallen into this fault . . . but . . . declare that such expressions were extort-
ed from me by the present view of the object, and imply no dogmatical
spirit, nor conceited idea of my own judgment, which are sentiments that
I am sensible can become no body, and a sceptic still less than any other"
(274).

Summary

Section VII marks the culmination of both Part IV and Book I. In its
early paragraphs Hume summarizes some of the main conclusions he has
reached in the book. These summaries are particularly valuable, because

they not only confirm those conclusions but state many of them in a succinct and unambiguous way. In the latter part of the section he completes his sceptical argument of Part IV, with the introduction of his "true" scepticism, which is unquestionably a major contribution to the history of sceptical thought.

But the section has another important dimension, one that is emotional rather than theoretical. In it Hume reveals himself as a human being, in a way that he had not done before. This is particularly true of its opening paragraphs, in which he speaks eloquently of his despair. Some commentators have criticized his language as unseemly. John Passmore, for example, writes: "The bewilderment Hume displays at the end of Book I of the *Treatise* is genuine enough, although, unable to resist the opportunity scepticism offers him for self-dramatization, he lapses into a stagey, melodramatic tone."[30] Others, however, have been more sympathetic to Hume. According to Barry Stroud, "Some of the most personal, and the most moving, passages in all of Hume's philosophical writings appear in that puzzling, confessional last section of Book I of the *Treatise*."[31] On this point I agree with Stroud; I find Hume's self-revelation in the section both poignant and moving.

CONCLUSION

At the beginning of this book I wrote that in it I would try to accomplish two aims: To elucidate Hume's philosophy by following the progress of his thought through Book I of the *Treatise* and to examine his arguments in order to give an evaluation of his epistemology and metaphysics.[1] I have devoted most of the book to the first task, mainly because Hume's theories are both novel and complex and his arguments sophisticated, subtle, and often extremely compacted, requiring detailed and lengthy interpretation. Throughout I have attempted to avoid "pre-textual" interpretation of Hume's philosophy, in favor of what I have called "post-textual" interpretation.[2] This procedure has required me to quote extensively from Book I. In doing so, I have endeavored to "get inside" of Hume's mind and follow his thought as he develops it in the course of the work. Throughout I have tried to avoid a "selective" reading of Book I but instead to base my commentary on a full and balanced account of what Hume actually says in it.

Although I have devoted considerably less space to my second task, I have tried to fulfill my obligation as a philosopher to examine Hume's theories critically. Rather than belaboring minor shortcomings in his arguments (which are often a result of his loose and ambiguous terminology), I have concentrated on what seem to me to be major inconsistencies in his philosophy. Although some of these are evident in the text itself, others lie in implications of his arguments that he did not himself draw. I have undertaken to uncover these and examine their major consequences.

In the introduction to the *Treatise* Hume wrote that he was proposing "a compleat system of the sciences, built on a foundation almost entirely new, and the only one upon which they can stand with any security" (xvi). The conclusion we must draw from this study of Book I is that he did not accomplish his goal. On the contrary, we have found that most of his central arguments collapse under the weight of their internal inconsistencies. Hume himself was aware of this fact, at least in part, as evidenced by his expression of despair in the early paragraphs of Section VII as well as by his confession, in his appendix note to Section VI, that he can give no viable account of the nature of mind. For philosophers, however, the fact that Hume's philosophy in Book I disintegrates raises a different question, of greater interest and importance. What are the causes of the disintegration? Although many factors are involved, the failure can be attributed to three main causes.

1. Hume's argument from the beginning has rested on an untenable epistemology. After all the criticisms that have been made of it over the centuries, it may seem hardly necessary at this late date to dwell on the inadequacies of empiricism. Nevertheless, it is important to emphasize that most of the numerous inconsistencies we have found in Book I result from his elaboration of views that are incompatible with his own empiricist assumptions. As we have seen, Hume's repeated use of the Empiricist Principle to demolish various philosophical views with which he disagrees is matched only by his own violations of the Principle. Classical empiricism truly found its executioner in Hume.

2. Although it did not make its appearance until Part IV, Hume's total scepticism has even more devastating consequences for his philosophy than his empiricism. His conclusion that all of our attempts to provide reasons in support of our beliefs are necessarily self-destructive, which he claimed to have proved in Section I, leads, as he acknowledges in Section VII, to the elimination of all science and philosophy. Not only does this make it impossible for him to carry out his project of constructing a science of human nature but it destroys the legitimacy of his philosophical endeavors as well.[3]

3. The third main problem in Hume's philosophy is more complex. It results from his *eclecticism*. Although Hume is traditionally labeled an empiricist, this is only a convenient tag, because he clearly did not contain himself within the narrow bounds imposed by that view. On the contrary, he was the great eclectic of modern philosophy, incorporating in the *Treatise* philosophical views from a wide variety of divergent and often conflicting sources, stitched together with original ideas of his own. Some of the main strands of thought included in Book I follow. (a) First is his empiricism, representing what is obviously a major theme in his argument, and stemming from both Locke and Berkeley. Throughout Book I Hume repeatedly appeals to the Empiricist Principle as the basis of his epistemology, even in situations in which he is in the process of violating it. But other theories, intentions, and modes of thought of equal importance appear in the book as well. (b) Part IV is dominated by his scepticism, in particular by his total scepticism of Section I and his "true" scepticism of Section VII, both of which are independent of his empiricism, and reveal the influence of both Bayle and the classical Pyrrhonists. (c) Hume gave the *Treatise* the subtitle "An Attempt to introduce the experimental Method of Reasoning

into Moral Subjects." It is reasonable to conclude, as many commentators have done,[4] that Hume was strongly impressed by Newtonian science and conceived of himself as the person who not only transferred the Newtonian methodology from the domain of "natural philosophy" to that of "moral philosophy" but also made the latter the "foundation" for the former. (d) Despite his denial of the existence of a material world, on several occasions Hume flirts with materialism. A good example is his appeal in Part II, Section V, to brain physiology as a way of explaining error. It is reasonable to conclude that he was influenced in this by developments in the natural sciences. (e) Equally important to Hume's thought is another domain of science—psychology. Much of Book I consists of psychological analysis, which, though valuable in its own right as well as historically important, often becomes a substitute for philosophical reasoning, with the result of confusion and inconsistency. (f) Theoretically important is Hume's notion of natural belief, or his view that, even though any attempt we make to support our beliefs rationally must end in failure, certain beliefs we have are ineradicable; we must accept them despite their irrationality, because we are the kind of beings we are. (g) Closely related to (f) is Hume's denigration of reason in favor of feeling, a thesis Norman Kemp Smith, in particular, has drawn to the attention of Hume scholars.[5] Although the view, which may have had its inspiration in Hutcheson's ethics, appears in several places in Book I, perhaps its most notable expressions occur in a paragraph in Part III, Section VIII (103), which I discussed in chapter 10, section 5, and in Hume's statement in Section I of Part IV that "*belief is more properly an act of the sensitive, than of the cogitative part of our natures*" (183). (h) Although Hume begins the *Treatise* with an epistemology based on the senses, the imagination gradually supersedes them. By the end of Part IV he has concluded that much of what we believe must be attributed to "suppositions" of the imagination rather than to the impressions of our senses. This change clearly reflects the disparity between his beliefs and his empiricism as well as between them and his total scepticism. (i) Hume's project, to develop a science of human nature, as well as the constructive philosophizing he does in Book I, rest on the general assumption of cognitivism, an assumption intellectually congenial to the eighteenth century. The advancement of knowledge is possible only if knowledge itself is possible. Hume clearly accepted this cognitivistic assumption, affirming it explicitly in the final section of Book I: "We might hope to establish a system or set of opinions, which if not true (for that, perhaps, is too much to be hop'd for) might at least be satisfactory to the human mind, and might stand the test of the most critical examination. . . . For my part, my only hope is, that I may contribute a little to the advancement of knowledge."[6] Hume is, thus, *both* a total sceptic and a cognitivist.

The theories and themes I have listed, as well as others of lesser importance, are interwoven throughout Book I in intricate patterns. They are often rewarding and illuminating in themselves, and display the richness and diversity of Hume's thought. But insuperable difficulties arise from his attempt to combine these diverse components into a coherent philosophy, because they are fundamentally incompatible with each other. Hume's eclecticism, more than anything else, is the root cause of the inconsistencies that permeate his philosophy in Book I.[7]

Nevertheless, despite these problems, Book I is well worth the attention that generations of scholars have devoted to it. In the remaining paragraphs I will review what seem to me to be the most important contributions to the history of thought Hume makes in it.

Hume was unquestionably one of the most important critical thinkers in modern philosophy. He had an acute awareness of the inadequacies of earlier philosophy and an ability to concentrate his attention on issues in epistemology and metaphysics that were not only of fundamental importance but that other philosophers had never raised. By doing so he was able to demolish many of the views of the scholastics and the rationalists, as well as of the empiricists, particularly Locke. Philosophy could never remain the same after the *Treatise*. Kant was the first to recognize this. In his remark that Hume aroused him from his dogmatic slumbers he paid one of the finest tributes ever accorded to the Scot.

But Hume's main interest was in constructive philosophy. In this, despite his general failure, he developed several theories that are of historical and theoretical importance. His most significant substantive contribution, I think most scholars would agree, is his epochal account of causation. Not only did this theory mark a radical departure from earlier philosophy, as well as from our ordinary ways of thinking, but Hume defended it by a series of arguments whose power must be respected even by those who disagree with him. That Hume's analysis revolutionized thought about causation is abundantly evident from the fact that his theory figures prominently in almost all philosophical discussions of the subject during the past century.

Another significant contribution concerns Hume's theory of imagination and the central role it plays in human "thought." It is important to recognize that Hume has, by his reliance on it, given a novel, and distinctive, characterization of man, as a "rational animal." "Imagination" replaces "reason" as the support for what we believe. Rather than turning to argument to ground our beliefs we must turn instead to feeling. Whether we find Hume's conclusion on this point palatable, we must recognize the historical importance of his denigration of reason. Far earlier than most others he challenged the sometimes too facile optimism of the Age of Reason, to become one of the first prophets of romanticism.

Still another major contribution of Book I is to psychology rather than to philosophy proper. This is Hume's theory of belief and, in particular, his theory of natural belief. Although most philosophers would probably disagree with Hume that all of our beliefs are irrational, we must, if we are candid, acknowledge that all too many of them are, if not positively irrational, at least nonrational. Also, Hume makes another, less controversial point about human beliefs. Certain of them are natural in the sense that they are unavoidable. How many of us, other than Berkeley, would not agree with Hume that we must believe in the existence of an external material world? One of the main tasks of philosophy, which Hume had much to do in setting, is to provide a rational justification for fundamental natural beliefs such as this one or else to show, in a compelling way, that it cannot be done.

Another contribution, whether one judge it positive or negative, that Hume makes to the history of philosophy in Book I is his scepticism. By this I do not mean his particular scepticisms but the general scepticism that appears in Sections I and VII of Part IV, which constitutes his "true" scepticism. That Hume considered himself to be a sceptic in the tradition of classical philosophy is evident. That he found a flaw in Pyrrhonism, as he understood it, with its "total" suspension of judgment, is equally evident. Finally, that his "true" scepticism, despite being vitiated by his total scepticism, is a sophisticated and, in some ways, attractive attempt at a revision of Pyrrhonism must be recognized. For this reason alone it constitutes a significant contribution to the literature of scepticism.

Finally, I should mention a contribution of great importance to philosophy that Hume made by not making it. Less enigmatically, I am referring to a problem he raised but never resolved but, in the very raising of it, advanced the cause of philosophy immeasurably. The issue arises early in Part III after he has distinguished between knowledge and probability (or opinion) in Sections I and II. Limiting the realm of knowledge to demonstration and, as a result, to algebra and arithmetic, he seeks some justification for our beliefs about matters of fact, beliefs whose truth cannot be demonstrated so cannot legitimately be claimed as things we know. Because he can find no rational justification for such beliefs he bases them on feeling. We believe because we want to believe, even though we can give no reasons to support our beliefs. The historical importance of Hume's treatment of our beliefs about matters of fact does not lie in its reception by subsequent philosophers; few have accepted his view. It is important, rather, because he raised and sharply posed the questions: Can we give any rational justification for our beliefs about matters of fact? Is there anything we can distinguish from knowledge, conceived as demonstration, that we can legitimately call reasonable belief? If so, what reasons can we give to justify our claim that our beliefs about matters of fact are reasonable? Although philosophers have wrestled perennially with these questions, and some have claimed to have resolved them, they remain for others the single most important outstanding set of issues in epistemology.

It is evident that Hume was not satisfied with Book I of the *Treatise*. Indeed, later in life he "repudiated" the entire work. In an advertisement appearing in an edition of his later works that was not published until after his death he described the *Treatise* as a "juvenile work" which "[he] never acknowledged." Although he never stated in any detail what he concluded its shortcomings to be, one can at least surmise that they included his realization that his account of mind in Book I was not viable. That he took this failure very seriously is evidenced not only in his appendix note to Section VI of Part IV but also in the absence of any serious discussion of the nature of the mind in his *Enquiry Concerning Human Understanding*. Could he have lived to witness it, Hume, the ironist, would undoubtedly have savored the irony in the fact that an individual who would two centuries later be acclaimed as one of the preeminent minds of modern philosophy should have himself been unable to give a satisfactory explanation of what a mind is.

The *Treatise*, which Hume later described as having fallen "dead-born from the press," was slow in returning to life. After being vilified at the hands of his contemporaries, it was little regarded for well over a hundred years. Only in the twentieth century has its true worth come to be recognized. As this is written, more than 250 years after its publication, philosophers and scholars, whatever conclusions they reach regarding its philosophical viability, agree in ranking the *Treatise* among the classics of Western thought.

Notes

Introduction

1. D. Hume, *A Treatise of Human Nature: Being an Attempt to introduce the experimental Method of Reasoning into Moral Subjects,* 2 vols. (London: Printed for John Noon, 1739). Book III was published as a separate, third volume in 1740 by a different publisher. In this book my citations will be from the second edition of the *Treatise,* ed. L. A. Selby-Bigge and P. H. Nidditch (Oxford: Clarendon Press, 1978). Since most of my citations will be from the *Treatise,* usually I will include the page numbers parenthetically in the text itself, following the citation, rather than in endnotes.

2. *The History of the Works of the Learned* (London, 1739), 6:362n. Although there has been considerable conjecture about the author of the review, no one has succeeded in identifying the person beyond question. E. C. Mossner, Hume's biographer, writes: "There is no direct evidence, but it may be conjectured that it was William Warburton, later the Bishop of Gloucester." E. C. Mossner, *The Life of David Hume* (Austin: University of Texas Press, 1954), 122–23. Mossner's attribution has, however, been questioned. See R. M. Ryley, "Did Warburton Review Hume's 'A Treatise of Human Nature'?" *Notes and Queries* 221 (1976): 354–55. Hume was less than pleased with the review, remarking in a letter to Francis Hutcheson that it was "somewhat abusive." J. Y. T. Grieg, ed., *The Letters of David Hume* (Oxford: Clarendon Press, 1932), 1:38.

3. J. Passmore, *Hume's Intentions,* 3d ed. (London: Duckworth, 1980), 1.

4. Similar observations about the difficulty of Hume can be found in other commentators. Norman Kemp Smith, for example, begins his book *The Philosophy of David Hume* with the statement: "Hume's *Treatise of Human Nature,* as its readers soon discover, is a difficult and often puzzling work. The ardour of mind and variability of mood in which it was composed, its loose and careless terminology, and other minor defects very excusable in a first and youthful work, also even its sheer bulk, account for many of the reader's difficulties. But the root-causes lie deeper, in the arrangement of the work as a whole." N. K. Smith, *The Philosophy of David Hume: A Critical Study of Its Origins and Central Doctrines* (London: Macmillan, 1941), 3.

5. Humean irony has been the subject of at least one book: J. V. Price, *The Ironic Hume* (Austin: University of Texas Press, 1965).

6. Robert Anderson distinguishes three different senses in which Hume uses the word "object." See his book *Hume's First Principles* (Lincoln: University of Nebraska Press, 1966), 46–47.

7. Passmore, *Hume's Intentions,* 131.

8. Some scholars who believe that the *Treatise* contains fundamental inconsistencies account for these by saying that Hume's philosophical views underwent substantial change as he was writing the book. See, for example, Constance Maund, *Hume's Theory of Knowledge: A Critical Examination* (London: Macmillan, 1937), 168ff. Although this theory may be correct, so may several other equally plausible explanations. I do not think the question is one we can resolve with any confidence at this late date.

9. For a good example of a commentary that emphasizes a particular interpretation of Hume's thought see N. Capaldi, *David Hume: The Newtonian Philosopher* (Boston: Twayne, 1975). In his book Capaldi defends the thesis that "Hume translated Newton into a philosophical system" (64).

10. D. W. Livingston, *Hume's Philosophy of Common Life* (Chicago: University of Chicago Press, 1984), 1. I should make it clear that, when I talk about "pre-textual interpretations" of Hume, I do not mean to imply that their authors have not based their interpretations on a reading of the *Treatise* but only that their method runs the danger of unduly emphasizing certain facets of Hume's thought at the expense of others.

11. Mossner, *Life of David Hume,* 70.

12. The letter is reproduced in full in *Letters of David Hume,* ed. Grieg, 1:12–18. According to Hume's nineteenth-century biographer, J. H. Burton, the letter, which may never have been sent, was addressed to Dr. George Cheyne, a London physician of Scottish birth. See J. H. Burton, *Life and Correspondence of David Hume* (Edinburgh: 1846), 1:42–47. Grieg accepts Burton's opinion but Mossner does not, adducing evidence to indicate the addressee was not Dr. Cheyne but another Scot practicing in London, Dr. John Arbuthnot. See E. C. Mossner, "Hume's Epistle to Dr. Arbuthnot, 1734: The Biographical Significance," *Huntington Library Quarterly* 7 (1944): 135–52.

13. Grieg, ed., *Letters of David Hume,* 1:13. Italics added.

14. C. W. Hendel, *Studies in the Philosophy of David Hume* (Princeton: Princeton University Press, 1925), 25. In a new edition of his book (1963), Hendel added an appendix in which he discusses various interpretations of the "new scene of thought" passage. See C. W. Hendel, *Studies in the Philosophy of David Hume,* new ed. (Indianapolis: Bobbs-Merrill, 1963), 483–92. In this appendix Hendel alters his view on how the passage should be understood. After reviewing several different interpretations commentators had given, he concludes: "The evidence here adduced from the correspondence, the *Treatise,* and the *Abstract,* offers some warrant for every one of the interpretations of Hume's discovery and the new scene of thought" (489).

15. J. Laird, *Hume's Philosophy of Human Nature* (London: Methuen, 1932), 20.

16. Smith, *Philosophy of David Hume,* 12–13.

17. D. G. C. Macnabb, Introduction to David Hume, *A Treatise of Human Nature, Book I* (Cleveland: World, 1962), 8–9.

18. D. Forbes, *Hume's Philosophical Politics* (Cambridge: Cambridge University Press, 1975), 17.

19. Passmore, *Hume's Intentions*, 131.

20. Smith, *Philosophy of David Hume*, 11.

21. Ibid., 14. Italics added.

22. R. Brandt, "The Beginnings of Hume's Philosophy," in *David Hume: Bicentenary Papers*, ed. G. P. Morice (Edinburgh: University of Edinburgh Press, 1977), 117–27.

23. Ibid., 118–19.

24. While this book was being written David Pears published a book that, from its title, might appear to parallel mine. See his *Hume's System: An Examination of the First Book of His Treatise* (Oxford: Oxford University Press, 1990). But Pears's book is quite different from this one, in both organization and contents.

25. My commentary will also include Hume's *Appendix* (which appears on pages 623–39 of the Selby-Bigge and Nidditch second edition of the *Treatise*). Hume apparently wrote the notes that appear in the appendix during the time between the publication of the first two volumes and the final volume of the *Treatise* (1739–40). For further details see P. H. Nidditch, *An Apparatus of Variant Readings for Hume's* Treatise of Human Nature (Sheffield, Eng.,: University of Sheffield, Department of Philosophy, 1976), 7–9. The appendix must be considered an integral part of Book I (to which its notes are devoted). In it Hume supplements and amends views contained in the main text, sometimes in significant and illuminating ways. In this book I will discuss these appendix notes at the same time I am commenting on the points in the text to which they are appended.

A second supplement to the *Treatise* needs our attention as well. In 1740 a short work, *An Abstract of a Book lately Published; Entituled, A Treatise of Human Nature, &c.*, by an anonymous author, was published in London. It consists of brief but often clarifying summaries of the main theories and arguments of the *Treatise*, Book I in particular. The *Abstract* remained virtually ignored until early in this century when J. M. Keynes and P. Straffa republished it. See their edition of *An Abstract of a Treatise of Human Nature* (Cambridge: Cambridge University Press, 1938). In their introduction Keynes and Straffa argued the case that the *Abstract* was the work of Hume himself. Most scholars agree with their conclusion about the authorship of the *Abstract*. But not all. It has been challenged by John Nelson. See J. O. Nelson, "Has the Authorship of *An Abstract of A Treatise of Human Nature* Really Been Decided?" *Philosophical Quarterly* 26 (1976): 82–91, and "The Authorship of the *Abstract* Revisited," *Hume Studies* 17 (1991): 83–86. But, on the other hand, see D. Raynor, "The Authorship of the *Abstract* Revisited," and D. F. Norton, "More Evidence that Hume wrote the *Abstract*," *Hume Studies* 19 (1993): 213–15 and 217–22. The *Abstract* is included in the Selby-Bigge and Nidditch edition of the *Treatise*, 643–62. I will refer to it in this book on several occasions, with the understanding that its authorship has not been established beyond question; it probably was, but *may not* have been, written by Hume.

26. *Treatise*, 272. Italics added. The same claim is repeated in the *Abstract*. "This treatise therefore of human nature seems intended for a system of the sciences" (646).

CHAPTER 1: INFLUENCES AND INTENTIONS

1. D. Hume, *My Own Life*, reprinted in Mossner, *Life of David Hume*, 611.

2. See Introduction, section 4.

3. D. Hume, "Letter to a Physician," in *Letters of David Hume*, ed. Grieg, 1:16. According to Hume's biographer this period of independent reading, writing, and study covered a total of five years, from 1729 to 1734. However, Hume may have begun his concentration on philosophy only around 1731. See Mossner, *Life of David Hume*, chap. 6.

4. Hume, *My Own Life*, in Mossner, *Life of David Hume*, 611. Arnoldus Vinnius (1588–1657) and Johannes Voet (1647–1713), whose writings Hume neglected in order to "devour" Cicero and Virgil, were both influential professors of law at the University of Leyden, scholars whose works were widely used as textbooks in Scotland during the early eighteenth century. For further information about Vinnius and Voet see R. Feenstra and C. J. D. Waal, *Seventeenth-Century Leyden Law Professors and Their Influence on the Development of the Civil Law* (Amsterdam: North-Holland, 1975), esp. chap. 1 and chap. 3, section 2.

5. For these memoranda and Mossner's commentary on them see E. C. Mossner, "Hume's Early Memoranda, 1729–1740: The Complete Text," *Journal of the History of Ideas* 9 (1948): 492–518.

6. Mossner, *Life of David Hume*, 78.

7. See [D. Hume], *A Letter from a Gentleman to his friend in Edinburgh*, ed. E. C. Mossner and J. V. Price (Edinburgh: For the University Press, 1967).

8. A copy of Hume's letter, which is dated "Orleans, August 31, 1737," can be found in R. H. Popkin, "So Hume Did Read Berkeley," *Journal of Philosophy* 61 (1964): 773–78.

9. Hume matriculated at the University of Edinburgh on 27 February 1723, just over a month before his twelfth birthday. He remained there for upwards of three years, leaving in either 1725 or 1726 (the exact date is unknown), without earning a degree (a common practice of the time). It is clear from the age of its students and the subjects taught that the institution was closer to what a later era would call a secondary school than to a university.

10. Norman Kemp Smith offers an apt appraisal both of Hume's dependence on his predecessors and of his independence from them. "A chief reason why it is so difficult to be certain as to the precise influences that determined Hume's development . . . is the independence which he adopts in relation to each and every one of them, and his consequent departures from this and that influence, under the very impetus given by it." Smith, *Philosophy of David Hume*, 43. For excellent accounts of the wide and varied roster of earlier writers to whom Hume turned for ideas, arguments, and illustrations the reader can consult Laird, *Hume's Philosophy of Human Nature;* D. F. Norton, *David Hume: Common-Sense Moralist, Sceptical Metaphysician* (Princeton: Princeton University Press, 1982); and J. P. Wright, *The Sceptical Realism of David Hume* (Minneapolis: University of Minnesota Press, 1983).

11. *Treatise*, 17. The "discovery" to which Hume refers is Berkeley's explanation of general ideas.

12. See *Treatise,* 2 n. 1.

13. J. Locke, *An Essay Concerning Human Understanding,* ed. A. C. Fraser (Oxford: Clarendon Press, 1894), 1:121–22.

14. G. Berkeley, *A Treatise concerning the Principles of Human Knowledge,* in *The Works of George Berkeley Bishop of Cloyne,* ed. A. A. Luce and T. E. Jessop (London: Nelson, 1949), 2:41.

15. *Treatise,* 4. In a footnote Hume explains his use of the terms "impressions" and "ideas." See *Treatise,* 2 n. 1.

16. Several years ago the historian of philosophy Richard Popkin questioned Hume's indebtedness to Berkeley, writing: "It is, I believe, highly questionable whether Hume ever read Berkeley, or derived any views from him." R. H. Popkin, "Review of G. Boas, *Dominant Themes of Modern Philosophy: A History,*" *Journal of Philosophy* 56 (1959): 71. This statement generated a long controversy among scholars, some of whom cited Hume's references to Berkeley in the *Treatise* and elsewhere. These left Popkin unmoved, however, and he was convinced he was in error only after being confronted with the passage from Hume's letter to Michael Ramsay that I quoted earlier in this chapter. See Popkin, "So Hume Did Read Berkeley," 773–78. On this topic see M. Morrisoe, "Did Hume Read Berkeley? A Conclusive Answer," *Philological Quarterly* 52 (1973): 310–15. I will discuss Hume's relationship to Berkeley later, particularly in chapters 2, 5, 15, and 16.

17. See *Treatise,* 638–39. The appendix item is described by Hume as a note to page 64, where the discussion concerns the question of our possible knowledge of an external world.

18. A full account of Hume's student days at the University of Edinburgh can be found in Mossner, *Life of David Hume,* chap. 4. See particularly 38–43.

19. I. Newton, *Philosophiae Naturalis Principia Mathematica,* 2d ed., ed. R. Cotes (Cambridge, 1713); 3d ed., ed. H. Pemberton (1728); *Mathematical Principles of Natural Philosophy,* tr. A. Motte (1729).

20. See *Treatise,* xvi–xvii. Hume is, of course, not historically correct in crediting Bacon with introducing the experimental method into the natural sciences in the modern world; this had happened well before his time.

21. Newton, *Philosophiae Naturalis Principia Mathematica,* "Scholium Generale."

22. Although Newton renounced speculative or nonempirical hypotheses in his scientific work, he did not eliminate them. In particular, he believed it necessary to appeal to the activities of God in order to give a complete explanation of nature. For a detailed and balanced account of Newton's ambivalent views on scientific hypotheses, and their relationship to Humean thought, I recommend J. Noxon, *Hume's Philosophical Development: A Study of His Methods* (Oxford: Clarendon Press, 1973).

23. I. Newton, *Opticks: or, a Treatise of the Reflections, Refractions, Inflections and Colours of Light,* 4th ed. (London: William Inrys, 1730), book 3, part 1, quest. 31.

24. Smith, *Philosophy of David Hume,* 41–42. Italics added.

25. *Treatise,* xvii.

26. Shaftesbury (Anthony Ashley Cooper, Third Earl of Shaftesbury) published his major work, *Characteristicks of Men, Manners, Opinions, Times* (which was a collection of earlier essays), in 1711.

27. Hume's side of the correspondence with Hutcheson on these matters can be found in *Letters of David Hume*, ed. Grieg, vol. 1, letters 13, 15, and 16.

28. Grieg, ed., *Letters of David Hume*, 1:58. For a detailed discussion of this incident, with a discussion of the reasons why Hutcheson might have opposed Hume's appointment at Edinburgh, see W. R. Scott, *Francis Hutcheson: His Life, Teaching and Position in the History of Philosophy* (Cambridge: Cambridge University Press, 1900), 126–30.

29. F. Hutcheson, *An Inquiry into the Original of Our Ideas of Beauty and Virtue*, 2d ed. (London, 1726), 135.

30. Evidence of Hume's fondness for the ancient moralists can be found in a letter to Hutcheson (Letter 13) in which he remarks: "Upon the whole, I desire to take my Catalogue of Virtues from *Cicero's Offices*, not from *The Whole Duty of Man*." Grieg, ed., *Letters of David Hume*, 1:34. (*The Whole Duty of Man*, stern in its moral demands, was published in 1659.) Further evidence on this point, as well as on Hume's indebtedness to Hutcheson, can be found in his letter of 1745 (see note 7, above). There he writes, "He [Hume] hath indeed denied the eternal Difference of Right and Wrong in the Sense in which *Clark* and *Woolaston* maintained them. . . . In this Opinion he concurs with all the antient Moralists, as well as with Mr. Hutchison." Hume, *A Letter from a Gentleman*, 30.

31. Grieg, ed., *Letters of David Hume*, 1:32. Unfortunately for the theory of Hutcheson's influence on Hume's ethics, the bulk of the letter consists of points on which Hume disagrees with his comments. However, in a letter he wrote to Hutcheson about six months later Hume says: "Since I saw you, I have been very busy in correcting & finishing that Discourse concerning Morals, which you perus'd; & I flatter myself, that the Alterations I have made have improv'd it very much both in point of Prudence & Philosophy." Grieg, ed., *Letters of David Hume*, 1:36. So perhaps Hutcheson did exert considerable influence on Hume's final formulation of Book III of the *Treatise*.

32. Few of the writings of the classical sceptics have survived—except in fragments—into modern times. An exception is the works of Sextus Empiricus (second–third centuries AD). Latin translations of Sextus began to appear in the sixteenth century and he was translated into both English and French during the seventeenth and early eighteenth centuries. These translations were probably available to Hume through the Advocates' Library in Edinburgh. Although he may well have read Sextus himself, Hume probably got most of his information about the classical sceptics indirectly, through the *Dictionaire Historique et Critique* of Pierre Bayle (which I will discuss in section 6).

33. Sextus Empiricus, *Outlines of Pyrrhonism*, tr. R. G. Bury, Loeb Classical Library (London: Heinemann, 1933), 7, 9.

34. *Treatise*, 183. Sextus, always wary of committing himself, is generally less positive in his statements of scepticism than Hume. In *Outlines of Pyrrhonism*, for example, he writes: "For the Sceptic, having set out to philosophize with the object of passing judgement on the sense-impressions and ascertaining which of them are true and which false, so as to attain quietude thereby, found himself involved in contradictions of equal weight, and being unable to decide between them suspended judgement" (19). Sextus would probably, on the basis of the statement from

Hume I have just reproduced, label him an Academic sceptic rather than a Pyrrhonist. See *Outlines of Pyrrhonism*, 3.

35. See Mossner, "Hume's Early Memoranda," nos. II:4–8, 10, 14, 16, 19, 21, 28–30, 32–34 (pages 500–502). In his introductory remarks to the memoranda, Mossner suggests that some of Hume's citations of Bayle may have come to him secondhand but adds that other memoranda, for which no citations are given, may well have come from Bayle as well.

36. See the quotation from Hume's letter, reproduced in section 1 of this chapter.

37. Bayle published his *Dictionaire Historique et Critique* in Rotterdam in 1697. It was translated into English in 1710. Thus it was available in both languages during Hume's early lifetime.

38. The three alternative theories are that space is (a) infinitely divisible, (b) mathematical points, (c) physical points. In both Bayle and Hume most of the discussion consists in the attempt to refute the theory of infinite divisibility. For comparisons between the two see particularly P. Bayle, *Dictionaire Philosophique et Critique*, 4th ed. (Amsterdam, 1730), vol. 4, Article "Zenon d' Elee," Note (G), 540 ff., and Hume, *Treatise*, 26–27, 39–40. However, almost the whole of Part II of the *Treatise* can be profitably compared with the article "Zenon"; the similarities between the two are unmistakable.

39. See Bayle, *Dictionaire*, vol. 4, Article "Zenon d' Elee," Note (I), 544 ff., especially 545, and Hume, *Treatise*, Part II, Section V, especially 54–55.

40. *Treatise*, 243, and Bayle, *Dictionaire*, vol. 4, Article "Spinoza," 253–71.

41. See Hume, *Treatise*, 244, and Bayle, *Dictionaire*, vol. 4, Article "Spinoza," Note (N), 260.

42. Bayle, *Dictionaire*, vol. 4, Article "Spinoza," 259.

43. The question might be raised whether Hume ever read Spinoza himself. Norman Kemp Smith, at least, thinks not, writing, "Hume had, it is evident, no knowledge of Spinoza's teaching, save what he derived from Bayle." Smith, *Philosophy of David Hume*, 325. It is not clear to me how Smith could be so positive on this point.

44. See Bayle, *Dictionaire*, vol. 3, Article "Pyrrhon," 731–36.

45. Ibid., Note (B), 733. The "learned theologian" is presumably Bayle himself.

46. A. Flew, *David Hume: Philosopher of Moral Science* (Oxford: Basil Blackwell, 1986), 2. For another account of Hume's indebtedness to Descartes, see Wright, *The Sceptical Realism of David Hume*, especially chap. 3.

47. *Treatise*, 158 n. 1. The note reads: "See Father *Malbranche*, Book vi. Part 2. chap. 3. and the illustrations upon it."

48. N. Malebranche, *Recherche de la Vérité*, in *Oeuvres Complètes*, ed. G. Rodis-Lewis (Paris: J. Vrin, 1963), 2:309.

49. Ibid., 314.

50. There are several other clues in Hume's discussions of causality that point to the influence of Malebranche. For example, both illustrate their views concerning the opacity of physical causes by using the same image—that of the collision of billiard balls. See Malebranche, *Recherche*, 2:313, and Hume, *Treatise*, 164. The billiard-ball example also forms the centerpiece of the discussion of causality in the *Abstract*.

51. See *Treatise,* 249 n. 1. Hume's citation actually reads, "As father *Malebranche* and other *Cartesians.*" The passages in which Malebranche presents his views on divine causality can be found in *Recherche,* book VI, part II, chap. 3. As he puts it, "All natural forces, thus, are nothing but the will of God, which is always efficacious" (2:314).

52. *Treatise,* 160. Hume offers a similar argument on page 248 as well as another objection to Malebranche's view of God as the sole causal power in the universe on the following page, where he argues that, if this be true, God must be responsible for the evil as well as the good actions of human beings.

53. Malebranche, *Recherche,* 2:315.

54. *Treatise,* 632. The quotation is taken from the appendix to the *Treatise,* in a note appended to page 161 of the text.

55. Following eighteenth-century usage, Hume made a distinction between "natural" philosophy and "moral" philosophy. The first was the study of the non-human world, a study a later age would label natural science, the second the study of humanity, which, besides disciplines within philosophy like ethics, includes what came later to be called social science.

56. See *Treatise,* xiii–xix. In the "Advertisement," which he inserted just before this Introduction, Hume writes, "*My design in the present work is sufficiently explain'd in the* introduction" (xii).

57. *Treatise,* xviii–xix. As we will see as we study Book I, Hume often follows the procedure he describes here. But not always. Frequently he makes himself the object of his experiments.

Part 1: Hume's Empiricist Epistemology

1. For some information on this historical point see H. Aarsleff, *From Locke to Saussure: Essays on the Study of Language and Intellectual History* (Minneapolis: University of Minnesota Press, 1982), 142 n. 23.

Chapter 2: The Elements of Hume's Philosophy

1. See *Treatise,* 4. I introduced the term "Empiricist Principle" in chapter 1, section 2. I will discuss the Principle in detail in section 3 of this chapter.

2. My designation of the section or sections from the *Treatise* with which I will be concerned in each of my own sections will not always be exact. Although I will be focusing my attention on the material in the section indicated, I will occasionally refer to other parts of Hume's writings (particularly Book I of the *Treatise*). When I do so, I will mark the fact in the text, by the insertion of a page number (if from the *Treatise*) or a note.

3. "Perception" is the word Hume uses to replace Locke's and Berkeley's word "idea." See chapter 1, section 2, and *Treatise,* 2 n. 1.

4. *Treatise,* 67. Hume reiterates his identification of thoughts with ideas in his later book *Enquiry Concerning Human Understanding,* where he writes: "Here therefore we may divide all the perceptions of the mind into two classes or species, which

are distinguished by their different degrees of force and vivacity. The less forcible and lively are commonly denominated *Thoughts* or *Ideas.*" D. Hume, *Enquiry Concerning Human Understanding and Concerning the Principles of Morals,* ed. L. A. Selby-Bigge, 3d ed. (Oxford: Clarendon Press, 1975), 18.

5. In my commentary I will use Hume's terms "inconceivable" and "unintelligible" in the way I have just described. In his *Enquiry Concerning Human Understanding* Hume makes this point in an explicit and forceful way, saying that words used in this way are meaningless. "When we entertain . . . any suspicion that a philosophical term is employed without any meaning or idea (as is but too frequent), we need but enquire, *from what impression is that supposed idea derived?* And if it be impossible to assign any, this will serve to confirm our suspicion." Hume, *Enquiry Concerning Human Understanding,* 22.

6. *Treatise,* 1–2. Two qualifications must be made to this distinction. The first concerns feelings like pleasure or pain, which, although they do not arise from the five senses, are nevertheless impressions. I will discuss the second in section 5.

7. Ibid., 4. Hume adds a complication to this account but it does not affect the view that simple ideas are exact copies of their correspondent impressions. I will discuss the complication in section 2.

8. See chapters 15 and 16.

9. Later in Part I (particularly in Sections IV and V), however, Hume uses the term "object" in a way that suggests that he is referring to physical objects. Whether his intention in these passages is actually to talk about physical objects is difficult to say. In any case readers can make the necessary adjustments, simply by remembering that Hume has earlier identified objects with perceptions.

10. The importance of the Empiricist Principle is emphasized in the *Abstract* as well, where it is characterized as "the first proposition [Hume] advances" (647).

11. *Treatise,* 4. In this preamble we have another statement of Hume's intentions in writing the *Treatise,* to add to those in the introduction.

12. Hume discusses this point in more detail later in Book I (Part III, Section V). I will review that passage in section 1 of chapter 8.

13. In the final paragraph on page 9 Hume suggests, with his example of the historian, that he means the same by "form" as he does by "order."

14. Hume speaks to this point in the appendix, in reference to a question raised later in Book I. He writes: "[The imagination] may set [ideas], in a manner, before our eyes in their true colours, just as they might have existed" (629).

15. Hume inserts a footnote in Section III (9) referring to "Part III. sect. 5," which indicates that he will return to a further examination of these topics later. Perhaps we will find that his later discussion will resolve the problems of his initial account of memory and imagination. In any case, I will comment on his views, as they appear in Part III, in sections 2–7 of chapter 8.

Chapter 3: First Fruits of the Empiricist Principle

1. Hume does not use the word "inconceivable" here but instead denies that the traditional notion of substance has any "meaning" for us (16). As he makes clear

in the paragraph, his reason for saying this is that there is no such idea as the "idea of substance." In other words, we have nothing before our minds when we utter or hear the word. For my discussion of this point see chapter 2, section 1.

2. Locke, *Essay*, 1:390–91.

3. G. Berkeley, *Three Dialogues between Hylas and Philonous*, in *The Works of George Berkeley*, ed. Luce and Jessop, 2:221.

4. Locke, *Essay*, 1:215.

5. Hume uses the terms "abstract" and "general" ideas synonymously (17). I will follow this usage.

6. *Treatise*, 17. The main statement of Berkeley's views on abstract and general ideas appears in the introduction to his *Principles of Human Knowledge* but another can be found in his *Alciphron*. See *The Works of George Berkeley*, ed. Luce and Jessop, 2:27–38 and 3:331–35. Berkeley disagrees with Hume on one point. Instead of identifying general ideas with abstract ideas, he distinguishes between the two, accepting the former but rejecting the latter. See *Works*, 2:31. From his admiring reference to Berkeley in the opening paragraph of Section VII, it is apparent that Hume was greatly impressed by his work. This is supported by his comment in his letter to Michael Ramsay in 1737. See chapter 1, section 1.

7. But see chapter 2, section 9.

8. In an appendix note to his discussion of the role of resemblance in his account of general ideas, Hume says that the requirement that resembling ideas must share some common circumstances does not apply to simple ideas (637). The appendix note is important because it raises questions about the possibility of our finding resemblances among simple ideas.

9. The same point can be made in another way. Why do just the figures Hume mentions—which are both triangles—"immediately crowd in upon us"? Why not figures like parallelograms or pentagons as well? The answer is clear. We recognize that the first are triangles and the second are not.

10. *Treatise*, 25. The "kind of reflexion" Hume describes in this statement must be distinguished from his impressions and ideas of reflection. The latter are emotions but it is an activity in which the mind draws distinctions between the different respects in which objects bear resemblances to each other.

Part 2: Space, Time, and Existence

1. Antony Flew, for example, has said: "Part II of Book I of the *Treatise* is by common consent the least satisfactory—perhaps it is also the least satisfactory in all Hume's publications. He himself when he came to compose the first *Enquiry* found little here fit for salvage." *David Hume*, 38.

2. The development of the calculus by Newton and Leibniz, working independently, generated probably the most famous, as well as acrimonious, dispute in the history of mathematics. Followers of the two great figures argued for years the question of which of them should be credited with this achievement, even drawing the principals themselves into the controversy. For an account of this important episode in the history of thought see A. R. Hall, *Philosophers at War:*

The Quarrel between Newton and Leibniz (Cambridge: Cambridge University Press, 1980).

3. See chapter 1, section 6.

CHAPTER 4: SPACE AND TIME AND THEIR IDEAS

1. See *Treatise*, 26. In his *Enquiry* Hume attacks the "geometricians and metaphysicians" even more harshly, writing: "No priestly *dogmas*, invented on purpose to tame and subdue the rebellious reason of mankind, ever shocked common sense more than the doctrine of the infinite divisibility of extension, with its consequences; as they are pompously displayed by all geometricians and metaphysicians, with a kind of triumph and exultation." Hume, *Enquiry Concerning Human Understanding*, 156.

2. See *Treatise*, 26–27. In fact, Hume devotes most of his effort to space, treating time in a relatively brief and cursory way.

3. *Treatise*, 28. Although Hume's remark is directed to a single kind of error, its importance lies in the fact that it recognizes that our senses can mislead us.

4. Ibid., 29. From the context of the remainder of the paragraph it seems apparent that the "objects" Hume is referring to in the sentence are external physical objects.

5. Later in Book I Hume seems by implication to repudiate such a view. See *Treatise*, 191–92.

6. See chapter 2, especially sections 1, 3, and 6.

7. See sections 9 and 10 of this chapter and also chapters 5, 15, and 16 for further discussions of this problem.

8. In a footnote (30 n. 1) Hume states an objection to his conclusion, to the effect that, although an infinite number of "*aliquot*" (constituent) parts of extension implies an infinite extension, an infinite number of "proportional" (interpretable as fractional) parts does not. He dismisses this distinction as "frivolous," arguing that, whatever we call the parts, none can be smaller than the smallest parts we can conceive.

9. *Treatise*, 30 n. 2. M. de Malezieu, a French mathematician, was tutor to the Duke of Burgundy, grandson of Louis XIV. He is the presumed author of *Elémens de Géométrie de Monseigneur le Duc de Bourgogne*, first published in 1705.

10. Hume adds a second brief argument against the infinite divisibility of time, to the effect that the nature of motion establishes that the infinite divisibility of space implies the infinite divisibility of time. Since the former is impossible so, too, must the latter be. He does not elaborate this argument. See *Treatise*, 31.

11. *Treatise*, 32. The term "mathematical points" Hume introduces here refers to the ultimate, indivisible parts of extension. I will discuss these "points" in detail in section 6.

12. Ibid., 33. Hume says we acquire the idea of extension from the sense of touch as well as that of sight. However, in his discussions he concentrates on visual impressions as the primary source of this idea. I will do the same. It might also be noted that in the passage I have reproduced Hume appears to identify objects with bodies.

13. Ibid., 34. Hume is here presumably reporting on a simple experiment he has conducted. Any reader can conduct a similar experiment, just by looking at a table. Would his senses convey to him what Hume found?

14. Ibid., 20. For my discussion of Hume's theory of abstract ideas see chapter 3, sections 3 and 4.

15. Ibid., 35. Because succession is an essential ingredient in the generation of the idea of time, the parts (or moments) of which this idea is composed cannot, Hume points out, be coexistent. Such coexistent parts characterize our idea of space, distinguishing it from that of time. See *Treatise*, 36.

16. The same problem I raised in the previous section about space as an abstract idea applies to time as well. To have an abstract idea of time we must have ordinary ideas of individual "times." But these, Hume says, we do not have.

17. Another requirement, which Hume does not mention in this context, is memory. If I am to be able to count the successive flute notes and conclude that I have heard five, I must be able to hold the first four in my memory until I hear the fifth. The place of memory in our thinking is an important issue that I will discuss in detail in chapter 8.

18. Hume talks also of the "solidity" of the mathematical points. This results from his view that the idea of extension comes to us through touch as well as sight. As I pointed out in chapter 1, section 6, much of this argument is derived from Bayle, except for Hume's last, positive assertion about mathematical points.

19. See *Treatise*, 43. Hume's argument is a non sequitur. When he says that anything we can conceive of must be possible, all he is justified in concluding (as he himself acknowledges) is that the thing does not involve a contradiction. It does not at all follow that it can exist "in nature."

20. In a footnote Hume attributes this argument to *L'Art de Penser*. See *Treatise*, 43 n. 1. He is referring to a book bearing the title *La Logique ou L'Art de Penser*, by Antoine Arnauld and Pierre Nicole, first published in Paris in 1662. This book has come to be known as the *Port Royal Logic*, after the Jansenist abbey with which its authors were associated.

21. The implication of Hume's account of space—that it does not exist in external reality—seems to have a further important consequence. If external material objects must occupy space there can be no such entities. Hume addresses this issue at some length in Part IV. For my discussion see chapters 15 and 16.

22. Isaac Barrow (1630–77) was a noted mathematician at Cambridge University and the teacher of Isaac Newton.

23. In an appendix note Hume adds that we neither have nor need a definition of equality. See *Treatise*, 637.

24. Hume apparently later changed his views on geometry. See *Enquiry Concerning Human Understanding*, 25.

25. The same conclusion follows if we appeal to the sensation of touch or feeling; we cannot generate a positive idea of a vacuum from the deprivation of tactile sensations. Throughout Section V Hume appeals to touch as well as to sight in his arguments and illustrations. I will limit myself to the latter; the necessary transfers can easily be made.

26. *Treatise*, 59. Hume adds that the fictitious idea of distance not only resem-

bles the real idea of filled distance but that, when fictitious distance is converted into filled distance, it is its cause. "As the first species of distance is found to be convertible into the second, 'tis in this respect a kind of cause" (62).

27. It is interesting to note that earlier in Part II, in connection with the question of whether we have an idea of extension, Hume writes: "Now 'tis certain we have an idea of extension; for otherwise why do we talk and reason concerning it?" (32).

28. *Treatise,* 64. In a note in the appendix added to this passage (638–39), as well as in an ambivalent statement in the text itself (64), Hume betrays an indecision over the question of whether there really is empty space. In the appendix he seems to be leaning in the direction of accepting its existence. "If it be ask'd, whether or not the invisible and intangible distance be always full of *body,* or of something that by an improvement of our organs might become visible or tangible, I must acknowledge, that I find no very decisive arguments on either side; tho' I am inclin'd to the contrary opinion" (639). He concludes the note with his only reference to Newtonian science in the *Treatise,* admonishing scientists not to pursue questions like that of the existence of empty space, because the understanding of such matters exceeds "all human capacity" (639).

29. Ibid. Italics added. Hume concludes this passage by saying that his philosophy explains the causes of our impressions and ideas. But in Section II of Part I he had written "[Impressions of sensation arise] in the soul originally, from unknown causes" (7). I will have more to say on this subject in section 1 of chapter 8.

30. C. D. Broad, "Hume's Doctrine of Space," *Proceedings of the British Academy* 47 (1961): 176.

31. Noxon, *Hume's Philosophical Development,* 115.

Chapter 5: Existence and External Existence

1. *Treatise,* 66. Hume adds a paragraph to his discussion here (67) in which he points out that his argument about the distinction of ideas without any real difference (which appears in Part I, Section VII) is not relevant to the issue under consideration in this section. My discussion of the section to which he refers appears in section 5 of chapter 3.

2. That this, despite the vagueness of his language, is Hume's intention is evidenced by the fact that in the second paragraph of the section (66) he writes as though the words "perception" and "object" are synonymous.

3. If we understand the word "occasion" to mean the same as "cause," which seems reasonable, Hume is here reaffirming the view he stated on page 64 about the cause of our perceptions and repudiating the view he stated on page 7. But this is not his final word on the matter. He returns to the issue in Section V of Part III. For my discussion see chapter 8, section 1.

4. H. A. Prichard, *Knowledge and Perception* (Oxford: Clarendon Press, 1950), 196. Italics added.

5. At the end of Section VI Hume writes "But of this more fully hereafter" and adds a footnote, "Part IV. sect. 2" (68). But this reference apparently is only to the fact that he will return to the general problem of our possible knowledge of an

external world in that later section. I find nothing in Part IV, Section II, that directly addresses the question of whether external objects are specifically different from or specifically like perceptions, let alone a definition of the phrase itself. However, it does contain at least one statement that, although it does not use the "specifically different" terminology, addresses the same issue. See the next note. Also, in Section V of Part IV Hume returns to the question of "specifically different" and possible knowledge. See n. 10, below.

6. *Treatise*, 216. Italics added. The clause with which Hume begins this passage, "we suppose external objects to resemble internal impressions," merits comment, partly because it repeats a statement he makes on page 68: "Generally speaking we do not suppose [perceptions and external objects] specifically different." Both of these are statements about human psychology, describing the way in which the imagination works. The word "suppose" is a rough equivalent to the words "presume" or "believe." In his discussions in the latter part of Book I, Hume makes it clear that when we "suppose" something we have no rational grounds for our supposition.

7. It is hard to determine what Hume's intention in his use of this distinction was. He simply does not give us enough information to allow us to make a definite judgment. Perhaps he was attempting to justify his conclusion that, although we ordinarily "suppose" external objects to be specifically identical to our perceptions—our perception "tree," we believe, exactly resembles the tree in the meadow—we are mistaken in this supposition. See the previous note.

8. *Treatise*, 68. Hume does not mention the possible conceivability of external objects specifically identical to our perceptions, supposing any such objects to exist; but, since, as we have already seen, we cannot in principle determine into which of the classes any object would fall, the distinction has no point.

9. Ibid., 241. Italics added. This statement is excerpted from a longer passage in which Hume raises the question of whether we can know if the relations among our impressions are applicable to external objects. His view is that we cannot know this if we start from our impressions because we have no way of knowing that the objects resemble the impressions. However, if we start from the objects we can make the comparison because, as he says, "the quality of the object, upon which the argument is founded, must at least be conceiv'd by the mind; and cou'd not be conceiv'd, unless it were common to an impression" (242). This is, of course, just a cumbersome (and slightly misleading) way of making the same point I made earlier in this section—that we cannot compare perceptions with external objects but only with other perceptions.

10. There is an additional problem in Hume's account of the nature of relative ideas. It assumes that we can have ideas of relations themselves. But this assumption is dubious. I have spoken to the point earlier, in chapter 2, section 9.

11. In the passage from Section V of Part IV that I have reproduced (*Treatise*, 241), Hume gives an alternative to our conceiving an external object as "a relation without a relative." That is "to make it the very same with a perception or impression." This, of course, makes it internal to the mind, rather than external: "All impressions are internal and perishing existences" (194).

12. Why Hume introduced his remark about a relative idea of external objects

is puzzling. I suggest that he was simply being deferential here to Locke, who had written of our "relative idea of [material] *substance in general.*" Locke, *Essay,* 1:392.

13. *Treatise,* 188. Hume adds a footnote to this statement, referring the reader to "Part II. sect. 6." Hume's statements and my commentary on them in this chapter make it clear that, since he cannot support a distinction between objects specifically different from and objects specifically identical to perceptions and since both categories of objects are, in any event, inconceivable, the insertion of the phrase "when taken for something specifically different from our perceptions" adds nothing to this statement. Therefore, Hume is implying that he has shown in Section VI that the notion of an externally existing object is absurd.

CHAPTER 6: KNOWLEDGE AND PROBABILITY

1. See *Treatise,* 13–15. In that early section Hume had distinguished between *natural* relations and *philosophical* relations, adding that, of the seven philosophical relations, three—resemblance, contiguity (which is a subspecies falling under relations of time and place), and causation—are natural relations as well. For my discussion of Hume's original analysis of relations see chapter 2, section 9.

2. See *Treatise,* 70. However, later in Part III Hume uses the word "objects" in such a way that its meaning is ambiguous. See, for example, the statement on page 73 to which note 3 refers. Sometimes it seems apparent from the context that Hume is referring to material objects in an external world. But we now know that he should not mean that because he has concluded in Section VI of Part II that such objects are inconceivable. In any event it is usually possible to read him as meaning by "object" simply "perception." For the sake of clarity, I will use his terminology with the understanding that, unless I stipulate differently, by "object" I mean "perception."

3. *Treatise,* 73. *All* reasoning, of course, includes that, leading both to knowledge and to probability.

4. See chapter 2, section 9.

5. See, for example, Part I, Section IV. For my discussion see chapter 2, section 8.

6. In Part II Hume makes a similar statement about the ability of the mind to intuit relations. "'Tis evident, that the eye, *or rather the mind* is often able at one view to determine the proportions of bodies, and pronounce them equal to, or greater or less than each other." *Treatise,* 47. Italics added.

7. For Hume's earlier account of the nature of geometry see Part II, especially pages 44, 50–53. For my comments on his views see chapter 4, section 7.

8. *Treatise,* 71. Italics added. It might be noted, in passing, that Hume does not include logic in his list of disciplines here. He gives no reason for not including it but simply passes it by without recognition.

9. The most famous defender of this conception of knowledge in the history of modern philosophy is, of course, Descartes.

10. In the first sentence of Section II Hume describes the four relations he discussed in the previous section as the "foundation of science" (73). In this context we should take the term "science" to be equivalent to "knowledge" rather than to "empirical science."

CHAPTER 7: THE RELATIONS OF CAUSATION

1. Hume does not introduce this example explicitly in Section II (but see 76–77); however he does so later in Part III. See *Treatise*, 164. See also *Abstract*, 649.

2. *Treatise*, 75. In talking of "distant objects" here Hume seems clearly to be referring to material bodies in an external world, as he does throughout much of Part III. On this point see my remarks in chapter 6, particularly n. 2.

3. Ibid., 76. Hume is somewhat diffident about this argument but does not give any reasons for his hesitancy, simply adding that "the affair is of no great importance" (76).

4. Ibid., 77. In the final clause of this statement Hume raises the possibility that, to account for our idea of necessary connection, it may be necessary to give up the Empiricist Principle. To anticipate his later discussion, it is safe to say that he believes a way can be found to resolve the issue without resorting to such a drastic expedient.

5. It might be noted, however, that in a third reference to memory, in the middle of the paragraph, Hume refers to it neutrally, as a "perception" (83).

6. Whether we have an impression of the relation of contiguity, it seems safe to say that Hume is mistaken in his claim that we have one of the relation of succession.

CHAPTER 8: HUME'S REVISED THEORY OF MEMORY

1. Hume's discussion of the second thing appears mainly in Section VI of Part III and of the third in Section XIV. See my chapters 9 and 12.

2. See *Treatise*, 64, 67. For my discussions of these opposed views see chapter 2, section 6; chapter 4, section 10; and chapter 5, section 2.

3. See chapter 6, section 1.

4. On the page following the passage I have reproduced, Hume complicates the situation further. Speaking of the impressions of pain and pleasure, he writes: "Bodily pains and pleasures . . . arise originally in the soul, or in the body, *whichever you please to call it*, without any preceding thought or perception" (276—italics added). This statement is, to say the least, puzzling. Does Hume reduce the soul to the body or the body to the soul? Is he, in other words, embracing materialism or idealism? Or does he reduce neither one to the other but simply identify the two, thus embracing neutral monism? I will not pursue this intriguing metaphysical speculation further because the passage is not part of Hume's argument in Book I.

5. I will discuss it in chapter 17.

6. *Treatise*, 79. I have discussed Hume's argument in chapter 7, section 2.

7. See chapter 2, section 6.

8. See *Treatise*, 8–10. I have discussed Hume's original theory of memory in detail in chapter 2, section 7.

9. *Treatise*, 85 (second and fifth italics added). Hume adds an appendix note to this paragraph. I will discuss it in section 3.

10. This statement, it should be noted, is a denial of what Hume said in his original account of memory and imagination in Part I, where he wrote that "the

imagination is not restrain'd to the same order and form with the original impressions; while the memory is in a manner ty'd down in that respect, without any power of variation." *Treatise*, 9.

11. Later in Book I Hume refers to the liar again, confirming the conclusion he had reached in Section V. "Liars, by the frequent repetition of their lies, *come at last to remember them*" (117—italics added).

12. For comparison the original Empiricist Principle reads, "*All our simple ideas in their first appearance are deriv'd from simple impressions, which are correspondent to them, and which they exactly represent*" (4).

13. Hume concludes Section V with a paragraph in which, besides reiterating his revised theory of memory, he introduces a new concept—belief. The points he makes are somewhat obscure, mainly because, at this stage of Book I, he has not yet explained what he means by belief. But he will do so later in Part III, particularly in Sections VII–X. I will devote chapter 10 to these sections.

Chapter 9: Constant Conjunction and Mental Causation

1. See *Treatise*, 78, and my chapter 7, section 1.

2. *Treatise*, 87. To "call to mind" the past is clearly another way of saying "recollect" the past. I think all Hume commentators would agree with me here. At least I have found none who tries to explicate Hume's argument about constant conjunction in terms of his revised theory of memory.

3. Hume writes in Section VI: "Thus in advancing we have insensibly discover'd a new relation betwixt cause and effect. . . . This relation is their CONSTANT CONJUNCTION. Contiguity and succession are not sufficient to make us pronounce any two objects to be cause and effect, unless we perceive, that these two relations are preserv'd in several instances" (87).

4. For an explanation and defense of this statement see *Treatise*, 85, and my chapter 8, especially section 6.

5. See chapter 7, section 4.

6. In Part III, Section I, Hume limited discursive knowledge to demonstration. I have commented on his view in chapter 6, section 1.

7. This is the same distinction Hume made in Section I of Part III. I have discussed it in chapter 6, particularly in the introduction.

8. I have discussed this theory in section 8 of chapter 2, noting that there is a gap in Hume's explanation of the causal relation between the natural relations of ideas and the uniting activity of the imagination.

9. *Treatise*, 94. Hume adds, however, that it is only because causation is also a natural relation that produces a union of ideas in the imagination that "we are able to reason upon it, or draw any inference from it" (94). Hume devotes a paragraph on the previous page to an interesting but subsidiary point, noting that, because we have associated words with objects (e.g., "flame" with flame), the mere hearing of a word will cause us to make a transition to its related idea ("flame" to heat), without our needing to reflect on the original idea itself. "The imagination . . . is so accustom'd to pass from the word to the idea, that it interposes not a moment's delay betwixt the hearing of the one, and the conception of the other" (93).

Chapter 10: Belief

1. *Treatise*, 107. He does, however, qualify this claim in several ways, some quite important. I will discuss his qualifications later.

2. Ibid., 94. Hume had made the same point earlier in the *Treatise*, in Section VI of Part II. For my discussion of that passage see chapter 5, section 1.

3. See *Treatise*, 95–96. Hume makes it plain that his argument does not apply to beliefs based on "intuition or demonstration" (95) but only those resulting from causal "reasonings" about "matters of fact." The phrase "matters of fact" might be misleading here. Hume equates it with "the existence of objects or of their qualities" (94). In our ordinary thinking this would be the equivalent of saying that matters of fact refer to objects in the external world. But we now know that Hume cannot mean that because such objects are inconceivable. A bit later in his discussion he makes it clear that he is using the word "object" as a synonym for "impression" (96).

4. See *Treatise*, 96. Hume modifies his account of belief in three appendix notes, two of considerable length, added to Section VII. I will discuss these appendix modifications in section 2.

5. *Treatise*, 119–20. Later Hume writes, "A strong propensity or inclination alone, without any present impression, will sometimes cause a belief" (210).

6. Barry Stroud offers a somewhat different commentary on this passage from the one I have given here. See his book *Hume* (London: Routledge and Kegan Paul, 1977), 71–72.

7. See *Treatise*, 97 n. 1. The footnote also contains a misstatement. Speaking of conception, judgment, and reasoning, Hume writes of "what we may in general affirm concerning these three acts of understanding." Setting aside algebra and arithmetic, the action of the mind when we make "judgments" or engage in "reasoning," Hume had concluded in Section VI, is *not* a function of the understanding but of the imagination. Thus it is not a rational process. I think we must conclude that Hume is using the term "understanding" in a wider and looser sense than he had earlier in his argument. Hume also, late in the note, reduces both judgment and reasoning to conception. But in explaining why he does so, he contradicts statements he has made earlier in the note, as well as in the text. It is difficult to understand why he does this; a possible reason is his realization that we have no ideas of relations.

8. In this section I will discuss the first two of these appendix notes, which are relatively long and make several substantive points. The third note consists in a general statement, in which Hume explains why the other two notes are appropriate additions to the text.

9. *Treatise*, 626–27. The concluding phrase of the statement, "without producing any distinct impression," rules out the two suggestions Hume had offered, for to have an idea of existence one would have to have an impression of existence and to have an idea of reflection one would have to have an impression of reflection.

10. Although the concepts I have listed in (2) and (3) do not form part of Hume's *definition* of belief in Section VII, they all appear in the text there. See page 97 and page 97 n. 1. So he has not added substantively to his view about the

"feel" of a belief in this note. In the *Abstract* the terms used to describe the special feeling of belief are approximately the same (654).

11. *Treatise,* 629. One might ask whether the adjectives Hume uses to characterize belief succeed in distinguishing belief states from other states of mind. Could we not, for example, use the same adjectives to describe states of disbelief or "incredulity" (95)? Also, would these adjectives not be appropriate descriptions of memories as well?

12. Ibid., 636. The first error to which Hume alludes in this passage occurs on page 58 and concerns our knowledge of the distance between two bodies.

13. Ibid., 108. I will discuss this passage further in section 7.

14. Ibid., 92. Italics added. See also page 97.

15. Hume's only acknowledgment of the epistemological component in the concept of belief in Section VII appears in the long footnote I discussed earlier. He writes that "the only remarkable difference, which occurs on this occasion, is, when we join belief to the conception, and are perswaded of the truth of what we conceive" (97 n. 1).

16. Hume adds an appendix note to this example (*Treatise,* 630) consisting of an excerpt from Cicero's *De Finibus,* in which the author describes a walk through the gardens of the Academy, during which a friend notes that his emotions are more aroused by his being in the place where Plato and other famous figures once taught than by his hearing of their deeds or reading their works.

17. See chapter 9, section 5.

18. *Treatise,* 102. See also pages 103–4.

19. For example, this is one of the main points Hume makes in the introduction to the *Treatise.*

20. *Treatise,* 104. Hume uses this point to reinforce his denial that our belief that instances of things of which we have no experience must resemble those of which we have is based on reasoning, on the grounds that, if such a view were true, we could not make the immediate "inferences," without any process of reasoning, that we do in the river example.

21. Ibid., 108. It is important to note that Hume is careful in his language here. He does not refer to either system as a reality.

22. Ibid., 115. By "the gunpowder treason" Hume is presumably referring to the attempt of Guy Fawkes, a Catholic, to blow up Parliament on November 5, 1605. The massacre of St. Bartholomew was perpetrated by the French Catholic nobility against the Huguenots in Paris on August 24, 1572.

23. Although Hume does not use the word "judgment" in the note, he does elsewhere, to refer to our probable "reasonings." Since his use of the word is different from the normal one it can be considered a technical term of his philosophy. To make clear that he is not using it to describe an activity of reason, I will put "judgment" in quotation marks, as I have "inference" and probable "reasoning."

24. However, in the appendix note Hume dismisses the effects of poetry on belief, in relation to those of experience. He writes: "Whatever emotion the poetical enthusiasm may give to the spirits, 'tis still the mere phantom of belief or persuasion" (630). Going on, he writes: "Where the vivacity [of an idea] arises from a customary conjunction with a present impression; tho' the imagination may not,

in appearance, be so much mov'd; yet there is always something more forcible and real in its actions, than in the fervors of poetry and eloquence" (631).

25. *Treatise*, 123. Italics added. A similar denigration of poetry, as opposed to history, appears in the appendix note. "A poetical description may have a more sensible effect on the fancy, than an historical narration. . . . It may seem to set the object before us in more lively colours. But still the ideas it presents are different to the *feeling* from those, which arise from the memory and the judgment. There is something weak and imperfect amidst all that seeming vehemence of thought and sentiment, which attends the fictions of poetry" (631).

Chapter 11: Probability

1. D. G. C. Macnabb, ed., *A Treatise of Human Nature, Book I* (Cleveland: The World Publishing Company, 1962), 177 n. 21. D. C. Stove, however, is less impressed with Hume's achievement. See his *Probability and Hume's Inductive Scepticism* (Oxford: Clarendon Press, 1973), 127.

2. Hume discusses causal determinism, in relation to the possibility of free will, at some length later in the *Treatise*. See Book II, Part III, Sections I and II.

3. *Treatise*, 146. In the course of his discussion of our beliefs about history Hume notes that there is "one very memorable exception" to the view that our beliefs diminish as chains of testimony on which they are based lengthen and adds a footnote reference to "Part IV. sect. 1" (146). He footnotes this same section later in Section XIII on a related point (153 n. 1). I will discuss this point in chapter 14.

4. For my discussion of this argument see chapter 10, section 9.

5. It is also plagued by several confusions resulting mainly from Hume's inaccurate usage of his main concepts, like "reason," "understanding," "judgment," and "general rules."

6. Just before giving his iron cage illustration Hume writes: "In almost all kinds of causes there is a complication of circumstances, of which some are essential, and others superfluous; some are absolutely requisite to the production of the effect, and others are only conjoin'd by accident" (148).

7. See Part III, Section VI.

8. See *Treatise*, 117–18 n. 1. Since all "reasoning" about matters of fact is the work of the imagination, so too is "judgment." Completing his general summary of his account of probable "reasoning" at the end of Section XIII (153–55) Hume concludes: "Without considering these *judgments* as the effects of custom on the imagination, we shall lose ourselves in perpetual contradiction and absurdity" (155—italics added). The distinction Hume is making on page 149 between "judgment" and "imagination" is, as he makes clear, a distinction *within* the imagination. It is the same as the "inaccurate" distinction between imagination and probable "reasoning" he described in his footnote on pages 117–18. I have discussed this point earlier. See chapter 10, section 8, including note 23.

9. Hume concludes the section with a long discussion of the effects of open and concealed language and action on social relationships; though interesting, the discussion does not contribute anything of significance to his philosophy.

CHAPTER 12: NECESSARY CONNECTION

1. For a detailed analysis of Hume's theory of causation and a closely reasoned defense of a theory based on it I recommend T. L. Beauchamp and A. Rosenberg, *Hume and the Problem of Causation* (New York: Oxford University Press, 1981). For an imaginative reconstruction of Hume's views on causation see G. Strawson, *The Secret Connexion: Causation, Realism, and David Hume* (Oxford: Clarendon Press, 1989).

2. J. L. Mackie, *The Cement of the Universe: A Study of Causation* (Oxford: Clarendon Press, 1974), 3.

3. See *Treatise*, 87–88.

4. Hume had already offered criticisms of some of these views, in Section III. See *Treatise*, 80–82.

5. In a footnote Hume writes "See Mr. *Locke;* chapter of power" (157 n. 1). The reference is to Locke, *Essay*, book 2, chap. 21.

6. In a footnote (*Treatise*, 158 n. 1) Hume acknowledges his debt to Malebranche, who had criticized such views, using language much like that of Hume. For quotations from Malebranche on this point, see chapter 1, section 7.

7. Hume does not mention Malebranche by name in his argument, referring simply to "the *Cartesians*" (159), but the view in question was one Malebranche held. See chapter 1, section 7.

8. *Treatise*, 160. Hume makes no mention of an obvious further point—that we have no impression of God, let alone of his causal power. He ends his statement with a verbal concession to religion that can hardly represent his true opinion.

9. Ibid., 633. Hume adds a footnote to this appendix note, including another concession to religion. Here, however, he imbeds in his (questionable?) piety an attempt to explain God's "power" in terms of his own theory. Hume presents a longer and more detailed criticism of the will-power theory of causation in his *Enquiry*, including a number of counterexamples. See Hume, *Enquiry Concerning Human Understanding*, 64–69. The criticism is also repeated in the *Abstract*. See 655–56.

10. *Treatise*, 161. For Hume's account of abstract ideas see Part I, Section VII. I have commented on this theory in chapter 3, sections 3–4. Throughout his argument in Section XIV Hume uses the terms "power," "efficacy," "necessity," and "necessary connection" interchangeably.

11. Ibid., 8. His theory of causation is the only place, but an important one, in which Hume makes a theoretical use of impressions of reflection in Book I.

12. It is hardly necessary to note that "cause" and "effect" are technical terms of Hume's philosophy.

13. *Treatise*, 128. Italics added. The word "produc'd" is equivalent to "caused." "The idea of *production* is the same with that of *causation*" (90).

14. For my discussion of mental causation see chapter 9, section 5.

15. *Treatise*, 128. Italics added. See note 13, above.

16. In a similar statement a bit earlier in the section Hume implies that the notion of "objective" mental causation is unintelligible. "The uniting principle among our internal perceptions is as unintelligible as that among external objects, and is not known to us any other way than by experience" (169).

17. See chapter 8, sections 6 and 7, and chapter 9, section 3.

18. For an explanation of what is involved in the recollection of the past see *Treatise,* 85 and chapter 8, especially section 6.

19. See chapter 9, section 3.

20. Although Hume does not mention the point here, people also believe in other forms of "objective" causation—body to mind, mind to body, and mind to mind.

21. *Treatise,* 168. Yet it should be mentioned that Hume does occasionally talk about the operation of causes in the external world, although he almost always adds that such causes are unknown to us. A good example of his ambivalence on this point can be found on page 64.

22. For Hume's definitions of philosophical and natural relations see *Treatise,* 13–14.

23. See, for example, J. A. Robinson, "Hume's Two Definitions of 'Cause,'" *The Philosophical Quarterly* 12 (1962): 162–71.

24. T. Penelhum, *Hume* (London: Macmillan, 1975), 55. David Pears expresses the same opinion. See his *Hume's System,* 118–19.

25. Wright, *The Sceptical Realism of David Hume,* 25.

26. Stroud, *Hume,* 92.

27. For a short but incisive review of problems raised by Hume's definitions of "cause" see Mackie, *The Cement of the Universe,* 3–5.

28. Later in Book I Hume implies that it is impossible for causal connections to exist in the external material world. See *Treatise,* 223.

29. *Treatise,* 10. On page 92 Hume gives further support to the view that our minds are not rigidly determined to make transitions from causes to effects.

30. Ibid., 110. But on page 128 he softens this by saying that "the mind is determin'd by custom to pass from any cause to its effect, and . . . upon the appearance of the one, 'tis *almost impossible* for it not to form an idea of the other." Italics added.

CHAPTER 13: CAUSAL RULES AND ANIMAL "REASON"

1. Hume inserts two other short sections on animals into the *Treatise.* Both appear in Book II and are devoted to the feelings or emotions animals experience. See *Treatise,* 324–28 and 397–98.

2. However, it should be noted that Hume cannot mean "external material object" because he has long since concluded that such "things" are unintelligible so it would be impossible for him to talk meaningfully about their causal relations.

3. At one point earlier in the *Treatise* Hume referred to the vagaries of human psychology, in connection with the causal "inferences" we make. He wrote that "the thought has evidently a very irregular motion in running along its objects, and may leap from the heavens to the earth, from one end of the creation to the other, without any certain method or order" (92). In other words, any thing may produce (or cause) any thing.

4. The point in Hume's theory of causation that the second interpretation emphasizes is that the necessary connection the theory requires is not quite *neces-*

sary. The transition of the mind, with our anticipation of an effect when we observe a cause, is, as he says at the beginning of Book I, only "a gentle force, which commonly prevails" (10). See the previous note.

5. Hume's statement, in Rule 3, that the "constant union" of cause and effect "chiefly . . . constitutes the [causal] relation" (173) is not quite accurate. What chiefly constitutes the causal relation is necessary connection, which is a feeling of anticipation in an observer's mind, itself an effect of constant conjunction.

6. This question, of course, refers to the problem of induction. See *Treatise*, 89.

7. My third question raises a deeper issue about Hume's rules. To uncover this issue we can ask: Why does he call them *rules?* His language indicates that he has shifted from a descriptive account of our causal "inferences" to a normative account of what these "inferences" ought to be. This conclusion is supported by a statement he makes about the rules earlier in Part III. "We shall afterwards take notice of some general rules, by which we ought to regulate our judgment concerning causes and effects" (149). If we ought to follow these (or any) rules Hume needs to explain why we ought to do so. Given his account of the nonrational nature of our causal "reasoning," the question arises: *Can* he give any satisfactory explanation?

8. See J. S. Mill, *A System of Logic*, book 3, chap. 8, section 6.

9. See T. Hobbes, *The English Works*, ed. W. Molesworth (London: John Bohn, 1839), 1:122–23.

10. It might be worth adding a general note to Hume's eight rules. They seem more extensive and complex than necessary to accomplish their purpose. Hume prefaces the rules with the statement, "Since . . . 'tis possible for all objects to become causes or effects to each other, it may be proper to fix some general rules, by which we may know when they *really* are so" (173—italics added). It seems fair to say that for Hume a cause-effect relation *really* exists whenever the situation satisfies the requirements of his theory of causation. These requirements include Rules 1 to 3 (although these are not unexceptionable), plus the following: 4. Someone must observe the constant conjunction and remember having observed it. 5. The observer must, on a present appearance of the cause, have a feeling of anticipation that the effect will follow. Whenever these requirements are met we have an example of a *real* cause-effect relation. So Hume's Rules 4 to 8 are unnecessary. This raises the question: Why did he add them? I think the only plausible answer is that he failed to realize that, on his own theory of causation, they were redundant.

11. I have not italicized the word in speaking of this kind of animal reasoning, as I have the first kind. Hume makes it clear that the first kind of "reasoning" is analogous to human "reasoning" about matters of fact, which is the work of imagination rather than of reason, so is nonrational. He does not, however, categorize the second kind of animal reasoning, limiting himself to a comment on its "sagacity."

PART 4: SCEPTICISM

1. It might be noted that the word "scepticism" seldom appears in Parts I to III.

2. See chapter 9, section 5.

3. The *Abstract* contains the following remark: "The reader will easily perceive, that the philosophy contain'd in [the *Treatise*] is very sceptical" (657).

CHAPTER 14: HUME'S TOTAL SCEPTICISM AND IRRATIONALISM

1. I have discussed Part III, Section I, in detail in chapter 6, section 1.

2. *Treatise*, 180. As he indicates in the next paragraph, by "demonstrative sciences" Hume is referring specifically to algebra and mathematics. This corresponds to his earlier listing of demonstrative sciences in Part III as "algebra and arithmetic" (71). I will use the term "mathematics" to include all of these.

3. This is not, of course, a new conclusion but rather a reiteration of the view Hume expressed in Part III about the epistemological status of nonmathematical "reasoning."

4. Hume comes close to acknowledging my conclusion earlier in Section I. He writes: "There is no Algebraist nor Mathematician so expert in his science, as to place entire confidence in any truth immediately upon his discovery of it, or regard it as any thing, but a mere probability. Every time he runs over his proofs, his confidence encreases" (180).

5. At the end of Book I Hume agrees with this criticism. See *Treatise*, 268.

6. *Treatise*, 183—italics added. The phrase "all the rules of logic require . . . " that appears in this sentence merits some attention. This is one of the few places in Book I that Hume explicitly appeals to logic, in the strict sense of that term. His doing so, however, raises a problem. If logic requires him to reach a certain conclusion and, further, if that conclusion, being based on logic, is therefore cogent, it cannot be a sceptical conclusion. Having just proved it, he knows it to be true, thus he is by that very fact forced to concede the existence of knowledge. Hume might reply by making the point, as he did in connection with "all demonstrative sciences," that, although their rules are certain, we make errors when we apply them. But then his appeal to logic would fall prey to his two-step argument and therefore should (for him at least) be destroyed, so he could not legitimately draw the conclusion he does.

Logic and logical reasoning are, unfortunately, subjects to which Hume devotes almost no attention in Book I. Consequently it is difficult for a commentator to be sure what his conception and evaluation of logic might have been. John Passmore offers a reconstruction of what he believes to be a Humean conception of logic. See his *Hume's Intentions,* 3d ed., chap. 2.

7. It is clear from the way Hume uses the term "evidence" in his argument that he is not talking just or even primarily about empirical evidence but is employing the term broadly to characterize any kind of rational justification we might give in support of a belief.

8. *Treatise*, 183. Hume's use of the term "total scepticism" departs somewhat from ordinary philosophical usage. That his argument should destroy all "evidence" or justification for our beliefs would ordinarily be considered sufficient to render his conclusion a case of total scepticism. So it would not be necessary to add the psychological point, that it destroys our beliefs as well. That Hume would accept this distinction is evident from the way he develops his argument later in Section I.

9. In his original discussion of intuitive knowledge in Part III Hume seems to leave open the possibility of error even regarding it. See *Treatise*, 70. So, although he does not specifically apply his two-step argument to this "knowledge," such an application would not appear inappropriate, especially since it would justify his conclusion that his scepticism is total.

10. *Treatise*, 183. It should be noted that Hume's repudiation of scepticism in the passage I reproduced earlier is somewhat ambiguous. He does not deny being "one of those sceptics, who hold that all is uncertain," but says only that no one is ever "sincerely and constantly of [the sceptical] opinion." His real point is his view that the "question is entirely superfluous" because, as he then goes on to explain, we *must* believe.

11. Ibid., 183. In defense of the Pyrrhonists, it should be mentioned that Hume is probably misstating their position, because they did not advocate the total suspension of judgment. According to Sextus, Hume's target here should have been the "Academics" rather than the Pyrrhonists. See Sextus Empiricus, *Outlines of Pyrrhonism*, 3.

12. See *Treatise*, Book I, Part III, Sections VI–X, and my discussion in chapter 9, section 5. See also chapter 10, section 5.

13. The classical Pyrrhonists were more careful than Hume on this crucial point. They did not attempt to offer an argument that would "destroy" reason and "prove" scepticism; thus they avoided the trap into which Hume fell. Sextus, distinguishing between the Academic sceptics and the Pyrrhonists, writes: "The adherents of the New Academy [the Academic sceptics], although they affirm that all things are non-apprehensible, yet differ from the Sceptics [Pyrrhonists] even, as seems probable, in respect of this very statement that all things are non-apprehensible (for they affirm this positively, whereas the Sceptic regards it as possible that some things may be apprehended)." Sextus Empiricus, *Outlines of Pyrrhonism*, 139.

Chapter 15: Belief in an External Material World

1. *Treatise*, 188. Hume adds a footnote to this statement, referring the reader to "Part II. sect. 6."

2. Ibid., 67–68. I have discussed Hume's argument in this early section in detail in chapter 5, section 2.

3. For a lengthy and detailed analysis of Section II see H. H. Price, *Hume's Theory of the External World* (Oxford: Clarendon Press, 1940). Price's commentary clarifies some of the difficult arguments in Section II but occasionally it makes questionable extrapolations from Hume's text.

4. It is clear from the context that Hume is using the word "object" as a synonym for "body" or "material object" here.

5. See Locke, *Essay*, particularly book 2, chaps. 1 and 8. Locke's theory of representational realism is, of course, more sophisticated than a simple "image" view.

6. Hume's use of the term "reason" in paragraphs 14 and 47 may be misunderstood. He is not talking about demonstrative reasoning but about the kind of "reasoning" we engage in regarding matters of fact, which is a function of the imagination. Unfortunately, he is quite loose in his terminology in these passages.

7. See *Treatise*, 212 (paragraph 47). Hume summarizes this argument briefly toward the end of the paragraph on page 193.

8. In the following paragraph (194) Hume refers to our impressions of figure, extension, color, sound, and heat as being of this kind. We can assume that in general he thought of the impressions of primary and secondary qualities as ones to which we ordinarily attribute an existence outside of consciousness while we deny it to the impressions of tertiary qualities.

9. Elsewhere in Section II Hume says we "suppose" that some impressions continue to exist outside of consciousness. From his conclusion that impressions are internal to the mind, it follows that such suppositions, attributions, or beliefs must be false. In his discussion Hume uses the terms "impressions" and "percep- tions" without distinction. This is reasonable. Since our perceptions are our im- pressions and our ideas (which are copies of our impressions), if our impressions are internal so must be our ideas, hence all of our perceptions.

10. *Treatise*, 194. It is clear that in his discussion of constancy and coherence Hume is using the term "objects" as equivalent to "contents of impressions" and not as "material objects." But his use of language is often loose.

11. In a footnote (198) Hume refers to "Part II sect. 4."

12. Hume's metaphor of the galley, it should be noted, violates his theory of imagination, as well as his empiricist epistemology. His claim that the imagina- tion gives a greater coherence to the objects of our perceptions than we actually sense assumes that it can perceive "objects" without having had any impressions of them. But, since the contents of the imagination consist solely in ideas that are copies of impressions, this is impossible. The imagination cannot continue the voyage on which Hume tries to launch it.

13. More precisely, we are looking at what we call the "sun." It is essential to keep in mind that Hume is talking at this point about our internal or conscious experience and is not begging any question about the existence of external mate- rial objects.

14. Hume's analysis apparently presupposes that our perceptions, even when we gaze fixedly at some object, are not continuous but broken. This is consistent with his view that they are perishing. Since the problem he has to resolve concerns the identity of objects the perception of which is unquestionably broken, the issue of the correctness of his analysis at this stage of his argument is immaterial.

15. *Treatise*, 202. Hume continues this "vulgar" usage until page 211. I will fol- low him in it. He does point out (rightly) that the identification of external mate- rial objects with perceptions is not a practice confined to the vulgar. All of us, in- cluding philosophers, think that way most of the time. As he puts it, "almost all mankind, and even philosophers themselves, for the greatest part of their lives, take their perceptions to be their only objects, and suppose, that the very being, which is intimately present to the mind, is the real body or material existence" (206).

16. Ibid., 204. Hume gives a succinct statement of his argument in a footnote on pages 204–5.

17. Ibid., 206. Italics added. Hume adds that he will explain this distinction later and makes a footnote reference to "Sect. 6." This is a distinction I will dis- cuss in this section and also in section 11 and in section 5 of chapter 16.

18. Ibid., 207. Since I will devote much of chapter 17 to an analysis and examination of Hume's theory of mind I will not discuss it here.

19. Ibid., 208. It is clear from the context that the term "sensible objects" in this statement means "material objects that are sensed."

20. Although he does not mention his name here, it seems clear that on this point Hume is expressing his disagreement with Berkeley. In his *Principles* Berkeley wrote: "For as to what is said of the absolute existence of unthinking things without any relation to their being perceived, that seems perfectly unintelligible. Their *esse* is *percipi*, nor is it possible they should have any existence, out of the minds or thinking things which perceive them." Later he adds, "The very notion of what is called *matter* or *corporeal substance*, involves a contradiction in it." G. Berkeley, *A Treatise Concerning the Principles of Human Knowledge*, in *The Works of George Berkeley*, ed. Luce and Jessop, 2:42, 45. Although Hume seems clearly to be disagreeing with Berkeley, John Cook, in a carefully argued paper, has concluded that Hume must acknowledge that unperceived perceptions are logically impossible. See J. Cook, "Hume's Scepticism with Regard to the Senses," *American Philosophical Quarterly* 5 (1968): 1–17.

21. *Treatise*, 209. Italics added. In this statement Hume says only that the fiction of the continued existence of *perceptions* is false. The question may still be raised whether the fiction of the continued existence of *material objects* is also false. Nevertheless, we must remember that Hume is thinking at this point with the vulgar, who identify perceptions with material objects. This passage offers a possible clue to Hume's ontology. I will keep it in mind to see if he clarifies it further.

22. See *Treatise*, 96. For my discussion see chapter 10, particularly section 1.

23. *Treatise*, 94—italics added. Hume is here using "God" simply as an illustration of the meaning of "belief." It would be a mistake to conclude from his language that he *really* has an idea of God or believes in God's existence. Later Hume repeats his conception of belief. "'Tis certain we must have an idea of every matter of fact, which we believe" (101).

24. See chapter 5, section 2.

25. *Treatise*, 209. That Hume is here talking about bodies is confirmed at the end of the sentence where he writes, "[this] makes us believe the continu'd existence of body."

26. For Hume's meaning of conceivability and inconceivability see chapter 2, section 1. That Hume's introduction of "fictions," as something we believe in but have no idea of, is illegitimate is apparent. On his philosophy "fictions" simply cannot exist. No more can the imagination "feign" anything. All it can work with are ideas and these it does not need to "feign" because they are copies of impressions. Hume's account in Section II of the way in which the imagination leads us to a belief in an external material world must, therefore, be discarded.

27. See note 26, above, and chapter 2, section 1.

28. Just prior to this, in paragraph 43, Hume summarizes his four-step account of the way in which the imagination leads us to believe in the existence of body. With the exception of his remark that the fiction of a continued existence is false, which I have noted in section 9, that paragraph contains nothing new.

29. *Treatise*, 210. It should be remembered that Hume is still following the

vulgar in equating perceptions with external material objects. Thus he is implying that the natural propensity to ascribe a continued existence to such objects is a fallacy.

30. Ibid., 210. Again, we must remember that Hume is still thinking with the vulgar, in which perceptions and material objects are the same. So, in concluding that the former have no continued and independent existence, he must also be concluding that the latter have none either. Although he uses the term "perceptions" throughout the discussion that follows, the appropriate transfers can easily be made.

31. The argument I have been reviewing in this section is not Hume's last word on unperceived perceptions. He returns to them briefly in Section V. I discuss his remarks in that section in chapter 16, section 5.

32. *Treatise*, 190–91. Although the passage I have reproduced has been extracted from an argument on a somewhat different point from the one with which we are now concerned, the passage itself is relevant to our inquiry.

33. This interpretation can explain Hume's other references to our body and its organs scattered through Book I. See, for example, his statements on pages 60–61 and 64 and my discussion of them in chapter 4, sections 8–10. It might be added that such an interpretation is required by Hume's epistemology.

34. *Treatise*, 211. Hume notes at this point that he will return from the vulgar to the philosophical way of speaking and thinking by accepting this distinction.

35. Ibid. Italics added. As we will see later, however, Hume thinks the philosophical system has certain advantages over the vulgar one.

36. Ibid. In his discussion Hume replaces the terms "understanding" and "fancy" with "reason" and "imagination." See 211ff.

37. See *Treatise*, 212. I have reviewed this argument earlier in the chapter, but from a different perspective. See section 3.

38. *Treatise*, 214. Italics added. Hume's vague qualification, "in a manner," does not alter the substantive conclusion he reaches.

39. Hume presumably had Locke, at least, in mind here. No less obvious is his implicit reference to Berkeley, as representative of the "extravagant sceptics," who, he adds, never seriously believed their conclusion.

40. He wrote, for example, that "philosophers . . . distinguish (as we shall do for the future) betwixt perceptions and [material] objects." *Treatise*, 211.

41. Ibid., 218. I have put together portions of the last two sentences of the paragraph that begins page 218 in this quotation. It is important to note that Hume includes himself in his indictment.

42. There are interesting similarities between Sections I and II of Part IV: (1) Hume gives the two sections parallel titles, (2) in both he reaches sceptical philosophical conclusions, and (3) in both he refuses to believe the conclusions he reaches.

43. At least one Hume scholar sees Hume's conclusion in a less ambiguous light than I do here. Robert Fogelin writes: "I am not suggesting that Hume actually accepts Berkeley's argument: on the contrary, he is anxious to reject it. The difficulty is to find any systematic reason for his doing so." See his *Hume's Skepticism in the Treatise of Human Nature* (London: Routledge and Kegan Paul, 1985), 78.

CHAPTER 16: CRITIQUE OF PHILOSOPHERS AND THEOLOGIANS

1. *Treatise*, 220. Although he could have written more clearly, it is apparent that Hume is referring to an "object" as a "content of perception" and not a "material object" here, and throughout the rest of Section III.

2. Ibid. First two italics added. That the material substance the imagination feigns is *unknown* confirms Hume's view that we have no knowledge of an external material world. By adding that it is unintelligible presumably he means at least that, because we can have no perception of it, it is inconceivable. These, of course, are conclusions he had reached as early as Part II, Section VI. Hume expands on this discussion in Section VI of Part IV, adding a number of illustrations to illuminate his points. See, particularly, *Treatise*, 255–58.

3. See *Treatise*, 167–68. I have commented on this passage in chapter 12, section 8.

4. *Treatise*, 223. Italics added. Hume did make one remark in Part III that confirms this view by implication. See page 171. Nevertheless, one can still question whether he holds this position without qualification, because he has made numerous statements in Book I that seem inconsistent with it.

5. Ibid., 225. Hume returns to this distinction within the imagination in the final section of Book I. But there he does not make a claim for the superiority of certain principles of the imagination over others but condemns all equally. See *Treatise*, 267–68.

6. Ibid., 227. In his list of sensible qualities Hume does not include feeling or touch, discussing it separately later in the section. In this he follows Locke. See Locke, *Essay*, book 2, chaps. 3 and 4. It should be noted, however, that Hume includes it by implication, in his reference to "other sensible qualities."

7. *Treatise*, 229. Hume seems, by his use of the pronoun "our," to be including himself as a representative of the "modern philosophy" here. This inclusion seems to be assumed throughout Section IV.

8. In his *Enquiry* Hume states both his agreement with, and difference from, Berkeley in concise terms. Speaking of Berkeley's "sceptical" arguments, he writes that "*they admit of no answer and produce no conviction.*" Hume, *Enquiry Concerning Human Understanding*, 155 n. 1. In other words, Berkeley is right as a philosopher but no one believes his conclusion. It might just be added that, although Hume certainly did not believe his conclusion, Berkeley himself presumably did.

9. The "atheists" are represented by Spinoza. Hume in a footnote (243) says, "See *Bayle's* dictionary, article of *Spinoza*." For this article see Bayle, *Dictionaire*, Article "Spinoza," 4th ed., 4:253–71.

10. Hume's constant references to "body" in this section, after he has concluded in Section IV that no material world exists, may be questioned. It may be compared to his return to the notion of memory as recollection of the past in Part III, Section VI, after he had given up that notion in Section V. The situations, however, are not parallel. Hume used memory as an ingredient in his theory of causation but he isn't using body as any part of his own philosophy in Section V, only referring to it as a basic concept within the context of the materialists' metaphysics, which he is examining in this section.

11. *Treatise*, 233. This was a standard definition of "substance" in Hume's time.

12. Ibid. Italics added. The final clause of the penultimate sentence of the passage requires a comment. When Hume says that "[perceptions] have no need of any thing else to support their existence," he means, as he makes clear on the next page, that they do not need to inhere in a substance, not that they exist unperceived.

13. Ibid. It might be noted that Hume offers no definition of "substance" of his own. This omission, I think, is deliberate. If the term is meaningless, as he has implied, how could one define it?

14. See *Treatise*, 207–8 and 210–11. For my discussion see chapter 15, sections 9 and 11.

15. See his example of the "relishes" of the fig and the olive, page 236.

16. *Treatise*, 243. During the course of his argument against the theologians Hume discusses the question of the "specific difference betwixt an object and impression" (241). I have analyzed this argument at some length earlier in the book. See chapter 5, section 2.

17. Ibid., 247. In the course of his argument Hume digresses briefly to examine Malebranche's theory that the cause of mental events is the activity of God rather than of bodies. See pages 248–49. Much of his argument is a repetition of points he had made earlier. See, for example, *Treatise*, 159–60.

18. Ibid., 248. Although Hume does not mention the fact here, on his theory of causation our experience of constant conjunction is the cause of the determination of our mind to "infer" an effect from a cause, which is the relation of necessary connection essential to causation.

19. It is hard to be sure of the full significance of Hume's condemnation of theologians and materialists. We can definitely say that, when he concludes that the notions of material and mental substance are unintelligible, he means that they are inconceivable, because we can have no idea of either. But he seems to mean more than this, speaking of both notions as involving contradictions and absurdities and of having no meaning for us. Does he therefore mean that neither substance exists? That is the conclusion he had found himself forced to draw at the end of Section IV about matter. Does he reach the same conclusion about mind? This is a question I will pursue in chapter 17.

CHAPTER 17: HUME'S MIND

1. See *Treatise*, 253–58. The earlier arguments appear on pages 219–20. Hume had also discussed the topic in Section II of Part IV.

2. See above, chapter 15, sections 7 and 8, and chapter 16, section 1.

3. Almost every commentator on Hume understandably devotes considerable attention to Section VI of Part IV. Not only is the notion of mind central to Hume's philosophy but it is also of special interest to everyone. Although I refer only occasionally to the secondary literature in this chapter, it will be evident from what I write that I have profited from my study of it.

4. I will follow Hume in concentrating on the "identity" of the self. He has little to say about the characteristic of "simplicity," disposing of it in a single paragraph at the end of the section (263).

5. *Treatise*, 252. This is not Hume's first statement of this view in Book I; he has said these things about perceptions several times before. See, for example, page 233.

6. See chapter 15, sections 9 and 11, and chapter 16, section 5.

7. *Treatise*, 634–35. This statement seems to involve a non sequitur. It does not follow from the fact that the self cannot survive the cessation of perceptions that the two are the same, for perceptions may only be necessary conditions for the existence of the self. Nevertheless it is clear that Hume holds them to be the same.

8. See, for example, *Treatise*, 259, where Hume writes that "every distinct perception, which enters into the composition of the mind, is a distinct existence, and is different, and distinguishable, and separable from every other perception." See also page 636.

9. See, for example, *Treatise*, 219–20. The discussion in Section VI is mainly an expansion of this account.

10. See chapter 15, section 10.

11. *Treatise*, 260. In his original discussion of the association of ideas at the beginning of Book I Hume had listed three uniting principles—the relations of resemblance, contiguity, and cause and effect (11). However, in his account in Section VI, he drops contiguity, which, he writes, "has little or no influence in the present case" (260).

12. Ibid. Hume's introduction of the Berkeleyan word "notions" here should be noted. He is careful not to say that we have an idea of personal identity, or of an enduring mind. However, the statement contains one possibly misleading phrase. Hume speaks of "a train of connected ideas." The ideas are not themselves connected; rather we connect them.

13. Ibid. Special note should be taken of Hume's statement "that succession of perceptions, which constitutes his mind." This is a reiteration of his metaphor of the actors.

14. Hume is clearly appealing to his original theory of memory here, not his revised theory.

15. *Treatise*, 261. Hume follows this statement with another analogy, comparing the mind to "a republic or commonwealth" (261). This analogy, unfortunately, is singularly inapt.

16. Ibid., 261–62. Italics added. Hume continues his account by pointing out that our self-identity extends beyond the range of our memory, but he does not explain how this is possible.

17. See *Treatise*, Part I, Section III, and Part III, Section V. I have discussed these theories in chapter 2, section 7, and chapter 8, sections 2–7.

18. *Treatise*, 635. Hume adds a footnote here, referring the reader back to "Book I. page 260."

19. See, for example, Fogelin, *Hume's Skepticism in the Treatise of Human Nature*, 93.

20. I have discussed this point already, early in the book. See chapter 2, section 8.

21. See Introduction, note 4.

22. My concern here is not simply with conclusions Hume actually reached but

also with conclusions to which his philosophy leads, even though he never drew them.

23. One might consider adding to this list of real entities two others—space and time. However, we have long since seen that, whatever Hume's beliefs may have been about them, his arguments in Part II lead to the conclusion that neither exists. For my discussion of both see chapter 4, section 6.

24. J. Bennett, *Locke, Berkeley, Hume: Central Themes* (Oxford: Clarendon Press, 1971), 35.

25. For example, see J. Bricke, *Hume's Philosophy of Mind* (Princeton: Princeton University Press, 1980), 72.

26. *Treatise,* 234. I have discussed these passages in chapter 16, section 5.

27. See, especially, *Treatise,* 227–28 and 231, and my chapter 16, section 3.

28. See *Treatise,* 207–8 and 210–11. For my discussion see chapter 15, sections 9 and 11. See also note 20 of chapter 15.

Chapter 18: Hume's "True" Scepticism

1. James Beattie, for example, wrote, in a clear reference to Hume: "Those unnatural productions, the vile effusion of a hard and stupid heart, that mistakes its own restlessness for the activity of genius, and its own captiousness for sagacity of understanding, may, like other monsters, please awhile by their singularity; but the charm is soon over; and the succeeding age will be astonished to hear, that their forefathers were deluded, or amused, with such fooleries." J. Beattie, *An Essay on the Nature and Immutability of Truth; in Opposition to Sophistry and Scepticism* (New York: Garland, 1983), 502. First published in 1770.

2. Hume makes a footnote reference here to "Sect. 4." The reference is to the final paragraph of that section (231), which states the same conclusion in even more explicit terms. For my discussion of the earlier statement see chapter 16, section 3.

3. *Treatise,* 265. The word "true" performs no function in Hume's statement. Because we cannot bring the past back to compare our memory ideas with it, we cannot say that these ideas are "true" pictures, "distorted" pictures, or any pictures of the past at all. For my detailed discussion of this point see chapter 8, section 4.

4. Ibid., 183. For my discussion of this argument see chapter 14, sections 2–4.

5. I have discussed Hume's irrationalistic response to his total scepticism in Section I in chapter 14, section 5.

6. *Treatise,* 267–68. Italics added. Hume adds a footnote to this statement, referring the reader back to "Sect. I." In this statement his scepticism applies to *all* propositions, including those of "common life," not just to theoretical ones.

7. Ibid., 268. Although Hume realizes that his problem is logically irresolvable, he suggests (also on page 268) another, practical way of resolving it—just forget about it.

8. See *Treatise,* 8–9 and 85. Hume would have clarified the distinction considerably if he had given precise information about the point in decreasing vivacity at which memory ideas become imagination ideas. But perhaps it is impossible to do this.

9. See, particularly, Part III, Sections VI and VIII. In this early part of the

Treatise Hume distinguishes between the understanding or reason and the imagination (88–89) but the important conclusion he reaches, even at this point, is that "reasoning" is mostly the work of the imagination. See, particularly, pages 101–3. I have commented on his arguments at some length, especially in chapters 9 and 10.

10. *Treatise,* 267. The distinction Hume makes within the imagination is between "the trivial suggestions of the fancy" and its "general and more establish'd properties" (267). It should be remembered, however, that all of these mental processes are nonrational, in the sense that Hume can offer no reasons in support of any conclusions he reaches.

11. This conclusion prompts the suggestion that Hume may have mistitled Book I. Instead of calling it "Of the Understanding" perhaps he should have entitled it "Of the Imagination."

12. *Treatise,* 9. Hume repeats this distinction in his revised theory of memory on page 85.

13. See chapter 17, particularly section 4.

14. One can interpret some of the statements Hume makes in these parts as being (implicit) expressions of the theory. For example, he writes, in his discussion of causation, that "the mind has a great propensity to spread itself on external objects" and adds, "the same propensity is the reason, why we suppose necessity and power to lie in the objects" (167). It is reasonable to assume that he is talking here about our natural belief in "objective" causation.

15. Most of our beliefs, such as my belief that I am correctly interpreting Hume's theory of natural belief, would not be natural beliefs on Hume's theory.

16. Smith, *The Philosophy of David Hume,* 126.

17. I have discussed this point in detail earlier. See chapter 15, section 10.

18. See, particularly, chapter 17, section 4.

19. I place the word "true" within quotation marks to indicate the ambivalence in the interpretations one can give of the term, as Hume uses it in Section VII. See the introduction to this chapter.

20. Hume does not introduce this concept formally as a new theory in Section VII but instead simply begins, midway through the section, to describe the practice of philosophy itself and its effects on the practitioner. His account starts with paragraph 8 and continues through much of the remainder of the section. In my commentary I will attempt to organize Hume's thought somewhat more systematically than he does; this will require me to reproduce passages in an order different from that of their appearance in the text.

21. From his description of it in both the *Treatise* and the *Enquiry* it seems apparent that Hume did not have a full understanding of Pyrrhonism. See *Treatise,* page 183, and *Enquiry Concerning Human Understanding,* Section XII, Part II. I have commented on this matter earlier; see chapter 14, notes 11 and 13.

22. Hume gives several illustrations of the kinds of problem he has in mind. See *Treatise,* 269.

23. In this phase of his activities Hume does not suspend his judgment completely, as he had accused the Pyrrhonists of doing, but only his theoretical judgment. He writes: "The course of my animal spirits and passions reduce me to this indolent belief in the general maxims of the world" (269).

24. A bit later in the section Hume contrasts philosophy with religion hedonistically (271–72), arguing that the former is more "agreeable" (271) than the latter. The passage is heavily ironic, particularly about religion but about philosophy as well. Hume ends it with the remark, "Generally speaking, the errors in religion are dangerous; those in philosophy only ridiculous" (272). Many people would, I think, find religion preferable to philosophy on hedonistic grounds. Clearly Hume was not one of them.

25. *Treatise*, 270. Hume's appeal to hedonistic considerations in "justification" of what we believe is apparent here.

26. Ibid., 273. The sceptics to whom Hume is referring, who are "so overwhelm'd with doubts and scruples, as totally to reject [philosophy]," are presumably the Pyrrhonists. From the context it is apparent that, when he says "a true sceptic will be diffident" about his philosophy, Hume is implying that he will not take it too seriously.

27. The word "philosophizing" should be interpreted broadly, to include any kind of intellectual activity.

28. More correctly, this is an idealized self-portrait. The language he uses in the section suggests that Hume recognized that he fell short in his own attempt to realize the ideal of the "true" sceptic.

29. See *The History of the Works of the Learned* (1739), 6:357n. My earlier reference appears in the Introduction, section 1.

30. Passmore, *Hume's Intentions*, 133.

31. B. Stroud, "Hume's Scepticism: Natural Instincts and Philosophical Reflection," *Philosophical Topics* (1991).

CONCLUSION

1. See the Introduction, section 1.

2. See the Introduction, section 3.

3. I make no comment here on Hume's response to his total scepticism; namely, his total irrationalism. Whatever questions it raises are psychological and moral, rather than philosophical.

4. See, for example, the quotation from Nicholas Capaldi in the Introduction, n. 9.

5. See chapter 1, section 4.

6. *Treatise*, 272–73. Needless to say, the notion of an eclectic system of philosophy is an oxymoron.

7. Hume's eclecticism can, I think, explain why Hume scholars have given so many—and such diverse—interpretations of his philosophy in Book I.

INDEX

OLIVER A. JOHNSON is Emeritus Professor of Philosophy at the University of California, Riverside, where he was a founding member of the faculty in 1953 and first chair of the Department of Philosophy. He is the author of numerous scholarly articles as well as several books, among them *Rightness and Goodness* (1959), *Moral Knowledge* (1966), *The Moral Life* (1969), *The Problem of Knowledge* (1974), and *Skepticism and Cognitivism* (1978). Professor Johnson is the editor of six volumes, including *Ethics* (now in its seventh edition), *The Individual and the Universe, Heritage of Western Civilization* (now in its eighth edition), and *Sources of World Civilization.*